Shopping Secrets of Southern California

by Mindy Glazer

A **H**elpful **P**ublication
Los Angeles, CA

Copyright © 1992 by Mindy Glazer

Helpful Publications
P. O. Box 24447
Los Angeles, CA 90024-0447

ISBN 0-9633263-0-9

All rights reserved. No part of this book may be used or reproduced in any manner without written permission of the publisher.

Cover design by Alec Bernstein
Computer imaged by Bonnie Montoya

Library of Congress Catalog Card Number 92-90768

Table of Contents

Introduction	v
Accessories	1
Handbags	1
Gloves	5
Antique Malls, Flea Markets and Swap Meets	6
Appliances	14
Art Supplies	18
Audio and Video	22
Beauty Products and Services	26
Books	29
Building and Remodeling	36
Cameras and Photographic Equipment	40
Carpet and Flooring	42
Cars and Automotive Needs	46
Cellular Phones	52
Charity Sales	53
China, Crystal, Silver and Candles	55
Clothing	62
Children's Clothing	62
Men's Clothing	69
Men and Women's Clothing	77
Leather Apparel	91

Swimsuits		94
Tees and Sweats		97
Women's Clothing		99
Bridal and Formalwear	116	
Lingerie	122	
Maternity Clothing	127	
Women's Large Sizes	129	

Computers	133
Craft Supplies	135
Department Store Outlets	138
Discount and Variety Store Chains	144
Drapes and Window Treatments	147
Dry Cleaners	149
Entertainment	151
Fabric	154
Food	161
Furniture	171

Baby Furniture	177
Beds	179
Decorating Services	181
Used Furniture	182
Outdoor Furniture	183
Barbeques and Fireplaces	184
Office Furniture	185

Giftware	187
Hobbies	191
Housewares	193
Jewelry	195
Light Fixtures and Ceiling Fans	200
Linens	204
Luggage	213
Marine Supplies	216

Table of Contents

Medical and Optical Needs	218
Musical Instruments	221
Office Supplies and Equipment	223
Outlet Malls	226
Paint and Wallpaper	232
Party Supplies and Paper Goods	234
Boxes, Moving and Mailing Supplies	236
Wholesale Paper Houses	236
Printing	237
Pet and Equestrian Supplies	238
Plants, Planters and Flowers	244
Pool Supplies	249
Records and CDs	250
Shoes	252
Sporting Goods and Athletic Wear	264
Tools	276
Toys and Games	278
Travel	281
Uniforms	283
Warehouse Buying Clubs and Wholesale Grocers	287
Southern California Sale Calendar	288
Alphabetical Index	297
Index of Discount Catalogs, Books and Other Sources	302
Geographical Index	303
Index of Chainwide Clearance Centers	318
Discount Coupons	
Reader Response Card	

Introduction

Some people remember the day the circus came to town, the day the local movie theater played its first show. I remember the day Loehmann's moved into our neighborhood. A new adventure had begun. It wasn't like any other kind of shopping: nothing was orderly, merchandise was widely disparate in quality and in taste, and you could spend hours in there, combing through every piece, and come home with nothing or bags full of beautiful things, at a fraction of what they cost at far more mundane stores. From those early days I developed a passion for trophy shopping, great finds with tiny price tags. I became a seeker of secret sources and discount hideaways.

Shopping secrets have always enabled those in the know to get more for their money. With lifestyles seemingly constricting around us, more consumers want, indeed *need* in on these buying secrets. This book is for them. Many of these stores I have frequented for years, the balance came from referral and research. Each store has been visited, undercover. I came and went as a shopper, asked questions, made my own judgments, didn't take anybody's word for anything (bought a lot of fabulous stuff).

And I realized something. As we watch newscasters walking empty malls on prime holiday shopping weekends it's becoming clear that we consumers set the price for the goods we desire. We do this by simply refusing to pay inflated prices. But what many shoppers don't realize is that the very structure of manufacturing and retail sales generates windows of opportunity for discount shopping. These are the shopping secrets that enable you to find quality merchandise, *often identical to what is being sold at retail*, and buy it at greatly reduced prices.

In a perfect retail world, the manufacturer creates a perfect product, sells it to the retailer for the cost of materials plus whatever the manufacturer deems a fair profit. The retailer then adds a mark-up and sells the product to the consumer, for whatever the retailer deems a fair profit. The manufacturer gets a profit, the retailer gets a profit, the consumer gets the shaft. But, since we don't live in a perfect retail world, you don't have to shop in one. The above scenario is only one option in the shopping story; its many alternatives will enable you to save bigtime, to decide what you want to pay, and find an outlet that carries what you want at your price.

Savings Inherent in the Structure of Manufacturing and Retail Sales

Manufacturer	Retailer
FIRST QUALITY PRODUCT	PRODUCT AT RETAIL PRICE
SAMPLES	RETURNED GOODS
ONE-OF-A-KINDS	LIQUIDATORS
JOBBER/LIQUIDATOR	SALES
KNOCK-OFFS	CLEARANCES
IRREGULARS	CLEARANCE CENTERS
SECONDS	UNCRATED STOCK
DAMAGES	SCRATCH AND DENT
OVER-RUNS	LIQUIDATED STOCK
CLOSE-OUTS	BANKRUPT STOCK
MILL ENDS	
BOLT ENDS	
REMNANTS	
FREIGHT DAMAGE	
SHIPPING ERRORS	
DISCONTINUED MERCHANDISE	
FACTORY OUTLETS	
OUTLET MALLS	

In the chart above, first quality goods, with no flaws or imperfections, are sold to retailers at the wholesale price (cost of materials, labor, manufacturing and profit). Those bought by consumers at full retail price are removed from the picture. Everything else, *every other type of merchandise or situation below the line* is grist for the discount shopper, and *an opportunity to save money.*

Savings Inherent in the Manufacturing Process

Before a product is manufactured, it is generally sold on the basis of a *SAMPLE*, a representation of the goods to be sold. Sometimes SAMPLES become *ONE-OF-A-KINDS*, when the piece does not wind up being manufactured. SAMPLES and ONE-OF-A-KINDS are not sold to retailers, but they are sold to someone. Because there are so few pieces involved, they are sold below the wholesale price, to a "Discount" store, a *JOBBER* or *LIQUIDA-*

TOR (who will sell to another retailer, or to an end-user, you). These buyers are starting out at a lower price than retailers; even if the same mark-up is tacked on, the final price is lower.

Designer goods, typically clothing but often other items, are sold with the name of a designer on the label. The clothing has intrinsic value, i.e., the cost of fabric, workmanship and shipping costs, but the designer's name also has a value. You can pay more for the name than the intrinsic value of the merchandise. *KNOCK-OFFS* are copies of designer styles, often *made of the same fabric, in the same factories, by the same people*, but without the designer name on the label. Unless you wear you clothing inside out it can be hard to distinguish knock-offs from the real thing.

In the course of the manufacturing process, some items are not made perfectly, but imperfections are so slight they would not be noticeable unless you knew they were there, may not be noticeable under any circumstances, and do not affect product durability or life. These are *IRREGULARS*, which cannot be sold as first quality merchandise to retailers. Also manufactured are goods whose imperfections are somewhat greater, although still often not visibly apparent: *SECONDS*. SECONDS may not be as structurally sound as first quality pieces, and may not carry warranties. Pieces where flaws are visible are called *DAMAGES*. All these pieces cost the manufacturer money to produce, and are sold to someone, again, often JOBBERS or LIQUIDATORS.

In order to insure they can fill their orders, manufacturers produce more then they need, and at the end of the buying season, they may be left with *OVERRUNS*, first quality merchandise for which they have no buyers. These are often sold as *CLOSE-OUTS*, odd lots of leftover merchandise. Similarly, *MILL ENDS*, *BOLT ENDS* and *REMNANTS*, pieces too small to sell to large volume users (of carpet or fabric, for example), are sold to small "Discount" retailers.

In the course of doing business, accidents happen. Sometimes cartons are *FREIGHT DAMAGED*, appliances suffer *SCRATCH AND DENT*, or arrive too late for use by retailers. In any of these cases, if retailers refuse delivery these goods are sold to someone, below the regular wholesale price, though the merchandise may be completely unharmed and first quality.

At the end of a season fashion always changes, and so styles are *DISCONTIN-UED*. Styles of everything are discontinued eventually, and whatever stock of discontinued merchandise remains has to be sold somewhere. The only potential problem in buying discontinued goods can be in getting replacement parts. Eventually this is a problem in buying just about anything.

Some manufacturers profit from their own mistakes, opening **FACTORY OUTLETS** where they sell these pieces (damages, irregulars, seconds, discontinued merchandise, close-outs and over-runs) directly to the public. They profit by getting rid of goods often at wholesale prices, and the public enjoys great savings. The proliferation of these outlets has lead to the rise of **OUTLET MALLS**.

All of these errors, overages, bits and pieces have value, and wind up sold to someone other than major retailers carrying first quality product. They wind up in the shops on the pages that follow, where you can buy them below retail.

Savings Inherent in the Structure of Retail Sale

On the retail level, first quality goods are initially sold at full price. Say you buy an item. You take it home, try it on, decide you don't like it. You return it. What happens to it? The store can't sell it again; they dont know what you did in or with it. **RETURNED GOODS** often wind up at LIQUIDATORS, which sell them "as is".

When an item doesn't sell at all, you know what happens. It goes on **SALE**. If it still doesn't sell, even after being reduced, and reduced, and reduced, it goes on **CLEARANCE**, which means that store will not sell that item at a lower price. That's the lowest price it will ever sell for in that store. And if it doesn't sell at clearance? Some stores send it on to their **CHAINWIDE CLEARANCE CENTER**, where marked-down merchandise is reduced even further, sometimes as much as 90% (off the *marked down* price, hence up to 95% savings). Not all stores have clearance center. Some sell clearance merchandise to LIQUIDATORS.

If the piece is an appliance, and it has developed a cosmetic flaw in the showroom, or maybe from being banded too tightly in its crate, it's called a **SCRATCH AND DENT** and discounted, even though mechanically there's nothing wrong with it. **UNCRATED STOCK** is generally white goods that have for some reason been taken out of their boxes, and can be cheaper because of it.

If the retailer doesn't manage to lure customers in, he may sell off his stock cheaply to jobbers to raise cash; this is **LIQUIDATED STOCK**. If the business eventually goes belly-up, it provides an opportunity for other retailers and jobbers to come in and purchase **BANKRUPT STOCK**, i.e., remaining inventory, sold to pay creditors.

Introduction   ix

All these processes occur daily in manufacturing and retail, and business owners have provisions for all of them. Every manufacturer has an outlet, a place where goods can be disposed of. Most retail chains have an outlet as well. What you need to know is where the outlets are. That's what the rest of this book is about.

I've reported here on my observations of hundreds of stores. I saw hundreds more but these were the best values I found. I do not guarantee that you'll find what I found. Indeed, if a store has changed, please let me know. Or tell me if you've found a store you think I've overlooked. There are stores represented for all tastes and all pocketbooks. What they have in common is *value*.

A word about *RESALE*. I'm not wild about it. I've included some of the better resale shops. You can find many more in your local Yellow Pages. If you want to buy someone else's wardrobe (and that can be a great idea), try garage sales. You can buy used clothing, in some cases by name designers and barely worn, and cut out the middle man. Drive around your neighborhood on a Saturday morning, look for signs on telephone poles. And if you don't like your neighbors' taste, cruise the better neighborhoods nearby.

Acknowledgements

I discovered in the writing this book how many friends I have, and how talented they all seem to be. Beyond encouragement and support I got a lot of concrete help; without them this effort could not have turned out as well as it has. So thank you, to Carlyn, for saying "You should write a book" every time I told her about a new outlet. And to Alec, who created one great cover and then did it all over again. To Bonnie and Franz, who helped me with computers, and art, and shepherded me through the land of printing and typesetting, talked about the possibilities far more than they wanted to, and offered input every step of the way. To Liz for art ideas, and Liz and Teri, for good shopping company and support. To Rachelle for bringing lots of new stores to my attention. To Irene, for introducing me to garage sales, and teaching me to start out by offering a quarter. To Dorit who came through in a pinch. To Claire and Jeff, for marketing ideas. To Logger, my attorney, proofreader and cohort in the never-ending search for *drastic* reductions. To my mother, who can spot a designer dress at one twelfth its original price at 50 paces, and who taught me to love the hunt. And, most especially, to my father, who often financed this training, and every time we came home laden with bags and bargains, wanted to see all the money we saved. His interest and encouragement during the production of this book not only made difficult things interesting, it made impossible things possible.

There is a Reader Response Card in the back of this book. If you liked a store, or hated one, if you think there's a place I should check out or one I should remove from the book, please let me know. Thanks in advance for that.

In some cases I couldn't list all addresses of a chain. Where there are two they are listed, in cases of three, you get one address and the phone numbers of two; beyond that, the cities are listed until that number hits 10, then "see Geographical Index".

Discount Catalogs and Resale Stores are at the end of each product category.

Abbreviations and Symbols

AE	American Express
ATM	Automatic Teller Machine Card
CB	Carte Blanche
CCC	Chainwide Clearance Center
COD	Cash on Delivery
D	Discover
DC	Diner's Club
GC	Gift Certificate
L	Layaway
MC	Master Card
MO	Money Order
SC	Store Card
TC	Traveler's Check
V	Visa
($###)	A price in parenthesis denotes the *actual retail price*, as opposed to the price the item currently sells for

Accessories

Handbags

Bag Lady
COUPON
31954 San Luis Rey, Cathedral City (619) 323-5062
Mon.-Sat., 9:30-5; Sun. 11-4
Terms: MC, V, Check. Exchanges.   Parking

When you enter this store your eye won't know where to settle first—metallics, jeweled evening bags, rhinestone studded casual bags, leather bags painted with gold—purses are glittering and glinting all over the place. Handbags, belts, and a few leather jackets are here at prices that begin at about 25% less than in department stores. There are also bargain tables, where merchandise is further discounted. Prices range $25 to $250, and this is a pleasant place to shop. *Use the coupon for 5% off your next purchase.*

Bijoux Medici
493 S. Robertson Blvd., Suite 1, Beverly Hills (310) 271-8591
The Citadel, City of Commerce (213) 728-2690
Hours vary by location.
Terms: MC, V, AE, Check. Exchanges.   Street parking

The bags and belts here are made in Italy, of precious hides in unique colors, the kind you've seen at the best department stores (probably imported for them by Bijoux Medici). Inventory is on the pricey side, but if you're looking for crocodile or lizard for less, this is the place. A pink crocodile bag here is $600, a fraction of what you'd pay at Neimans. An ostrich shoulder pouch retailing for $355 was here for $189. There were bags at $100 to $200; a replica Chanel, made of the same French kidskin, was $169; and a handwoven leather shoulder bag was $119. There was a great leather and 24K gold plated brass snake belt reduced to $105. The Citadel has a larger selection of moderately priced bags.

Coach Value Store
Factory Merchants of Barstow (619) 253-2772
Mon.-Sat., 9-8
Terms: MC, V, AE. Final sale. Parking

This is the final resting place for irregular and discontinued Coach inventory, at savings of 20% to 50%. In addition to their classic handbags, the shop carries mens and women's small leathergoods, travel accessories, organizers, key rings, belts, briefcases, men's socks, ties, braces and a few overnight bags.

European Natural Leather Bags
12265 Ventura Blvd., Suite 204, Studio City (818) 752-2790
1730 1/4 Westwood Blvd., Westwood (310) 475-8118
Tues.-Fri., 11-5; Sat., 11-4
Terms: MC, V, AE, Check. GC. Exchanges. Street parking

If you love Bree leather bags, visit this store. These are the same bags (minus the Bree imprint), made in the same factory, in a greater variety of styles, sold at discounts of 33% to 50%. Available are shoulder bags, satchels, traveling bags, briefcases, backpacks, fannypacks, wallets and small leathers in raw cowhide, pigskin and calfskin. Cowhide backpacks and shoulder bags begin at about $75; briefcases at about $100; calfskin is more expensive. Should a problem arise with a bag, it can be brought back for repair or exchange. Their major sale is is in June, and students always get a 10% discount.

Fallbrook Handbag Outlet
6739 1/2 Fallbrook Av., Canoga Park (818) 348-6910
Mon.-Sat., 8-6
Terms: MC, V, Check. Final sale. Parking

If you really need a shopping fix at 8 a.m., try finding this store. (Hint: It's also a shoe repair shop.) If you like metallic leather there are a number of bags here for you, in the the $50 to $75 range. The best buys are on the "Sale" rounder, at $19, and some interesting brasstone metal evening bags shaped like eggs and seashells. The softest leather Chanel knock-off I've found was here, in a medium size, at $75.

Fashion West
71-846 Hwy. 111, Rancho Mirage (619) 773-3361
Hours vary with season.
Terms: MC, V, AE, Check. Exchanges. Parking

The walls lining this shop are full of handbags. Most start at discounts of 20%

to 25%, but there are a few clearance racks with bigger discounts, and the back houses the sale wall, where merchandise is marked down again, 30% to 80%. There are many beautiful purses here, from top designers. A selection of belts and several display cases of unusual costume jewelry are also offered, and the saleswomen are helpful without being high-pressure. The problem in a store like this is choosing between all the things you want.

Handbag Hang-up
8580 Washington Blvd., Culver City   (310) 870-0762
Mon.-Sat., 10-5:30
Terms: MC, V, D, Check. Returns.   Parking

In what may be the largest hand-bag inventory available to the public, Handbag Hang-up has a front room featuring hundreds of styles discounted 25%, and a back room of slight irregulars, odd lots and promotional items discounted at least 50%. There is also a stock of "vintage" handbags, dating from the store's opening in 1961 on, which are discounted from their *original prices*. Looking for a lime green leather clutch for $2.99? Some of these are wonderfully trendy, and considering what they're made of, incredibly cheap. There is also a selection of attache cases, luggage and small leather goods, discounted at least 25%, and because you can't see a lot of the inventory, you get a lot of patient sales help.

Le Club Handbag Company   COUPON
860 S. Los Angeles St., Los Angeles (213) 623-8709
Mon.-Sat., 9:30-5:30; Sun., 11-5
Terms: V, MC, Check. Exchanges.   Street Parking

LeClub features a wide assortment of bags and accessories, ranging from pretty beaded belts and evening bags at $9.99, to Bally, Finesse, Ann Turk, and Brahmin handbags at $450 to $700 (selling for at least 25% more at better department stores). They also carry Liz Claiborne and Frenchy of California in the more moderate price range. Small leather goods, gloves and accessories are also offered at discount prices. A new addition at Le Club is Adolfo hats; they have become the factory outlet for several lines, offering you savings of up to 80% on hats that retailed for as much as $300. This is a store worth getting to know. *The coupon entitles you to 10% off your next purchase.*

Marlene Gaines Handbags
6000 Reseda Blvd, Unit Q, Tarzana (818) 344-0442
Mon.-Sat., 10-5:30
Terms: V, MC, Check. Returns.   Parking

Marlene Gaines offers some unusual and exquisite handbags, and you can generally buy them for 10% below the already discounted price on the sticker. Some are manufactured expressly for Marlene, so it's hard to comparison shop, but the bags are high quality, and prices, while objectively high, seem reasonable for what you're getting. Of course, if you stop in when there's a sale—usually in December and June, and always advertised in the *Los Angeles Times*—discounts go as low as 70%.

Millie's Bags and Shoes
101 W. Ninth St., Los Angeles (213) 623-6175
Mon.-Sat., 10-6
Terms: MC, V, D, Check. Exchanges.   Street parking

This shop offers a collection of handbags, shoes, attaches and small leathergoods at discounts of 10% to 50%. Some of the designer names I saw were Liz Claiborne and Perry Ellis, and they stocked matching purse accessories. Borganza beaded evening bags started at $12, and special sale racks—where all sizes, shapes and qualities of purses are offered at low prices—had lots of good buys. The store also sells shoes; there are bins for $19.99 to $29.99 (including Impo, Allure, Golo, 9 West, Garolini and Via Spiga), even *sale shoes* in sizes 2 1/2 to 3 1/2.

Shirley's Shoes & Handbags
71-843 Hwy. 111, Rancho Mirage (619) 340-4955
31-930 San Luis Rey, Cathedral City (619) 323-3737
Mon.-Sat., 10-6; Sun., 12-5
Terms: MC, V, D, Check. Final sale.   Parking

These two shops offer an assortment of shoes and handbags, discounted, then discounted again. (The shop in Cathedral City also has a small selection of men's shoes.) Bags range in price from $20 to $150, are discounted initially 25%, and there's usually a sale running on top of that, with further reductions of 30% to 50%. Styles go from missy to trendy.

See also
    California Mart Saturday Sales
    Shoes by Shirley
    The Deerskin Place

Gloves

Gloves by Hammer
7210 Melrose Av., Los Angeles (213) 938-0288
Mon.-Fri., 9-5
Terms: Cash and Check only. Final sale.   Street parking

This store is reminiscent of another era. Here you can buy gloves from the person who makes them, and though they aren't cheap (you're probably paying here what you'd pay in a better department store), here you're getting real quality. There are unlined gloves for men, women and children, in kid or suede(linings became popular to mask inferior grades of leather). A pair of women's wrist length kid gloves were $49. You can also special order here, where Hilda makes gloves for the film studios.

> **Garage sales are a great place to find costume jewelry, gloves, handbags, scarves, beautiful things someone once treasured. Buying carefully from someone else's attic, you often wind up workmanship never to be seen again, at unbeatable prices.**

Antique Malls, Flea Markets and Swap Meets

Antiques are rarely discounted, yet there are often ways to get a better deal on them. Antique shows and malls provide vendors with shared space to show their wares at low overhead, and the savings can be passed on to you. Generally the further out of a metropolitan area you go, the cheaper prices get. Many vendors at antique and flea markets accept cash and checks only.

Antique Malls

Antique Exchange
31251 Outer Hwy. 10, Yucaipa   (714) 794-9190
Daily, 10:30-5; closed Wed.
Terms: Cash and Check only.   Parking

The Antique Exchange consists of over 50 shops selling dolls, jewelry, pottery, porcelain, coins, furniture and glass.

The Antique Guild's Showcase Gallery
8800 Venice Blvd., Los Angeles   (310) 838-3131
Mon.-Fri., 10-7; Sat., 10-6; Sun., 11-6
Terms: MC, V, AE, D, Check.   Parking

The Antique Guild's Showcase Gallery has 44 shops full of antiques and collectibles, costume and fine jewelry, vintage watches, pottery, toys, religious objects, china, silver and silverplate, pressed glass and more.

Antique Palace Mall
8044 Van Nuys Blvd., Panorama City   (818) 786-3441
Mon.-Sat., 10-5:30
Terms: MC, V, Check.   Parking

Here there are over 7,000 square feet of collectibles, furniture, quilts, sterling, jewelry, paintings, and gift items.

The Antique Warehouse
212 S. Cedros Dr., Solano Beach (619) 755-5156
Daily, 10-5; Closed Tues.
Terms: MC, V, CB, DC, Check.   Parking

This large mall boasts 101 shops featuring antiques, collectibles, American and European furniture, jewelry, and primitives.

Best of Times Antique Mall
434 W. 6 St., San Pedro (310) 514-2970
Daily, 10:30-5:30; Closed Wed.
Terms: MC, V, AE, D, Check.   Street Parking

Best of Times houses 35 dealers featuring furniture, collectibles and jewelry.

Broadway Antique Mall
7945 Broadway, Lemon Grove (619) 461-1399
Mon.-Fri., 10-9; Sat.-Sun. 10-6
Terms: MC, V, Check. L.   Parking

Here you will find 30 dealers offering collectibles and antiques. You can have pieces appraised here as well.

Country Antique Fair Mall
21546 Golden Triangle Rd., Saugus (805) 254-1474
Daily 10-5
Terms: MC, V, Check.   Parking

This mall is home to over 100 dealers offering antiques, collectibles and gifts.

El Cajon Antique Mart
143 E. Main, El Cajon (619) 588-7877
Daily, 10-5; Fri., 10-8
Terms: Cash and check only.   Parking

Here there are 40 shops full of antiques, collectibles, furniture, jewelry, porcelain and dolls.

Frontier Village Antique Mall
114 N. Monte Vista, San Dimas (714) 592-7611
Tues.-Sat., 11-5:30; Sun., 11-4
Terms: MC, V, Check.   Parking

Twenty-six dealers offer furniture, collectibles, primitives, jewelry, quilts and more.

Harbor Antique Mall
211 N. Harbor Blvd., Fullerton (714) 680-0532
Mon.-Sat. 10-5; Sun. 12-5
Terms: MC, V, AE, D. Check.   Parking

Twenty-five dealers offer a variety of antiques and collectibles, large and small.

King Richards Antique Mall
12301 Whittier Blvd., Whittier (213) 696-1066
Mon.-Tues., Sat., 10-6; Wed.-Fri., 10-9; Sun. 12-5
Terms: MC, V, Check.   Parking

This is a three story, 75,000 square foot mall with over 250 dealers, featuring furniture and collectibles of every description.

Lincoln Antique Mall
1811 Lincoln Av., Anaheim (714) 778-2522
Daily, 10-6
Terms: MC, V, Check.   Parking

There are 125 dealers in 12,500 square feet, whose wares include fine antiques and collectibles, china, pottery, furniture, bears, primitives, and jewelry. Lincoln also hosts a bi-monthly outdoor antique faire.

Newport Antique Mall
12141 Brookhurst, Suite 101, Garden Grove (714) 537-4552
Mon.-Sat., 10-6; Sun. 10-5
Terms: Cash and Check only.   Parking

Here you'll find 35 dealers offering a large selection of furniture, glassware, jewelry, books and decorator items.

Olde Towne Pomona Antique Mall & Collectibles
260 E. 2 St., Pomona (714) 622-1011
Mon.-Sat., 10-6; Sun., 12-5
Terms: MC, V, D, AE, Check.   Street parking

This space houses more than 60 dealers in over 8,000 square feet, offering vintage clothes, china, toys, costume jewelry, cameras, and military, ocean liner and sports memorabilia.

Pasadena Antique Center
480 S. Fair Oaks Av., Pasadena (818) 449-7706
Daily, 10-6
Terms: MC, V, AE, Check.   Parking

Approximately 65 dealers in a two story space offer antiques and collectibles, sports memorabilia, dolls and jewelry.

Penny Pinchers
4256 Valley Fair St., Simi Valley (805) 527-0056
Mon.-Sat., 10-5; Sun., 11-5
Terms: MC, V, D, Check.   Parking

This is a 10,000 square foot mall, where approximately 60 dealers offer furniture, pottery, artwork, rugs, collectibles, and jewelry.

Robbins Antique Mart
200 East 2 St., Pomona (714) 623-9835
Daily 10-5
Terms: MC, V, DC, CB, Check. L.   Parking

Robbins Antique Mall is three floors of antiques and collectibles from glassware to furniture and linens. There are over 140 shops here.

Santa Monica Antique Market
1607 Lincoln Blvd., Santa Monica (310) 314-4899
Mon.-Sat., 10-6; Sun. 12-5
Terms: MC, V, Check.   Parking

Featuring quality antiques, collectibles and lots of quilts in a 20,000 square foot space, this mall offers valet parking, which you'll appreciate as soon as you see the lot.

Sherman Oaks Antique Mall
14034 Ventura Blvd., Sherman Oaks (818) 906-0338
Sun. 12-5; Mon.-Sat., 11-6
Terms: MC, V, Check.   Street parking

Here you'll find 74 dealers offering Victorian and Art Deco, furniture, collectibles, sterling, glassware, toys, jewelry and pottery.

T&R Antiques Warehouse
4630 Santa Fe, San Diego (619) 272-0437
Mon.-Fri., 9-5; Sat., 10-5; Sun., 11-5
Terms: MC, V, Check.　　　　Parking

T&R specializes in furniture and collecitbles from Italy, France and Austria. They offer over 15,000 square feet of imported antiques at warehouse prices.

Treasure Mart
293 Redlands Blvd., San Bernardino (714) 825-7264
Mon.-Sat., 10-5:30; Sun., 11-5:30
Terms: MC, V, Check. L.　　　Parking

This space consists of 80 shops featuring antiques, primitives, period furniture and collectibles.

Westchester Faire Antique Mall
8655 S. Sepulveda Blvd., Los Angeles (310) 670-4000
Mon-Sat., 10-6; Sun., 12-5
Terms: MC, V, Check.　　　　Parking

Westchester Faire boasts 30,000 square feet of antiques and collectibles on two levels, featuring 75 shops and three cafes.

Westlake Antique Center
2900 Townsgate Rd., Westlake Village (805) 496-1225
Mon.-Sat., 10-5; Sun., 11-5
Terms: MC, V, Check.　　　　Parking

Here 25 dealers offer furniture, porcelain, crystal, silver, jewelry, prints and collectibles.

Antique Auctions

Santa Margarita Auction Barn
P. O. Box 702, Santa Margarita, CA 93453

Write to be put on the mailing list for notification of upcoming auctions.

Flea Markets

While small flea markets are held sporadically, advertised in local papers, you can find the following, month after month in the same locations, and they're anything but small. Take cash or a checkbook, plastic's no good.

Long Beach Flea Market
Long Beach Veterans' Stadium (310) 420-4018
Third Sunday of the Month, 8-3; $3   Parking

There are 700 dealers here, selling pottery, vintage clothing, quilts, jewelry, collectibles, primitives, furniture, china, glass, toys and dolls. This place is almost as big as the Rose Bowl. An interesting collection to look at, fun to people watch. Refreshments and restrooms off to one side of the market. Three hours at a brisk pace.

Pasadena City College Flea Market
1570 E. Colorado at Hill, Pasadena
First Sunday of the month, 8-3, free   Parking

This is a small flea market with old and collectible merchandise. There is some furniture, but mainly smaller items: costume jewelry, pottery, ceramics, glass and crystal. An hour if you rush, two hours to see it all. Refreshments.

Rose Bowl Flea Market
The Rose Bowl, Pasadena (213) 588-4411
Second Sunday of the month, 9-3; rain or shine; $3   Parking

The largest of the local flea markets, The Rose Bowl features new, swap meet type merchandise on the outer rim of the stadium; and collectibles, furniture, vintage clothing, linens, and jewelry to the left as you enter. There are two schools of thought on this Flea Market. The Get There First or All the Good Stuff will be Gone folks show up when the gates open to make sure they don't miss anything. The more laid-back, Get There

Late and See What You Can Get For a Song crowd know that when you're in the market for larger pieces, dealers negotiate differently come 2:30, if they don't want to *schlep* that breakfront home again. Either way, take a hat; even at a good clip this can be an all day event. Purchase a cold drink when you pass a refreshment stand rather than waiting till you get thirsty; by the time you realize you're parched you'll be diametrically across the Rose Bowl from refreshments. (You've heard of the Law of the Jungle. This is the Law of the Flea.) Restrooms.

Swap Meets

Swap meets offer new goods at discount prices, from clothing to housewares and small electrics, produce, even computers. Some also sell collectible merchandise. Many dealers don't take plastic; plan accordingly.

The Orange County Swap Meet
88 Fair Dr., Costa Mesa (714) 723-6616
Sat.-Sun. 7-4; .50 admission, children under 12 free; Parking

With over 1200 dealers, this may be the biggest swap meet in California. The preponderance of merchandise is new, a small percentage of dealers offer collectibles.

The Roadium
2400 Redondo Beach Blvd., Torrance (213) 321-3920
Daily, 7-4; $1.50/car and driver,.50/passenger   Parking

About 250 dealers sell new merchandise here on weekends. During the week merchandise is a mixture of new goods and collectibles.

Saugus Swap Meet
22500 Soledad Cyn. Rd., Saugus (805) 259-3886
Sundays, 9-3; $1 per person   Parking

The Saugus Swap Meet features over 800 vendors selling new and used merchandise around Saugus Speedway. (Remember that hat.)

The Valley Indoor Swap Meet
14650 Parthenia, Panorama City (818) 892-0183
and
Valley Indoor Swap Meet of Pomona
1600 S. Holt Blvd., Pomona (714) 620-4792
and
Woodland Hills Indoor Swap Meet
6701 Variel, Woodland Hills (818) 340-9120

These three swap meets each offer over a hundred vendors selling new merchandise. They are open Fridays and Saturdays, from 10 to 4, admission is $1, kids and seniors enter free.

Antique Shows

The Glendale Show
1401 N. Verdugo Rd., Glendale (213) 380-2626
First Sunday of the month, 9-3, $3 Admission   Parking

Over one hundred antique dealers participate.

The Pickwick
1001 Riverside Dr., Burbank (310) 455-2886
Fourth Sunday the month, 9-3, $3 Admission   Parking

The Pickwick features over 140 antique dealers.

Interested in receiving updates
of this book?
Please fill in and mail the Reader
Response Card on the last page.

Appliances

It's advisable to do some homework before making a major purchase of this kind. *Consumer Reports* rates brands and models of appliances and back issues are available at the library. If you find a model that's right for you, don't try to find that same model number at the "discount" chains; model numbers on their appliances are generally not the same as the manufacturer's model numbers. As far as I can see, all this does is prevent effective comparison shopping. At the stores below you have a better chance of finding your appliance by number, or a comparable or better model, at a great price.

ABC Premiums
7266 Beverly Blvd., Los Angeles (213) 938-2724
Mon.-Sat., 10-7; Sun., 11-5
Terms: MC, V, AE, D, Check. Exchanges. **Street parking**

ABC carries all major brands of appliances, including Caloric, Sharp, Maytag, Hotpoint, Amana, Frigidaire and Litton, as well as cameras (Nikon, Minolta, etc.), video and audio equipment (RCA, Sony, Panasonic, Zenith), and every small electric you might ever need, and all at discount prices. They also stock housewares. They won't quote prices over the phone but if you visit you'll probably find several things you need, and at a good price.

Albee's Discount Appliances
6305 Wilshire Blvd., Los Angeles (213) 651-0620
Mon.-Sat., 9:30-7; Sun., 11-5
Terms: MC, V, AE, D, Check. Exchanges. **Parking**

Albee's sells just about everything in the way of electronics and major appliances, and chances are it's cheaper here then where you bought it (unless you bought in at another store mentioned in this section.) They carry kitchen appliances—large and small—microwaves, audio and video, televisions, cameras, vacuums, faxes, office equipment, etc., etc., etc. Pricing is 5% to 10% above cost.

Algert Appliances
2121 E. Del Amo, Carson (310) 632-7777
Mon.-Fri., 8:30-5:30; Sat., 9:30-4:30
Terms: MC, V, Check. Final Sale. *Parking*

Algert has a warehouse full of washers, dryers, refrigerators, freezers, stoves, cook-tops televisions, a few microwaves and air conditioners, and if you look around you at the volume of business they're doing, you'll understand how they can offer such deeply discounted prices. A Whirlpool stack washer/dryer combination was $799; microwaves began at $83; a Westinghouse washer and dryer set was $600 and stoves began at $285. There are always a few items on special, so if you're in the market for an appliance, call or come by and check out what's been reduced. Delivery is $35, including installation.

Aztec Appliances
665 15 St., San Diego (619) 236-0616
Mon.-Fri., 8:30-5:30; Sat., 10-3
Terms: MC, V, D, Check. C.O.D. Final Sale. *Parking*

Aztec is a clearance center for Hotpoint and G.E. appliances. Here you'll find models that are discontinued, some scratch and dent and bankrupt stock, at discounts of 20% to 60%. There are refrigerators, stoves, washers, dryers, dishwashers, air conditioners and trash compactors, although stock constantly varies. A 27" full size stack washer/dryer was $666, and a 24 cu. ft. Jenn Air refrigerator with ice and water dispenser was $999. There is a $25 local installation charge, which includes carting away your old appliance.

Barrett's Appliances   **COUPON**
2723 Lincoln Blvd, Santa Monica (310) 392-4108
Mon.-Fri., 8-6; Sat., 8-5; Sun. 11-3
Terms: MC, V, Check. Exchanges. *Parking*

Barrett's has been discounting appliances since 1946, and with the advent of the "discount" appliance chains, business has only gotten better. Here you'll find Amana, Kitchenaid, Magic Chef, Sub-Zero, Viking, Maytag, Whirlpool, and White Westinghouse washers, dryers, stoves, microwaves, built-ins, refrigerators and dishwashers, and Barrett's services everything they sell. All items come with a warranty, and you can get extended warranties from the manufacturer, so if you move out of the state the warranty is still good. Barrett's also rents appliances. While outright purchase is cheaper, should you need to rent-to-own, with good credit you'll save as much as 50% over the major rent-to-own company servicing the Los Angeles area. *Receive free delivery in Barrett's delivery area (value to $95) upon presentation of the* *coupon.*

Friedman's
5515 Stearns, Long Beach (310) 598-7756
Mon.-Sat., 10-6; Sun., 10-5
(also in Costa Mesa, Encino, Orange and Pasadena)
Terms: MC, V, D, Check. Exchanges. **Parking**

Friedman's carries G.E., Amana, Panasonic, Sanyo, Tappan, Sharp, RCA, Quasar, Frigidaire, Toshiba and Magic Chef microwave ovens, and it has a price guarantee: if you find your microwave for less in 60 days they'll refund the difference. Should you buy an oven and find you want a different model, there is a 60 day full credit exchange. They take old microwaves for trade-in, and offer free microwave cooking classes to their customers forever. (I really could have used this; after six years, I'm just learning the subtleties of defrost.) They do repairs, and give free loaners if there's a parts delay.

Lincoln Appliances
1674 20 St., Santa Monica (310) 829-2442
Thurs., 12-5; Fri.-Sat., 10-5; Sun., 10-5
Terms: MC, V, Check. Return w/restocking chg. **Street Parking**

If you've ever driven down Olympic Blvd. in Santa Monica, this is the place with the sign "The store that looks like Sears blew up." Lincoln Appliances is full of value, because its stock is mainly Whirlpool, Kitchenaid, Roper and Estate appliances, uncrated but unused, bankrupt stock or, in some cases, prizes not won on quiz shows. Merchandise comes with full warranty, and some pieces are scratch and dent, the flaws frequently not visible once installed. You can save about 20% off others' "lowest prices" on stoves, washers, dryers, refrigerators (bar and full-size), freezers, microwaves, cooktops and vent hoods. If you're looking for an item with particular features, call to see if they have what you want. The place is enormous; odds are you'll find what you're looking for.

Pacific Sales
2080 Washington Av., Torrance (310) 212-2700
Tues.-Fri., 10-5; Sat., 10-5
(also in Buena Park, Irvine, and City of Industry)
Terms: MC, V, Check. Returns. **Parking**

Pacific Sales carries major appliances, plumbing fixtures, and audio and video, and all at rock bottom prices. In addition, you will find service here. A bulletin board notes clearance items and specials are tagged on almost everything. They carry all major brands of household appliances, free-standing and built-in, and many models come with service specials, like a second year service contract free (first year included with purchase). There is no delivery charge, generally no charge for colors other than white, and they will haul away your old appliance. There is also a plumbing showroom, with fixtures and hardware for kitchen and bath remodeling, also at competitive prices.

The Sewing Machine Warehouse
COUPON
16141 Nordhoff St., West Hills (818) 893-5005
Mon.-Sat., 9:30-6
(also in Torrance (310) 543-2425, West Los Angeles (310) 477-0448)
Terms: MC, V, Check. L. Exchanges.   Parking

Sewing Machine Warehouse is the second largest independent Singer Sewing Machine dealer; they also carry machines by White and Bernina, and stock over 45 styles. Machines begin at around $150, and discounts generally range from 30% to 50%, but may go lower if a machine is on clearance, or a volume purchase has been made. Lessons and service are included in the purchase, and they take trade-ins. Extended warranties are offered, and service is done on premises, with factory trained mechanics. *The coupon entitles you to purchase an extended warranty at half price when buying a sewing machine.*

Discount Catalogs

ABC Vacuum Cleaner Warehouse
(512) 459-7643
Terms: MC, V, D, MO, L, COD. Returns.

Here you'll find Royal, Panasonic, Kirby, Electrolux, Hoover, and Eureka Vacuums. They are bought from distributors who find themselves overstocked, so not all manufacturers' models are available at any particular time, but if you're interested in what ABC has in inventory, you can save up to 40%. They also carry carry tools and accessories for models they sell.

Art Supplies

Aaron Brothers Art Mart
5640 E. La Palma, Anaheim   (714) 779-9844
Mon.-Sat., 10-9; Sun., 11-6
(36 additional locations; see Geographical Index)
Terms: V, MC, Check.   Returns.   Parking

Aaron Brothers carries art supplies, framing needs, and furniture for the artist's studio. Although a retail store, they frequently have "20% to 50% off" sales on paints, brushes, papers, pens, markers, portfolios and studio furniture. They also have One Cent Frame Sales (seemingly monthly); buy one picture frame, poster frame, or custom framing job at the regular price, and get a second of equal or lesser value for a penny. There is also a low price guarantee on custom framing.

The Art Store
7301 W. Beverly Blvd., Los Angeles   (213) 933-3284
Mon.-Fri., 9-7:30; Sat., 9:30- 5; Sun., 11 - 5
(also in West Los Angeles, Pasadena, Universal City, Fullerton, and Newport)
Terms: MC, V, D, Check.   Returns.   Parking

Here there are consistent discounts of 10% to 35% on a wide selection of artist's colors, brushes, accessories, paper, pens and markers, air brushes, portfolios, studio furniture and graphics products. There are also advertised specials, ranging from half price sales on frames to discounts on furniture.

Art Supply Warehouse
6672 Westminster Blvd., Westminster   (714) 891-3628
Mon.-Fri., 9:30-6; Sat., 10-5; Sun., 11-4
Terms: MC, V, Check ($5 min.).   Returns.   Parking

There is over 12,000 square feet of merchandise here, and just about all of it is reduced. Illustration mat and poster board are discounted to 21%; watercolors to 35% and oils to 26%; markers to 40%, technical pens to 66%. The staff is friendly and knowledgeable, and there is a video rental library of how-to tapes.

Flax Art Supplies
8801 S. Sepulveda Blvd., Westchester (310) 641-7995
10852 Lindbrook Dr., West Los Angeles (310) 208-3529
Mon.-Fri., 9-5:30; Sat., 10-4
Terms: MC, V, D, AE, Check. Exchanges.   Parking

Flax has a number of ongoing sales, and the studio furniture section always has some buys. Stretched canvas, when purchasing six or more, are discounted 40%. Grumbacher water colors and Winsor & Newman oils are also 40% off. There were various taborets, and a variety of drafting tables, reduced from 30% to 50%. Lamps, chairs and stools are comparably reduced. There is a students' discount of 10%, but not on sale items.

Graphaids   *COUPON*
3030 S. LaCienega Blvd., Culver City (310) 204-1212
12406 Santa Monica Blvd., West Los Angeles (310) 820-0445
Mon.-Fri., 9-6; Sat., 9-5
Terms: MC, V, AE, D, Check. Exchanges.   Street parking

Graphaids sells graphics supplies, fine arts supplies, airbrush supplies and some studio furniture at discounts of 30% to students with valid I.D.'s (from any school, at any age), and 20% to professional accounts. There is free delivery on orders of $40 or more, and the Culver City store is the warehouse, offering a bit more variety. They have two annual sales, one around Christmas and the other in the summer. *The coupon entitles you to a 20% discount on all future purchases.*

Michael's Art Store
1518 Highland Av., Hollywood (213) 466-5295
Mon.-Fri., 8:30-6:30; Sat., 10-6
Terms: AE, MC, V, Check. Exchanges.   Parking

Everything at Michael's is always discounted 10% to 50%. Brushes are 40% off, picture frames, 50%. There is a close-out corner, where overstocked and discontinued items are discounted 50%; last time I found tempera and liquetex poster paints there. During periodic sales, prices are further reduced. Pick up a flyer as you enter.

Pacific Airbrush
1207 W. Center St.
150 W. Lincoln, Anaheim (714) 250-0774
Mon.-Fri., 9-5:30; Sat., 10-4
Terms: MC, V, Check. Exchanges.   Parking

This store carries a large selection of airbrushes, including Paache, Badger, Iwata, Thayer & Chandler, discounted 20% to 25%. Compressors, paints, stencil media, books and other accessories are also discounted.

Picture Frames

The Golden Frame, Inc.
6422 Maple St., Westminster (714) 893-2294
Mon.-Sat., 10-6
Terms: Cash or Check only. Returns.   Parking

With over 75,000 frames in stock, this is an amazing store. Inventory ranges from 3x5 to 36x48 in a large assortment of styles and finishes from from raw wood to whitewash, colored and neutral, to gilt and rosebuds. A 3x5 gilt frame with a linen liner was $2.96; an 8x10 whitewashed frame with linen liner was $10.90. A 14x18 carved whitewashed frame was $19, a 4x5 oval frame with a walnut burl finish was $3.50. The prices are bargain basement here, better then discount stores, and the quality and variety are top drawer. Frames come without glass, which can be provided. They also custom frame, at competitive prices.

See also
   Mainly Seconds
   Tuesday Morning

Discount Catalogs

Art Supply Warehouse
(800) 243-5038
Terms: MC, V, Check.

Art Supply Warehouse regularly discounts merchandise up to 60%. Among the items reduced are paints, inks, markers, brushes, boards, books, canvas, studio furniture, paper, sculpture and silk painting supplies. They ship free within the continental U. S. and there are volume discounts for orders exceeding $500.

Cos-Tom Picture Frame
(800) 854-6606
Terms: MC, V. Returns.

This catalog is full of put-together-yourself frames of varying styles and materials. There are lots of close-outs, overstocked and discontinued frames, discounted from 25% to 50%. A broad selection of finishes is represented: driftwood, walnut, gold, silver, cherry, antique gold and brass, to name a few. Most choices include a mat or liner.

Daniel Smith
(800) 426-6740
Terms: MC, V, Check. Returns.

Daniel Smith offers watercolors, oils, acrylics, pastels, paper, brushes, canvas, materials for printmaking, frames and studio furniture, all at discount prices. Many items are cheaper in volume.

Audio and Video

Adray's
11201 W. Pico Blvd., West Los Angeles (310) 479-0797
Mon.-Fri., 10-8; Sat. 10-6; Sun., 11-5
(also in Van Nuys, Ventura, Torrance, Lakewood, Canoga Park, Los Angeles)
Terms: MC, V, Check. ATM. Returns.   Parking

Adray's is a discount department store, carrying audio and video products, televisions, cameras, housewares, giftware, small appliances, jewelry, home office equipment, baby furniture, you name it, they've got it. There is a discount for cash and a low price guarantee: if you find the same item cheaper, within a year, they will refund the difference plus 10% (with some exceptions). Jewelry seems to be a concession; Adray's policies may not apply; check before you buy.

Crystal Sonics
1638 S. Central Av., Glendale (818) 240-7310
Mon.-Fri., 9-6; Sat., 10-3
Terms: MC, V, D, AE. Returns.   Parking

Crystal Sonics offers discounted electronics for the automotive audiophile. They will send you a catalog for $2, or come in and pick one up free. They offer cellular phones (they will do the hook-up), car stereos, the equipment to install car stereos, installation of car stereos, radar detectors, antennae, and anti-theft devices. In addition to their low prices—often discounted as much as 60%—there are close-outs, priced even lower. Among the lines offered are Panasonic, Pioneer, Sony, TDK and Clarion. They are working on a deal for the best prices on personal pagers, which may be in place by now.

DAK Outlet Store
8200 Remmet Av., Canoga Park (818) 888-8220
Mon.-Fri., 10-6; Sat., 11-5
Terms: MV, C, AE, Check. Returns.   Parking

Dak puts out an electronics catalog, and the outlet sells returned goods which have been factory reconditioned, and deemed A-one. An auto-bake bakery was $90 ($130); a 200 name memory phone was $60; a halogen executive desk lamp was $40. There were lots of computers and computer accessories, radios, stereos, and CD players.This is a fun place to shop for the person who has everything, and definitely a hard place to categorize.

Discount Sales Stores
2253 S. Sepulveda Blvd., West Los Angeles (213) 473-5015
Hours vary by location.
(also in Arcadia, Carson, Huntington Beach, Upland, Burbank, Covina, Corona and Anaheim)
Terms: MC, V, Check. Exchanges.   *Parking*

Discount Sales sells televisions, ceiling fans, and phones, and though they have a big stock of these items, the thing you remember most after one visit is *video cameras*. It looks like there must be hundred different models, by Sony, Panasonic, JVC, Canon, RCA, Minolta and more; and they'll take your old video camera in trade. They also rent video cameras.

L. A. Tronics
12121 Pico Blvd., West Los Angeles (310) 820-8444
Mon.-Fri., 10-9; Sat.-Sun., 10-6
(also in Encino, Huntington Beach, West Hills, Pasadena and Torrance)
Terms: MC, V, AE, D, Check. Returns.   *Parking*

Among the best of the new discount audio and video stores is L. A. Tronics. If you're looking for brand name televisions, VCRs, stereo systems, phones, radios, camera equipment or small appliances, check their prices.

The Sharper Image Outlet   CCC
Wilshire at Grand, Los Angeles (213) 622-2351
Mon.-Sat., 9-6; Sun., 11-5
Terms: MC, V, AE, Check. Final sale.   *Street parking*

The back of this Sharper Image location houses the chainwide clearance center for the 74 Sharper Image retail stores. Here you'll find all kinds of gizmos of modern life reduced 10% to 50%. In addition to electronics there are watches, jewelry, luggage and clothes. The burgundy stripe in the carpet denotes the beginning of the outlet; everything beyond it is reduced.

Speaker City U.S.A.
10615 Vanowen St., Burbank (818) 508-1908
Mon.-Sat., 10-6
Terms: MC, V, Check. Exchanges.   Parking

Speaker City offers name brand speakers for home, car, and some for heavy duty commercial use. Everything is discounted, and there are a lot of choices. A listening room is provided, so you can hear how the speakers sound before you buy them. There is something here for every budget.

See also
ABC Premiums
Albee's appliances
Algert Appliances
Pacific Sales

Discount Catalogs

Crutchfield
(800) 336-5566
Terms: MC, V, AE, DC, CB, O, D. Returns.

Crutchfield sells home office equipment, phones, video equipment, computers, security equipment, audio and car stereo equipment, and prices are often discounted to 55%. They have three distinct catalogs, so ask for the particular product line that interests you. The catalogs are packed with information, in fact in places it feels more like you're reading a magazine, comparing specifications and diagramming installations. After the sale they offer toll free customer service and technical assistance, as well as a repair department.

J&R Music World
(800) 221-8180
Terms: MC, V, AE, D, Check. Exchanges.

J&R's catalog offers compact discs, audio products, computers, peripherals, home office products, televisions, VCRs, video accessories, professional sound equipment, car stereos, radar detectors, CB radios, scanners, home security products, watches, electronic keyboards, cameras, home appliances, telephones, calculators, software and instructional videos, all at discounted prices. They will quote prices over the phone and if you're looking for anything in the above list, it would be worth it to give them a call; they are often cheaper than local sources.

Wholesale Tape & Supply Co.
(800) 251-7228
Terms: MC, V, AE, D, Check. Returns.

WTS sells audio cassettes, audio accessories, duplication equipment and services, microphones, open-reel tape, video equipment, accessories and video tape. If you use any of this in quantity, you can get it cheaply here. (Quantity prices start at orders of ten, and savings can go as high as 50%.) Among the brand names offered are Maxell, TDK, Sony DAT, and Ampex. They can duplicate compact discs, cassettes or videotapes, again, cheaper in quantity.

See also
47th Street Photo

Have I left our your favorite discount store? Please let me know where it is.
Shopping Secrets of Southern California
Box 24447
Los Angeles, CA 90024-0447

Beauty Products and Services

Lora's
18737 Ventura Blvd., Tarzana (818) 705-4030
11677 San Vicente Blvd., Brentwood (310) 826-6159
Mon.-Sat., 9:30-6:30
Terms: MC, V, Check.　　　　　Parking

Lora's offers perfumes discounted from 10% to 50%. In addition to the most popular brands, Lora's has many fragrances you won't find elsewhere. Some make-up products are discounted as well.

Perfume City
12215 Ventura Blvd., #204, Studio City (818) 763-1875
Tues.-Sat., 10:30-6:30
Terms: MC, V, Check.　　　　　Parking

Here you'll find current brands of perfumes and colognes for men and women at discounts ranging from 10% to 50%.

Perfumes West
2099 Westwood Blvd., Westwood (310) 470-8556
Mon.-Sat., 10-6; Sun., 12-5
Terms: MC, V, Check.　　　　　Parking

Perfumes West sells brand name perfumes at a discount; they also offer some make-up and hair care items, also marked down.

Prestige Fragrance
The Citadel, City of Commerce (213) 887-1135
Plaza Continental Factory Stores, Ontario (714) 944-5881
Hours vary by location.
Terms: MC, V, Check.　　　　　Parking

Prestige carries discounted perfumes, make-up and sundries. Halston Spray Cologne (1 oz.) was $12 ($28.50); Tea Rose Eau de Toilette Spray (2 oz.) was

$16 ($25.95). There is also a selection of make-up, including Germaine Monteil, Almay, Max Factor, Orlane, Borghese and Countess Isserlyn.

Prima Beauty Center
2130 Westwood Blvd., Westwood (310) 474-0903
Mon.-Fri., 9-7; Sat., 10-7; Sun., 11-5
Terms: MC, V, D, Check.   Parking

Prima is a friendly place to shop. They carry well known perfumes at discounted prices. If your favorite scent is more obscure, they can probably order it for you. They also carry haircare products, accessories and make-up.

See also
Lace and Scents

Department store make-up counters offer make-overs using their products, by appointment, and there is no obligation to buy. Why not schedule an appointment before a date, or New Year's Eve? (You could pay $100 for this in a salon.) You may discover you want some of the products that made you so ravishing, or, if you hate the look, you already own soap and water.

Services

If you're adventurous, you can procure the services of manicurists and hair stylists dirt cheap by having yourself beautified by a student, under supervision.

Gino Robair Beauty College
3582 Adams, Riverside (714) 785-5270
Tues.-Fri., 9:15-4:30; Sat., 8:15-4:30
Terms: Cash and Check only.   Parking

Here you can get a manicure for $3.50, a pedicure for $7 and a haircut for $4.50. Perms start at $15 and color starts at $10.50.

Hairmasters University
210 W. Highland Av., San Bernardino (714) 882-2987
Tues.-Sat., 9-4
Terms: Cash and Check only.   Parking

Haircuts here are $4.75, perms begin at $12.25, and color begins at $10.50. Manicures are $2.50 and pedicures, $6. They also have a Fontana location.

Marinello Beauty School
6288 W. 3 St., Los Angeles (213) 938-2005
Tues.-Fri., 9:30-2:30; Sat., 8-2:30
(14 additional locations; see Geographical Index)
Terms: Cash and Check only.   Parking

Marinello is a large chain of beauty schools, and pricing may vary from location to location, but haircuts are around $5.50, perms from $11.95 to $22.95, and one process color, $17.50. Manicures are $2.95 and pedicures, $6. If you call early you can generally come in the same day.

Richards Beauty College
200 N. Euclid Av., Ontario (714) 620-8277
Tues.-Sat., 9-4:30
Terms: Cash and Check only.   Parking

Haircuts here are $4.75, perms start at $25, and color starts at $9.95. Pedicures are $5.95 and manicures, $2.50. There is generally no need for an appointment. There is a second location in San Bernardino.

Vidal Sassoon Beauty School
1222 Santa Monica Mall, Santa Monica (310) 393-1461
By appointment only.
Terms: MC, V.   Street parking

At Vidal Sassoon they give manicures at 9:15, Tuesdays through Fridays; you have to bring your own polish, and the charge is $4. Haircuts are $12 Monday through Friday, $16 on Saturday. They ask that you allow two to three hours for consultation, wash, cut and blow dry. Perms are $38, and color is $18 for a touch up. If you want a Saturday appointment, call at least two weeks in advance; for a weekday appointment, two to three days is sufficient.

Books

New Books

Bookstar
11000 West Jefferson Blvd., Culver City   (310) 391-0818
Mon.-Sun., 9-11
(11 additional locations; see Geographical Index)
Terms: MC, V, D, AE, Check. Returns.   Parking

Not only are these stores open thirteen hours a day, every day, but each contains over 100,000 discounted books. Hardcovers, paperbacks and children's books are discounted 10%, with lots of sale racks at greater reductions. *New York Times* hard cover best-sellers are discounted 40%.

Book Warehouse
The Citadel, City of Commerce   (213) 722-7210
Hours vary by location.
(also in Ontario, Barstow and San Ysidro)
Terms: MC, V, Check. Final sale.   Parking

Remaindered books at discount prices is what you'll find at this chain. They have a few $1 tables, where I found *Jo Bob Goes back to the Drive-In* ($10.95). A good selection of year-old travel books were $3.99 and $4.99, 1990 Mobil travel guides were $1.99 ($10.95). This is the kind of store that may have something you want; if so it will be substantially reduced. There is also a frequent buyer program: purchase $100 worth of books and get $10 worth of free merchandise.

Crown Books
326 Wilshire Blvd., Santa Monica   (310) 394-5445
Mon.-Sat. 10-9:30; Sun., 10-6
(91 additional locations; see Geographical Index)
Terms: MC, V, Check. Returns.   Parking

Crown sells books and magazines at discounts beginning at 10%; *New York Times* best-seller hard backs are discounted 40%, paperbacks, 25%; audio cassettes are reduced 20% and there are lots of sale books and remainders in addition. Super Stores carry a greater selection.

Discount Reader Bookstore
8651 Lincoln Blvd., Westchester (310) 410-1069
Mon.-Sat.,9-9; Sun.,9-6
Terms: MC, V, Check. Returns.   Parking

Discount Reader offers a 25% discount on all *Los Angeles Times* best-sellers, and 10% off everything else. There are sale tables where books are more deeply discounted. They will order books, giving you the 10% discount whenever possible.

Hunter's Books
414 S. Lake Av., Pasadena (818) 793-8139
1111 Prospect, La Jolla (619) 459-3707
Mon.-Fri., 9:30-9; Sat., 9:30-6; Sun., 12-5
Terms: MC, V, Checks. Returns.   Street parking

Hunter's sells new books at a 10% discount, but it also stocks lots of remainders. With these it's possible to wind up paying as little as *10% of the original retail price.*

> **The chain bookstores are going crazy coming up with deals to lure you back from the discounters. There are savings cards and frequent buyer plans, but joining them costs money. Discounters are still the best value.**

Used Books

Acres of Books
240 Long Beach Blvd., Long Beach (310) 437-6980
Tues.-Sat., 9:15-5
Terms: Check and Cash only. Final sale.   Parking

As the name implies, there are a lot of books in this warren of aisles and nooks, with little side rooms dedicated to special subjects. There are large sections of cookbooks and old fiction (including out of print titles). Hardcovers are priced as marked, and most modern paperbacks are half the cover price. Acres does buy books: if they find something of yours they're interested in they'll make you a cash offer; if you choose to take store credit, you get 20% more.

Bargain Books
14426 Friar, Van Nuys (818) 782-2782
Tues.-Fri., 10-6; Sat., 10-5
Terms: V, MC, D, Check. Final sale.   Street parking

Bargain Books has been around for 33 years and sells used books on all subjects, with specialties in technical and art books. About half the stock is paperbacks; newer ones generally sell at half the cover price. If you tell them you're looking for something they'll keep an eye out and call you if it comes in. They're picky about what they'll buy, but if they want some of your books you'll get 20% to 30% of the cover price in cash; 30% more in credit.

Bodhi Tree Used Bookstore
8585 Melrose Av., Los Angeles (310) 659-3227
Mon.-Sat. 11-7
Terms: MC, V, Check. Final sale.   Street parking

Though specializing in metaphysics, this shop around the corner from The Bodhi Tree has new and used books of all kinds. To sell your books you'll have to leave them for a few days to be priced, and then they'll offer you cash, or 33% more in credit, which can be used in the new bookstore as well.

Book Again
5039 Torrance Blvd., Torrance (310) 542-1156
Tues.-Sat., 11-6; Sun., 12-5
Terms: Check and Cash only. Final sale.   Street parking

While over half of Book Agains' stock is paperbacks, they do have a substantial number of hard-cover books. Most current paperbacks sell for half the cover price, but Book Again offers weekly sales where they pick a few letters of the alphabet, and books by authors whose names begin with those letters sell for 25% of the cover price. They have two-for-one sales once or twice a year (typically March and late summer). They'll buy your books, generally for credit.

The Bookie Joint
7246 Reseda Blvd., Reseda (818) 343-1055
Mon.-Fri., 11-6:30; Sat., 10:30-5:30; Sun., 11-3
Terms: Check and Cash only. Final sale. Street parking

The Bookie Joint offers a large selection of used paperbacks and hard covers. Recent paperbacks are half price, there is usually a section of paperbacks for a quarter, and a $2 hard cover section. They will buy your old books, selectively, for cash or credit, and they have a search service for out-of-print books.

Cliff's Books
630 E. Colorado Blvd., Pasadena (818) 449-9541
Mon.-Sun., 10:30-Midnight
Terms: AE, Check. Final sale. Street parking

Cliff's has over 100,000 books, records, and comics, so if you don't see what you're looking for, *ask*; they have books stowed in the attic, in the garage, in *someone else's* garage.... Their strongest areas are metaphysics, technical specialties, cookery and children's books. They have collector and out-of-print books, a search service and keep a want list. They buy for cash or twice as much in credit.

Marlow's Books
2314 Lincoln Blvd., Santa Monica (310) 392-9161
Mon.-Fri., 10-8; Sat., 10-6; Sun., 12-6
Terms: V, MC, Check. Final sale. Street parking

Marlow's sells hard and soft cover used books, as well as tons of magazines, piled in not much order. Reasonably current magazines sell for half price, but they do have rare issues at collector's prices. Pocket books are $1, and they will accept three of yours in trade for one of theirs any time. They buy books for cash or store credit.

Once Read Books
4174 Woodruff, Lakewood (310) 420-1034
Mon.-Sat., 10-7; Sun., 12-5
Terms: MC, V, AE, Check. Final sale. Street parking

Once Read Books has a large selection of used paperbacks and hardcovers. While specializing in Western Americana, there are books on every subject. Recent paperbacks go for half the cover price, other books are as marked. They will take books for cash but you'll get more if you opt for credit.

New and Used Books

Brand Bookshop
231 N. Brand Blvd., Glendale   (818) 507-5943
Mon.-Thurs., 10-9; Fri., 10-10; Sat. 11-6
Terms: MC, V, AE, D, DC, Check. Final sale.   Parking

Brand carries mostly used books. Recent paperbacks sell for half the cover price and all other prices are as marked. There is a general selection of fiction and non-fiction and they buy books for cash and credit (50% more if you choose credit, to be spent on used books only).

Carl's Pocketbook Exchange
1040 W. Gardena Blvd., Gardena   (310) 327-9331
Mon.-Sat., 11-5
Terms: Check and Cash only. Final sale.   Street parking

Carl's carries mainly pocketbooks, and used books generally sell for half the cover price, new pocketbooks are 15% off. They have lots of bargain books at four for $1. They'll take your books for store credit, applied to purchase of used books.

Dutton's Brentwood Bookstore
11975 San Vicente Blvd., Brentwood   (310) 476-6263
Mon.-Fri., 9:30-9; Sat., 9:30-6; Sun., 11-5
Terms: MC, V, AE, Check. Exchanges.   Parking

This is the largest new book bookstore in L. A., with over 180,000 titles. They sell both new and used books: new hard-cover fiction is 20% off the cover price, and most used paperbacks are $1 or less. They do take books in trade, offering more credit than cash. This store is *not* related to the Dutton's in the valley.

Dutton's Bookstore
5146 Laurel Canyon Blvd., North Hollywood (818)769-3866
Hours vary by location.
(also in Burbank, (818) 840-8003; and Los Angeles (213) 683-1199)
Terms: MC, V, Check. Exchanges.   Parking

Dutton's is half new books and half used; they are strong in literature, fiction and history. New fiction hardcovers are discounted 20%, non-fiction, 10%. They buy used books, for cash or credit. They also carry some rare books.

The Paperback Trader
1510 Wilshire Blvd., Santa Monica (310) 394-8147
Mon.-Thurs., 10-8; Fri.-Sat., 10-10; Sun., 12-8
Terms: Check and Cash only. Final sale.   Street parking

The Paperback Trader offers new books at the same price as Crown, and used books at half their cover price, to $1.97. Strong in romance, science fiction, mystery, adventure and literature, they will look over your books and purchase what they need for store credit toward the purchase of used books, offering you 25% of the cover price. This is a comfortable store, a place where you find patrons sitting on the floor, reading a chapter before deciding to buy.

Valley Book City
5249 Lankershim Blvd., North Hollywood (818) 985-6911
Mon.-Thurs., 11-7; Fri.-Sat., 10-8; Sun., 11-6
Terms: MC, V, Check. Final sale.   Street parking

Valley Book City sells mostly used books, so they buy used books, and they're more generous with credit than cash. Newer paperbacks are half the cover price, and they have something for everyone, from cannibal recipes to worm ranching, everything in between, and lots of things more appetizing.

Friends of the Libraries Sales

Most libraries hold these sales periodically. They are generally announced in the paper, as well as in the library. The Beverly Hills Sale is ongoing.

Beverly Hills Friends of the Library Sale
Beverly Hills Public Library
444 North Rexford Dr., Beverly Hills (310) 288-2244
Mon., Wed.-Sun., 12-4; Tues. 11-3
Terms: Cash only. Final sale.   Parking

A small room off the entrance to the new library is home to the Friends of the Library sale. Here books on all subjects sell at a fraction of original prices.

Discount Catalogs

Barnes & Noble
(800) 242-6657
Terms: MC, V, AE, DC, Check.

Barnes and Noble offers reference books, children's books, history, language, math and science books, as well as videos, CDs and cassettes, at discounts up to 70%.

Daedalus Books
(800) 395-2665
Terms: MC, V, AE, Check.

Daedalus offers remaindered and new books at discounts from 10% to 90%. They carry books published by trade and university presses, as well as some small presses. Though there are sections of children's books, and some genre books, this catalog is full of contemporary literature.

Edward R. Hamilton
Falls Village, Ct. 06031-5000
Terms: Check.

Once on the Edward R. Hamilton mailing list you will receive a 32 page newsprint tabloid monthly, full of remainders, publishers' closeouts and overstocks on all subjects. Books are mainly hard cover, there's something to appeal to every taste, and discounts run as high as 90%.

Garage Sales are a great place to buy used books. Paperbacks often sell for a quarter.

Building and Remodeling

Air Conditioning Exchange
COUPON
6900 San Fernando Rd., Glendale (818) 845-8544
Mon.-Sat., 8:30-5
Terms: MC, V, D, Check. Returns.   Street parking

Here you'll find a variety of ways to save on air conditioning and heating. For the do-it-yourselfer, there's everything you'd need to install equipment by manufacturers such as Carrier, Lennox, Tempstar and Heil, and the units can be purchased at discount prices. The Air Conditioning Exchange can design your ductwork, and if you have a problem mid-install, call and they'll help you out. For those with great intentions but not much follow through, you can do part of the job, and they'll do the rest. Or if you're like me, (and want someone else to do it), you'll be glad to know they install at reasonable prices. They also sell scratch and dent models, discounted up to 20% more. Financing, extended warranties, maintenance contracts and replacement parts round out the service. *The coupon entitles you to 10% off one purchase.*

Art Glass Designs and Doors
7139 Vineland Av., North Hollywood (818) 765-0217
Mon.-Fri., 8:30-5
Terms: Cash and Check only. Final sale.   Parking

As you'll see by the entrance, Art Glass manufactures wooden doors inset with etched and beveled windows (many looking like leaded glass). They come in poplar, fir, mahogany and oak, finished or unfinished, and can be purchased at 15% to 20% less than what you'd pay through a contractor. There is a wide selection of styles, and prices range from $395 to $985. There are also a few beautifully carved wooden fireplace mantles.

Deco Brass
18919 Ventura Blvd., Tarzana (818) 345-5481
Mon.-Fri., 8-5; Sat., 9-4
Terms: V, MC. Returns.   Parking

Deco-Brass specializes in hardware for every room of the house, from brass hinges to porcelain doorknobs, mailboxes and door numbers to the doors themselves, plumbing, locks and hinges, manufactured by such names as Baldwin, Lamp, Bates & Bates, Artistic Brass, Keller and Jado, at discounts ranging from 25% to 40% everyday, with an occasional sale when prices are further reduced. Be prepared to take a number and wait; it's always busy.

The Fence Factory
29414 Roadside Dr., Agoura (818) 889-2240
Mon.-Fri., 9-5; Sat., 9-3
(also in Goleta, Ventura and Santa Maria)
Terms: MC, V, Check. Exchanges.   *Parking*

Right off the 101 Freeway is the Fence Factory, in business for twelve years, supplying pre-fabricated and custom fences at reasonable prices. Stock ranges from wood (redwood to picket fence panels) to chain link to wrought iron to PVC to concrete; everything but masonry, and prices are based on the volume and dollar amount purchased. They will quote you on custom work, but as you might expect, stock items will be cheaper.

Kitchen & Bath Clearance Center   CCC
13035 Saticoy St., North Hollywood (818) 982-5524
Tues.-Sat., 8-5
Terms: MC, V, Check. Final sale.   *Parking*

At this new store all stock is below cost, because this is the clearance center for the Familian line of kitchen and bath fixtures, where you can save up to 60% on everything, everyday. Featured are sinks, tubs, kitchen appliances and accessories. Stock is discontinued models and colors, and there isn't much inventory, so if you want it you'd better buy it soon (like now). A single handle kitchen faucet, retailing at over $140, sold here for $42. Cooktops start at $150. Merchandise always varies but quality is consistently high. If you can find what you're looking for here, you'll save a bundle.

Kitchen and Bath Specialists
7820 Balboa Blvd., Van Nuys (818) 781-8990
Mon.-Fri., 8-5:30; Sat., 9-5
Terms: MC, V, Check. Exchanges.   *Parking*

Kitchen and Bath Specialists carries tubs, sinks and plumbing fixtures, as well as kitchen and vanity cabinetry, at discounts beginning at 25%, going as low as 60%. They carry the newest merchandise, and there's always stock on hand. If you know what you're doing you can install your purchases yourself, or they can do the installation for you.

The Kitchen Warehouse   **COUPON**
2093 W. Washington Blvd., Los Angeles (213) 734-1696
Mon.-Sat., 9-5
Terms: MC, V, D, Check.   Parking

There are over forty kitchens on display here. Kitchen Warehouse can install a complete custom kitchen, or replace a cabinet or two, and their prices are very competitive. They carry over 14 lines of cabinets, and all you have to do is bring in the dimensions of your kitchen and sit down with one of their designers; with the help of their computerized kitchen designing system, you'll create a great looking kitchen for less. *Use the coupon to save 5% on your next purchase.*

Panel It, The Kitchen Store   **COUPON**
6322 W. Slauson Av., Culver City (800) 726-1745
Mon.-Fri., 8:30-8, Sat., 8:30-5:30; Sun., 9:30-3
Terms: MC, V, D, Check. Returns.   Parking

Panel It offers paneling, closet organizers, window greenhouses, tub enclosures, mirrored doors and vanities, almost any kind of small home improvement you can think of you'll find here, and discounted. The bulk of business seems to be in custom kitchen and bath cabinets. A factory outlet for ten different cabinet manufacturers, Panel It has what you're looking for in any price range. They will help with how-to instructions, or their contracting staff can remodel your kitchen. *The coupon entitles you to free delivery in the Los Angeles area.*

See also
Froch's Woodcraft Shop

Discount Catalogs

The Renovator's Supply
(800) 659-2211
Terms: MC, V, Check.

Renovator's Supply carries architectural accents, hardware, lighting, plumbing and decorative accents you can't find anywhere else, and one of the easiest paint strippers on the market. If you like to putter around the house, you'll appreciate their catalogs.

Discount Hardware Chains

These stores are springing up all over Southern California, offering one-stop hardware shopping, mazes of aisles featuring widgets you can't imagine a use for, and prices lower then local hardware stores.

Builders Discount
12580 Saticoy St., North Hollywood (818) 982-5900
Mon.-Fri., 7-9; Sat., 7-8; Sun., 8-6
(also in Los Angeles, Chatsworth, Simi Valley, and Northridge)
Terms: MC, V, D, Check, SC. Returns.   Parking

Carrying everything from hardware to housewares to lawn and garden needs, outdoor furniture and fixtures, Builders Discount has low prices everyday, and weekly advertised specials.

Contractors Warehouse
601 E. Imperial Hwy., La Habra (714) 447-1009
1680 W. Mission Blvd., Pomona (714) 622-4675
Mon.-Fri., 5:30-9; Sat., 6-8, Sun., 7-7
Terms: MC, V, Check. Returns.   Parking

This new entry into the discount hardware business claims lower prices than the other guys; call for a quote.

Home Base
8341 Canoga Av., Canoga Park (818) 407-1224
Mon.-Fri., 6-9; Sat., 7-8; Sun., 8-7
(20 additional locations; see Geographical Index)
Terms: MC, V, AE, D, SC, Check. Returns.   Parking

Home Base promises to have the lowest prices on anything. If you find the same item elsewhere cheaper, Home Base will beat the price by 5%. If you have a Home Base nearby, call the other guys for a price first.

Cameras and Photographic Equipment

Bagnall Camera Show and Sale
Box 5165, Irvine, CA 92716 (714) 786-8183

COUPON

Call or write to get on the mailing list for notification of Bagnall Enterprise's monthly Camera Show and Sale. Admission is $4, and once inside, you have access to over 140 dealers of photo equipment, both new and not so, including camera bodies, lenses, film, filters, accessories and darkroom equipment. Here you can haggle a little. The show is held monthly in Buena Park and semi-annually in Santa Barbara, generally in January and August. They may soon be branching out to other locations; the mailings will give you details. *The coupon entitles you to one free admission to the show.*

Bel Air Camera
1025 Westwood Blvd., Westwood (310) 208-5150
Mon.-Fri., 9-6; Sat. 9:30-6
Terms: MC, V, AE, Checks. Returns.   Street parking

Bel Air stocks cameras, lenses, film, paper, printing supplies, enlargers, darkroom supplies, audio components, video cameras and televisions. Their prices are competitive with the lowest price camera shops, and the store is large and well organized. They carry all major brands, and they will quote prices over the phone (lowest prices are for cash). There is a pro department and they do film processing. A few times a year they host a camera show, where you can find new products and talk to manufacturers' representatives. Call for information on the next planned show.

Frank's Highland Park Camera
5715 N. Figueroa St., Los Angeles (213) 255-1543
Mon-Sat., 9:30-6 (Sun., 4-11 in Dec.)
Terms: MC, V, AE. Exchanges.   Street parking

If you can't come in you should get a catalog from Frank's, but even with its 160 pages of photo bargains, the catalog doesn't do this place justice. There's something of the attic about Frank's: you can find used models of scores of cameras (including a few made in the former Soviet Union); lenses and accessories for many of them; if you've got a camera but lost the manual, hunt through their stack; and if you've lost your camera case, check out the pile on the floor, there's bound to be one that'll fit. You can get new hardware here, as well as film, paper and chemicals. There is a 2% discount for cash, and most prices are heavily discounted. They have everything you could want (the catalog has *seven pages* of tripods). There are bags, filters, video cameras and underwater cameras. They have a pro department and take film in for processing. They will gladly quote you prices over the phone, and that catalog means a mail order business.

Freestyle
5124 Sunset Blvd., Los Angeles (213) 660-3460
Mon.-Fri., 9-5:30; Sat., 10-5; Sun., 11-4
Terms: MC, V, Checks. Returns   Parking

Freestyle has been selling photographic equipment at low prices since 1946. They carry Samsung, Minolta and Pentax cameras and camera accessories, but they are a huge source for film, paper and chemistry, and they may have the largest selection of darkroom supplies in Los Angeles. As you enter, pick up a catalog for seasonal bargains, but do browse, items around the store are on special as well. They do a large mail-order business and ship postage free within the continental U. S. Their toll free number is (800) 525-1011.

Samy's Camera
271 S. La Brea, Los Angeles (213) 938-2420
Mon.-Fri., 8-9; Sat., 9-6
Terms: MC, V, D, AE, Checks. Returns.   Parking

Samy's sells cameras, lighting equipment, photo and darkroom supplies and film, all at discounted prices. They have a pro department, do photo finishing, carry all major camera brands and will quote prices over the phone. If what you want isn't in stock, they can special order for you. Their original store (7122 Beverly Blvd.) was burned during the civil disturbance; they expect to be at the current location through mid-1993 at least, but do plan to return to the old location when feasible.

See also
47th Street Photo

Carpet and Flooring

The Carpet Club *COUPON*
16681 Roscoe Blvd., North Hills (818) 892-2082
Mon.-Fri., 9-8; Sat., 9-6; Sun., 1-4
Terms: MC, V, Check.   Parking

The Carpet Club offers a variety of ways to save money. In their 6,000 square foot showroom you'll find new carpet, wood and vinyl flooring, remnants, and sometimes carpet seconds and pull-ups, (carpet that has been gently used, or put down and pulled back up because of a color mistake, a change in taste, or a slight flaw in an inconvenient place). While all merchandise is discounted, high quality pull-ups are available at $7 to $12 a yard (including installation and padding), and represent carpets originally retailing for up to $40. Pull-ups showing greater wear are much cheaper, good for use in utility rooms. They don't always have pull-ups, so if you're redecorating at a leisurely pace, let them know what you're looking for and they'll call if it comes in. They also do custom carpet inlays, border work, carpet carving, and logos, and they service and clean carpets and floors. *The coupon entitles you to $50 off a $500 purchase, $100 off a $1000 purchase, or $200 off a purchase of $5000 or more.*

Carpetland Mills *COUPON*
6951 Reseda Blvd., Reseda (818) 609-0339
Mon.-Fri., 10-9; Sat., 10-6
Terms: MC, V, Check.   Street parking

This shop carries a huge selection of flooring, from marble tile (retailing at $11.99, here $7.99), to wood flooring (from $2.95 a square foot), to linoleum, to carpet from over 100 mills, including Camelot, Queen, Horizon, Salem, Wellington, Dupont Stainmaster, Cabin Crafts and Diamond, and here you may pay as little as 5% above cost. A Dupont Stainmaster nylon carpet, regularly $34 a yard, was $18.99, and a Diamond Diamolon originally $26 was $18 (including padding and installation). They also offer custom area rugs. *The coupon entitles you to $100 off on a purchase of $1,000 or more.*

Carpet Showcase
8975 Tampa Av., Northridge (818) 886-8300
Mon.-Fri., 9-9; Sat., 9-6; Sun. 11-6
Terms: MC, V, Check.   *Parking*

Carpet Showcase offers carpet from $10.99 installed, which includes removing your old carpet and cleaning up after the installation. Brands available include Bigelow, Mohawk, Philadelphia, Horizon, Hallmark, Cabin Crafts, Bulistan, Salem, Atlas, Columbus and Queen. Anso Crush Resistant Carpet was $17.99, and Dupont Extra Life Stainmaster, $19.99. The walls and back warehouse are lined with remnants, on which you can get a better deal. Purchase over a hundred square feet of carpet they'll upgrade your padding.

Culver Carpet Center
4026 S. Sepulveda Blvd., Culver City (213) 870-5797
Mon.-Fri., 9-5:30; Sat., 9-4:30
Terms: MC, V, Check.   *Street parking*

This showroom has swatches of hundreds of carpets, including Mohawk, Royalty, Monticello, Salem, Cabin Craft, and Catalina, all of which is 15% over cost (padding and installation additional). If you want a better bargain, go to the warehouse down the block; there you'll see carpet selling in some cases below wholesale. Culver Carpet Center buys goods at distressed prices from mills and carpet companies that are strapped for cash, and since that seems to be a common occurrence lately, you have a wide choice of carpet bargains. The store and warehouse also sell vinyl.

Jenkins Products
1841 S. San Gabriel Blvd., San Gabriel (818) 280-3110
Mon.-Sat., 9-5:30
Terms: MC, V, Check.   *Parking*

Jenkins Products is a store seemingly without end. You enter one showroom full of carpet, which leads to another and another; there are a few rooms of linoleum, and when you think you've seen it all you realize there are rooms of carpet *behind* the rooms of carpet. And it's *all discounted*. Jenkins offers linoleum roll ends, mill ends, room size carpet remnants and manufacturers' discontinued styles and overruns. Among the carpet lines are Philadelphia, Cabincraft, Evans & Black, Queen and Columbus; on carpet you can save about 30% (installation additional). On vinyl your savings can go as high as 70%, and wide rolls are available. (If you're doing the installation, you won't have to seam pieces together). They will quote prices over the phone.

Liberty Carpet
1330 W. Venice Blvd., Los Angeles (213) 748-4517
Mon.-Fri., 8-4:30; Sat., 8-12
Terms: MC, V, Check.   Parking

Nothing at Liberty Carpet is over $12.50 a yard, and here you can find carpets that retail for up to $30. They sell second quality pieces of the finest carpets, and 90% of carpet seconds have undetectable flaws. Should you see a streak or line, it can often be cut away in installation, making your second quality carpet, to all appearances, first quality. Retails on these carpets in first quality range from $17 to $30 a yard; buying seconds saves you about half. If you have a particular color in mind, stop in; they'll peruse their list of what's available and show you a sample of the first quality piece. If you like what you see, give them a deposit, and when the order comes in you inspect it; if you find a flaw

---
Quality carpet seconds at about half price
---

you can't live with, your deposit is refunded. If not, they'll install your carpet and you'll save lots of money. (Padding and installation are additional.) Liberty also gets pull-ups from time to time, ranging in price from $4.50 to $7.50 (retailing at $10 to $15, sometimes more); most pieces are barely used. Tell them the color you're looking for and they'll let you know if it comes in.

Ceramic Tile and Stone

Tile seconds are also called Builder's Grade. Most do not have noticeable flaws; they look so good, in fact, that some retailers are selling them as first quality. If the carton says "Builder's Grade," or *any* print is red, it's probably second. When working with seconds, add an additional 10% to your square footage.

California Wholesale Tile
1656 S. State College Blvd., Anaheim (714) 937-0591
Tile Importers
1320 S. State College Blvd., Anaheim (714) 533-9800
Mon.-Fri., 7:30-5; Sat., 8-4:30
Terms: MC, V, Check. Final Sale.   Parking

These two stores offer ceramic tile for use indoors and out. They import tile directly from Italy, and so can save you 30% to 40% off retail prices. The stock is varied and tremendous, from floor and wall tiles (field, decorated and hand painted) to quarry and terra cotta tile, to pool tile.

Discount Tile Center   (COUPON)
8627 Venice Blvd., Los Angeles (310) 202-1915
Mon-Fri., 10-6; Sat., 9-5
Terms: MC, V, Check. Final sale.   Parking

This store carries an immense array of ceramic tile, as well as marble, slate, and limestone tile for kitchens, baths, foyers, almost anywhere in your home. Much of it is discounted, averaging 30% off. Tile is available in country as well as sophisticated looks, matte and gloss finishes, in relief, and with coordinating border patterns. ***The coupon will save you $25 on a purchase of $300 or more.***

Discount Catalogs

Johnson's Carpets, Inc.
(800) 235-1079
Terms: MC, V, AE, D, Check.

Johnsons manufactures carpet and sells direct, offering you savings of as much as 80%, and samples are available. If you want to order the carpet of other manufacturers through Johnson's you can also save, just give them the manufacturer and model number. They also offer discounts on padding and area rugs.

Warehouse Carpets, Inc.
(800) 526-2229
Terms: Cash, Check, TC.

Warehouse Carpets is a carpet wholesaler that can save you about 50% on carpets from all major lines, as well as padding, vinyl and area rugs. Give them the manufacturer's name and style number, and they'll give you a price; they will set up shipping via common carrier (ranging from $50 to $150, depending on distance and carpet, but you'd probably be paying that much in sales tax).

Cars and Automotive Needs

New Cars

Consumer Reports Auto Price Service
Consumer Reports
Box 8005, Novi, MI 48376

To get the best deal on a new car, you need to know what the dealer paid. *Consumer Reports* offers print-outs of the list price and dealer cost of any new car, plus prices on the options you've chosen. They also recommend equipment that promises a safer and more comfortable ride in each car. The cost is $11 for one car, $20 for two, $27 for three, $5 for each additional car.

Mickey's Auto Sales and Leasing
5554 Reseda Blvd., Tarzana (818) 996-9601
Mon.-Fri., 9-5:30
Terms: Cash or Cashier's Check.   Parking

Mickey's is the oldest auto broker in Los Angeles, in business since 1957. You may not have heard of them because they don't advertise; business is by referral, and they represent you in shopping for the best deal in a new car, sometimes finding it *below* dealer's invoice. Just tell them what you're looking for, the features you desire, and they'll search to find that car at the best price. They will take your old car as a trade-in. They suggest you call them last, confident that they can beat whatever price you've found. There is no charge for the service, and they can arrange financing.

National Auto Brokers, Inc.
23011 Moulton Pkwy., Suite I-11, Laguna Hills (714) 740-7441
Mon.-Fri., 9-6:30
Terms: MC, V, Check.   Parking

National Auto Brokers doesn't advertise, 85% of its sales are repeat business or referrals, because over the last 20 years Nationwide has managed to get thousands of Southern Californians the car of their dreams at fleet prices. They sell and lease cars, and since they're volume buyers, your savings can range from $500 to $5000, depending on your choice. Tell them what you're looking for, all the options, and they'll give you a price; no negotiating, no being passed off to a closer, no histrionics; if you want it, give them a $300 deposit you can generally have your car the next day. You can arrange financing, or they will; they offer you extended warranties, window tinting, and all other dealer services, at a fraction of the the dealer's price.

See also
> **Fedco**
> **Costco**
> **Pace Membership Warehouse**
> **The Price Club**

Used Cars

City of Los Angeles Salvage
(213) 894-5162

From time to time the City of Los Angeles auctions off surplus material and vehicles no longer in use. Call to be put on the mailing list to receive catalogs, dates and times of auctions.

Nationwide Commercial Auctioneers
13005 E. Temple Av., City of Industry (818) 330-9529

Held monthly on a Sunday, these auctions sell some amount of miscellaneous merchandise, including office equipment, computers, bikes, audio, video and photographic equipment, as well as vehicles "incidental to narcotics investigations." That means confiscated in drug raids, so you'll see a few Bentleys and Maseratis here, but also cars municipalities are upgrading from, so there are Citations and Caprices, too. You can find almost anything, trucks, step vans, minivans, RVs, sedans and sportscars. Cars can be inspected prior to the sale, to the extent that you can look at them, start them, and drive them about a foot in each direction. The cars are driven from the lot into the auction ring, so you're assured they run a few hundred feet. If you know anything about cars and prices you can get some good buys here, but there are no returns. A friend of mine got a Ford station wagon for $700; 100,000 miles later all he's had to change was the tires.

Parts and Accessories

Auto Parts Club
2500 Marine Av., Redondo Beach (310) 644-8822
Mon.-Fri., 8-7; Sat.. 9-5; Sun., 10-4
(also in Long Beach, Anaheim, San Diego, El Cajon, Santa Clara and Fountain Valley)
Terms: MC, V, Check. Returns.   Parking

This is a membership club for car parts and accessories. Annual dues are $10.83 and entitle two people to shop at this warehouse of wholesale auto parts, a haven for the auto-mechanically inclined. It isn't necessary to be a member, you'll just pay 10% more. They quote prices over the phone.

Covercraft Outlet Store   (COUPON)
20675 Nordhoff St., Chatsworth (818) 407-5555
Mon.-Fri., 7:30-4
Terms: MC, V, Check. Final sale.   Parking

Here you'll find discontinued car covers, bras, tonneau covers, tailgate nets, dash and seat covers, at prices one third to one half less than auto accessory stores. The stock is organized by car type and model, and constantly varies, so if you dont find what you need, keep coming back. Tailgate nets were $17.50, Durango seat covers were $19.95, and a poly/cotton car cover was $49.95. Rear and wing spoilers sold for $1. *The coupon entitles you to 10% off your next purchase.*

Four Day Tire Stores
2120 W. Main St., Alhambra (818) 282-0689
Wed.-Fri., 8:30-8; Sat., 8:30-5
(22 additional locations; see Geographical Index)
Terms: MC, V, Check. Returns.   Parking

Four Day Tire Stores actually *do* save you money by being open only four days. You can find a tremendous assortment of tires for cars, trucks, RVs, and trailers, at discounts of up to 30%. All come with a manufacturer's warranty, but for an additional 6% you can get a 4 Day Guarantee, which includes tire inspection and rotation every 4,000 to 6,000 miles.

Cars and Automotive Needs 49

Wesco Auto Parts
1705 W. Garvey N., West Covina (818) 814-2311
Open 24 Hours
(also in El Monte, Buena Park, Rowland Heights, Santa Ana, and Covina)
Terms: MC, V, Check. Exchanges.   *Parking*

For you home mechanics who manage to doodle away most of Sunday, then discover you need a part at about 10 p.m., you'll want to know about Wesco. They never close. You do pay a slight premium for 24 hour service, but the prices they quoted me were lower than those of many stores calling themselves "discount". They also have frequent sales, when you'll pay close to the lowest prices around. Any time, day or night.

See also
> **Fedco**
> **Costco**
> **Pace Membership Warehouse**
> **The Price Club**

Used Parts

Capital Auto Parts
15325 S. Figueroa St., Gardena (310) 323-4242
Mon.-Fri., 8-5
Terms: MC, V, Check.   *Street parking*

Capital offers parts for cars from 1984 on, some with warranties.

Hub Caps
4228 S. Sepulveda Blvd., Culver City (310) 559-1200
Mon.-Fri., 9-5; Sat., 9-4
Terms: Check and Cash only.   *Street parking*

As the name implies, you'll find hub caps here for almost every make of car, and you can sometimes save as much as 50% over a dealer's price.

Lakenor Auto Salvage
10950 S. Norwalk Blvd., Santa Fe Springs (310) 944-6422
Mon.-Fri., 7:30-5:30; Sat., 8-1
Terms: MC, V, Check. Exchanges.   *Parking*

Here you'll find parts for General Motors and Ford cars manufactured within the last ten years. All parts are warrantied for six months or 6,000 miles.

Marv's Auto
11020 Tuxford St., Sun Valley (818) 767-6615
Mon.-Fri., 8-5
Terms: MC, V, D, Check. Exchanges. Parking

Marv's carries parts for American-made cars from 1983 to the present. Some parts are warrantied, from 30 days to 6 months.

Pomona Swap Meet and Car Show
L. A. County Fairgrounds, Pomona (714) 544-7004
Admission: $6 Parking

This is an antique car swap meet and show, held monthly. While there may be no bargains here, it may be the only place you can find the part you're looking for for pre-1975 collector cars.

Smog Checks

Alpine Automotive
906 G St., San Diego (619) 236-9056
444 Mission Blvd., Pacific Beach (619) 273-0440
$16.95, plus $7 Certificate
Hours vary by location; by appointment.
Terms: Cash only.

Arco Smog Pro
800-SMOGPRO for nearest location
$19.95 plus $7 certificate, pass or don't pay.
Hours vary by location.
Terms: Check and Cash only.

Zeig Smog
11685 Saticoy, North Hollywood (818) 765-3318
$12.95 plus $7 certificate, pass or don't pay.
Mon-Fri., 8-6; Sat., 8-5
Terms: Check and Cash only.

Discount Catalogs

Euro-Tire
(800) 631-0080
Terms: MC, V, AE, Check. Returns

Euro-Tire has been in the mail order business since 1974. They carry first quality radials, wheels and shock absorbers. Among the brands offered are Pirelli, Bridgestone, Uniroyal and Michelin tires, discounted as high as 50%; and Bilstein, Boge and Koni shock absorbers, discounted 33%.

Books

The Car Buyer's Art, How to Beat the Salesman at His Own Game ($6.95)

Lease Cars, How to Get One ($6.95)

Used Cars, How to Buy One ($5.95)

all by Darrell Parrish
Published by Book Express; available at your local bookstore.

Darrell Parrish is a one man crusade against the tyranny of car salesmen. He used to be one, and knows the ins and outs of the trade. If you're interested in a new car, a used car, or leasing a car, knowledge is power, and after reading these books you'll feel armed with a club, able to defend yourself against rip-offs.

The Car Buyers Art tells how the dealer and his flunkies are manipulating you, and offers strategies for manipulating them right back, gaining the upper hand, and paying the price you want for the car you want. (If this sounds impossible, look on it as an acting exercise.)

Lease Cars will show you when leasing makes sense, how to set your own terms on a lease, and what to do when the lease term is over. Also included are a glossary of industry buzz words and a table of lease payment costs.

Used Cars explains how you can find a reliable car at a low price, negotiating strategies of salesmen, and some strategies you can use right back to wind up with a quality car for less.

Cellular Phones

Cellular Fantasy Cellular Phones
11668 Gateway, West Los Angeles (310) 478-5440
Mon.-Fri., 9-7; Sat., 9-6
Terms: MC, V, AE, Check. Final sale.   Parking

Cellular Fantasy sells cellular phones often below cost, and often up to $100 below current market prices. I priced several of the most popular models, and on each one Cellular Fantasy was $100 lower than just about anyone.

Cellular Wholesalers
4200 Lincoln Blvd., Marina Del Rey (310) 827-8885
Mon.-Fri., 9-5
Terms: MC, V, AE, Check. Final Sale.   Street parking

Cellular phones has hand held models for as low as $195, installed models from $275 (including labor), and transportable phones beginning at at $295. They carry all major brands, and discount most of them 20%.

See also
Crystal Sonics

Charity Sales

The Annual Great Beverly Hills Garage Sale
Beverly Hills High
241 Moreno, Beverly Hills (310) 286-2433
Terms: Cash only. Final sale.   *Street parking*

Held on a Saturday in June, this neighborhood garage sale features clothing, appliances, furniture, books—you name it—to benefit the Beverly Hills Public Schools. (Who'd have thought they needed *our* money?)

Center for Independent Living Rummage Sale
Santa Monica (310) 451-2350
Terms: Cash only. Final sale.   *Street parking*

You can buy "Everything from blue jeans to sable" at these monthly sales of little-used, quality clothing for men and women, held near the Santa Monica Promendade. Call for taped information as to date and location. They also schedule private appointments for group sales.

The Colleagues Glamour Sale
2018 Broadway, Santa Monica (310) 828-1619
Fridays, 10-2 (closes for the summer)
Terms: Cash only. Final sale.   *Street parking*

The Colleagues is a cross between a thrift and a resale shop, held to benefit the Children's Institute, a charity geared toward preventing child abuse. There are clothes for men and women here as well as good quality used furniture, some china and linen. A man's Polo knit shirt sold for $4, a Complice cotton bustier dress was $20, and a small Louis Vuitton roll bag in need of zipper and handle repair was $3. There are designer names a-plenty, the clothing is in excellent shape, and everything is a bargain.

Junior League Sales
The Junior League of Los Angeles (213) 937-5566
The Junior League of Long Beach (310) 494-4389
Terms: Cash only. Final sale. Parking

These sales, held annually in March (call for dates and locations), benefit the charitable work done by these organizations (including aiding the homeless, children, and those with AIDS). People arrive at these sales with *empty suitcases*, and pile in as much as they can carry of the housewares, linens, clothing, shoes, sporting goods, books, furniture, craft items, and collectibles. Go early for best selection, but if you happen to be a late riser, you may find some merchandise at half price by mid-afternoon. The last time I hit the Los Angeles sale I collected silk outfits by Calvin Klein and Carole Little, a gold

> *People arrive at these sales with empty suitcases, and pile in as much as they can carry*

lurex knit tank dress by Esprit, an off the shoulder wool sweater from Chaus, a chambray skirt and a flowered rayon skirt, and suddenly it was half price time. I added a baby pillow embroidered "Sweet Dreams" and my total came to $8! Merchandise is a mixed bag, in taste and quality, but there are some very good names. Try it once, you may get hooked

Town Fair Bazaar
317 S. Crocker St., Los Angeles (213) 626-0902
Second Saturday of every month, 9-3
Terms: Cash and Checks, $1 admission. Final sale. Street parking

This sale benefits the City of Hope and there is generally a line to get in; if you go after 12:30 you won't have to wait, but by then the eggs (.50 a dozen) will be gone. The merchandise is new, donated by civic minded shopkeepers, selling at prices well below half, and includes food, drug sundries, baby wear, shoes, men's and women's clothing (including maternity), lingerie, tools, books, and hardware. A short list of the buys I found were $5 electric can-openers, a baby comforter and bumper set for $30, a king size bedspread for $30, four bags of bread or rolls for $1, kids, mens' and women's designer jeans (without labels) for $5, L. A. Gear shoes for $20. Everyday drug sundries were reduced as much as 85%.

China, Crystal and Silver

Almost and Perfect English China
14519 Ventura Blvd., Sherman Oaks (818) 905-6650
Mon.-Sat., 10-5
Terms: MC, V, GC, Check. Exchanges.   Parking

Here you can find china and crystal by Royal Doulton, Wedgwood, Spode, Villeroy & Bosch, Rosenthal, Baccarat, Lalique and others, at discounts of 20% to 70%. If you don't see what you're looking for among the shelves of beautiful things, they can special order it for you at a 15% discount. There are sales twice a year, in January or February and August, and occasional parking lot sales, advertised in the *Los Angeles Times*. A bridal registry, phone orders, shipping, and gift wrap are among their services.

The Crystal Factory
8010 Beach Blvd., Buena Park (714) 952-4135
Sun., 11-5; Mon.-Fri, 10-6:30; Sat., 10-6
Terms: MC, V, Check. Exchanges.   Parking

This large showroom features crystal of every description from all over Europe, and the smaller showroom behind it has capodimante pieces. All but a few lines are discounted. Most pieces have been marked down at least once, often twice; with the many specials around the store, some pieces sell at half their retail price or lower. There is a bridal registry, they engrave and gift wrap.

Dansk Factory Outlet
2550 N. Palm Canyon Dr., Palm Springs (619) 320-3304
Mon.-Sat., 9:30-5:30; Sun. 11-5
Terms: V, MC, Check. Exchanges.   Parking

Here you'll find tabletop and kitchenware seconds at discounts of 20% to 50%. There are placemats reduced 35% to 50%, candlesticks reduced 35%, silverware discounted from 23% to 50% ... and the savings go on through the entire Dansk line, from teak bowls to crystal vases. There were platters, open stock china patterns, and enamel-coated cast iron cookware as well. Join their preferred customer mailing list for notification of special sales.

English China House
22776 Ventura Blvd., Woodland Hills (818) 340-1129
Mon.-Sat., 10:30-7
Terms: MC, V, AE, D, Check. Final sale.   Parking

If you like Spode or Royal Worcester, the English China House is a place you'll visit again and again. Some items are first quality, and sell at regular price or slight discounts, but some pieces are discounted as much as half, sometimes more, because they're seconds, although it's almost impossible to find a flaw. On the first floor are sets and place settings; upstairs are odds and ends, in case you need to replace something, or want to try a new pattern in a salad or desert plate without spending a fortune. The second floor also displays tea and coffee pots, jam jars, mugs and tureens.

General Wax & Candle Company
6863 Beck Av., N. Hollywood (818) 765-6357, Ext. 326
Mon.-Fri., 9-5; Sat., 9-2
Terms: Cash and Check only. Final Sale.   Parking

This shop sells candles and candle-making supplies. Retail prices here are lower than general merchandise stores, because the factory is in the back. But wait! Is that a Close-out Room? There I found 12" tapers, in a variety of colors and styles, at 12 for $1.99. Dinner candles in the 8" size were $1.50 a dozen; and columns were $1.50 for 3"x 6", and $2.25 for 3"x9". Birthday candles (24) were .15. Something's on sale every other month and the big sale is in December (including Christmas candles), where discounts average 20%, sometimes going as high as 50%.

Irish Crystal Company
1655 Thousand Oaks Blvd., Thousand Oaks (805) 496-8363
Tues.-Fri., 10-5; Sat., 10-4
Terms: MC, V, Check. Final sale.   Parking

The Irish Crystal Company carries Tyrone Crystal, which is hand blown, hand cut and hand polished. If you're a fan of Waterford you may find that once you check the price of this stuff, you're a fan of Tyrone. One reason is that many of the pieces are direct knock-offs of Waterford; the lead content is the same, but generally the Tyrone pieces contain more crystal. Leonard McDonald, the charming proprietor, has a few pieces of Waterford on hand for comparison purposes: a Waterford egg paperweight is $144, the Tyrone variety, $28. Napkin rings by Waterford are $51, Tyrone's all but identical piece, $14. A Waterford goblet, $128, Tyrone's, $38 (if you buy 12 or more of one piece there may be an additional discount). Waterford centerpiece, $1800, Tyrone centerpiece, $300. They also manufacture crystal sold under the labels of very expensive boutiques, so if you want something you've seen elsehwere, check

Knock-offs of Waterford at one fourth the price

The Irish Crystal Company out first. They can monogram, they ship everywhere, and they will custom engrave any image in glass.

Lenox Factory Store
Factory Merchants of Barstow (619) 253-7668
Mon.-Sun. 9-8
Terms: MC, V, Check. Exchanges.   Parking

This store carries mainly seconds of china, giftware, stemware and flatware, discounted to 50%, with special sales sending costs even lower. Place settings of fine china range from $70 to $90 ($140 to $180), and stemware discounts range from 50% to 60%. Paul Revere Silversmiths silverplate serving pieces are also sold here, as is Lenox silverplate flatware and Orrefors crystal giftware. Reduced table linen rounds out the inventory. They will ship or supply a gift box at a nominal charge. The hardest part of shopping here is deciding which of these beautiful things to buy.

Luna Garcia
201 San Juan Av., Venice (310) 396-8026
Mon.-Fri., 9-5; Sat., 9-2
Terms: Cash and Check only. Final sale.   Street parking

Luna Garcia makes pottery at this studio, where you can find a wall of seconds, representing most pieces in their Gigante line, at half price. The pottery is matte-finished and available in *gigante* sizes, the most gigantic of which is the 13" buffet plate. There are 12" dinner plates, 10" salad plates and 9" luncheon plates, cups, saucers, mugs, pitchers, vases, large serving bowls, pasta bowls and platters, ranging in price from $11 for a cup or saucer to $100 for a pitcher. They are available in cobalt blue, black, mustard, fuschia, green and violet.

Mikasa Factory Store
10642 South Fordyce Av., Carson (310) 537-9344
Hours vary by location.
(also in Palm Springs (619) 778-1080, San Ysidro (619) 428-2022)
Terms: V, MC, Check. Returns.   Parking

This warehouse full of Mikasa china, crystal, stemware and stoneware, all first quality and all discounted, is the ideal stop for picking up a wedding or anniversary gift. Twenty piece sets of every style of Mikasa bone china are discounted 30% to 70%. A lovely cake plate and server set, available in six patterns, was $25 ($60). Studio Nova stoneware was half the $70 retail for a 20 piece set, and their new Maxima line was a minimum of half off. There are tables filled with china by the piece; if you can put together a set you'll get an even better bargain. Stemware was discounted 35% to 50%, as were canisters, cookware, tea sets, placemats and napkins, trinket boxes, vases, napkin rings, candlesticks and candles. They will special order, and they ship or supply a gift box for a nominal fee. People emerge from this store with shopping carts piled high. Their annual sale is in June.

Munns
209 W. Wilson, Glendale (818) 241-2776
Tues.-Sat. 10-5
Terms: MC, V, Check. Final Sale.   Street parking

There's something Dickensian about this shop, which sells beautiful sterling flatware, candlesticks and a smattering of jewelry. Maybe it's that it's so dark, the better to display the silver. If you're looking for a particular item in sterling or plate, call or stop by; they represent Wallace, Reed & Barton, International Silver, Towle, Gorham, Kirk Steiff, just about all the silversmiths, and your price is always 10% above cost. There isn't a lot of stock here, but I noticed estate silver sets starting at $1000 (77 pieces). They also buy gold and silver, but not after 3 p.m.

Pfaltzgraff Stoneware
Desert Hills Factory Stores at Cabazon (714) 922-9038
Mon.-Sun., 9-8
Terms: MC, V, D, Check. Returns.   Parking

The company that calls itself the oldest stoneware manufacturer in America has set up an outlet featuring first and second quality goods discounted 25% to 33%. Their dinnerware is oven, freezer, dishwasher and microwave safe, and there are platters, pots, mugs, canisters, cookie jars, even *picture frames* in their signature patterns, as well as coordinating dish towels, placemats and napkins. They also carry discounted Durand and Anchor Hocking glass.

The Pottery Ranch
248 W. Huntington Blvd., Monrovia (818) 358-1215
Mon.-Sat., 9-6; Sun., 10-6
Terms: MC, V, Check. Returns.   Parking

The Pottery Ranch sells planters, birdbaths and lawn statuary as well as fine china, crystal and flatware, discounted at least 20%. They have a large selection of china patterns from Wedgewood, Sango, Mikasa, Internationl China, Noritake and Pfaltzgraff, as well as Portmeirion. The day I stopped in,

Wilton Armetale factory seconds were discounted 40%. They offer a bridal registry and will gift wrap.

The Pottery Shack
1212 South Coast Hwy., Laguna Beach (714) 494-8217
Hours vary with season.
Terms: MC, V, Check. Returns.   Parking

Yes, there is a discount store in Laguna Beach. Driving down South Coast Highway you can't help but notice it: it's that brown thing with all the china nailed to it. The Pottery Shack carries china, crystal, flatware, giftware, glassware and tabletop accessories. A sampling of the names here are Mikasa, Noritake, Fitz & Floyd, Royal Worcester, Villeroy & Bosch, Spode, Towle, Johnson Brothers and Franciscan, and prices are akin to department store sale prices. There are special sales where another 20% may be lopped off glassware or Wedgwood or Lenox for the day, but without advance warning. For even bigger savings, stop at the Bargain Barn in back, paradise for those who love to root around for a deal. You'll find serving pieces, individual pieces and sets, canisters, placemats and glassware, all reduced an additional 20% to 75%. A 15" oval ceramic platter originally $42, sold for $9. Ceramic canister sets started at $27. Bargain Barn merchandise is final sale.

Regal Rents Annual Sale
9925 Jefferson Blvd., Culver City (310) 204-3382
Held Annually on a Saturday in March, 9-3
Terms: MC, V, Check. Final sale.   Parking

There's a lot to buy at this sale, and there is bargain frenzy in the air, so beware! Regal sets up thousands of parties each year, and during this sale they turn over a huge number of used table cloths, napkins, folding chairs, banquet tables, flatware, china and stemware. (They also sell new flatware, stemware and china.) The used merchandise is a clear bargain, provided it isn't stained or broken. A 70" round table cloth is $3.95; cloth napkins are .25, 12' banquet cloths are $6, and all come in a wide range of colors. New Rogers Silverplate, bought in lots of twelve of each piece, averaged out at about $40 a place setting, and china sold for $15 a place setting. There were a variety of paper napkins, hot drink cups and candles at 60% off retail. A mob forms before the gate, and once it's opened, people run; I got in in the second wave, by then the serving pieces remaining were clearly blemished. Weigh your options, and wear tennis shoes. The lot fills up by 8:45 so if you don't come early, look for street parking.

Royal Doulton Direct
Factory Merchants of Barstow (619) 253-2161
Desert Hills Factory Stores at Cabazon (714) 849-4222
Mon.-Sun., 9-8
Terms: V, MC, AE, Check. Exchanges.   Parking

This shop features the patterns of Royal Doulton, as well as some figurines and stemware. The regular discount for first quality merchandise is 40%, and seconds on some patterns are further reduced. In addition to formal china they have everyday china, and baby china of Beatrix Potter, Bunnykins and Brambly Hedge. They also offer Royal Albert and Royal Doulton lead crystal, discounted 40%. They will take phone orders, they special order merchandise, and they have a bridal registry. For a nominal fee they'll ship anywhere,

The Treasure House
22741 Lambert St., Suite 1511, Lake Forest (714) 770-3285
Tues.-Sat., 10-5:30
Terms: V, MC, D, Check. Exchanges.   Parking

The motto here is "You'll like our low prices," and for china, giftware, and silver (sterling and plate) they aren't kidding. Everyday prices are discounted 20% to 60%, *better than department store sale prices*. A few of the names they carry are Royal Doulton, Lenox, Noritake, Dansk, Villeroy and Bosch, Wedgwood, Mikasa, Towle, Oneida, Reid and Barton, and Wallace International, but if you're looking for something else, try anyway: if they don't carry it, they can get it. There is a bridal registry, and they will gift wrap; they take phone orders and ship merchandise. Call for a price; they'll be glad to assist you over the phone, and you probably won't find what you're looking for any cheaper. Every January there is a clearance sale of stock on hand.

See also
Champagne Taste/The 2nds Shop
Corning/Revere Factory Outlet
Import Outlet
Arte D'Italia
Libbey Glass Factory Store

Discount Catalogs

Barrons
(800) 538-6340
Terms: MC, V, D, Check. Returns.

Barrons carries fine china, crystal and giftware at prices 30% to 50% below retail. Among the lines available are Lenox, Block, Aynsley, Dansk, Sasaki, Royal Doulton, Minton, Royal Albert, Royal Crown Derby, Wedgwood, Mikasa, Noritake, Fitz & Floyd, Franciscan, Johnson Brothers, Gorham, Hutschenreuther, Nikko, and Royal Worcester-Spode.

Midas China and Silver
(800) 368-3153
Terms: MV, V, AE, D. Returns.

Midas offers savings of 20% to 60% on china, crystal, flatware and giftware from such names as Kirk Steiff, Wilton Armetale, Reed and Barton, Towle, Waterford, Baccarat, Orrefors, Sheffield, Mikasa, David Winter Cottages, Portmeirion, Villeroy & Bosch, Noritake, Christian Dior, Lenox, Oneida, Aynsley, Spode, Wedgwood, Royal Worcester, Royal Doulton, and Gorham. They also have a large listing of estate silver patterns, and a bridal registry.

Nat Schwartz & Co.
(800) 526-1440
Terms: MC, V, AE, Check. Returns.

Nat Schwartz sells fine china, sterling, crystal and giftware at discount prices. They carry all the best names, including some you don't see everywhere else, like Coalport and Haviland Limoges. Their discount range is from 10% to over 50%, depending on the piece, how many you're buying and time of year. Send for their catalog for a glimpse of what they offer.

The Silver Queen
(800) 262-3134
Terms: MC, V, Check, Returns.

The Silver Queen carries estate silver, and at the best prices I've seen so far. There are a number of popular patterns, and prices start at $65 for a four piece place setting, ranging up to $250. They also sell new silver, beginning at $115 a place setting. They're located in Florida, open business hours during the week and Saturday, but that's Eastern Time, so time your call accordingly.

Clothing

Children's Clothing

Baby Guess
860 S. Los Angeles St., Los Angeles (213) 629-5833
Mon.-Sat., 9:30-5:30; Sun., 11-5
Terms: MC, V, Check. Final sale.   Street parking

This store is notable for the racks of samples for infants, toddlers and children priced from $5 to $10. Other pieces—seconds, overstocks, and discontinued merchandise—are reduced, but not as greatly. Children's jeans were $14; denim jackets, $32; overalls, $16; a girl's denim jumper was $16, an infant denim quilted jacket $12.

Bergstroms
200 Alto, Anaheim (714) 774-5050
Mon.-Fri., 10-9; Sat., 10-7; Sun. 11-5
(also in Costa Mesa, Irvine, Glendale, and West Los Angeles)
Terms: MC, V, Check. I. Returns.   Parking

Bergstrom's features clothing, furniture and accessories for newborn to pre-teen kids at competitive prices. Sales every two or three months reduce about half the stock by 50%, the balance by 20%. The Irvine store carries only baby furniture and needs, and if you know the magic words ("Baby Furniture Clearance Center," open Mon.-Sat., 10-6) they'll direct you to the basement, where you'll find discontinued items and floor samples discounted an additional 40%. There are no holds or layaways here, and you really get the feeling you've stumbled onto a secret.

C. W. Designs
18720 Oxnard St., #106, Tarzana (818) 343-0823
Mon.-Tues., Fri., 7:30-3:30; Wed.-Thurs., 7:30-5:30; Sat., 9:30-3:30
Terms: Cash and Check only.   Parking

C. W. Designs makes party and special occasion dresses for pre-teen and adolescent girls, though petite women may find clothing here as well, since the styles are youthful but not girlish. The clothing is not inexpensive: dresses range from $100 to $200, but many pieces on the racks in back of the factory are overruns, and reduced 20% to 50%. Prices aren't marked; you have to ask about each item.

California Kids
801 Lakeview Av., Placentia (714)779-1170
8659 Base Line Av., Rancho Cucamonga (714) 941-1004
Tues.-Sat., 10-6
Terms: MC, V, Check. Returns.   Parking

California Kids offers clothing for newborns to adolescents at prices discounted 15% to 20%. They carry Cutler, Quicksilver, Body Glove, Esprit, Guess, Bryan, Le Top Baby, Ocean Pacific, Buster Brown, and other top brands. There is a mailing list to be informed of their regular sales (when large sections of the store are reduced another 50%), generally four times a year: back to school, holiday, February clearance and Easter.

Flap Happy Kids
3516 Centinela Av., West Los Angeles (310) 398-3527
Mon.-Fri., 10-5; Sat., 11-4
Terms: MC, V, D, AE, Check. Final sale.   Parking

This is an outlet for 100% cotton seconds and discontinued styles of play clothes for kids from newborn to size 4T by manufacturers like Lollytogs, Wibbies, and Flap Happy, discounted up to 50%. First quality merchandise is also offered, at discounts of 20% to 30%. There are bargain bins, featuring baby bedding, underwear, socks and tons of hats.

For Kids Only
746 N. Fairfax Av., W. Hollywood (213) 650-4885
19367 Victory Blvd., Reseda (818) 708-9543
Mon.-Sat., 10-6; Sun., 12-5
Terms: MC, V, Check. Exchanges.   Parking

Here you'll find European and American designer clothing and shoes for kids, from newborns to size 14, at 30% to 60% savings. The clothing is unusual, a little funky, a little sophisticated, definitely not what every kid is wearing. Even with the hefty discounts, a baby's two piece play suit can still run $35 to $40, ($70 to $80) a party dress is $50 ($100), as is a boy's three piece set of slacks, shirt and vest with *faux* tie ($99). There's a mailing list to be notified of the end-of-season sales, around July and January or February, where savings start at 30%, and, at the tail-end of the sale, hit 50%.

Hang Ten Outlet
119 Pasadena Av., South Pasadena (213) 256-8851
Lake Elsinore Outlet Ctr.
Hours vary by location.
Terms: MC, V, Check. Returns. Parking

This is the outlet for Hang Ten knitwear for toddler girls, girls sizes 7-14, juniors, and women. The merchandise is first quality, and the discount is 35%, except on close-out racks, where garments are further reduced. There I found a women's jumper reduced to $10 ($60), a toddler sweatshirt reduced to $4 ($14), a companion skirt at $5 ($17); a girl's overshirt and skirt, each piece reduced to $9 ($31). There is a mailing list for notification of sales.

John Fulmer Company Factory Outlet Store
6868 Acco St., City of Commerce (213) 722-8300
Fridays, 11:30-1:30
Terms: Cash only. Final sale. Parking

A corner of this factory is filled with racks of infant to pre-teen girls' clothing, women's and maternity wear. The merchandise consists of closeouts, irregulars, overruns, and damages (generally marked). Prices aren't marked, but most pieces (mainly casual separates and knits) were around $2, with an occasional maternity dress at $10. Infant separates were $1; girls' short sets were $3; and a girls' knit dress painted with hearts was $3. Toddler tees with cartoon characters were $2 as were girls' leggings. Maternity dresses in cotton and blends were $5 and $10, and oversized tops, to size XL, were $2 and $3. There is no fitting room, little semblance of order, and lots of children milling around, so careful where you step.

Kids for Less
1701 S. Grove Av., Ontario (714) 923-5119
1487 E. Foothill Blvd., Upland
Thurs.-Sat., 9-5
Terms: Cash only. Final sale. Parking

These shops carry mainly girls' clothing, in sizes toddler to 14, and prices don't generally go above $7.95. Infants' short suits, with hat, were $3.99; infants sweatsuits were $4.99. Girls' tees were $4.99 and short sets were $6.99. In the back, clearance racks feature clothing at $2.50 and under.

Kid's Mart/Little Folks
1416 Third Street Promenade, Santa Monica (310) 394-4197
Mon.-Sat., 10-6; Sun., 11-5
(over 90 additional locations; see Geographical Index)
Terms: MC, V, D, AE, Check. L. Returns.   Parking

Discounted clothing for children from newborns to size 14 is available in abundance at this chain. Name brand goods are reduced at least 15%, often a whole lot more. The longer an item stays in the store the less it costs, and discounts can get as high as 60%. There are also frequent sales *on top of* these reductions. The clothing comes from manufacturers like Jordache, Cherokee, Buster Brown, Little Gems, Fame, Harley, Bryan, Bebe Terrifique and Carters. Little Folks is the slightly upscale chain, the difference being they carry Guess? apparel. Both chains will match anyone's lower price on anything in stock, paying you the difference plus 10%. Some of the buys I caught were on a "take 40% off everything" day: a Carters infant playsuit was $9 ($20), a Diane Von Furstenberg girl's party dress, $17 ($36), a toddler boy's Sahara Club cotton sweater, $8 ($27), and Ocean Pacific Coveralls, $18 ($36). A Preferred Customer Card is available for $5 annually, entitling you to an additional 10% off purchases, extended layaway, and advance notice of sales.

Kids R'Us
10900 Jefferson Blvd., Culver City (310) 398-5905
Mon.-Fri., 9:30-9; Sat., 9:30-7; Sun., 11-6
(11 additional locations; see Geographical Index)
Terms: MC, V, AE, D, Check. Returns.   Parking

Clothing here ranges from infants to preteens and is about a third off retail. Brands like Bugle Boy, Levi's, Oshkosh B'Gosh, Carters, Gitano, Rosanna, Mona Lisa, Palmettos, Ocean Pacific, Fast Moves, Izod Sport, Caitlyn Scott and Little Gems are discounted another 25%, when they're reduced for clearance at the end of the season. There is a mailing list for notification of sales.

Oshkosh B'Gosh Factory Store
The Factory Merchants at Barstow (619) 253-5230
Mon.-Sun., 8-9
Terms: MC, V, Check. Exchanges.   Parking

While this store does carry some women's clothing, most of their wares are for kids, infant to size 14. The clothing is both firsts and seconds, and the tags are color coded to differentiate between them. Irregular jeans in sizes 7-14 were $14.50, a girls 4-6X denim pinafore was $13.55, a toddler denim pinafore was $12.95. Infant overalls in sizes from 3-24 months were $11.50 and a two-pack of boys brightly colored briefs were $4.80. They also stock socks, shoes, and hats.

Sacks SFO Kids *COUPON*
7018 Melrose, Hollywood (213) 935-2590
1439 W. Olive, Burbank (818) 840-0571
Mon.-Sat., 10-7; Sun., 11-6
Terms: MC, V, Check. Exchanges.   Parking

These two shops are doing for kids what Sacks SFO does for the rest of us, bringing trendy fashions to little people at low prices. Merchandise ranges from infant sizes to size 14, it's first quality, the kids' stuff is cute, the young adult clothing is *au courant*, and most of it is about half price. The labels are those usually seen in Southland department stores. An infant knit cotton romper was $17 ($32); a boy's shirt was $14 ($28); a $30 girl's jumper sold for $17 and toddler cordoruy overalls, originally $40 were $20. The Sacks SFO stores in Tarzana and West Los Angeles have sections of children's clothing. *The coupon entitles you to 10% off one purchase, Monday through Thursday.*

Star Baby
The Citadel, City of Commerce (213) 888-2781
Mon.-Sat., 10-9
(also in Century City (310) 286-7841 and San Ysidro (619) 690-5270)
Terms: MC, V, Check. Exchanges.   Parking

This factory direct retailer offers 100% cotton clothing at prices discounted 20% to 50%. There is a wide variety of playwear and separates for newborns to girls' size 6x and boys' size 7, and several rounders with special sales. There is a small play area with a few toys to keep the kiddies busy. Sign the mailing list to be apprised of sales.

The Stork Shop *COUPON*
1868 La Cienega Blvd., Los Angeles (310) 839-2403
Mon.-Sat., 10-5:30
Terms: MC, V ($20 min.) Check. Returns.   Parking

The motto here is "At our prices it pays to have babies." The Stork Shop offers a huge selection of top quality infants', childrens' and pre-teen clothing at savings of 25% to 70%, as well as discounted baby furniture and accessories. The goods are first quality, generally close-outs, odd lots and samples. You can find playclothes as well as hosiery and underwear, and they specialize in pre-teen party dresses. I overheard a woman purchasing a dress for her daughter say that she'd seen the same one Bullock's, for twice the price. There is a always a close-out rack of clothing previously retailing from $30 to $100, now selling for $9.95. *The coupon offers you a $5 discount with a purchase of $45 or more.*

See also
- Esprit
- Move It Outlet
- Cole of California Outlet
- Sutter Place/La Petite Factorie
- Mother Harts
- PCH Clothing Co.
- Men and Women s Clothing Section

> Garage Sales are an excellent source for children's toys, clothing and furniture. Think of it as original resale.

Resale

Children's Exchange
23812 Via Fabricante, A-4, Mission Viejo (714) 859-4397

Children's Exchange
12113 Santa Monica Blvd., West Los Angeles (310) 826-6967

Children's Orchard
13771 Newport Av., #7, Tustin (714) 832-7373
(also in El Toro (714) 951-0444, Laguna Niguel (714) 249-3736)

Christine's Place
18822 Beach Blvd., Huntington Beach (714) 965-1449

Everything for Kids
24407 Hawthorne Blvd., Torrance (310) 373-4863

Kids Cottage
3415 Magnolia Blvd., Burbank (818) 842-5023

Kids Double Time
4405 Torrance Blvd., Torrance (310) 542-4497

Kids' Store
16202 Nordhoff, Sepulveda (818) 894-1545

Kids Stuff
4159 1/2 W. Redondo Beach Blvd., Torrance (310) 214-0911

Little Ones Reruns
7332 Center Av., Huntington Beach (714) 895-1508

Little Orphan Overalls
1938 E. Colorado Blvd., Pasadena (818) 793-5990

Make Room for Baby
12324 Venice Blvd., Los Angeles (213) 398-7177

Mother Goose Garment Exchange
22474 Barton Rd., Grand Terrace (714) 783-4666

Young Seconds
436 Heliotrope, Corona del Mar (714) 673-2120

When does buying discontinued merchandise present a problem? See the Introduction

Men's Clothing

Academy Award Clothes, Inc.
811 S. Los Angeles St., Los Angeles (213) 622-9125
Mon.-Fri., 9-5:30; Sat., 9-5
Terms: MC, V. Exchanges.   Street parking

If you're into self-serve men's shopping this place is set up for you. Not that there isn't a helpful staff ready to assist you, but if you want they'll point you in the right direction and let you browse through suits aligned by color and style, and within those, size. Among the brands are Givenchy, Bottany 500, Pierre Cardin, Bert Pulitzer and Halston. Suits begin at $189 and are discounted anywhere from 30% to 50%. There is a 2% discount for cash.

Alandales
10500 W. Pico Blvd., West Los Angeles (213) 838-8100
Tues.-Fri., 10-7; Sat., 10-6
Terms: V, MC, AE, Check. Exchanges.   Parking

If your look is high quality European, you like Armani, Hugo Boss, and lots of personal attention, but you're not wild about spending $1,000 a suit, Alandales is an alternative. Here you will find a quality product, selling at about half of what you would find it for elsewhere. The clothing is made from the same fabric and along the same lines as the best European names, but at Alandales suits range from $475 to $895 (comparable retails $950 to $1400), with most suits selling from $495 to $695. There is also a lovely selection of silk sport coats, shirts, ties and accessories. If all that looking in the mirror has made you realize you're in need of a trim, there's a hair studio here, too.

Big Fella Warehouse Store
13120 Saticoy St., North Hollywood (818) 764-6989
Mon.-Sat., 9-5; Sun., 9:30-4:30
Terms: MC, V, Check. Final sale.   Parking

This is the warehouse store for the Big Fella chain, and this place *looks* like a warehouse operation. Prices are 20% lower here for current merchandise. They don't sell suits or sport jackets, but knit shirts by Van Heusen, Highway One and Members Only, in sizes 1X to 7X, are available at $20 to $30. If you're looking for slacks by Haggar, Sansabelt and Sergio Valente in sizes 42 to 80, look no further. Dress shirt sizes go to 22 collar and 38 sleeve. They also carry robes, windbreakers and sweaters, and extra long silk ties are $20.

C&R Clothiers
6301 Wilshire Blvd., Los Angeles   (213) 655-6466
Mon.-Fri., 9:30-9; Sat.,9:30-6; Sun. 10-5
(31 additional locations, see Geographical Index)
Terms: MC, V, AE, D, SC, Check.   Returns.   Parking

What a difference an ad campaign makes; you'd have to live in a *cave* not to know about C&R's discount suits, sport coats, slacks and shirts. The chain carries designer names like Pierre Cardin, Givenchy and Adolfo, as well as unbranded suits and sport coats in wools, silks and blends, and there are a lot of ways to save money. "Wardrobe prices" are discounts for purchasing more than one item within a "wardrobe group", i.e., buy a suit and if you buy a top coat, leather jacket, rain or sport coat, you get further reductions. Dress shirts, ties, belts, and raincoats round out the inventory (lined trench coats are as low as $79). Alterations are free if an item is not on sale at or lower than half it's ticketed price. Express tailoring is offered at additional charge, but the lifetime alteration policy is free. The Executive Club is also gratis at many C&R locations, and offers pressing, shoe shining, and a gift registry.

Compagnia Della Moda, Inc.
31192 La Baya Dr., #F, Westlake Village   (818) 706-8177
Mon.-Fri., 9-5; Sat., 10-4
Terms: MC, V, Check. Final sale.   Parking

Compagnia Della Moda is an importer and wholesaler of fine men's clothing, supplying better department stores. You can buy their overstocks here at substantial discounts. There are a lot of beautiful clothes to choose from, mainly in standard sizes. Featured are silk jackets ($300) and slacks ($100), wool and blend suits ($250 to $650), wool slacks ($75), some dress shirts ($60) and ties. Prices are wholesale and below. From time to time they have a sale, so sign the mailing list. There is a 2% discount for cash.

Dorman Winthrop
12301 Wilshire Blvd., West Los Angeles   (310) 447-7813
Mon.-Fri., 11-8; Sat., 10-6; Sun., 12-5
(also in North Hollywood (818) 984-1114 and Westminster (714) 847-3303)
Terms: MC, V, Check (2% discount). Returns.   Parking

Dorman Winthrop is a huge showroom of top quality men's clothing, discounted 20% to 60%. Among the brands in their inventory of 4,126 suits, are Hugo Boss, Donald Brooks, Chaps, Hickey Freeman, Givenchy, and Halston.

Suits generally fall into the $300 to $500 range; some retail as high as $1100. Sport coats generally range between $150 and $250. They also carry slacks, shirts and ties.

Eddy's For Men
860 S. Los Angeles St., Los Angeles (213) 624-9755
Mon.-Sat., 9:30-5:30; Sun., 11-5
Terms: MC, V, Check. Final sale.   Street Parking

Eddy's sells men's shoes and sportswear at discount prices. They feature Generra 100% cotton pants and shirts, retailing elsewhere from $55 to $70, for $30. Wool gabardine pants are $60 ($110) and they have a variety of dress and sport shirts at reduced prices.

Europa, The Suit Club   (COUPON)
4087 Glencoe Av., Marina del Rey (310) 578-0094
Mon.-Fri., 11-6; Sat., 11-5; Sun., 11-4
(also in West Los Angeles, Woodland Hills, and San Gabriel)
Terms: MC, V, Check. Exchanges.   Parking

This is a store for the man who wears a suit and tie daily. The suits, jackets, and slacks are Italian wool, and cost up to 50% less than in better department stores. Suits range from $150 to $347, with at least a hundred suits in every size. Wool blazers are $169, (to $450) and wool and cashmere blends are $229, (to $695). Two, three and four pleat pants are two pair for $120 and Italian leather belts are two for $30. There is also a suit club: a $10 annual membership buys you a complimentary tie, notification of sales, and special sales when the store is closed to everyone but members. There are also benefits in buying multiples; buy two of those and three of these and get something for free. There are a lot of ways to save money, including several major sales, generally in January, May or June, and September. *The coupon entitles you to free membership in the suit club with the purchase of a suit.*

Geoffrey Beene Factory Outlet
Desert Hills Factory Stores at Cabazon (714) 849-4490
Lake Elsinore Outlet Ctr. (714) 245-4779
Mon.-Sun., 9-8
Terms: MC, V, Check. Returns.   Parking

This shop carries high quality men's sportswear manufactured under the Geoffrey Beene name. Long-sleeved, 100% cotton casual shirts were reduced from $52.50 to $30, and sweaters were $30 ($60). Dress shirts were $29 ($40) and silk ties were $11.99. Washed twill slacks sold for $25.99 ($45) and tees originally $30 were $12.99.

Harris & Frank Outlet
13451 Sherman Way, North Hollywood (818) 764-4872
Mon.-Sat., 9-5; Sun., 12-5
Terms: MC V, Check. Final sale.   Parking

Here high quality men's clothing has already been marked down at least once, and when it hits these racks it is reduced another 35% to 50%. I found a Christian Dior rayon robe, once $54, now $27; a Countess Mara shirt, $30 ($80); a Geoffrey Beene long sleeved cotton shirt, $12.50 ($36); and a wool Geoffrey Beene suit at $250, half price. A good spot for business clothing.

Hathaway Factory Store
Plaza Continental Factory Stores at Ontario (714) 941-1800
1863 E. Ventura Blvd., Oxnard (805) 988-1788
Mon.-Sat., 10-9; Sun., 10-6
Terms: MC, V, Check. Returns.   Parking

This shop features Puritan knits, Chaps shirts, ties and slacks, and Christian Dior Monsieur shirts, ties, and sportswear, all at discounts of 35% to 50%. The emphasis is casual; there is a large selection of sport shirts, sweaters, slacks and outer jackets, and some Jack Nicklaus polo shirts and sweaters.

Max Levine & Son, Inc.
845 S. Los Angeles St., Los Angeles (213) 622-2446
Mon.-Fri., 8-5:30; Sat., 9-5
Terms: MC, V, AE, D, Check. Exchanges.   Street Parking

Max Levine has been selling suits for over 50 years, and you can count on lots of personal attention, as well as saving about $100 over what you'd pay for these suits in a department store. Among the designers here are names like Lanvin, Daniel Hechter, Calvin Klein, YSL, and Perry Ellis. Their selection in standard sizes is ample, in European and American cuts, with fabrics to fit every taste.

Men's Wearhouse
8160 Mira Mesa, San Diego (619) 222-6301
Mon-Fri., 10-6; Sat., 11-5
(Five additional locations in the San Diego area)
Terms: MC, V, Check. Exchanges.   Parking

Men's Wearhouse offers discounts of about 25% off men's brand name suits by designers such as Yves St. Laurent, Oscar de La Renta, Oliver Hunt, and Nino Cerutti. Wool worsted pants were $75 ($110), and silk ties were $6.99. Dress shirts, accessories, and shoes are also available. Tailoring is additional, but future alterations are at no charge. If you find a suit you like and they don't have your size, they can check the computer to see if any of their other stores statewide have it; if so, it'll be yours in three days.

Mona's Custom Tailors
5446 Del Amo Blvd., Long Beach (310) 420-3219
Mon.-Fri., 9-6:30; Sat., 9-5:30
Terms: V, MC, Check.   *Parking*

One day at the Cooper Building I found myself browsing next to a very well dressed man. We got into a conversation about discount shopping—I'll tell you mine if you tell me yours—and he introduced me to Mona's, where he, and now all his friends, buy suits. At Mona's one third of the business is alterations, one third is custom made suits, and the rest is the sale of men's ready made suits, jackets, slacks and accessories. Many of the garments here are identical to

Garments identical to those at better stores, but without the label and at a fraction of the price

those at better department stores, but without the labels and at a fraction of the price. The suits are generally in the $150 to $250 range, and compare to the better stores at $450 to $650. Sport coats range from $165 to $175; comparable jackets go for up to $400. Size range is 36 to 60 and alterations are free. Suits are mostly wool, the jackets are silk, wool, camel hair, or cashmere and wool blends. Custom made suits are about $400 to $450—you can design your own—and take about four weeks. Ready made suits can, in a pinch, be altered the same day. You can also buy custom made shirts, of pinpoint and Sea Island cotton, at $55. When I asked Bob, the owner, about a return policy he told me that no one ever wants to return anything, he makes sure his customers are happy before they leave.

Paul Jardin Outlet   CCC
13333 Sherman Way, North Hollywood (818) 503-4411
Hours vary by location.
(also in West Hills (818) 710-0169 and City of Commerce (213) 721-6400)
Terms: MC, V, Check. Final sale.   *Parking*

Clothing that took too long to move in the other Paul Jardin locations winds up here at further reductions, and you can find all manner of merchandise at these stores. Ties start at $5.99, there were racks of long sleeved sport shirts for $6.99 and $9.99. I found Pierre Cardin leather loafers for $59, and a wool Harve Bernard Suit with a retail price of $560 sold here for $225. Dress shirts began at $19.99.

PCH Clothing Company   COUPON
4478 Cerritos Av., Los Alamitos (714) 761-0144
Mon.-Sat., 10-6
Terms: MC, V, Check. Returns.   Parking

This is the outlet for PCH mens and boyswear, and everything in the store is discounted at least 35%. Clearance racks of older merchandise, samples, and special promotional discounts on current merchandise can bring markdowns to 80%. Men's cotton tees were $9.99, boys, from $6; boys jeans were $11.99 and a pair of men's cotton slacks were $5. There were long and short sleeved cotton sport shirts at about half price ($10 and $11), shorts as low as $2, baseball jackets, jerseys, and a full line of men's and boy's coordinated sportswear. They have a mailing list to alert you of their regular sales, where merchandise is reduced even further. Toddler clothing is a new addition. *The coupon entitles you to $5 off a purchase of $50 or more.*

Politix Outlet Store   CCC
The Citadel, City of Commerce (213) 887-1140
Mon.-Sat., 9-8; Sun., 10-6
Terms: MC, V, AE, D, Check. Final sale.   Parking

The outlet for the Poltiix chain features trendy European-style sportswear and shoes. Jackets previously selling for $299 were $199, trousers once $115 were $59, and jeans began at $29. There is a nice selection of leather shoes, many made in Italy, from $50 to $90. There is a mailing list to be notified of their occasional sales. (The Politix store in the Santa Monica Place Mall gets much of the chain's sale merchandise.)

Rick Pallack
4554 Sherman Oaks Av., Sherman Oaks (818) 789-7000
Mon.-Fri., 10-8; Sat., 10-6; Sun., 11-6
Terms: MC, V, Check. Exchanges.   Parking

This is discount Rodeo Drive shopping, so to get a full appreciation of what you'll be seeing, browse Beverly Hills before coming here. Rick Pallack, who supplies clothing to lots of TV hosts, offers high-end sportswear and suits at what they call "value prices"; the clothing is manufactured under their label at the same European factories that manufacture Armani and Hugo Boss. While the price range for suits is $400 to $700, you will find comparable suits elsewhere at $700 to $1100. Dress shirts begin around $70, there are tuxedoes, footwear and slacks (this is not the kind of place that sells *pants*). A silk baseball jacket in your choice of colors is $130, and the purple suede variety is about $300. What do you wear with a purple suede baseball jacket? The staff will be glad to coordinate an outfit, or a wardrobe for you. The atmosphere here is boutique, the service, excellent.

Roger Stuart Clothes, Inc.
729 S. Los Angeles St., Los Angeles (213) 627-9661
Mon.-Sat., 9-5:30
Terms: MC, V, D, DC, CB, AE, Check. Exchanges. Street parking

Roger Stuart sells men's suits, jackets, and tuxedoes at 30% to 60% below what you'd find the same suits for in department stores. There is a lot of variety, even in hard-to-fit sizes, and suits in the outer room average $250. If you're looking for a European cut and a somewhat finer grade of wool, try the back room, where suits are $400 to $500, and retail in the $900 to $1100 range.

Rosenman Associates
2211 E. Olympic Blvd., Los Angeles (213) 622-6266
Mon.-Sat., 11-6; Sun., 11-5
Terms: MC, V, Check. Final sale. Parking

This warehouse features suits, jackets, tuxedos, slacks, shirts, ties and shoes at discount prices. Silk ties began at $10.99, tie and cummerbund sets were $26. An Adolfo tuxedo, retailing for $570, sold here for $300. Nino Cerutti sports coats were $98 ($300), and suits were $300 ($420). Other designers were Givenchy, Pierre Cardin and Yves St. Laurent. Cotton long sleeved shirts ranged from $20 to $40 and wool worsted slacks began at about $60.

Royal Mode
831 S. Los Angeles St., Los Angeles (213) 623-9907
Mon.-Sat., 10-6; Sun., 11:30-5
Terms: MC, V, AE, Check. Exchanges. Street parking

This shop offers suits, sport coats, slacks, dress shirts and tuxedoes at discounted prices, but the big draw is that it's a distributor for the designer Ted Lapidus, whose wool suits can be found here at $359 to $459.

Steven Craig Wholesale Clothiers
19365 Business Ctr. Dr., #9, Northridge (818) 701-7474
Wed.-Fri., 10-5; Sat., 10-4:30
Terms: MC, V. Final sale. Parking

Steven Craig is a wholesaler of suits, sport coats, slacks and shirts that opens its doors to the public Wednesday through Saturday. This is a no-frills operation; no tailor, the fitting room is an office, but you can find famous maker suits like Pierre Cardin and Yves St. Laurent here for under $300; private label suits under $200. All garments are lightweight wools; sport coats range from $120 to $180, and slacks are under $60. Dress shirts are $12; silk ties, $19. Sportswear shows up irregularly. A stop for businesswear.

Zachary All, Inc.
5467 Wilshire Blvd., Los Angeles (213) 931-1484
Mon.-Fri., 10-6:30; Sat., 9-6; Sun. 10-5
Terms: MC, V, Check. Final sale.   Parking

Zachary All has been in the discount clothing business for 36 years, and while you'll never see a "compare at" price, the feel of the garments, as well as the buying power of this long-established retailer, will tell you you're getting a special deal. The store is almost as wide as the block of Wilshire it's on, and it's full of men's suits, jackets, slacks, and tuxedos, with names like Botany 500 and Oleg Cassini, in sizes that include extra short to portly long, with variety even in hard to fit sizes. Suit prices begin at $129 and range up to $350; jackets begin at $39. Alterations, done on premises, are extra.

See also
Thai Silks

Discount Catalogs

Huntington Clothiers & Shirtmakers
(800) 848-6203
Terms: MC, V, AE, DC, CB, Check. Returns.

Huntington Clothiers and Shirtmakers sells business and casual wear at discounted prices. Silk neckties start at $19.50, as do pinpoint oxford shirts; Egyptian cotton broadcloth shirts start at $27.50. Suits are available in a wide variety of fabrics, all in traditional styles, and in certain fabrics you can buy a suit in pieces (jacket in one size, trousers in another), and they guarantee the pieces will match. Their "alternative to the $225 poplin suit" is $132.50 and $450 tropical weight worsted wood suits are under $235. They also offer shoes, Byford of England socks, and a variety of accessories.

Resale

Bailey's
109 E. Union St., Pasadena (818) 449-0201
Tues.-Sat., 11-5
Terms: MC, V, AE, Check. Final sale.   Street parking

COUPON

Bailey's offers men's clothing that is no more than two years old, mainly natural fibers, as well as an assortment of shoes and some cowboy boots. There is a selection of jackets, suits, ties (some great buys at $6 and $12 for Polo and Valentino silks), leather and suede jackets and vests, and slacks. I saw some pieces by Armani, Hugo Boss, and other designers. An Armani suit was $449, and probably cost about $950 new. Armani and Hugo Boss sweaters were $49. Some items still have store tags on them, so not everything in this shop is pre-owned or pre-worn. Sizes generally range from 38-48; if you're an odd size, don't count on much. There is a Bargain Basement downstairs, open the last Sunday of the month, where everything in the store six months or more winds up; merchandise here is marked down 50%. *The coupon entitles you to 10% off one purchase.*

Men's and Women's Clothing

Apparel Designer Zone
8250 Camino Santa Fe, La Jolla (619) 450-3323
Mon.-Fri., 11-8; Sat., 11-6
(also in El Cajon (619) 460-4370, and Pacific Beach (619) 483-5150)
Terms: MC, V, AE, Check. Final sale.   Parking

What happens to the clothing you order from catalogs like Spiegel, J. Crew, Victoria's Secret, Tweeds and J. Smythe, that you decide you to return? Well, they can't just re-package it and sell it to someone else. (*Who knows what you were doing in it?*) Give up? (Never really thought about it, did you?) Some of it winds up here, discounted 50% to 90%. Some items on the racks are irregulars, discontinued styles and damages, but many are customer returns. Also in stock are some first quality pieces from places like Esprit and The Gap. The highest price in the store is $49.99. Bras from Victoria's Secret were $6,

2/ $10, and panties were $3, 2/$5. There were also robes, nightgowns and pajamas. The more mentionable of the Victoria's Secret offerings, the Moda International line, was here in profusion, from suede skirts at $19.99 to evening dresses at $24.99. Jeans for men and women were $14.99 (including some Guess?), and men's Gap chinos were $10. There were rounders of shirts from Bugle Boy, The Gap, and Smythe at $12.99. There is a mailing list for

---

Sales so big they're held at sports arenas and convention centers

---

notification of sales, which include liquidations of store chains and catalog merchandise, so big they're held at sports arenas and convention centers.

Arrow Shirts
Desert Hills Factory Stores at Cabazon
Mon.-Sun., 9-8
Terms: MC, V, D, Check. Returns.   Parking

Moderately priced sportswear for men, boys, and women is available at this outlet. Women's shirts were marked down 30%, and sweaters, featuring such names as Outback Red, were reduced as much as 45%. Menswear, including Colours by Alexander Julian and Arrow Shirts, was marked down 30% to 40%. Munsingwear was discounted 25%.

Beno's
1500 Santee St., Los Angeles (213) 748-2222
Mon.-Fri., 9:30-6; Sat., 9-5; Sun., 11-4
Terms: MC, V, D, Check. L. Returns.   Parking

Beno's is a discount department store for the whole family. Clothing for infants, kids, young adults, men and women (including large sizes) is discounted 20%. Further reductions are available on the many clearance racks. Levi's 501's are $19.60, pre-washed 501's are $27.20, and there's a five pair Levi's limit. There is a mailing list to be advised of sales.

Big Dogs Sportswear Factory Outlet
6 E. Yanonali St., Santa Barbara (805) 963-8727
Factory Merchants of Barstow (619) 253-3908
Hours vary by location.
Terms: MC, V, Check. Final sale.   Street parking

These are outlets for Big Dogs Sportswear, on which, you guessed it, there's a graphic of a Big Dog. The clothing is youth oriented and includes camp shirts, sweats, shorts and polo shirts; accessories include beach towels and totes; discounts on all merchandise range from 20% to 40%. Twill walking shorts were $25 ($35); cotton camp shirts in wild prints were $20 ($32), polo shirts were $25 ($38), and Big Dog shoulder totes were $17 ($30). There are plans for a Big Dogs Outlet in Santa Monica.

Bugle Boy Factory Store
Factory Merchants of Barstow (619) 253-3436
Mon.-Sun., 9-8
Terms: MC, AE, V, Check. Exchanges.   Parking

Sportswear and jeans for the entire family are featured in this large shop, where some merchandise is irregular, but the bulk is first quality. Discounts begin at 25%; but clothing on the many sale rounders is discounted up to 70%. Huskie boys' jeans were $18 ($31), men's jeans were $28 ($37), and boys' jeans jackets were $14 ($39). Women's jeans were as low as $8.99 ($43).

The California Fit   CCC
9460 Central Av., Montclair (714) 626-2495
Mon.-Fri., 10-9; Sat., 10-7; Sun., 11-6
Terms: MC, V, AE, D, Check. Final sale.   Parking

The California Fit is the last stop for clothing from Millers Outpost. Some is priced identically to the Millers Outpost Clearance Center, but some is even cheaper: $10 for one or *two pair* of jeans is common. Among the brands are Bugle Boy, Jordache, and their own Anchor Blue. Shortalls are $15, and men's long sleeved knit shirts are $8. A woman's Dockers long sleeved shirt, originally $32, was $6. Ties were $2, as were leather belts. The selection is varied, the atmosphere all but nil. Clothing here for the whole family.

California Mart Monthly Saturday Sales
Olympic & Los Angeles Sts., Los Angeles (213) 623-5876
Third Saturday of the month, 10-4
Terms: Cash only. Final sale. $1.50 admission.   Street parking

The California Mart is home to over 170 name brands, representing 300 lines of clothing and accessories for men, women, juniors and children. Once a month they sell their samples to the public in what resembles a big indoor swap meet, and samples often sell below wholesale: I found lines of designer clothing selling for about *one quarter* of department store prices. Featured are sportswear for the whole family, leather jackets and accessories, men's suits and furnishings, women's lingerie, exercise wear, watches, handbags, silk ties, hats, kidswear, just about anything you can think of, though most boothes feature clothes for women. The merchandise is first quality, but check for damages. The "fitting rooms" are curtains to change behind, often without mirror. Try this sale once; if it's your style you'll be back monthly.

Designer Labels for Less   COUPON
4726 Admiralty Way, Marina Del Rey   (310) 827-5115
Hours vary by location.
(20 additional locations; see Geographical Index or call 1-800-FOR FASHion during business hours)
Terms: MC, V, AE, Check. Exchanges.   Parking

At "Always 40% to 80% off", this chain offers first quality merchandise by some of the most popular designers on the scene today. In the men's department, Bill Blass cotton shirts regularly sell for $14.90 ($40); the day I visited they were marked down an additional 50% to $7.45. Motto shirts were $19.90 ($48), also 50% off, down to $9.95. The stores that offer menswear carry suits, pants, jackets and sweaters. The women's stores feature tons of Carole Little. A burgundy velour party dress was on sale for $68.60 ($188). Many other designers are represented, featuring sports, athletic and some showy beaded evening wear, and some locations carry Lily of France and Christian Dior lingerie at 50% off retail. Merchandise here is always current, and savings are tremendous. *The coupon entitles you to an additional 10% off one purchase on all but marked down merchandise.*

Designer Labels for Less Clearance Center   CCC
6100 Canoga Blvd., Woodland Hills (818) 999-9030
1808 E. Dyer Rd., Santa Ana   (714) 261-6678
Mon.-Sat., 10-7; Sun., 11-6
Terms: MC, V, AE, Check. Exchanges.   Parking

An outlet store for a discount chain, that's what I call shopping! In these warehouses there are racks and racks of $5, $10 and $15 finds in famous maker sportswear; generally first quality but also some "as is" goods, so check purchase carefully. Men's and women's sportswear, suits, and accessories are available here. A portion of the space is for merchandise at their regular low prices. A browser's heaven.

Eddie Bauer Outlet
The Citadel, City of Commerce   (213) 725-1858
Mon.-Sat., 9 - 8; Sun. 10 - 6
(also in Cabazon (714) 922-9202 and San Ysidro (619) 428-7611)
Terms: MC, V, Check. Returns.   Parking

These shops feature discounts of 30% to 70% on seconds, discontinued and overstocked items, and there is a wide variety of merchandise here, from men's suede jackets at $125 ($199) and goretex parkas at $100, to nylon fanny packs at $10, men's and women's flannel shirts, slacks, sweaters and many weights of outdoorwear. Women's dresses, robes and nightgowns are also available, as well as a selection of shoes.

Evan Picone/Gant Factory Outlet
Desert Hills Factory Stores at Cabazon (714) 849-4335
Mon.-Sun., 9-8
Terms: MC, V, AE, Check. Returns.   Parking

Classic clothing for men, women and boys from labels such as Gant, Izod, Palm Beach, Hunter Haig, and Evan Picone sell here at discounts of 40% and more. Mens' Gant flannel shirts were $21.99 ($58) and cotton/poly sport shirts were $19.99 ($35). An Izod wool jacket was $120 ($225), and dress shirts ranged from $12.99 to $24.99. Men's sale suits were $199. Women's separates were available in misses and plus sizes, discounted to 50%. Jackets were $99 ($170), matching skirts, $69 ($120). Trifari jewelry was discounted 25%.

The Gap Outlet
The Citadel, City of Commerce (213) 726-0432
Mon.-Sat., 9-8; Sun., 10-6
Terms: MC, V, Check. Returns.   Parking

This entire store isn't an outlet; stick to the side with the "Sale" signs and you'll find a selection of discounted Gap clothing for the whole family. Some irregulars and seconds are mixed in, and are generally marked. The outlet offered jeans for $16.99, ($38), and women's cotton pique shirts at $12.99 ($38). Racks of baby and children's cotton knits included baby rompers at $6.99 ($17). The find of the day were men's silk rep ties in classic colors, originally $25, marked down *five times,* to $1!

Gitano Outlet   CCC
Desert Hills Factory Stores at Cabazon (714) 922-2220
Hours vary by location.
(also in Commerce, Barstow, San Ysidro, Ontario, and Lake Elsinore)
Terms: AE, D, MC, V, Check. Exchanges.   Parking

Casual clothing for men, women (including plus sizes), juniors, boys and girls is offered here at substantial savings. Adult jeans begin at $19.97, kids at $12.97, and there is a huge assortment of tops, sweaters, jackets and shirts marked down at least once, often to $10 and under.   The Cabazon store incorporates the Chainwide Clearance Center, where items are reduced again, as much as 50% and often 70%. Here you can find jeans under $10.

Guess Outlet
860 S. Los Angeles St., Los Angeles (213) 629-4438
Desert Hills Factory Stores at Cabazon (714) 849-1585
Hours vary by location.
Terms: MC, V, Check. Final sale.　　　　Parking

If you're looking for that magic Guess? triangle on the butt, you've found it. Here seconds, irregulars, overruns and discontinued Guess? jeans sell for $35. Overalls are $45; denim skirts, $25; sweatshirts and sweaters imprinted with the Guess? logo are $25 and shirts, rayon and cotton, striped and flowered, are $28. Denim jackets are $50. Some pieces are in odd colors, but there is plenty of blue denim.

Intermoda Exchange
100 N. LaCienega Blvd., Suite 103, Los Angeles (310) 657-4777
Mon.-Fri., 10-7; Sat., 10-6; Sun., 12-5
Terms: MC, V, AE, Check. Exchanges.　　　Street parking

Intermoda is quite a find. (It may be the mother lode.) While there are some women's suits and separates, the emphasis here is on menswear by Armani, Gianni Versace, Claude Montana, Gianfranco Ferre, Ungaro, and Valentino. The proprietors are importers who sell to other wholesalers, and the pricing

---

Armani, Gianni Versace, Claude Montana, Ungaro and Valentino below department store sale prices

---

policy is to keep current goods at prices below department store sale prices (and department stores only reduce prices at the end of a season), so you don't have to wait for a sale. Armani suits range from $299 to $599 ($899 to $1299), other suits are in that range or slightly lower. There are also tuxedos and sport coats, all in sizes 36 to 58. A smattering of women's clothing included Thierry Muglier, Valentino and Gianni Versace. No tailor on premises (can't have everything). Their mailing list informs you of new shipments.

Jerry Pillers
937 E. Colorado Blvd., Pasadena (818) 796-9559
Mon.-Sat., 10:30-6
Terms: MC, V, Check. Final sale.　　　Street parking

This is a hodge podge of designer and not-so clothing, leathers, accessories and shoes for men and women, though the women's department is larger than the men's. There are some phenomenal savings—the odd designer piece that will compliment your wardrobe reduced by 50%, then another 50%—but finding it may be like finding a needle in a haystack. On a recent visit there was a rack of Romeo Gigli separates, very reasonably priced, and an old Norma Kamali strapless, still interesting, that began life at $500, now $50. Tony Lambert long sleeve sport shirts were $35 ($90). The shoes are beautiful, many Italian, discounted 50%, then another 20%. The back has slightly older shoes discounted 75%.

John Anthony Apparel Company
1424 Third St. Promenade, Santa Monica (310) 394-8400
Mon.-Tues., 10-7; Wed.-Thurs., Sun., 10-9; Fri.-Sat., 10-11
Terms: MC, V, AE, Check. Exchanges.   Street parking

When you walk into this store full of jeans, Lycra, denim and mini skirts, it looks like almost everything is on sale. Actually *everything is. Always.* Trendy separates for men and women sell at unbeatable prices: jeans begin at $10; men's rayon slacks start at $15.99; long and short sleeved rayon shirts are $19.99 and denim jackets are $26. Women's long lacey skirts are $19.99, Lycra mini-dresses are $15.95; long, retro print dresses, $42.

Leading Designer Outlet
Factory Merchants of Barstow (619) 253-5333
Mon.-Sun., 8-9
Terms: MC, V, AE, Check. Returns.   Parking

This large shop sells clothing, shoes and accessories for men, women and children, as well as a selection of linen, by one of the biggest designers around. Some savings are amazing considering what this merchandise originally sold for. Women's woven leather pumps were $179 ($365), and crocodile loafers in your choice of colors were $379 ($895). A women's wool and nylon blazer had been marked down several times to $150 ... from $1500. A suede sarong skirt was $199 ($620). Men's suits ranged from $99 to $499 (to $1,000); trousers began at $60 (to $195); irregular knit short sleeved signature shirts were $25.99 ($65), and casual loafers were $169 ($340). Boy's long sleeved knit jerseys were $15 ($35); and short sleeved knit signature shirts, $22.99 ($32). Irregular sheets, pillowcases and comforters in current styles were discounted 40% to 70%.

Levi's Outlet
Factory Merchants of Barstow (619) 253-5561
San Diego Factory Outlet Center (619) 662-1244
Mon.-Sun., 9-8
Terms: MC, V, D, Check. Returns.   Parking

This is a store full of jeans and sportswear for the whole family. Levis' 501's were $21.99 and $24.99, 550's were $24.99, Dockers were $21.99; men's long sleeved chambray shirts were $11.99; boys, $7.99. Boys' 2T-4T jeans were $11.99, sizes 4-7 jeans and denim jackets were $19.99. Infant overalls were $19.99, and girls 4-6x cotton knit tops were $9. Women's Brittania jeans were $19.99, denim jumpers were $19.99 and denim shorts were $9.99 and $14.99.

The Liquidation Club   **COUPON**
19032 Vermont Av., Gardena (310) 715-6500
Mon.-Wed., Fri.-Sat., 10-6; Thurs., 10-8; Sun., 10-5
Terms: MC, V, Check. Exchanges.   Parking

While this store calls itself a club, there is no membership fee. It's a store for "the professional black belt shopper." If at first it looks a little odd and less then special, look closer: those Guess? jeans are *$24.99*. I started nosing through the men's department and found Nino Cerutti wool blazers, single and double breasted, labels removed, for $79.99. A Burberry suit in a quiet wool plaid was $165, and a Perry Ellis Portfolio wool blend was $129. A Bill Blass Harris Tweed type jacket was $70. For women there were dressy dresses (a Jessica McClintock velvet and taffeta dress was $45), everyday dresses, sweaters (two for one the day I was in), playclothes and lingerie (an Eileen West flannel robe was $25). There were bras, teddies and stockings too. Men's shirts were not a big buy at $18, but that day if you bought anything for $17 or more, you received a second item of the same or lower price free. Rainbow Body Wear for kids was two pieces for $8. I started noticing a preponderance of store private labels among the clothes; turns out a lot of the stock is store returns. Check the bulletin board as you enter for the sale of the day. *Take 10% off your next purchase with the coupon.*

London Fog Factory Store
Factory Merchants of Barstow (619) 253-3434
Lake Elsinore Outlet Ctr. (714) 245-0450
Hours vary by location.
Terms: MC, V, Check. Returns.   Parking

Concentrating on more mature folk, these shops sell jackets, coats, sportswear and accessories at discounts close to 50%. On one of my visits, a woman's fur-trimmed satin lined parka was $90, reduced from $190. (Women's sizes range from petite to 24 1/2). Women's unlined trenches started at about $90; lined, $135. Men's unlined trenches began at $100; lined, $125. There were men's golf jackets discounted 30%, and winter coats at about half off. There was also a selection of men's Ultrasuede sport coats in a large variety of colors. Women's sportswear was in missy styles, and included separates in the $30 to $80 range. They also carried a line of leather handbags resembling Coach, at

$60 to $75. All merchandise is current and first quality, and there's a raincoat here for everyone.

Millers Outpost Clearance Center   CCC
333 S. E St., San Bernadino (714) 885-3804
Mon.-Fri., 10-9; Sat., 10-7; Sun., 11-6
Terms: MC, V, AE, D, Check. Final sale.   Parking

Here you'll find clothing from the Millers Outpost stores for men, women, young men and women, and some kids clothing, a host of accessories and some shoes, all reduced one third from marked prices. (Marked prices have been reduced at least once and frequently several times from original retail.) What this translates to is women's decorated baseball hats, once $9, now .66, Anchor Blue women's tees, originally $16, now $3; shortalls, originally $30, now $10; mens long and short sleeve shirts, originally $22, $8; Dockers slacks, originally $36, $16. There were tables of belts, underwear, shoes, handbags, and earrings, all at big discounts. Great for back to school shopping.

NaNa Outlet
8327 Third St., Los Angeles
Mon.-Sat., 11-8
Terms: MC, V, AE, Check. Final sale.   Street parking

The outlet for NaNa's Santa Monica store carries a large selection of shoes and boots in addition to clothing for young men and women. A pearl encrusted bustier was $20, and black Lycra dresses were $50 ($95). Flowered leggings were $10 ($33), and rayon dresses were about half price at $25 to $40. Men's clothing was also half price: rayon shirts were $35 ($70); navy cotton pants were $20 ($40), and jackets were $45 ($90). The shoes were in the $25 to $40 range, from platform pumps to stiletto-heeled boots for women to biker boots for both to two-toned wing-tips for men.

The Ninth Street Outlet
1124 W. 9 St., Upland (714) 985-5715
Mon.-Sat., 10-6
Terms: MC, V, Check. GC. Exchanges.   Parking

The Ninth Street Outlet sells men's and women's sportswear, and some boys' and girls' sportswear, at prices beginning at about one third off, going down to two thirds off regular retail price. There is a large selection of jeans and tops, jackets, casual and beach wear.

Pillers of Eagle Rock
1800 Colorado Blvd., Eagle Rock (213) 257-8166
Fri.-Sun.,10-5:30
Terms: MC, V, Check. Final sale.   Parking

Here men's and women's sport and casual clothing is discounted 50%, then reduced an additional 20% to 90%. Clothing takes up about two thirds of the store, the rest is shoes, which are three pair for the price of one, including some very pricey names like Charles Jordan, Sesto Meucci, Privilege, Xavier Danaud, and Phyllis Poland, French Shriner, Nunn Bush, Mario Brutini and

---
For $20 I walked out with a bag of shoes originally retailing for over $800

Bruno Magli. On the balcony women's shoes are three pair for $10. I spent $20 up there and walked out with a bag of shoes originally retailing for over $800! There are accessories, wallets, handbags, belts, lingerie and some leather goods. A mailing list to be notifies you of sales.

Sacks SFO   COUPON
114 Washington Blvd., Marina del Rey (310) 306-2623
Mon.-Tues., 10-6; Wed.-Fri., 10-8; Sat., 10-7; Sun., 11-6
(also in West Los Angeles, West Hollywood, Hollywood, Culver City, Long Beach, Studio City, Tarzana and Burbank)
Terms: MC, V, Check. Exchanges.   Parking

Sacks specializes in trendy sportswear at discounts of 40% to 70%, sometimes even greater with special buys. On a recent visit I found mens' slacks at $13.99 ($42), rayon and viscose jackets, $29.99 ($72), women's jeans were $16 ($40), retro print dresses, $49.99 ($57), patterned leggings, two for $20. Some separates from a very pricey New York department store were discounted 80%. They also offer accessories and occasionally have leather sales, where jackets run as low as $39.99; skirts, $19.99. The Hollywood and Burbank stores have kid's shops; Tarzana and West Los Angeles have children's departments within the store, featuring small clothes at similar discounts. *The coupon offers a 10% discount on one purchase, Monday through Thursday.*

See Me Color
625 E. Cochran St., Simi Valley (805) 527-9573
Mon.-Fri., 9-5
Terms: Cash and Check only. Final sale.   Parking

This is a factory outlet of cotton and cotton blend sportswear for women, juniors, and girls, with a smattering of boys' shirts. Most stock is bright knit tops, legging, shorts, pants and dresses at prices ranging from $2 to $10. The merchandise is over-production from their factory, and although mainly first quality, there may be some irregulars and seconds, check carefully.

Shipley's
Seacliff Village, Huntington Beach (714) 536-4700
Mon.-Fri., 10-9; Sat., 10-7; Sun., 10-6
(also in Orange, Los Alamitos, Costa Mesa, Placentia, Tustin, Anaheim, Long Beach and Lakewood)
Terms: MC, V, Check. Exchanges.   Parking

Shipley's has clothing for the entire family at savings of about 20%. They specialize in sportswear, jeans and beachwear, with more men's clothing than women's, including a sizeable big men's department. They advertise a new sale almost every week. When I visited, mens' B&B swim trunks were $9.99, and all boys Motto separates were $9.99. Women's swimwear ranged from $14.99 to $24.99. Men's Levi's began at $19.99; 501's were $21.99. Women's Guess shortalls and overalls were $49.99. Danskin athletic wear was discounted 45% and women's nylon warm up suits were $29 to $39.

The Shore Shop
2117 Main St., Huntington Beach (714) 536-4600
321 Seal Beach Blvd., Seal Beach (310) 594-8927
Mon.-Fri.,10-7; Sat., 10-6; Sun., 11-5
Terms: MC, V, AE, D, Check. Exchanges.   Parking

The Shore Shop has sportswear for adolescents, men and women, at discounts beginning at 20%. Sale rounders reduce that price again and again. Clothing featured ranges from moderately priced women's sportswear to Paris Blues and Esprit for females, and Quicksilver and other surf lines for males. There is also a selection of shoes, the deal of the day on my last visit: a thin soled Top-Sider for $19.50. There are wallets, purses and accessories and a mailing list to be informed of their sales, in January and July, their back to school sale in September, and their March preview. They offer a 10% discounts to students under 21 (sale merchandise excluded).

Thel's
4334 S. Sepulveda Blvd., Culver City (310) 390-2144
Mon.-Fri., 10-6; Sat., 10-5
Terms: MC,V, AE, Check. Final sale.   Street parking

Thels' sells first quality Levi and Lee jeans at a 10% to 20% discount. You can find jeans cheaper, but if you're one of those people whom jeans don't quite fit, buy them here because alterations are free. (They estimate that a tailor would charge you $5.50 for a hem, $12 for pegging and $3 to take in a waist.) There are also denim seconds, with labels removed: jackets are $29, jeans start at $8.

United Colors of Benetton
The Citadel, City of Commerce (213) 721-3676
Mon.-Sat., 9-8; Sun., 10-6
Terms: MC, V, Check. Final sale.   Parking

This is the sale store for the popular chain, where wool sweaters were marked down to $26.25 ($69), and rayon chiffon blouses were $33 ($69). A wonderful wool and nylon blend men's sport jacket in a choice of solids was $131 ($250). There are also children's clothes. If this is your look you're coming out around 50% off.

Van Heusen Factory Store
Desert Hills Factory Stores at Cabazon
Hours vary by location.
(also in Lake Elsinore (619) 674-1190, San Ysidro (619) 690-6028)
Terms: MC, V, D, Check. Returns.   Parking

Here you'll find men's Van Heusen dress shirts at $12.99, silk ties at $18.99 ($32.50), and tee shirts at $9.99 for three ($13). Authentic Sportswear sweaters were discounted from 40% to 50%. There was a selection of women's sportswear in misses sizes under the Van Heusen For Her line, discounted 25% to 40%.

Venice Beach Embroidery
801 Ocean Front Walk, Venice Beach (310) 399-1823
Mon.-Sun., 10-6
Terms: MC, V, Check. Exchanges.   Street parking

This is another hodge podge store, featuring samples, irregulars, damages and whatever they can buy cheaply to sell cheaply to you. Men's patterned tees were $5, a selection of men's jeans were $10, as were sweaters and bodysuits. There were a few suede skirts at $15.99 and Bila flowing pants at $10. Make sure you see the whole store, which is actually three adjacent spaces.

Warehouse Outlet
100 North Maclay, San Fernando (818) 361-0292
Mon.-Sun., 8:30-5:30
Terms: Cash and Check only. Exchanges.   Parking

As you near the Warehouse Outlet you realize there are signs plastered all over it, advertising men's first quality denim flare Levi's for $15.99. The store is full of Levi's and a couple of other brands, for boys, men and women, at low prices. Levi's 517's are $21.99 and 501's (preshrunk) are $25.99, with prices somewhat higher if you're a size 38 or larger. (Another incentive to put that cookie down. *Now*.) There are sweats at $9.95 per piece, some sweaters, shirts, underwear and socks, but the overwhelming impression is *pants*.

See also
Cole of California Outlet
Hang Ten Outlet

Catalogs

Lands' End
(800) 354-4444
Terms: MC, V, AE, Check. Returns.

Lands' End sells clothing for men, women and children, the quality is high, and the prices are generally lower than comparable merchandise at retail stores. Additionally there are often several pages of their "outlet" selection, offering markdowns of 50% and more on first quality merchandise.

Wintersilks
(800) 648-7455
Terms: MC, V. Returns.

Wintersilks offers silk underwear, sweaters and separates at factory prices, but they also have factory seconds and returned goods selling at 20% to 50% below catalog prices. A silk polo sweater, retailing at $39, is available in second quality for $19.95. A women's silk charmeuse slip, ordinarily $45, is $30, and men's silk briefs are $12.95 (first quality, $15.95). Seconds are not available in all styles, but if you find something in the catalog you like, ask.

Resale

Star Wares on Main
2817 Main St., Santa Monica (310) 399-0224
Mon.-Sun., 10-6
Terms: MC, V, Check. Final sale.　　Street parking
and
A Star is Worn
7303 Melrose Av., Los Angeles (213) 939-4922
Mon.-Sat., 11-7; Sun., 12-5
Terms: MC, V, AE, Check. Final sale.　　Street Parking

These are fun stores; as their names imply, many of the garments were previously owned or worn in movies by some of your favorite stars.　Want

---

Consider it the modern equivalent of Grauman's Chinese: try to fit your fanny into Cher's short shorts

---

Madonna's earrings, or Michael Jackson's jacket? Some items are collectibles, some are still fashionable, and they're almost new. Value is a real question. You *are* paying something for the famous body that previously occupied the outfit. But some of the money does go to charity and shopping here is as close as most of us will come to the rich and famous. You could consider it the modern-day equivalent of Grauman's Chinese: try to fit your fanny into Cher's short shorts.

It's a Wrap
2705 Burbank Blvd., Burbank (818) 567-7366
Mon.-Sat., 11-6
Terms: MC, V, Check. Final sale.　　Parking
and
Studio Wardrobe
3953 Laurelgrove, Studio City (818) 508-7762
Mon.-Sat., 11-5
Terms: Cash and Check only. Final sale.　　Street parking

These shops offer wardrobes from film and television productions. Clothing is for men, women, and children, and varies depending on the production wardrobe they've just received. Many pieces have hardly been worn, and if you find something you like they'll be able to you what show or movie it was worn in, and maybe by whom.

Leather Apparel

Fellini Leather
Fox Hills Mall, Culver City (310) 397-8202
Hawthorne Plaza, Hawthorne (310) 644-8308
Hours vary by location.
Terms: MC, V, Check. L. Exchanges.   *Parking*

Fellini leather is a store for the whole family, and there's usually a sale going on. While the prices on kids jackets are steep (little biddy pieces cost several times more than, say, hot pants or bustiers, which are little too but not *that* little), prices for adult jackets range from $100 to $300, with some pieces slightly higher. They also offer coats and several sportswear items. Women's leather shortalls, in a variety of colors, were $60, pants and skirts ranged from $120 to $200, and those hot pants and bustiers were about $50. They also did some intriguing things with leather and lycra. There are frequent sales.

Firenze Factory Outlet   **COUPON**
The Citadel, City of Commerce (213) 888-8577
Hours vary by location.
(also in Santa Barbara (805) 965-5723, and San Diego (619) 690-3378)
Terms: MC, V,AE, Check. Final sale.   *Parking*

If you think you'll never get a discount on all those exquisite, trendy leather and suede fashions the beautiful people wear, visit Firenze. They manufacture high fashion leathers for the best stores, and the outlet is packed with leather and suede, in great colors and styles, discounted 25% to 75%. For women there are bustiers, suits, skirts and pants in suede and leather, some embellished with studs and beading. A woman's butter-soft white leather strapless dress was $112.50. For men the most popular items are leather jackets, in many colors and styles, from fringes to baseball and bomber jackets, and once you put one of these jackets on, you won't want to take it off ... it's hard to stop stroking the leather. February and August are Firenze's semi-annual sales, when prices drop *another* 40% to 80%, but there is a sale rack everyday with a few markdowns. The atmosphere is boutique; stopping in here will change your notions of discount shopping. ***The coupon entitles you to 10% off your next purchase.***

The Leather Loft
The Citadel, City of Commerce (213) 721-0609
Hours vary by location.
(also in Cabazon, San Ysidro, Barstow and Ontario)
Terms: MC, V, Check. Exchanges.   Parking

The Leather Loft features luggage, handbags, small leather goods, belts and jackets. A variety of bomber jackets sold for $139 to $199 ($225 to $375); a large leather backpack was $110 ($172); a garment bag, $150 ($280).

Leather to the Limit
8342 Melrose Av., West Hollywood (213) 653-9155
Mon.-Fri., 10-7; Sat., 10-5
Terms: AE, Check. Final sale.   Street parking

Leather to the Limit manufactures custom leather clothing, and while prices are by no means cheap, they are comparable to retail at better stores, but you're getting a custom piece. Women's jackets begin around $500; skirts, $120. Men's jackets start at around $700. You'll be amazed at the diversity of hides, including lambskin, goatskin, calfskin and pigskin, and the grades, colors, and prints available. If they don't have it, it probably isn't made. Garments are produced first in fabric to assure fit, then in leather. Generally you can have your order within a few days. There is a book of styles for inspiration.

PTS Leather Warehouse
828 W. 12 St., Long Beach
Wholesale Leather Apparel
1406 E. Katella Av., Anaheim (714) 937-8924
Hours vary by location.
Terms: Cash only. Final sale   Parking

You'll feel intrepid looking for the Long Beach location, when you find it you'll feel accomplished, and once inside you'll understand what warehouse pricing really means. There are two "rooms" of leather here, full of jackets, skirts, pants and chaps at discounted prices. Men's biker jackets are $99, women's, $89. Women's short jackets are $129, and matching skirts are $39. Leather dresses are $79. Most men's jackets (with the exception of bikers) are $149. The Anaheim store has more regular hours, but the Long Beach location is only open Thurs. and Fri., 1-5. October through December they're open all week.

Remy Leather
1020 S. Los Angeles St., Los Angeles (213) 747-5493
Mon.-Fri., 10-4
Terms: Check and Cash only.   Street parking

Remy Leather sells lambskin and suede clothing at prices just above wholesale. They carry jackets, skirts, pants, and a few dresses. There's a wide choice of color, and the grade of leather you choose determines the price. Jackets average $300, skirts begin around $150. If you find something you like but want it in another color choice, no problem: they'll make one up for you. They also do minor alterations.

Wilson's House of Suede and Leather Outlet   CCC
1033 N. Hollywood Way, Burbank (818) 841-7789
Wed.-Sat., 10-6:30; Sun., 11-6
Terms: AE, MC, V, Check ($500 limit). Final sale. Parking

This is the only outlet in California for the popular leather chain. Nothing in the store is over $99.99, and most pieces are quite a bit under. The garments come in a variety of colors and up to the minute styles. There is always a rack with skirts at $9.99, and a men's jacket rack at $79.99. A white leather bustier dress with lace skirt was $19.99, as was a black suede low-back dress ($120). A man's brown suede coat was $99.99 ($250), and baseball jackets, in a variety of colors, were $79.99 ($225). A rack of men's bomber jackets were $69.99 and men's leather pants were $69.99 ($150). There are wallets, fanny packs and bags, and the scent of leather is so thick, it stays with you long after you've left.

Discount Catalogs

The Deerskin Place
(717) 733-7624
Terms: MC, V, Checks, MO.

The Deerskin Place sells deerskin, leather and suede garments and accessories at very affordable prices. Knee high suede lace-up boots are $45, and soft-soled suede ankle boot slippers are $16.95. Men's and women's sheepskin shearling coats are $295, and motorcycle jackets with quilted linings are $149; buckskin fringe jackets are $169, and there are several other jacket styles to chose from. There is also a selection of purses, wallets, gloves, and accessories.

Swimsuits

Atlantis Discount Swim and Sport
1806 Tustin Av., Tustin (714) 547-1552
Hours vary by season.
Terms: Cash and Check only. Final sale.   Parking

Atlantis offers name brand bathing suits, bikinis, cover-ups and playwear at discounts beginning at 20%. The store is separated into a juniors' section—with higher cut legs—and a women's section, with more demure suits and a little strategically placed control. The racks are full of labels like Rosemary Reid, Sassafras, and LaBlanca. They've been at this location for 15 years.

Blue Moon Exchange
608 Main St., Ventura (805) 643-2553
5122 Holister Av., Goleta (805) 967-0610
Mon.-Sat., 10-6
Terms: MC, V, Check. Final sale.   Parking

Blue Moon carries all kinds of clothing, from discounted junior sportswear to consignment clothing for resale, but they also carry bathing suits, which are $9.99 all the time. They are new, first quality, brand name junior swimsuits, in a variety of styles, in sizes 5/6 to 13/14.

Cole of California Outlet
6015 Bandini Blvd., City of Commerce (213) 724-4693
Mon.-Fri., 9-5; Sat., 9-4
(also in La Verne (714) 593-6415, and Northridge (818) 894-3422)
Terms: V, MC, Checks. Exchanges.   Parking

This is the outlet for Catalina, Hot Coles, Cole of California, Catalina Girl, Half Moon Bay and Bay Club separates and swimwear for the whole family. Catalina Girl swimwear was $3.99 and up, Half Moon Bay trunks were $9.99, and women's swimsuits began at $3.99; the current collection at $21.99 (plus sizes and maternity swimsuits are available too). A small group of Cathy Hardwick separates were $16.99; girls' cotton and Lycra Lee jeans were $11; boys' Winning Moves baseball jackets were $21.99; and Catalina men's windbreakers were $60. Some of the kids sportswear brands offered are King Cole, Jet Set, Lee Jeans and Donmoor, all reasonably priced.

Swimsuits

Everything But Water Sale Merchandise   CCC
10800 Pico Blvd., Westwood   (310) 470-4678
Mon.-Fri., 10-9; Sat., 10-7; Sun., 11-5
Terms: MC, V, D, Check. GC. Final sale.   Parking

In the off season a section of this store carries clearance merchandise from the Everything But Water chain. The goods are first quality, and represent manufacturers such as Gottex, LaBlanca, Body Glove, Too Hot Brazil, Sassafras, Jag and Hot Coles, in junior sizes to 13, women's to 16. There are also pareos, cover-ups, leggings, jackets, and some sportswear. The pricing policy is simple: anything that originally sold for under $20 is now $9.99; $20 to $50, now $19.99; over $50, $29.99. Since most of the suits are by better manufacturers, the bulk of the merchandise is $29.99.

Fresh Peaches Swimwear   COUPON
9293 Archibald Av., Rancho Cucamonga (714) 980-0172
Mon-Sat., 10-6
Terms: MC, V, Check. Exchanges.   Parking

Fresh Peaches manufactures swimwear, aerobic wear, and some sportswear in cotton and Lycra, and nylon and Lycra, and sells direct to you at great prices. At the shop you can hear the whir of the sewing machines as you peruse the

---
Custom-made swimsuits start at $40

---

goods. There are women's swimsuits in one and two pieces ($25 to $35, unless you want a leather bikini, that's $40), men's briefs and trunks ($12.50), and girls' bathing suits ($15). There is tons of exercise wear: leotards, unitards, leggings, crop tops and briefs, in wild prints and solids. Women's leotards range from $12.50 to $15, leggings from $10 to $15, and unitards from $20 to $25. They custom-make bathing suits and leotards, starting at $40. (Turn-around time gets longer the closer it gets to Spring Break.) They will do minor alterations on their ready made suits for free. There is one big sale, just after Valentine's Day, where bathing suits are $15, leotards are $10. *The coupon entitles you to 10% off on one purchase of ready made merchandise.*

Kirkpatrick Sales
8592 Washington Blvd., Culver City (310) 839-6455
Mon.-Sat., 10-6
Terms: MC, V, Check. Final sale.   Street parking

There are rooms full of bathing suits at Kirkpatrick, and all are heavily discounted. On my last visit, one-piece swimsuit seconds were $9.75; mix and match bikini tops and bottoms were $4 and a rack of two piece suits were $6. First quality swimsuits sell from $10 to $50. Mens trunks by Jantzen, Hobie, and Members Only range from $8 to $12. Cover-ups, sportswear and sunglasses are also discounted.

Time-off Apparel
6022 Reseda Blvd.,Tarzana (818) 344-2825
Mon.-Sat., 10-6
Terms: MC, V, D, Check. Final sale.   Parking

This shop carries a large selection of beach, resort and weekend wear for juniors and women, at discounts of 30% to 50%. Some of the brands here are LaBlanca, Roxanne, Sirena, Gottex, Too Hot Brazil, Citrus and Sassafrass. There is also a small selection of sandals and beach accessories, all under $10.

See also
Anne Klein Factory Outlet
Adrienne Vittadini Factory Store
California Girl
The Gigi Shoppe
The Robe Outlet
SpaGear

Discount Catalogs

The Finals
(800) 431-9111
Terms: MC, V, AE, D. Returns.

The Finals manufactures competition swimsuits that are fashionable and won't fall off. Styles for women were one and two piece, high- and not so high-cut, and for men, European, American and Master Cut (a fuller brief). Men's suits begin at $18, women's, $36. Suits are generally made of Antron and Lycra, a few in Ultra-tech, what they call "the ultimate performance swimwear". There are team discounts and a Grab Bag offers discontinued suits at about half price. They also carry goggles, caps, and other swim accessories. First time buyers spending $50 or more receive a free pair of goggles, and anyone ordering $100 or more at one time gets 10% off all future purchases.

Tees and Sweats

Shirts Mart
18007 E. Gale Av., City of Industry (818) 964-8615
Mon.-Sat., 9-8; Sun., 9-7
Terms: Cash and Check only. Final sale.　　　Parking

Shirts Mart offers tee and sweat shirts, underwear, socks and playclothes, in cotton and blends, imprinted and in solid colors, at near wholesale prices. Five tee shirts are $10, three pair of men's Fruit of the Loom briefs, $4.99. Infants sweat sets are $7.99, as are tank top and short sets. Adults cotton baggies are $7.99, kids' sizes, $6.99. Sweat tops are $6.99 and pants, $5.99. Women's cotton slacks and tee sets are $7.99.

Sweats and Surf
6733 Eton Av., Canoga Park (818) 340-4251
Mon.-Sun., 10-6
Terms: MC, V, Check. Exchange.　　　Parking

This store is huge, and filled with rounders of sweats, tees, tanks, shorts and miscellaneous clothing at $2 to $7. Sweats are $4, hooded sweatshirts, $7, and colored tees, $3. There are youth and adult sizes, and although much of the merchandise is first quality, damages are mixed in, so check carefully. Women's oversized cotton tees are $3, tanks are $5. In the back there are odds and ends, rounders of jeans for $4, mens shorts and trunks for $2, men's long and short sleeved shirts, sweaters, a few women's dresses and jumpsuits, most of which bear little stylistic relation to each other, at $5.

T-Shirt Warehouse
13317 E. Rosecrans Av., Santa Fe Springs (213) 921-9778
531 Beach Blvd., Buena Park (714) 955-6161
Mon.-Sat., 10-7; Sun., 10-5
Terms: V, MC, TC, Check. Exchanges.　　　Parking

This store offers kids' tee shirts, plain and screened, at five for $10, kids' sweats at $3.99, hooded sweat shirts at $6.99, and sweatsuits at $7.99. Jerzees adult sweats are $5.99 in sizes S-XL. Leggings are $7.99 and sweat shorts $3.99. Women's cotton tee shirt and pant sets are $9.99, and hand-painted sets, $17.99. Men's and boys' cotton polos are $5.99, and Hanes Beefy Tees, $3.

T-Shirts Warehouse, Inc.
10955 Sherman Way, Sun Valley (818) 764-1122
Mon.-Fri., 9:30-9; Sat.-Sun., 9:30-6:30
Terms: MC, V. Exchanges.   Parking

The big draw here is five tee shirts for $10 (50/50 blends and all cotton, imprinted and plain), but they also sell sweatshirts ($5.99), sweatpants ($4.99), and women's cotton tee shirt dresses ($4.50 short, $5.99 long). Six pair of tube socks are $4.99, two pair of Fruit of the Loom shorts, $4.99. Lycra stirrup pants are $6.99 and cotton and Lycra, lace edged shorts are $4.45. Men's cotton baggies are $8 and a rack of irregular cotton golf shirts in bright colors were $4.55 each. Hanes Beefy Tees were $3.

T-Shirt Wholesale Mart
17435 E. Gale Av., City of Industry (818) 810-4221
Mon.-Sat., 9-7; Sun., 9-6
Terms: MC, V ($20 min.). Exchanges.   Parking

This large store is packed with sweats, tees, socks, underwear, baggies and baby clothes in a variety of colors and styles. Tees were five for $10 ($2.50 each). This store had the widest variety of solid color tees, mostly 100% cotton, with pockets, at three for $10. Jerzees sweats were $4.95 adult, $3.95 for kid's size. Infant sweat sets by Trend Basics were $3.95.

These stores are becoming more and more popular. Those that follow have merchandise and pricing similar to the above.

T-Shirts Mart
701 E. 2 St., San Bernardino (714) 888-2996
Mon.-Fri., 9:30-8; Sat.-Sun., 10-7

T-Shirts Warehouse
Lockwood off Rose, Oxnard
New store, no phone yet.

T-Shirts Wholesale Warehouse
12643 Sherman Way, North Hollywood (818) 503-0315
Mon-Sun., 9-7

Women's Clothing

Adrienne Vittadini Factory Store
Desert Hills Factory Stores at Cabazon   (714) 922-2241
Mon.-Sun., 9-8
Terms: MC, V, AE, Check. Exchanges.   Parking

Here you'll find sportswear, evening wear, swimsuits and lingerie for women and petites, as well as some playwear for children, all designed by Adrienne Vittadini. Everyday discounts are 25% to 40%, but there are frequent additional markdowns, and on Presidents' Day, Memorial Day and Labor Day they usually have sample sales. Last time I visited a grey woolen suit jacket, regularly $320 was $192; there was an additional 25% off sale, making it $169. A cotton knit top was reduced from $82 to $39, reduced again by 25% to $29.75. There were sale racks in back with great bargains. I found beaded evening sheaths for $117 ($384).

Aileen Stores, Inc.
The Citadel, City of Commerce   (213) 724-1493
Hours vary by location.
(also in Cabazon, Ontario, Barstow and San Ysidro)
Terms: MC, V, Check. Exchanges.   Parking

Here you'll find first quality missy, petite and plus size cotton knit coordinating separates at discounts of 35% to 70%. There are always a few sale racks offering an additional 20% off, and there is a mailing list to be notified of upcoming sales. Sign up, they send out coupons.

Albert Nipon Factory Store
Desert Hills Factory Stores at Cabazon   (714) 922-9250
Mon.-Sun., 9-8
Terms: MC, V, Check. Exchanges   Parking

This is a find for sophisticated suits and dresses in sizes 2-14. Albert Nipon and Nipon Boutique separates, dresses and evening wear are discounted from 30% on up. I also found Castleberry suits at $99.99, Kasper suits and separates at 40% off and Breckenridge separates at savings of up to 74%.

All that Jazz Factory Outlet
341 W. 31 St., Los Angeles   (213) 747-8466
Mon.-Fri., 9-5; Sat., 9-1
Terms: Cash and Check only.   Exchanges.   Parking

This store is full of first quality day and evening dresses for girls, juniors, women, petites, and large sizes (to 30), sold under the All That Jazz and More Jazz labels. Prices range from $9.99 to $39.99 (retails are three to four times that), with most women's and junior styles at $22.99, most girls dresses (including some lovely party outfits), $13.99. Know your size before you come: there's no fitting room.

All Together
860 S. Los Angeles St., Los Angeles   (213) 614-0992
Mon.-Sat., 9:30-5:30; Sun. 11-5
Terms: MC, V, Check. Final sale.   Street parking

This large shop features a selection of traditional misses clothing by California Girl, A. C. Sport, Elizabeth Stewart, Nicole Miller, Oleg Cassini, Adolfo, Giorgio Sant'Angelo and others, in sizes to 16, at discounts beginning at 35%. I found a houndstooth cotton dress by California Girl at $35 ($144); a rayon challis two piece, $83 ($138). Most of the stock is in career and casual styles.

Anne Klein Factory Outlet Store
Desert Hills Factory Stores at Cabazon   (714) 849-1114
Mon.-Sun., 9-8
Terms: MC, V, Check. Exchanges.   Parking

This shop is tastefully crammed with Anne Klein sportswear, dresses, coats, swimwear and accessories, discounted 40% to 50%. When I happened in they were having a 50% off clearance sale, and several racks of sportswear, suits and evening dresses were selling for one third to one quarter of their *outlet prices*. A long mohair sweater was $40 ($159) and a peach coat and dress evening ensemble was $100 ($590). A selection of handbags was discounted 60%, costume jewelry was discounted 40%, and bathing suits were marked down 30% to 55%.

Ann Taylor Outlet   CCC
The Citadel, City of Commerce   (213) 725-7033
Mon.-Sat., 9-8; Sun., 10-6
Terms: MC, V, Check. Final sale.   Parking

I'm always amazed at how much high quality merchandise is packed into this store, and how great the values are. A silk and rayon jacket, originally $158 was $39.90, a Tahari silk charmeuse blouse was also $39.90 ($160), and $78 flowered rayon pants were the find of the day at $9.90. Shoes with the Ann Taylor name were also available; woven leather pumps were $89.90 ($198), and flats were $59 ($118). A selection of accessories rounded out the stock.

Arthur John's
2207 Main St., #24
2213 Main St., #33, Huntington Beach   (714) 960-5752
Mon.-Sat., 10:30-6; Sun., 9-5
Terms: MC, V, Check. Exchanges.   Parking

These two stores in the Seacliff Village Center feature unique and lovely clothing for sizes 4-14, at prices 30% to 70% below department stores. Outfits fall into the $100 to $200 range, and among the labels I found were Componix, Platinum, Hype, and Wild Rose, in styles and combinations seemingly more interesting than displayed at other shops. Since these are often samples, there is sometimes only one piece, and not always in your size (chances are better if you're a 6 or an 8), but if you like something that's not your size they'll try to order it for you. This is the perfect place to find unusual and beautiful clothes for work and special occasions, and they keep a register to note your favorite labels so they can notify you of new arrivals. The atmosphere is boutique, the saleswomen pleasant; Arthur John's has the feel of a high priced venue but without the price tag.

Azita J
2238 S. Sepulveda Blvd., West Los Angeles   (310) 478-1593
Mon.-Sat., 10-6; Sun., 12-5
Terms: Cash and Check only. Exchanges.   Parking

Azita J offers designers lines like Bis, Donna Karan, DKNY, Nolan Miller, Nancy Heller, Vertigo and Ann Klein II, at discounts of 50% and sometimes more. The clothing goes from casual to eveningwear, with lots of good sportswear and business clothing in between. Sizes are from 4 to 16.

Back Door Boutique
14331 Chambers Rd., Suite A, Tustin   (714) 544-9360
Thurs.-Fri., 12-4; Sat., 10-4
Terms: Cash and Check only. Final sale.   Parking

This back door takes you into a corner of the factory of Two Potato sportswear, where you'll find women's casual separates, dresses and jumpsuits in cotton gauze solids and rayon prints, sized XS to XL. They are samples, overruns and end-of-season merchandise. Skirts and pants had elasticized waists, and all pieces sold from $5 to $20. Most were first quality, but some damages were mixed in. Unlike most factories, there are fitting rooms.

Bizarre Bazaar
5539 Riverton Av., North Hollywood (818) 763-4361
Tues.-Sat., 10:30-4:30
Terms: Cash only. Final sale.   Parking

Around about September, when wool starts appearing in department stores and desert winds start blowing across the Southland, keep Bizarre Bazaar in mind. It's the factory outlet for New Hero Sportswear, a line of light and medium weight cotton gauze dresses, separates and jumpsuits, in regular and large sizes, at prices ranging from $12 to $35. A short bustier dress with elasticized back was $25, three tiered, full-skirted off the shoulder dresses were $23 and full skirts and peasant blouses were $12. Sizes are S to XL, and all pieces have elasticized waists. This stuff travels wonderfully well. (Even if it's just the freeway at rush hour.)

Black & White Wholesalers   COUPON
1250 S. Broadway, Los Angeles (213) 746-5841
Mon.-Sat., 10-5:30
Terms: V, MC, Check. Final sale.   Street parking

Black & White doesn't have a tremendous variety of stock, but the high quality merchandise at low, low prices kept me busy in the fitting room a long time. I found a beautiful line of raw silk separates, jackets $35, tops, pants and skirts $25. (No other store carrying this line sold it this low.) Dresses from Karen Kane and Sue Wong ranged from $30 to $45 and Karen Kane knit tees were $18. Styles are also available in petite sizes. *The coupon entitles you to 10% off your next purchase.*

Clothestime Outlet   CCC
821 Hacienda Blvd., La Puente (818) 961-2807
Mon.-Fri., 11-9; Sat., 11-8; Sun., 11-6
(also in Rialto (714) 877-5255 and Cuddahy (213) 771-0144)
Terms: MC, V, D, AE, Check. Final sale.   Parking

While Clothestime is a discount chain for trendy junior merchandise, these outlets are where Clothestime clothes go to die. Some of them are a bit deader upon reaching these stores than others. Here everything is 30% off the lowest marked price (some tags already have three or four markdowns), or 30% off the *only* marked price, which is $10 or less. About two thirds of the merchandise is on rounders marked "Damaged or Irregular," but the proportion of actual damages varies by store and season. If you're willing to look carefully, you can save a lot of money here. Jeans were reduced from $44 to as low as $7. Leggings and Lycra bike shorts were $4.20, denim shorts were reduced from $36 to $8.40; an L. A. Movers unitard was reduced to $7 (less than the manufacturers' outlet price). Dresses were $7, and linen and cotton blend blazers were $9. I doubt there was anything over $25 in the store. A bargain bonanza for the careful Clothestime shopper.

The Clothing Factory
6831 Tampa Av., Reseda (818) 609-7219
Mon.-Fri., 8-6; Sat., 10-5
Terms: MC, V, Cash. GC. Final sale.   Parking

If you're looking for boutique frills, pass this one by, but if you want poly/cotton knit separates reminiscent of the Units line, Eureka! The Clothing Factory sells coordinating solids and prints in sizes S-M-L, a few children's pieces and some workout wear, and nothing is over $25. Tee shirt dresses with padded shoulders were $19; a duster coat was $25; pants (all waistbands are elastic) ranged from $7 to $11; gored skirts were $9 and $13. Tees were $16 and tanks $6. Sundresses were $12 and cummerbunds were $3 or five for $10. A great place for a low-cost, coordinated wardrobe.

Collectibles
860 S. Los Angeles St., Los Angeles (213) 623-1155
Mon.-Sat., 9:30-5:30; Sun., 11-5
Terms: MC, V, Check. Final sale.   Street parking

Collectibles offers designer women's clothing at substantial savings. A velvet Anne Klein II skirt was $99.99 ($240); Nolan Miller Suits were less than half price, and a DKNY Denim Embellished Jacket was $60 ($125). DKNY jeans were $25 and there were six rounders of Bis separates, all pieces selling for $15. Included were some interesting sequined separates and a beautiful tie-dyed satin baseball jacket.

Contempo Casuals Outlet   CCC
18557 Main St., Huntington Beach (714) 841-0869
1505 S. Riverside Av., Rialto (714) 877-0560
Mon.-Fri., 10-9; Sat., 10-6; Sun., 12-5
Terms: MC, V, Check. Final sale.   Parking

For the woman without an ounce of fat, this is your flaunt-it-at-a-discount store, full of Lycra, short shorts, middie blouses and slinky dresses. Call and the recording will tell you how much everything is reduced that week (every time I've called it's been 65%). All merchandise is sold "as is," and some garments are damaged, but if you can find something you like there are great bargains: dresses and skirts originally up to $25 were $2; originally $26 to $40,

$4; and over $40, $6. I found suede and leather mini skirts at *$4*. There are accessories, also reduced, jewelry for $1, everything the Contempo chain carries, at deep discount.

Damone
1349 S. Main St., Los Angeles (213) 747-0355
Mon.-Fri., 9-5; Sat., 9-3
Terms: V, MC, AE, D, Check. Final sale.   Street parking

You must be a member to shop at Damone's, where the lifetime membership fee is $25, negligible if you buy suits by designers like Albert Nipon, George Simington, Oleg Cassini, Lilli Ann and Kaspar; or evening suits, cocktail dresses and gowns in missy styles, sizes 4 to 24, because you'll find prices here that begin at about one quarter off and go down from there, and you'll find beautiful things. There are two large rooms full of suits, with variety in every size. But the treasure house is the other side of the shop, where racks and racks of evening dresses and suits sparkle with beads and sequins on designs by Nolan Miller and Bob Mackie, among others, at prices from $99 to $2000. This is a space full of beautiful things, including a bridal selection, where discounts range from 20% to 50%. They can get you one-of-a-kind evening outfits, and they lavish attention on you. (Heated fitting rooms are a nice touch, as well as coffee and couches for the non-shopping members of the entourage.) They have a price guarantee: if you see the same dress for less, they'll meet the price and give you an additional 10% off.

Dressed Up
6000 Reseda Blvd., Units F and L, Tarzana (818) 708-7466
Mon.-Sat. 10-5:30
Terms: MC, V, AE, D, Check. Final sale.   Parking

Dressed Up offers designer suits and eveningwear at discounts from 40% to 80%. Unit F is for daytime career dressing, and Unit L houses eveningwear. The merchandise is current, and many top designers are represented. I found some intricately beaded sheathes for $150, and there were many suits under $300. They also carry coats in the Fall.

Esprit
Desert Hills Factory Stores at Cabazon (714) 922-2170
Mon.-Sun., 9-8
Terms: MC, V, AE, Check. Final sale.   Parking

It's more than a store, it's an attitude. Music blares as you walk in, stock is arranged in metal bins, theoretically grouped according to price. Juniors' and girls' clothing is offered here, and if you can find what you want you can save a lot of money. In one of the $29-and-under racks I found a rayon print top for $15 ($54 retail) and matching pants for $5 ($48). Relaxed fit jeans, originally $54 were $29. Teen jeans were $10 ($28); and mini kids leggings were $15 ($25). There were tables of shoes priced at $10; others were discounted at least 50%. The clothes seem to begin at a 45% discount and drop perilously from there. There's lots of sales help, with that same attitude.

Fantastic Sportswear, Inc.
860 S. Los Angeles St., Los Angeles (213) 627-4536
Mon.-Sat., 9:30-5:30; Sun., 11-5
Terms: MC, V, Check. Final sale.   Street parking

This store offers a large variety of designers at substantial savings. On a recent visit, d. b. waldo jackets were $60; skirts, $30. There was a rack of $10 Paul Stanley cotton skirts, and racks of dresses and jumpers at $10.99 and $12.99 featuring clothing by Talbots, Dennis Goldsmith, and a Pea in the Pod. BCBC Paris separates sold for $12.99.

$5 Clothing Stores
3002 S. Sepulveda Blvd., West Los Angeles (310) 473-5525
Mon.-Fri., 10-6; Sat., 10-7; Sun. 11-6
(32 additional locations, see Geographical Index)
Terms: MC, V, D, Check. Exchanges.   Parking

It's a sign of the times that there's nothing over $12 at $5 Clothing Stores. These shops are ideal for teens who need trendy, disposable clothes. The brand names I was familiar with were Gitano slacks and tops, Jerzees sweats, and Hanes Beefy tees. There were leggings and stirrup pants for $8, and cotton tees with shoulder pads in a rainbow of colors for $6. Can't beat the prices.

Gigi Shoppe
134 N. San Fernando Blvd., Burbank (818) 842-5084
Mon.-Sat., 9-6
Terms: MC, V. Final sale.   Street parking

This is another hodge podge store, with a little more than what you'd expect. A rack of Maxim's of Hollywood swimsuits were $5 to $20, Lee Jeans seconds—the labels cut out—were $12. Cotton ribbed, long sleeved turtlenecks were $12, and a collection of long evening dresses in synthetics for sizes up to 28 1/2 were $45 to $75. Matching polyester separates were about $20 per piece.

Harpers *COUPON*
8588 Washington Blvd., Culver City (310) 839-8507
Mon.-Thurs., Sat., 10-6; Fri., 10-7
(also in Woodland Hills, Encino and Thousand Oaks)
Terms: MC, V, D, Check. Final sale. Parking

You never know what you're going to find at Harpers, from sportswear to suits and sexy evening dresses. On a recent trip I found separates from a Beverly Hills boutique, selling for 10% to 20% of their retail prices. Cotton sweatsuits were $30, stretch animal print jeans were $10 and there were famous maker printed rayon dresses at $45 ($120). Sheer skirts in floral prints were $15 and

---

Separates from a Beverly Hills Boutique at 10% to 20% of original retail

---

a beautiful evening ensemble, long flowing tank dress and jacket with satin rosette accents was $39.99. This is a store to keep checking out. *Use the coupon for an additional 5% off your next purchase of $50 or more.*

Heidi's Warehouse Fashion Outlet
17320 Saticoy St., Van Nuys (818) 344-6841
Tues.-Sat., 10-5
Terms: Cash and Check only. Exchanges. Parking

You'd pass this place right by if you didn't know it was there. Heidi's is a little neighborhood discount store, full of samples in junior and women's sizes. There are racks of separates for $5 and $10; beautifully embroidered and lace embellished jeans and bustiers were $26.95, and similarly decorated jean jackets were $32.95, about the most expensive item here. There are dresses, jumpsuits, jeans, tops, skirts, and most everything is one-of-a-kind.

Hit or Miss
348 S. Mountain Av., Upland (714) 949-8151
Hours vary by location.
(also in Century City, Fountain Valley, La Mirada, Irvine, Tustin, Granada Hills, San Dimas, Brea, Westminster, Lakewood, and Garden Grove)
Terms: MC, V, Check. L. Exchanges. Parking

Hit or Miss features clothing for the professional woman (Who are the amateur women?) at discounts of 30% to 60%. The emphasis is on suits, separates and dresses, by names like Rafella, Karin Stevens and Maggy London. Suits begin at about $80, dresses and blazers at $40, skirts at $20. There is a mailing list to notify you of special sales.

JH Collectibles Outlet
Lake Elsinore Outlet Ctr. (714) 674-0578
Mon.-Sat., 10-9; Sun., 11-6
Terms: MC, V, Check. Exchanges.   Parking

This shop carries first quality merchandise of past seasons. Discounts begin at about 20% and go as high as 75%. The clothing is for misses and petite sizes and is mainly sophisticated separates, with a few coats.

Jackeez & Nicolz   COUPON
20000 Ventura Blvd., Woodland Hills (818) 999-0991
Mon.-Sat., 11-7
Terms: MC, V, Check. Exchanges.   Street parking

Jackeez & Nicolz looks like a pricey boutique; the merchandise is high fashion and there is a lot of attention paid to every customer, but price tags are a third to half less then what you'd expect these clothes to cost in this kind of place. On my last visit I saw some beautiful, sheer retro dresses, retailing around town for $130 to $150, here for $69.95. The lace version was $89.95. Separates range from $19 for a cotton ribbed poor boy tee to $49 for a lace skirt, and there are coordinating pieces to everything. If I lived in this neighborhood I'd be in here all the time. ***The coupon entitles you to $10 off your next purchase of $50 or more.***

Jay Jacobs Clearance Store   CCC
Sherman Oaks Galleria, Sherman Oaks (818) 995-0852
Mon.-Fri., 10-9; Sat., 10-7; Sun., 11-5
Terms: MC, V, D, AE, Check. Returns.   Parking

This is the sale store for the Jay Jacobs chain of junior and women's clothiers. Everything here is reduced from 50% to 80%, and styles run the gamut from cocktail dresses to jeans. Zena jeans, originally $42, were $20. Ramie and cotton blend sweaters, in a variety of colors, were $10 ($36) and $29 ($48). A rounder of rayon jackets in many styles and colors was priced in the $25 to $30 range ($55-$65), and a Paris Blues long, flowered retro dress was $19.99 ($69). Some of the other labels I spotted were Yes, Judy Knapp, All That Jazz, Area Code and La Belle.

Jess/Maddox   CCC
Westside Pavilion, West Los Angeles (310) 475-7751
Mon.-Fri., 10-9; Sat., 10-7; Sun., 11-5
Terms: MC, V, Check ($100 max.). Final sale.   Parking

This is the sale store for the chain of boutiques in Beverly Hills and the West

Side. The merchandise has a sexy continental flair, and while some pieces are not on sale, many are, at clearance prices of 50% to 70% below retail. Among the brands are BCBC Paris, Vertigo, and Bisou Bisou. The styles range from tailored, gabardine jackets (originally $250, now $125), with matching straight or pleated skirts (originally $150, now $75) to Lycra unitards and sheer party dresses. There is a mailing list to be notified of the arrival of new merchandise.

> *Joan Geddes Sportswear, available at better department stores, occasionally has a sale in their Canoga Park Factory. To get on the mailing list, call (818) 710-0095*

Judy's Outlet   CCC
19411 Victory Blvd., Reseda (818) 344-2044
860 S. Los Angeles St., Los Angeles (213) 627-9173
Hours vary by location.
Terms: MC, V, AE, D, Check. Final sale.   Parking

These are outlets for Judy's, where the clothes are trendy, and have generally been marked down at least once. The longer they stay in the store the further they're discounted, often up to 75%. They rarely have sales, but last time I wandered in there was a whopping 50% of all merchandise.

Lanz II Outlet   CCC
6150 Wilshire Blvd., Los Angeles (213) 857-5725
Mon.-Sat., 10-5:30; Sun., 12-4:30
Terms: MC, V, AE, D. Final sale.   Parking

Behind the main store you'll find the Lanz outlet. In addition to offering their trademark flannel nightgowns at $19, and cotton gowns at less than half price, they are the perfect place to go for an outfit for an afternoon wedding or garden party. The dresses are pretty, lots of flowers and lace, designed by the likes of Jane Singer and Scott McClintock, and selling from 30% to 50% off. There is a section for petites, a small section for sizes 18-24, and many rounders in the more popular sizes. Their major sale is the end of January or early February.

La Petite Factorie
5458 Moreno St., Montclair (714) 982-1866
Sutter Place
18577 Main St., Huntington Beach (714) 848-8280
Hours vary by location.
Terms: MC, V, AE, TC. Final sale.   Parking

These two stores are outlets for Jessica McClintock/Gunne Sax, makers of those romantic, lacey evening dresses, tea dresses and bridal gowns. The stores feature a good selection of styles in women's, petite, pre-teens', girls', toddler girls' and large sizes. There are a lot of bridal gowns (to size 20), mainly in the $200-$500 range, with a few as low as $100, in white, antique white and bone. There are also pastel and jewel tone dresses; you could outfit the female half of your bridal party here, for a summer or winter wedding, at big savings, as well as find clothing for any formal occasion. A Jessica McClintock taffeta evening suit was $75 ($295); and a pre-teen taffeta party dress was $34 ($125). There is also a selection of day dresses. For home sewers, the Montclair location has a fabric corner, where discounted taffetas, silks, laces, velvets, appliques, trims, and flowered-printed cottons provide everything you'd need to make yourself a dress in the Jessica McClintock style, at a fraction of the outlet price.

Laura M Contemporary Sportswear
19350 Business Ctr. Dr., Northridge (818) 885-1130
Mon.-Fri., 10-5:30; Sat., 10-6
Terms: MC, V, AE, Check. Exchanges.   Parking

This shop is full of discounts on women's sportswear and apparel, including lines like Opera, Laundry, Shelly Segal, Naf Naf, Ton Sur Ton, Christine de Castlenau and Claude Z. A Claude Z sweater retailing for $69 here sold for $30, Laundry jackets were $69.99; skirts, $29.99; pants, $39.99.

Leslie Fay Manufacturer's Outlet
Lake Elsinore Outlet Ctr. (714) 245-0255
Mon.-Sat., 10-9; Sun., 11-6
Terms: MC, V, Check. Exchanges.   Parking

This shop features women's dresses and suits by Leslie Fay, Kasper, and Breckenridge, to name a few (over 30 lines of clothing are represented by Leslie Fay), in sizes ranging from petites to half sizes, at savings beginning at 30% off nationally advertised prices, and dropping as low as 60%. The styles are discontinued, i.e., from previous seasons, but do we really have seasons in Southern California?

Lila's Women's Discount Boutique
31938 San Luis Rey, Cathedral City (619) 325-7383
Mon.-Sat., 9:30-5; Sun. 11-2
Terms: MC, V, D, Check. Exchanges.   Parking

Lila's is a small store with a large number of interesting pieces. Most items are reduced from 20% to 25%, but on clearance are reduced even further. There are separates and dresses, mainly casual wear with a formal edge; you'll find a subtle metallic knit tank top here, or a playdress with a little pizzazz. It's resortwear, but not stuffy or matronly; playclothes with a lot of style.

Lillie Rubin Outlet   CCC
La Jolla Village Square Mall, La Jolla (619) 453-7215
Mon.-Fri., 10-9; Sat., 10-6; Sun., 11-5
Terms: MC, V, AE, D, DC, CB. Final sale.   Parking

The sixty Lillie Rubin boutiques are full of beautiful, unusual, high-priced, high fashion women's clothing, and this is the nationwide clearance center. You will find an assortment of separates, playwear, suits and businesswear, cocktail and formal dresses, all at discounts beginning at about 50% and going

---
Clothing reaches the store discounted 33% to 50%, then is discounted another 25% to 50%

---

down from there. (Items reach the store *already discounted* 33% to 50%, and once in the store everything is marked down *an additional* 25% or 50%.) Floor length beaded gowns, originally selling for $1500, were $350. A lovely set of white silk separates with subtle beading were less than half price; the jacket, originally $425, was $140, and the skirt, originally $195, was $75. Prices like this buy ordinary separates anywhere; these clothes are anything but ordinary. Sizes are to 14, and stock is constantly changing. Why not look like a million?

Liz Claiborne
Lake Elsinore Outlet Ctr. (714) 674-1406
Mon.-Sat., 10-9; Sun. 11-6
Terms: MC, V, AE, D ($15 min.); Check. Final sale.   Parking

This shop features leftovers, overruns and odd lots of discontinued first quality merchandise for women, and a smattering for men, at discounts of 30% to 50%. The lines offered are all that Liz Claiborne makes: First Edition, Elisabeth, Lizsport, Liz Claiborne and petites. There are also belts and bags, and lots of clearance rounders, where the discount can be doubled.

Loehmanns
6220 W. Third St., Los Angeles (213) 933-5675
Mon.-Fri., 10-9; Sat., 10-7; Sun., 12-6
(also in Reseda, Fullerton, Palm Springs, Oceanside, Huntington Beach, Laguna Niguel and Arcadia)
Terms: MC, V, D, Check. Exchanges.   Parking

One of the first if not the original designer discount store, Loehmanns is a place where it pays to know good clothing. There are designer names aplenty, as well as some of the oddest garments you'll ever see, but if you know what an Anne Klein or a Ralph Lauren costs in Saks, you'll know how good, or great, a deal you're getting here. The Back Room has pricier sportswear and after-five dresses, while the rest of the store offers separates, suits, dresses, pants, swimsuits, playwear and cocktail dresses. If you're looking for a suit don't neglect the separates racks: if you find a piece you like take it to a clerk; by the color of the tag she'll be able to tell you if something coordinates to or even matches it. Then all you have to do is find it. Dressing rooms are communal, and everybody plays "Look nonchalant 'til she puts it back on the rack and then grab it." If your neighbor starts telling you how terrible something looks on you, suspect ulterior motives. This kind of shopping is best done on strong self-image days or with a friend.

Max Studio
The Citadel, City of Commerce (213) 721-2200
900 Allen Av., Glendale (818) 242-9300
Hours vary by location.
Terms: MC, V, AE, Check. Final sale.   Parking

This store features Leon Max sportswear, generally one collection behind the retail specialty shops' selection. Discounts are close to 50%, in back of the store markdowns are even lower: there a $72 skirt was $18; a $120 pair of trousers was $30.

M. Fredric Outlet Store   CCC
2235 S. Sepulveda Blvd., West Los Angeles (310) 478-4240
4706 Admiralty Way, Marina del Rey (310) 821-1772
Mon.-Sat., 10-6; Sun., 11:30-6
Terms: MC, V, Check. Final sale.   Parking

Here there are racks of $10, $15 and $25 dresses, skirts, shirts and slacks. Most items are 25% to 50% of the price in Fredric's retail stores. I found Bila sleeveless dresses at $29, and crew neck cotton sweaters, regularly selling for $50, were here for $35. The amount and variety of stock varies, but you can often find separates in the $20 range.

Morrie's
934 S. Maple, Los Angeles (213) 623-3083
Mon.-Sat., 9-4:30
Terms: MC, V, AE, Check. Final sale.   Street parking

COUPON

Morrie's is a large store offering women's separates, dresses, play and eveningwear, with high quality labels at very moderate prices, and moderately

A dress here marked "Irregular," and selling for $200 sold in I. Magnin the same day for $875

priced labels at what you might call dirt cheap prices. Their motto is if they can't sell it at 50% off or more, they just don't bother. While most pieces are first quality you will find some irregulars. (I saw a dress marked "Irregular" here, selling for $200, with no visible imperfections; later that day I saw the first quality piece at I. Magnin for *$875.*) Sale racks offer discounts of up to an additional 50%, and there are $5 and $10 racks. Accessories and designer sunglasses round out the inventory. *The coupon entitles you to 10% off one purchase.*

Multi-Factory Outlet
19441 Business Ctr. Dr., Northridge (818) 998-3089
Mon.-Fri., 10-6; Sat. 11-6; Sun. 11-2:30
Terms: MC, V, AE, D, Check. Exchanges.   Street parking

From toddler girls on up to women, this shop enables you to purchase cotton knit tops, pants, skirts, girls' dresses, even baby's rompers—hand painted or embroidered with lace, rosettes and pearls—direct from the manufacturer at savings of half and more over better retail stores. For $19 to $29 you can get a girl's dress with lace and rosettes, for $24.99 a woman's short or long sleeved top embellished with lace, a tee shirt and slacks outfit for $29.99, or a tee shirt and skirt for $39.99. To make washing easy, the romantic trim is attached with Velcro and pins. There are also less elaborately painted sets: $17.99 for a short sleeved top and leggings; and unpainted sets: $14.99 for a two piece long sleeved top and pants in queen size.

Multiples Modular Knits
The Citadel, City of Commerce (213) 888-9139
San Diego Factory Outlet Center (619) 662-4562
Hours vary by location.
Terms: MC, V, AE, Check. Exchanges.   Parking

Women's and girls' knit separates are available here, featuring coordinating and mix and match knit tops, pants, skirts, jackets, jumpsuits, dresses and belts, in prints and solids, at savings of 40% to 45% off retail prices. There are sale racks, where you can save additionally.

The Outlet
1240 S. Main St., Los Angeles   (213) 749-8033
Mon.-Sat., 10-3
(also in El Monte, Thousand Oaks and Ontario)
Terms: TC. Final sale.   Parking

The Outlet carries missy clothing of Graff CaliforniaWear, in sizes 6-20 and S-L. These are coordinating separates in polyester and poly/cotton blends, all priced extremely reasonably. The most expensive item was a zippered blouson jacket with an elasticized waist, in a choice of jewel tones, at $26. Coordinating pants, skirts and culottes (all below the knee), were $12. Tops and shirts range from $5 to $12. With prices like these there's often a line at the dressing room.

Ricci Clothestique
3100 Wilshire Blvd., Los Angeles   (213) 383-6868
Mon.-Sat., 10-6
Terms: MC, V, D, AE, Check. Exchanges.   Parking

This shop features close-outs and overruns from many designers, at prices ranging from 25% to 50% below retail. Among the brands I found were BCBC Paris, Laura Ashley, Ann Taylor, Gap, Sue Wong, Kasper and Karin Stevens. There were casual and business separates, dresses and a few pieces of eveningwear. Several clearance racks offered an additional 40% savings.

Saka's Outlet
1112 N. LaBrea Av., West Hollywood   (213) 465-3986
Mon.-Sat.,10-7; Sun.,11-7
Terms: MC, V, Check. Exchanges.   Parking

This is one of those neighborhood dress shops that's becoming harder and harder to find; current style and great prices. As you enter there are racks of $5, $10 and $15 merchandise. Included in the $5 rack are cotton tees with shoulder pads and contrasting leggings. For $10 you can purchase a translucent, long romantic dress, and when you get up to $25 and $30 you're talking about long and short Paris Blues dresses. Palmetto slacks and jeans were $15 and up, and they carried Nina K, Rampage and other designers.

Sara Designers Outlet   COUPON
18562 Sherman Way, Reseda (818) 609-1200
Mon.-Fri., 10:30-6:30; Sat., 10:30-5:30
Terms: MC, V, AE, Check. Exchanges.   Street parking

Sara's offers discounts of 50% and more on moderately priced designer apparel. There is a large selection of after-five wear, separates, dresses, suits, some jumpsuits, playwear and even a few silk short suits. Specials vary, and clearance merchandise can be discounted up to 75% (I found a blazer I'd seen at a department store for $150 here for $35). Sara also offers complimentary fashion shows for groups, and does individual wardrobe consultation, also gratis. If Sara's taste is yours, you've just found yourself a home. *The coupon entitles you to an additional 10% discount on one outfit.*

Seventh Avenue West
71-842 Hwy. 111, Rancho Mirage (619) 340-6555
Mon.-Sat., 9:30-5; Sun., 11-4
Terms: MC, V, AE, Check. Exchanges.   Parking

This shop is full of casual resortwear at discounts of 20% to 25%. You'll find a lot of shorts, and shorts and pants sets, in soft colors, as well as jumpsuits, sweaters, blazers and some high class sweat suits, generally in missy sizes and styles. In addition to regularly discounted merchandise, there are usually several sale rounders, where you can find bargains of up to 50%.

Susie's Deals
3861 Culver Center, Culver City (310) 559-0101
Mon-Fri., 10-9; Sat., 10-7; Sun., 11-6
(26 additional locations; see Geographical Index)
Terms: MC, V, Check. Exchanges.   Parking

Susie's Deals is a junior fashion discount chain, where most items are under $20 (generally 30% to 60% below department store prices). They feature tops, jeans, legging, dresses, skirts, jackets and accessories by names like Gitano, Judy Knapp, Cherokee and One Step Up, as well as imported merchandise. In addition to everyday bargains there are always clearance racks, where clothing is marked down another 20% to 40%.

Wet Seal Clearance Store   CCC
The City Mall, Orange (714) 634-8727
Mon.-Fri., 10-9; Sat., 9-6; Sun., 12-5
Terms: MC, V, AE, D, Check. Final sale.   Parking

This is the clearance outlet for the Wet Seal junior shops, and here all merchandise is a minimum of 50% off. There is quite an assortment, with many tables of separates at $5 and under, and rounders of clothing for $7 and $9. The merchandise in the front is first quality; in the back are racks full of damages and irregulars, but things do get mixed up, so check carefully. A Paris Blues flowered denim jacket was $13 ($52), matching shorts were $5 ($36). There were a large assortment of jeans, as well as cotton, rayon, and cotton and Lycra blouses for $10 and under. Sweaters were reduced to $8.88 ($34) and cotton knit pants were $5 ($35). Dresses were generally half price, most not more than $30.

See also
>John Fulmer Company Outlet Store
>Hang Ten Factory Outlet

Catalogs

Chadwick's of Boston, Ltd.
(508) 583-6600
Terms: V, MC, AE, D. Returns.

Calling itself "the original women's off-price fashion catalog," Chadwick's offers first quality women's dresses, formals, suits, separates, accessories, swimwear and sportswear, and some girls' dresses, all by well-known ready-to-wear designers, at prices ranging from 25% to 50% below retail.

Resale

Jean Stars' Apparel
15136 Ventura Blvd., Sherman Oaks (818) 783-3710
Tues.-Sat., 10-6
Terms: MC, V, AE, Check. Final sale.   Street parking
and
The Place and Company
8820 S. Sepulveda Blvd., Los Angeles (310) 645-1539
Mon.-Sat., 10-5:30
Terms: MC, V, Check. Final sale.   Street parking

These two stores are related only in the quality of product they carry, and the wonderful savings they offer. This is where women who can't be seen in the same dress twice dispose of their *haute couture* wardrobes, which means you can get high fashion designer clothing for up to *95% off the original price.* Both stores carry gowns, evening wear, suits and separates, and many of the pieces originally sold for *more than your car.* If you have designer taste but a knockoff budget, you *can* afford the real thing.

Other couture resale shops include:

Caroline's Designer Resale
24020 Vista Montana, Torrance (310) 475-5542

Designer Consigner
834 Kline, La Jolla (619) 459-1737

Mercedes Designer Resale
1775 N. Hillhurst, Los Angeles (213) 665-8737

P. J. London
11661 San Vicente Blvd., Brentwood (310) 826-4649

Past Perfect
12616 Ventura Blvd., Studio City (818) 760-8872

Recycled Rags
2731 E. Coast Hwy., Corona del Mar (714) 675-5553

Bridal and Formalwear

Bridal

Brides of California
1308 Crenshaw Blvd., Torrance (310) 320-2999
Mon.-Sat., 11-5; Sun., 10-3
Terms: MC, V, D, Check. L. Final sale.   Parking

Brides of California offers you access to over 5,000 bridal gowns, and 20,000 bridesmaids', mother-of-the-bride and pageant dresses. Gowns are purchased from overstocked manufacturers, and sold at discounts ranging from 40% to 75% (you'll save more if you don't put a gown on layaway). Sizes are from 2 to 30, and among the brands are Ilissa, Alfred Angelo, Jasmine, Scassi, and others. Veils and headpieces are $79.

Discount Bridal Services
(213) 418-8154
Terms: MC, V, Check. Final sale.

This is a direct buying service offering savings of 20% to 40% on bridal, bridesmaids', and debutante gowns, mother of the bride, and formalwear of the current season. You do the legwork, then call Leslie for a price. Whether you find your gown in a store or on the pages of a bridal magazine, chances are she can get it for you at a discount. DBS also offers discounts on wedding invitations and stationary.

Factory Bridal Imports
(213) 259-1740

This is the San Martin bridal factory in Eagle Rock. They hold occasional clearances on showroom samples, discontinued styles, and overstocks of bridal gowns and accessories, prom dresses, mother of the bride and bridesmaids' dresses; call to see if one is upcoming. Gowns retail from $400 to $2,000 and are sold at discounts as high as 80%.

Galaxy of Gowns
2292 Tapo St., Simi Valley (805) 526-4696
Tues.-Thurs., 10-5; Fri., Sat., 10-6; Sun., 12-5
Terms: MC, V, D, Check. Final Sale.   Parking

Galaxy of Gowns is full of bridal and bridesmaids' gowns, and some after-five dresses, and everything is reduced up to 70%. If you look closely at the price tags you'll realize that most of these gowns have come from other bridal shops, perhaps some you've already looked in. They are discontinued samples, and wind up here at great reductions. Because they're samples, sizes cluster around 10 and 12, but there are a few smaller and larger sizes. There are also some consignment (resale) dresses mixed in. There are a lot of beautiful styles to chose from, and some bridesmaids' gowns are available in sets. A lovely Jessica McClintock bridesmaids dress originally selling for $170 was here for $85. Veils and accessories are discounted as well.

Hacienda Brides International
275 S. La Cienega Blvd., Los Angeles (213) 652-8447
Mon.-Fri., 11-9; Sat., 10-6; Sun., 11-5
(also in San Gabriel (818) 282-7293, and Santa Ana (714) 241-1870)
Terms: MC, V, Check. L. Final sale.   Parking

There are hundreds of wedding gowns in these large shops, all priced under $500, and some discounted up to 80%. The San Gabriel store also offers bridesmaids' dresses, and all stores carry veils and accessories. Gowns are available in petite, regular and large sizes, in white and ivory, formal and informal. Alterations are not included.

Ibex Apparel, Inc.
836 S. Los Angeles St., Los Angeles (213) 627-7532
Mon.-Sat., 9:30-5:30
Terms: MC, V, D, Check. Final sale.   Street parking

Ibex offers bridal wear, evening wear, dresses, veils, shoes, hats and accessories, at discounts of 40% to 50%. There are scores of wedding gowns in stock and they do both tuxedo sales and rentals as well as bridesmaids' and mother of the bride clothing.   Alterations are extra.

Price-less Bridals
6633 Fallbrook Av., #204, West Hills (818) 340-6514
Mon.-Fri. 10-9; Sat., 10-7; Sun., 11-5
Terms: MC, V, Check. Final sale.   Parking

Price-less Bridals is the outlet for a local bridal manufacturer, and here you can buy the current line, to order, at regular retail, but gowns of past seasons, size 4 to 44, as well as some discontinued bridesmaids and mother of the bride wear, are discounted. Markdowns depend on how old the gown is, or if it was a showroom sample. Samples are marked down an average of 20%, and other gowns can be reduced as much as 50%. Most discounts are in the 20% to 35% range.

Priscilla's Bridal   (COUPON)
19441 Business Ctr. Dr., #120, Northridge (818) 349-4229
Hours vary, call first.
Terms: V, MC, AE, D, Check. Final sale.   Parking

Priscilla's Bridals offers a smorgasbord of choices for the bride. You can design your own gown, or order one you've seen elsewhere and save 20% to 40%. If you buy the gown elsewhere, come here for alterations, at a charge of $20 per hour. (They can *make* a bridal gown in five hours, so you have some idea of the upper limit on charges.) They manufacture their own line of gowns, and can get you just about any other gown, veil, headpiece, shoes, or accessory at a discount. They provide a comparison service, graphically illustrating how much more you'd be paying at other bridal stores for the same goods. They sell dresses for bridesmaids, flower girls and mothers of the bride, provide for tuxedo rentals, and offer discounts on invitations and other reception accessories. Bridal gowns range from $75 to $2000. *Redeem the coupon for a free headpiece with purchase of a bridal gown.*

See also
> **Sutter Place/La Petite Factorie**
> **J. C. Penney Outlet Store**
> **Damone**

Bridal Trimmings

L. A. Trimmings
702 S. Los Angeles St., Los Angeles (213) 623-3903
Mon.-Sat., 9:30-5:30
Terms: MC, V, Check. Final sale.   Street parking

If you have some handicraft ability, L. A. Trimmings can offer you much of what you need to make your own headpiece and accessories, and those of your attendants, thereby saving a small fortune. They sell fabric flowers, beads, trim, appliques and a range of crowns, tiaras, floral sprays and other accessories, including gloves.

Discount Catalogs

Petticoat Express
318 W. 38 Street, NY, NY 10018
Terms: Check, MO. Final sale.

If you need a full petticoat, write for this brochure. They offer four styles (three floor length, one tea length) to wear under full skirts. Sizes are 4 to 20, and you can save over 40% by buying direct from the manufacturer. Petticoats range in price from $18 to $26 and are made of taffeta.

Books

Bridal Bargains
Secrets to Throwing a Fantastic Wedding on a Realistic Budget
by Denise and Alan Fields
Windsor Peak Press, $9.95
Available at bookstores or directly, at (800) 888-0395

The Fields have put together an entertaining consumer guide to wedding planning in an attempt to steer you through the minefield of the bridal industry without undue damage to your bank account and mental health. In addition to a timetable for making necessary arrangements, they offer a variety of money-saving secrets, best buys and helpful hints on every aspect of the wedding, from clothing to flowers to food to entertainment, invitations to limousines to

> *If you don't save at least $500 by using their strategies, they'll refund the cost of the book*

affordable champagnes. And they offer a guarantee: if you don't save at least $500 using their strategies, they'll refund the cost of the book. Can't beat that. *If you order by phone, mention Shopping Secrets of Southern California and they'll waive the $2 postage and handling fee.*

Bridal Resale

Deja Vu
(310) 821-8460
Terms: Check, Payment Plans. Final sale.   Parking

This resale bridal boutique features gowns no more than three years old, headpieces and petticoats. Shoshana sells them on consignment, so if you want to sell or buy a wedding gown, give her a call. Her inventory averages 80 gowns at any one time, mainly sizes 4-14, with a few larger sizes. The average price range is $400 to $700, and some gowns have never been worn. (It isn't uncommon for a bride to buy a dress, then find another she likes better and buy it too.) Shoshana says her inventory is now the best it's ever been in terms of quality, with gowns retailing new at $500 to $3,500.

Second Heaven Bridal Resale
5353 E. 2 St., Long Beach   (310) 433-3466
Mon.-Fri., 12-6; Sat., 10-3
Terms: Cash and Check only. Final sale.   Parking

Second Heaven is a bridal consignment store, and it carries gowns which are no more than three years old. The average gown sells for $400, and gowns range in price from $200 to $2,000. Most gowns are sold at 50% below their original prices, and not all have actually been worn. If you're looking for a particular style of dress you've seen in a magazine, bring in a picture and the proprietor will keep her eyes out for a match. They also sell slips, veils and shoes.

Second Look Bridal Resale
434 El Camino Real, Old Town Tustin   (714) 730-4909
Mon.-Fri., 11-6:30; Sat., 11-5
Terms: MC, V, AE, Check. L. Final sale.   Parking

This bridal resale shop offers three rooms of bridal gowns, slips, headpieces, shoes and accessories, carrying 300 to 400 wedding gowns at any one time, priced from $100 to $1000, representing savings of 25% to 70% off original retail. Some gowns have never been worn. They will rent an occasional gown, but they do rent entire bridesmaids sets, and have identical outfits for up to *13 bridesmaids*. They also offer mother of the bride gowns and evening wear. If you're interested in selling your wedding dress, bridesmaid's or mother of the bride dress, call for an appointment. If you want to buy a wedding or evening dress, come on in. Alterations on the premises.

Formalwear

Half Price House
12152 Brookhurst St., Garden Grove   (714) 537-1231
Mon.-Fri., 10-9; Sat., 10-6; Sun, 10-5
Terms: MC, V, Check. Final sale.   Parking

While they do sell some sportswear, Half Price House specializes in formalwear, gowns, bridesmaids' and some wedding gowns, but heavy on mother-of-the-bride. They offer sizes from petite to 46 (beaded tops go to 4X), and discounts range from 25% to 50%. There are a great variety of long, tea and cocktail length formal and beaded dresses, tops and chiffony skirts.

He-Ro Designer Group Outlet
Lake Elsinore Outlet Ctr. *(714) 674-0274*
Desert Hills Factory Stores at Cabazon *(714) 922-9400*
Mon.-Sat., 10-9; Sun. 11-6
Terms: MC, V, AE, D, Check. Final sale.   Parking

I've been asked not to name the designers this shop carries, but if you have a formal function in your future, come here first. There are beautiful evening dresses, suits, and gowns at a fraction of their retail prices. Discounts begin at about 50%, and go to 78% off. I found full length beaded gowns beginning

---
Buying here can be cheaper then renting the identical dress

---

at $160, and a $900 strapless floor length knockout was reduced to $200. Beaded tops and jackets began at $125. Buying here can be cheaper then *renting* the identical dress.

See also
Lillie Rubin Outlet

Lingerie

Barbizon Outlet
Factory Merchants of Barstow *(619) 253-2850*
Desert Hills Factory Stores at Cabazon *(714) 849-5044*
Mon.-Sun., 9-8
Terms: MC, V, Check. Returns.   Parking

If you're interested in long and short nightgowns that are lacey and utilitarian, you'll be a satisfied customer here. Discounts range from 40% to 70% on nighties, and they also stock Vanity Fair slips are here at 30% off. Myonne briefs, available up to size 10, in nylon or cotton, are ten pair for $10.99, or five for $5.99. There is a small assortment of pretty sachets and boudoir accessories.

Beverly Hills Hosiery, Inc.
801 S. Los Angeles St., Los Angeles (213) 627-7705
Mon.-Sat., 9:30-5:30
Terms: MC, V, AE, Check. Exchanges.   Street parking

At this location for 54 years, Beverly Hills Hosiery sells first quality lingerie and hosiery at bargain prices. There is far more merchandise available then what is displayed, so if you don't see what you want, ask. Felina, Exquisite Form, Jezebel and Carnival are among the brands here, at discounts of around 50%. They carry slips, warm and sheer nighties, teddies (trashy and otherwise) stockings (the brand major department stores put private labels on, at a fraction of the price), as well as men's socks and briefs. The savings emphasis is on quantity: hose are cheaper by the half dozen and dozen. They also have a large queen size department.

Chic Lingerie Outlet
693 High Lane, Redondo Beach (310) 372-9352
The Outlet Store
3435 S. Broadway, Los Angeles (213) 233-7121
Hours vary by location.
Terms: Cash only. Final sale.   Parking

Once you've been browsing awhile you'll realize the Chic Lingerie Outlet is the factory store for the factory that's directly overhead. There are many lovely items here: negligee sets, robes, long and short nightgowns, baby dolls, teddies, lounging pajamas, caftans, summer dresses and jumpsuits, mostly made of polyester, some of which feels like silk. The prices are very reasonable; the two showrooms are jam-packed with dainty things beginning at under $10. Unfortunately, no fitting rooms.

The Hosiery Depot
19410 Business Ctr. Dr., Northridge (818) 885-6331
Mon.-Sat., 10-5:30
Terms: MC, V, Check ($15 min.). Final sale.   Street parking

This store features a little of this and a little of that, some leotards and leggings, some bras and panties, but a lot of stockings and tights, and socks for all members of the family. Most of the merchandise is irregular. Round the Clock Control Top Pantyhose were $2.99, if perfect $4; Givency hose were $2.99, if perfect, $6.50, and Christian Dior hose were $3.29, if perfect, $5.50. Prices get better in quantity. The small selection of leotards range in price from $11 to $15, and a few teddies and merry widows were available at $13.99.

Lace & Scents
9140 Owensmouth Av., Chatsworth   (818) 718-3900
Mon.-Fri., 9-5
Terms: MC, V, AE. Final sale.   Parking

Lace and Scents carries lingerie and perfume; both discounted. The lingerie is not of the utilitarian type: teddies, camisoles and tap pants, and short, sheer kimonos, all in slinky synthetics are available here. Teddies are $7, garterbelts, $2.75; bustiers and long line bras are $8 and bra and panty sets are $7. Perfumes are discounted 20% to 60%, and they also discount the Biotherm line. Get on the mailing list to be notified of two-for-one perfume sales.

L'Eggs/Hanes/Bali Outlet
Factory Merchants of Barstow   (619) 253-2850
Lake Elsinore Outlet Ctr.   (714) 674-3291
Hours vary by location.
Terms: MC, V, Check. Returns.   Parking

Bali bras, slips and underwear are available here, at discounts from 25% to 60%. L'Eggs and other famous maker hosiery, sold in packages of three, are discounted 35% to 50%. Available also are a variety of Hanes sweats and tees for men, women, and kids. Men's Hanes briefs were seven for $6.99, crew tees, six for $9.49. All goods are irregulars, but they guarantee you won't see a flaw.

Lingerie for Less   **COUPON**
2245 S. Sepulveda Blvd., West Los Angeles   (310) 477-8605
Mon.-Sat., 10-7; Sun. 10-6
(14 additional locations; see Geographical Index)
Terms: MC, V, Check. Exchanges.   Parking

These shops feature beautiful discounted nighties by designers like Christian Dior, sexy silk sleepwear from Ria Silk Lingerie, as well as the old reliable flannel nightgowns, robes and pajamas. Bras and panties from Jezebel, Olga, Felina, Lily of France and Christian Dior, in a huge range of styles and colors, sell here at one third to one half off regular prices. On the clearance racks, savings are even greater. They carry slips, teddies, merry widows, camisoles, tap pants, and also a line of silk robes, pajamas and boxer shorts for men. Tell your significant other about this place. Hint hint. *The coupon gives you an additional 10% off your next purchase.*

Lingerie Outlet
3720 S. Santa Fe Av., Vernon (213) 588-6917
Mon.-Fri.,10-3; Sat. 9-1
Terms: MC, V, Cash. Final sale.   Parking

This is the outlet for Shirley of Hollywood lingerie, and Intimate Attitudes for sizes 1X to 4X. Everything is first quality, and discounted 50%. You can get a feather boa for $7.50 and a front close bra piped with fringe for about $10. There are G-strings ($1.25), garter belts ($3), a merry widow-like teddy with snap crotch and garters ($18), tap pants and camisole sets ($10), even edible panties in a variety of flavors ($4.50, selling for two to four times that elsewhere). Nightgowns go from the sweet sleep shirt in pastels at $10, to the slightly less sedate black mesh ankle length gown with *faux* fur collar ($19.50). There were short kimono robes ($12.50), and Big Beautiful Girl panties ($4). There is usually a sale in November, when most items are $6.

Lore Lingerie Factory Sale
15115 Califa St., #4, Van Nuys (818) 901-8520
Mon.-Fri., 11-5:30; Sat., 11-3
Terms: Cash and Check only. Final sale.   Parking

Lore makes some of the most beautiful silk lingerie you'll find anywhere, sold in places like Saks Fifth Avenue, and they make it in Van Nuys. They sell close-out merchandise in a corner of the factory, and the greatest variety in stock is in late May and October. Prices are below wholesale on peignoir sets, slips, camisoles, tap pants, bras, long and short nightgowns and men's boxer shorts,

---
Silk lingerie at the same price as synthetics

---

mostly made of silk, some cottons. On a recent trip a peignoir set was $150, men's silk boxers were $23; chemises were $40; silk bras were $15, panties, $10. Tap pant and camisole sets were $41 and sueded silk bra and panties sets were $30. These are *average* prices for lingerie. If you're worried about caring for these, remember: silk worms pre-date dry cleaning; people with far less education than you have washed silk for centuries.

Maidenform
Desert Hills Factory Stores at Cabazon (714) 922-2266
Hours vary by location.
(also in Lake Elsinore (714) 674-7335, and San Ysidro (619) 662-0388)
Terms: MC, V, Check. Exchanges.   Parking

Here you will find bras, panties, all-in-ones, slips, nighties and chemises from

Maidenform, Oscar de la Renta, Dreamtime and Diane Gilman. There are racks of bras and panties reduced from 25% on down to 80%. Bras start at $2.99 and panties at $2. The selection is large, not just in every size but yours.

Olga/Warner's Factory Outlets
15750 Strathern, Van Nuys (818) 994-7963
Hours vary by location.
(also in Los Angeles, Torrance, Costa Mesa, and Ontario)
Terms: MC, V, Check. Exchanges.   Parking

In stock here are Olga, Warners, Valentino, and Ungaro undies which have been discounted, and are often on sale besides. The day I stopped in Valentino bustiers that began life at $45 were marked down to $3. Discounts range from 30% to 75% on bras (including maternity bras), panties, slips, nightgowns, robes and pajamas. There are different specials weekly. They also sell skiwear; lines such as Mountain Gold, Edelweiss and White Stag, at discounts of 30% to 40%. A White Stag jumpsuit, regularly $230, was $120, and ski pants were $89 ($170). Men's cotton sweaters, values to $40, were $15.

The Robe Outlet
2233 1/2 S. Sepulveda Blvd., West Los Angeles (310) 478-0197
Mon.-Sat. 10-6; Sun., 12-5
(also in Vernon, Torrance, Burbank, Montclair and Huntington Beach)
Terms: MC, V, Check. Final sale.   Parking

These shops feature a variety of robes, and while they comprise most of the stock, there are also racks of jumpsuits, sundresses, work and evening dresses, sweatsuits, swimsuits and a little sportswear at prices of half to three quarters less than what you'd pay in a department store. Polyester dresses start at $8 (petite sizes too), Carol Wior swimsuits begin at $17.50 ($45), long terry robes are $21 ($65), and long fleece robes, $30 ($90). Terry playsets are $22.50 and velour sweatsuits begin at $12

See also
**Designer Labels for Less
T.J. Maxx
Lanz II Outlet
Petticoat Express
Apparel Designer Zone**

Discount Catalogs

National Wholesale Co.
(714) 249-0211
Terms: MC, V, AE, Check. Returns.

National sells a variety of things I haven't seen in a long time. The most mundane merchandise is pantyhose (from size A to 4X), but in a dizzying assortment of types: sheer, support, control top, thigh thinning, non-run, regular and queen sizes; thigh high stockings, knee-highs, surgical support hose, even stockings with cotton ventilated soles. They have socks, girdles, camisoles, pettipants, culotte slips, pants' liners, dickeys, models' coats, and cobbler aprons, all at value prices.

Showcase of Savings
(919) 744-1170
Terms: MC, V, D, Check. Returns.

In case you don't want to drive to a L'eggs/Hanes/Bali outlet, one can come to you in the form of this catalog. Included are irregulars of all the L'eggs products (including some hard to find at retail), at savings that can be in excess of 50% (the more you buy the more you save); Hanes hose, Bali bras, briefs and slips are discounted 40%; men's Hanes cotton tees, briefs and boxers are discounted from 30% to 50%. They also feature a variety of sweats, socks and activewear.

Maternity Clothing

Dan Howard's Maternity Factory
22817 Hawthorne Blvd., Torrance (310) 375-2640
Hours vary by location.
(also in Woodland Hills, Cerritos, San Diego and Santa Ana)
Terms: MC, V, AE, D, Check. Exchanges.   Parking

Dan Howard manufactures maternity clothing, sold only in their outlets, in styles from playclothes to executive businesswear, selling at prices 25% to 40% lower than comparable quality at retail. Prices are reduced on occasional sales. There is also a full range of accessories for mothers-to-be, from pantyhose to nursing gowns and tops, to underwear. Nursing bras start at $19.

Maternity Ltd.
3372 S. Bristol, Santa Ana (714) 557-2768
Mon.-Sat., 10-6; Wed., Thurs. to 8; Sun., 12-5
Terms: MC, V, D, Check. Exchanges.   Parking

This shop offers casual wear, office clothing, and after-five ensembles for the expanding expecting. Discounts range from 10% to 50%, and sales, generally held monthly and advertised in *The Orange County Register*, bring prices lower. They also offer a full line of undergarments.

Mom's the Word   *COUPON*
1008 1/2 Fair Oaks Av., South Pasadena (818) 441-9692
Mon.-Fri., 10:30-7; Sat., 10-6
Terms: MC, V, Check. Returns.   Parking

Mom's the Word stocks a pretty selection of maternity sportswear, businesswear, eveningwear, underwear and lingerie, discounted 25% to 40%. In addition, there's always a sale rack with merchandise at greater discounts. The quality of the clothing is high both in design and material, and the store is a pleasant place to shop, with a boutique atmosphere. They do alterations, will provide you with a pillow to see what the garment will look like in a few months, and offer clothing for new and nursing moms. *The coupon entitles you to an additional 10% off one purchase.*

See also
    John Fulmer Company Outlet Store
    Shelley's/Apparel Warehouse
    Cole of California Outlet

Discount Catalogs

Bosom Buddies
(914) 338-2038
Terms: MC, V. Returns.

Here you will find an assortment of nursing bras, beginning at $17, and tees, nightgowns and nightshirts made for the nursing mother.

Mother's Place
(800) 829-0080
Terms: MC, V, D. Returns

Mother's Place offers maternity dresses, suits, casual outfits and bedclothes, at prices ranging from 25% to 50% below retail. While the catalogs are small, styles represent a broad variety of tastes. There is also a clearance catalog, reducing prices even further.

Resale

This is one of those times when resale makes sense; pregnant women don't stay one size long enough to wear clothes out. If one of these locations is nearby, you're bound to save money.

Stork Club Resale Maternity
4838 Rolando Blvd., El Cajon (619) 287-9449

Stork Club II
240 N. 2nd Av., Upland (714) 920-3688

Stork Club II
440 W. Selicita Av., Escondido (619) 747-3667

Women's Large Sizes

Betty's Large Sizes
860 S. Los Angeles St., Los Angeles (213) 629-8045
Mon.-Sat., 9:30-5:30; Sun., 11-5
Terms: MC, V, Check. Exchanges.   Street parking

Betty's offers business suits, casual and evening wear at discounts of 25% to 60%. Here a Nina Austin wool suit was $234 ($329), a Chez coat dress was $111 ($190), and a John Meyer of Norwich suit was $179 ($269). They carry many Pat Argenti Plus ensembles, as well as evening wear: a Spencer Alexis chiffon dress was $79 ($199), and a Jovani two piece lace evening dress was $200 ($300). Vanity Fair slips and camisoles, as well as several brands of pantyhose, are discounted 10%.

The Big, The Bad and The Beautiful
7632 Tampa Av., Reseda (818) 345-3593
Mon.-Sat., 10-7
(also in Simi Valley (805) 582-1921, and Lancaster (805) 723-1554)
Terms: MC, V, Checks. Exchanges.   Parking

This shop carries a wide variety of looks from lingerie to all dressed up (sometimes it's hard to tell the difference), all discounted, but what I like here are the coordinating knit separates manufactured under the Big Bad and Beautiful label, done in a modular approach. There are dresses, coats, tops, slacks and belts in a variety of solids to mix and match; the pieces average about $35, and you can make about ten different outfits out of the combinations. For additional savings, they offer Big Beautiful Bucks: for every $25 in cash or check you spend, they give you one to apply to your next purchase. There's a mailing list to keep you apprised of sales.

Esther's Full Fashions
18147 Ventura Blvd., Tarzana (818) 996-8323
Mon.-Sat., 10-6
Terms: V, MC, AE, Check. Exchanges.   Parking

Esther's offers discounts of about 20% on clothing for the office, evening wear, sportswear and playwear, and features pieces from Alexis, Bichie Vi, Joanna York, Chez, and Gilda. The size range here is from 12 to 52. They also carry undergarments and accessories. There are generally two major sales annually; look for them in February and August.

Full Size Fashions
The Citadel, City of Commerce (213) 728-4612
Desert Hills Factory Stores at Cabazon (714) 849-6845
Mon.-Sat., 9-8; Sun., 10-6
Terms: MC, V, Check. Exchanges.   Parking

This shop features dresses and eveningwear in sizes 16 1/2-32 1/2, and pants and skirts in sizes 30-48. Everything begins at a 15% discount and prices go down from there. There are jeans as low as $12.99, Better Half Dresses from $25 to $30 and separates from $20 to $40. There is a small selection of accessories and belts, as well as bras, girdles and slips.

Modern Woman CCC
19800 Hawthorne Blvd., Torrance (310) 370-3035
Mon.-Fri., 10-9; Sat., 11-7; Sun., 12-5
(also in Moreno Valley, Carson, Buena Park, Fullerton, Lancaster, Los Angeles, Montclair, Montebello, Pasadena, and San Diego)
Terms: MC, V, AE, D, Check. Returns.   Parking

This chain is dedicated to fashion for the larger woman at everyday savings of 20% to 50%. The Torrance store is where the bulk of the clearance merchandise winds up, so, in addition to regular discounts there are buys on the many clearance racks. Sizes are generally up to 26, but they do carry some special sizes in blouses and separates. The regularly discounted merchandise includes some stunning evening wear, as well as a variety of dresses, suits and separates, sophisticated and subtle in design. A translucent flowered skirt was $22 ($32), and a black crinkly crepe cocktail dress and jacket set was $60. Cotton pocket tees in a variety of colors, to size 3X, were two for $20. They carry a full line of undergarments, and bras start at $6.99. The clearance racks had loads of bargains, representative of which was a Piccalino Plus rayon and lace dress at $29.99 ($100). Among the brands carried are Blassport, Elisabeth, and A. S. Elliott. If you're handy with a needle, the Carson store is where most of the damages wind up.

P. S. Plus Sizes Plus Savings
3950 Hardwick, Lakewood (310) 634-1724
Hours vary by location.
(also in Santa Ana, Laguna Hills, Anaheim, Torrance, Panorama City, Arcadia, Alhambra, Montclair and Rowland Heights)
Terms: MC, V, AE, D, Check. Returns.   Parking

This chain offers discounts of 25% to 50% on fashions in sizes 16 to 52; and everything in the store is discounted. They carry brand name undergarments, slips, hosiery and lingerie, as well as evening, career and casual wear by Sharon Anthony, Donkenny, Russ, Koret, and Sherwood Suits, to name a few. There's a new sale every week here, and five major ones a year. Sign the mailing list to be kept informed.

See also
> Evan Picone/Gant Factory Store
> Damone
> Half Price House
> Aileen
> All that Jazz
> Sutter Place/La Petite Factorie
> Shelly's/Apparel Warehouse
> Liz Claiborne Outlet
> Leslie Fay Outlet
> Cole of California Outlet
> Bizarre Bazaar
> Beverly Hills Hosiery, Inc.
> Lingerie Outlet
> London Fog Factory Store

Resale

Big City Woman Resale Store
4185 Adams Av., San Diego (619) 521-0121
Tues.-Fri., 11-6; Sat., 11-4
Terms: MC, V, Checks. Final sale.   Parking

The shop offers clothing for size 16 and up. The clothing is generally of the better designer variety, and not more than three years old.

My Secret Place
18862 Beach Blvd., #116, Huntington Beach (714) 963-4743
Mon.-Fri., 11-7; Sat., 11-4
Terms: MC, V, AE, D, Checks. Final sale.   Parking

Here clothing is size 14 and up; it's businesswear, evening wear, matched separates, and not more than three years old.

Computers

A computer, like a car or a major appliance, can be a big investment, so some research is in order. Computer magazines regularly rate software and hardware, so check out these sources when you are configuring a system. Often the cheapest way to buy computers and software is through the mail, by scanning such publications as *The Computer Shopper* (a huge magazine, available in bookstores for $2.95, published monthly, containing over 800 pages of features and ads for mail order computer companies), and comparing ads and features. In some instances you can buy directly from computer companies. If you choose not to do this, the Business and Sports sections of the *Los Angeles Times* are good sources for current prices from local companies. Some local sources with frequent good buys and technical support follow.

Comp USA
11441 Jefferson Blvd., Culver City (310) 390-9993
Mon.-Fri., 9-9; Sat., 10-7; Sun., 11-6
(also in City of Industry, Fountain Valley, San Diego, and Torrance)
Terms: MC, V, AE, D, SC, Check. Exchanges.   Parking

Comp USA is a local discount chain offering configurations from several of the major names in computers, as well as many clones, printers, accessories, peripherals, software and games. Discounts on software can go as high as 65%, and you can find a computer in any price range. There is also a clearance section, with marked down hardware and software. They offer business leasing of computer packages, and give courses at all levels in the more popular word processing, graphics and utilities programs. Books are discounted 30%, clearance books marked down 50% (*The Computer Shopper* is $1.99 here). These stores are tremendous and often crowded; it may take you a while to get help or technical support, but hang in there; once they get to you their level of service is superb. They publish their own catalog monthly.

Computer Marketplace Show and Sale
(800) 800-5600
Monthly. $6 adults, kids 10 and under, free   Parking

This show is home to over 250 vendors, so you may be able to walk back and forth between a few to get the best price on what you want. The larger show is held once every three weeks at the Pomona Fairplex, and a smaller version with 100 dealers, is held monthly in Buena Park. A third show is in Reseda. You can find almost anything here, from thousands of pieces of software and games beginning at *$1*, to vendors offering furniture, disks, equipment and books. There is a consignment table, should you want to sell your own equipment. Get on the mailing list by calling the number above.

Egghead Discount Software Clearance Store   CCC
11651 W. Pico Blvd., West Los Angeles (310) 473-8115
Mon.-Sat., 10-7; Sun., 12-5
Terms: MC, V, AE, Check. Final sale.   Parking

The Egghead Discount Software chain sells discounted software all over the country, and this is the clearance center for all those stores. Here you'll find overstocks, close-outs and discontinued merchandise, and savings go as high as 90%, sometimes even higher. Among the items I found were computer games at $1 (there is a $1 table full of all kinds of goodies, serious and otherwise), IBM and Apple software for word processing, money management, spreadsheet programs, graphics and desktop publishing, fonts for laser printers, even imprinted and wildly colored form feed paper. If you're worried about buying discontinued software, see if what you're interested in comes with an update card.

Discount Catalogs

47th Street Photo
(800) 235-5016
Terms: MC, V, Check. Returns.

Anyone from New York knows 47th Street photo as a crazy, bustling place, full of good deals on electronics. Going there can be a nightmare; but shopping by mail gets rid of the wait and the crowds, and 47th Street Photo has some of the best prices on computers, cameras and electronics. They don't have a catalog, but will quote prices over the phone; check here before buying.

See also
> DAK Outlet Store
> Damark International
> Comb
> J&R Music World

Craft Supplies

Bev's Crafts & Lace
7620 Tampa Av., Reseda (818) 881-2257
Mon.-Sat., 10-6 (Mon. and Wed. to 8)
Terms: Cash and Check ($5 min.) only. GC. Final sale. Parking

This shop offers supplies for wearable arts and home crafts at discount prices, as well as a variety of silk and dried flowers. Hundreds of types of lace are available by the yard, and rosettes selling at fabric stores for .35 are here at three for .49. Boas were $2.99 a yard and 8" to 12" wooden hoops sold for .75. Tulip Glitter Slicks and Iridescent paints were $4.99 (4 oz.) and there are supplies and books on a large variety of crafts. Classes will be available when their new back room is finished.

Cheep Lace
17251-B East Gale Av., City of Industry (818) 854-0062
Mon.-Fri., 10-8; Sat., 10-6; Sun. 10-5
Terms: MC, V, Check ($10 min.). Final sale.   Parking

As it's name implies, this is a cheap place for lace. And ribbons, trim, fabric flowers, and all sorts of craft notions. For $1 you can buy five yards of 7/8" satin ribbon, or ten yards of 1/4". There are many styles of lace, and spools of eyelet trim were dirt cheap (or cheep, I guess). Spools of 8.5mm pearls (36 yds.) were $5, and the 2.5mm size were $6, or two for $10. Lace goes from collars and appliques to bolts of fabric. Call for a price on your craft needs.

Dawn's Discount Lace II   **COUPON**
8655 S. Sepulveda Blvd., Westchester (310) 641-3466
Mon.-Sat., 10-6; Sun., 12-5
(also at Orange County Swap Meet on Sat. and Sun.)
Terms: Cash and Check only. Final sale.   Parking

This little corner of the Westchester Antique Mall is full of lace and ribbons, wreath forms and straw hats, rosettes and charms, appliques, collars, and trims, and all at discount prices. Whether you're buying hundreds of dollars worth, or just spending a quarter, you'll get prices close to or in some cases below wholesale. One craftsperson I met was buying the charms Dawn stocks, resembling antique gold hearts and angels. They're hard to find, and begin at five for $1. They make great barrettes, pins and earrings, and here you'll find backings for these crafts as well. The ribbon roses that are sprouting all over crafts projects here sell for .99 a bag (quantity ranges from dozen to four depending on size and intricacy. I've seen the eight-to-a-bag size selling for .35 apiece at local fabric stores.). Rhinestones, sequined appliques, and yards of lace round out the inventory. Sample projects decorate the shop; Dawn will be happy to tell you how to make them. This small space contains a lot of beautiful merchandise at competitive prices. Get on the mailing list for information on sales. *The coupon entitles you to 10% off your next purchase.*

The Fabric Barn
3111 E. Anaheim, Long Beach (310) 498-0285
Mon.-Sat., 9-5; Sun., 10-4
Terms: Cash and Check only. Final sale.   Parking

The Fabric Barn is a hard store to categorize. They do have a smattering of interior decorating fabrics (Waverly ranges from $3.99 to $9.99 on sale); but most of their fabric is for quilting and home sewing projects. Peter Pan cotton prints can go as low as $3.75 a yard, and they carry a large selection of calicos and children's prints. Craft books are discounted 10% (*Quilt In A Day* books, 25%), and they have a selection of dried and fabric flowers. But what Fabric Barn is known for is California's biggest selection of ribbons and lace. They sell wholesale, but if you're buying retail the prices are deeply discounted, and if there's something you can't find elsewhere, chances are you'll find it here, in your choice of colors and widths.

Robertson's
18217 Parthenia, Northridge (818) 701-0168
Mon.-Sat., 10-5
Terms: MC, V, Check. Final sale.   Parking

Robertson's is a wholesale supplier of craft items, including silk and dried flowers, grapevine and twig wreathes, wedding supplies, ribbons, ceramics, clothing crafts supplies and seasonal items. They do not sell to the public, but if you are a member of one of the warehouse buying clubs, show your card here and you'll get in, and get goods at close to wholesale prices. Robertson's has a big sale Thanksgiving weekend, and various smaller sales year round. There is a minimum of $50 on your first purchase, and $10 minimum purchases thereafter. Credit cards are accepted for orders of $100 or more.

Super Yarn Mart
60 N. Lake Av., Pasadena (818) 584-YARN
Hours vary by location.
(20 additional locations; see Geographical Index)
Terms: MC, V, GC, Check. Returns.   Parking

Super Yarn Mart sells acrylic yarn, factory direct. There are always a variety of other yarns to choose from (sometimes a small variety) at discounted prices, they sell notions, and there are generally close-out bins with craft kits (including counted cross stitch and iron on wearables) at half price or less. Another money-saver for crafts projects can be their bags of tangled skeins, sold by weight. They also carry embroidery thread, rug-hooking yarn and canvas, and they will special order cross stitch and other craft kits, but these are not discounted.

See also
> World of Plants and Gifts
> The Bead Gallery

Discount Catalogs

Home-Sew
P. O. Box 4099, Bethlehem, PA 18018-0099
Terms: Check.

Home Sew offers laces, trims, ribbons, buttons and appliques, as well as jewelry findings and quilting supplies, at competitive prices, which get better in quantity. There are savings on supplies for all kinds of crafts.

If you use fabric scraps in craft projects, consider garage sales and the clothing racks of thrift shops. Prints are priced much lower per yard then at fabric stores.

Department Store Outlets

Did you ever fall in love with something at a department store, but even on sale it cost more than you wanted to pay? These clearance centers are the last stop for department store merchandise, and **discounts here can range up to 95% off** an item's original price.

Boston Stores Clearance Center   CCC
2225 N. Garey, Pomona (619) 593-0212
Mon.-Fri., 9:30-6; Sat., 10-6; Sun., 12-5
Terms: MC, V, SC. Check. L. Exchanges.   *Parking*

The clearance center for the Boston Stores is filled with discounts of 70% and more on clothing, accessories, linen, china and giftware. All merchandise has been marked down at least once, and much of it is discounted an additional 25% to 50%. Women's dresses range from petite to size 18; a print dress originally selling at $58, was $16.97; long flannel nightgowns were $10 ($32). Infant Carter's polo shirts were $5 ($11); a toddler girl's Oshkosh B'Gosh denim pinafore was $13.67 ($23), and PCH boys' shorts were $10 ($22). Men's Haggar blend sport jackets, originally $95, were $40; Oscar de la Renta ties were $7.50 ($26.50), and sport shirts were $10 ($30).

The Broadway Clearance Centers   CCC
Panorama Mall, Panorama City (818) 893-7811
Mon.-Fri., 10-9; Sat., 10-7; Sun., 11-6
Terms: MC, V, SC, Check. Final sale.   *Parking*

The chainwide clearance centers for the Broadway are located on various floors of this store: young men's clothing on one; children's, men's and women's clothing, and housewares on two; and furniture on three.

Before entering the clearance center, clothing has been marked down at least once; then tags are color-coded, denoting additional markdowns of 25%, 50%, 75% or 90%. The women's, men's and children's merchandise on the second floor has been separated, but it's not much more organized then that, and there is no fitting room. Men's Neil Martin chinos were reduced to $6.25, and a Chaps long sleeved shirt was $22.50 ($60). Among the men's brands were

Colours by Alexander Julian, Nike, Izod La Coste, Motto, and Union Bay. In the children's department a Catalina Girls Swimsuit was $16.99, marked down to $6.50; and a Rare Editions infant cotton romper was $15 ($36). Women's and junior's clothing ranged from sportswear to evening clothes, and featured such names as Lizsport, Paris Blues, Rampage, Carole Little and Leslie Fay.

The Home Center was small, containing odds and ends; king size down comforters were $55, a Diane Von Furstenberg Garment Bag in a tapestry pattern was $20 ($75), and a Black & Decker one cup coffeemaker was $10.

The furniture section offered variety, and everything was marked down at least 40%. From sofas and upholstered chairs to bedroom and dining sets, there were great bargains here. A pine corner table was $270 ($530), and a pair of pecan lamp tables, once $649 each were $260. Couches ranged from $300 to $800 and sleepers were in the $600 to $700 range. A Meeting House queen pencil post bed was $1000 ($1825), and a beautiful carved pine king bedroom set (four poster, dresser, mirror and bedside chest) originally $3500, was $1780. There were lamps, day beds, wicker, even mattresses, at great savings.

Bullock's Grand Finale   CCC

Clark & Del Amo, Lakewood (310) 634-5111
5500 Grossmont Center Dr., Grossmont (619) 698-6422
Mon.-Fri., 10-9; Sat. 10-7; Sun., 11-5
Terms: MC, V, SC, Check. Final sale.   Parking

Months ago I saw a Jane Singer dress I loved, for $170. I didn't buy it. Some time later I stopped into the Bullock's clearance center, the top floor of the Lakewood store (in Grossmont it's in the basement), and there it was, reduced to $79.99. Tempting, but more than I wanted to pay. But that day all clothing was *75% off the ticketed price*. The dress was *$20!* And mine. The pricing policy here is usually 25%, 50%, 75% or 90% off the lowest marked price depending on the color of the ticket (intermediary markdowns taken before garments arrive). Generally there is a smattering of children's and men's clothing, with women's and juniors' predominating. I found an ABS California metallic skirt for $12.50 ($150); a Tahari jacket was $42.25 ($280), and an Ellen Tracy white linen skirt was $16.25 ($90). In the men's department I picked up a few cotton long sleeved sport shirts, in beautiful colors, for $7 ($50). Women's shoes sell at 25% or 50% off the lowest marked price. They are theoretically separated by size, and if you can find a shoe in your size you *deserve* to own it (unless you're a five or a six; *every* rack featured fives and sixes). Communal fitting rooms close a half an hour before the store does, and the check-out line stops forming 15 minutes before closing time. The line can be long, so be patient. Count up how much money you've saved.

J. C. Penney Catalog Outlet Store CCC
6651 Fallbrook Av., West Hills (818) 883-3660
Mon.-Fri., 10-9; Sat., 10-7; Sun., 10-6
Terms: MC, Visa, AE, SC. Returns.   Parking

This store is packed with overstocks, store returns and clearance items, and anything you can find in the catalog may be waiting for you here, at half price or less. There is clothing for men, women, (including maternity, large and petite sizes) and children; shoes, housewares, linens, sporting goods, lighting, sewing machines, accessories, underwear, lingerie and furniture. Men's Levis were $19.99 ($42.99), misses 100% cotton ribbed knit tops were $4 ($15). Women's high top Free Style Reeboks, in lavender suede, were $24.95 (if you were a size 7). Nurses' uniforms were $19.99 ($45), and bridal gowns (to size 24 1/2), ranged from from $50 to $175.

The May Company Clothing Clearance Center CCC
6067 Wilshire Blvd., Los Angeles (213) 938-4211
8450 La Palma, Buena Park (714) 827-4000
Mon-Sat., 10-9
Terms: MC, AE, D, SC, Check. Final sale.   Parking

Everything here is generally 50% off the lowest marked price (sales may bring it to 60%), and most things have been marked down at least twice before arriving. There are buys for the whole family, and the store is neatly divided into sections for men, women, juniors, boys and girls, but within the sections things are chaotic. If it doesn't have a price tag and you can't find another one (it took you half an hour to find *this* one), you're out of luck. A women's multi-tone cotton and Lycra blazer was $5 ($48), a Scott McClintock strapless cotton dress was $36.67 ($180). Mens' Bugle Boy Jeans were $15 ($38), a Nino Cerutti viscose and wool sport coat was $65 ($245), and a Bugle Boy ramie and cotton sweater was $7 ($36). This is a store requiring time and patience.

The May Company Home Clearance Center CCC
8252 Van Nuys Blvd., Panorama City (818) 509-4575
1530 West Covina Pkwy., West Covina (818) 338-5253
Hours vary by location.
Terms: MC, AE, D, SC, Check. Final sale.   Parking

They sell everything but clothing here, from furniture and televisions to lamps and napkins. Linens are an especially good buy: polyester table cloths of all sizes were $4.77 (values to $19.99); napkins were as low as .47. Sheets by manufacturers such as Wamsutta were $10.77, king; $8.77, queen; $6.77, full; and $3.77, twin; the day I dropped in they were reduced an additional 25%.

There is also furniture, including a large assortment of chairs, sofas, recliners and sleepers. A leather sofa was $765 ($1500), the matching loveseat $729 ($1400). A washed oak armoire/entertainment center was $1100 ($1850), and a Broyhill pine armoire was $680 ($1400). Magnavox video cameras were as low as $397. There were mattresses, lamps, and sleeper sofas, and folding chairs were reduced from $17.99 to $9. Giftware is discounted 50%.

Montgomery Ward Clearance Centers   *CCC*
8341 "A" La Palma Ave, Buena Park   (714) 521-4709
Mon.-Fri., 10-8; Sat., 10-6; Sun., 11-5
(also in Garden Grove, Santa Ana and Norwalk)
Terms: MC, V, AE, SC, Check. Final sale.   *Parking*

These stores are full of furniture, appliances, TVs and mattresses, with a pinch of other goods thrown in. While some of the furniture was soiled, there wasn't anything that couldn't be cleaned. Side chairs began at $100 ($300), recliners at $179 ($399), loveseats began at $119; a twin sleeper loveseat was $199 ($439) and full size couches and sleepers began at $249. Wooden country dining tables seating six were $124 ($399). A Panasonic Palmcorder Flying Erase Head video camera was $509 ($700), and washers, dryers, refrigerators and stoves were discounted about 30%. There was a small collection of lawnmowers; a Murray 3.5 hp 20" High Wheel Mower was $94 ($179); and a Rally Self-Propelled Lawn Mower 5.0 HP, 20" was $159.99 ($279.99). Bring a truck if you make a large purchase, because they don't deliver.

Nordstrom Rack   *CCC*
21490 Victory Blvd., Woodland Hills   (818) 884-6771
Mon-Fri., 10-9; Sat. 10-7; Sun., 11-6
(also in Santa Ana, Chino and San Diego)
Terms: MC, V, AE, SC, Check. Returns.   *Parking*

The quality at the Rack is every bit as high as at the retail stores, the prices are just a lot lower. This is the most well-organized department store clearance center, where some items have been marked down several times, some only once. Whatever the savings combination there are great buys for men, women and kids in clothes, shoes and accessories, and shopping carts are provided so you can really load up. I found a Tahari dress for $70 ($290), silk ties for under $20, a man's Burberry long sleeved cotton shirt was $29.98, and suits that had sold for $525 were now $250. There is footwear for the whole family, much at about half price, in a well-organized department that makes it easy to find your size in dress, casual and athletic shoes. There are also underwear and sleepwear sections. And, unlike most of the other clearance centers, this one takes returns, because even though they're cheap, they're still Nordstroms.

Robinsons Clearance Centers   CCC
600 W. 7 St., Los Angeles (213) 488-5522
Mon.-Sat., 10-6
Terms: MC, V, AE, SC, Check. Final sale.   Parking

Robinson's downtown store has clearance centers in on several floors: children's clothing is on two, some junior clearance is on three, men and women's is on four, and furniture is on six. (A new linen clearance center is planned for the second floor.)

Clothing clearance prices are based on taking a percentage (25%, 50%, 75% or 90%) off the lowest marked price, depending on the color code of the tag. In the children's section I found an infant's Buster Brown romper for $3.50 ($10), and a short set with matching hat for $4 ($14). Bugle Boy jeans were $9 ($36) and Not Guilty girls' denim overalls were $20 ($54). In the Ready to Wear Clearance Center on the fourth floor, the mens portion is usually smaller than the women's, which takes up most of the floor, with women's clothes for

---

*Customers purchase ten pieces of clothing
and get change back from a twenty*

---

every occasion. I found a Cachet lace and chiffon evening top, originally $180, reduced to $90, and marked down to $45. Dan Brooke suede Pants were $32 ($134). A Shelly Segal jacket had been marked down, several times, winding up at $15 ($122). There is a large selection of dresses and some very snazzy evening wear. In the men's section a friend picked up a $300 suede jacket for $70. The first of the month is generally when prices drop, and that's when you'll find a line outside the door half an hour before the store opens. Savvy shoppers can wind up with high-priced clothing for peanuts. There is an Express check-out, 10 items or less, because people buy by the armload. Keep your eyes open; you'll be amazed to see customers purchasing *ten* items and getting *change back from a twenty!*

In Furniture Clearance, a leather recliner was $600 ($1200); a wing chair was $200 ($575); a pine entertainment center was $999 ($2400), and an upholstered queen size sleep sofa was $650 ($1300). A pair of drop-end pine tables were each $299 ($850). Delivery charges range from $35 to $70 per piece.

In January and July, the downtown and Pasadena stores host the semi-annual Warehouse Sale. Large areas are cordoned off for sale tables, where housewares sell at low prices. These areas are mobbed, there are long lines to pay and great values to be found. Check the hours: the sale has hours of its own.

Sears Outlet   CCC
9045 Adams, Huntington Beach   (714) 963-2666
Mon.-Fri., 10-9; Sat., 10-6; Sun., 11-6
(also in Upland, Norwalk, LaHabra, Simi Valley, San Diego)
Terms: D, SC, Checks. Final sale.   Parking

This store promises 20% to 70% off most items, and features a selection of products found in Sears or the Sears catalog. A women's Gitano cotton and ramie sweater was $16 ($26), cotton skirts were $6 ($12), cotton and linen blend blazers, $8 ($24). Shoes for men, women and children were half price. Twenty piece china sets were $25 ($45), and an upright vacuum was $169 ($350). There were microwaves, typewriters, ceiling fans, air conditioners, drapes, toys, tires, wheels and furniture. An exercise cycle featuring dual action with calorie monitor was $75 ($199). A Craftsman power blower with vacuum was $37 ($60). Men's long sleeved sport shirts were $6 ($21.99), and men's jeans were $10 ($17.99). An infant's two piece warm-up suit was $6 ($10), and a little girl's embellished denim jacket $18 ($45). They don't have everything, but what they do have is often a great value.

Discount Catalogs

Grand Finale
(800) 995-9595
Terms: MC, V, AE, D. Check. Exchanges.

Grand Finale is the discount catalog for some pricier mail order catalogs, i.e., The Horchow Collection, Trifles and SGF. There is a $3 charge for a series of catalogs, refundable with your first purchase. The merchandise is discounted 25% to 70%, and includes women's clothing, linens, quilts, china and tabletop pieces, and assorted chatchkas of modern life.

Discount Chains

Some people can't stand these stores, but they're worth getting to know. Try each to discover which carry your kind of merchandise, which make your skin crawl. This is crap shoot shopping, but prices can be so low that if you have the time and the inclination, one day the odds are bound to be in your favor.

K-Mart
6310 W. 3 St., Los Angeles (213) 933-7306
Mon.-Sat., 9-9; Sun., 10-8
(30 additional locations; see Geographical Index)
Terms: MC, V, Check. Returns.   Parking

K-Mart carries everything, but best buys include housewares, small electrics, sporting goods, auto parts and car care sundries, candy and foodstuffs, baby items and whatever's on sale. The best clothing value seems to be in women's underwear, which look like knock-offs of styles found in better lingerie departments, but at a third the price. Party and paper goods were an excellent buy as well.

Marshalls
6221 Bristol Pkwy., Culver City (310) 337-9158
Mon.-Sat., 9:30-9; Sun., 11-6
(32 additional locations; see Geographical Index)
Terms: MC, V, AE, D, Check. Returns.   Parking

Marshalls offers clothing and shoes at discounts of 30% and more; with frequent sales and numerous clearance racks, discounts can run much higher. There is clothing for women, petites, large sizes, and juniors, featuring Liz Claiborne, Adolfo, Calvin Klein, Chaus, Adidas, Gloria Vanderbilt, Jordache, Esprit, and Guess?, although there may be only one piece in any one style. Kidswear brands include Carters, Oshkosh B'Gosh, Guess?, London Fog, Palmettos, B.U.M. Equipment and Ocean Pacific. Menswear ranges from casual wear to dress suits, and brands run the gamut, from Arrow, Haggar, Bugle Boy, Calvin Klein and Dockers to a small suit selection (where I found a $900 Polo suit by Ralph Lauren at $399).

Ross Dress for Less
4315 Pacific Coast Hwy., Torrance   (310) 373-0784
Hours vary by location.
(also in West Hollywood, Tarzana, Chatsworth, Culver City, Westwood, Northridge, and San Diego)
Terms: MC, V, Check. Returns.   Parking

Ross has discounted clothing, accessories, and shoes for the whole family, including many nationally advertised better brands.   Among the labels here are Edwin, Forenza, Liz & Co., Leslie Fay, Evan Picone, Burlington, Jordache, Dockers, LaCoste, Generra, Arrow, John Henry and Calvin Klein, at discounts beginning at 30% and going down to 70%. Athletic shoes, underwear, hose and lingerie are always a good buy.

T. J. Maxx
11020 Jefferson Blvd., Culver City   (310) 390-7944
Mon.-Sat., 9:30-9:30; Sun., 11-6
(18 additional locations; see Geographical Index or call (800) 926-6299)
Terms: MC, V, D, AE. Checks. Returns.   Parking

T. J. Maxx carries clothing, jewelry, giftware, linens, luggage, and shoes. Discounts begin at 30% and can go considerably higher, particularly if they're having a sale. Better to moderate name brands are available in clothing and shoes. T. J. Maxx is also a liquidator for some better department stores; you can find their end-of-season clearance merchandise here, sold at a fraction of the original price, often with store tags or inside labels still on the garments.

Variety Store Chains

99 Cents Only Stores
(30 locations; see Geographical Index or call (213) Lucky-99)
Mon.-Sun., 9-9
Terms: Cash. Final sale.   Parking

These stores feature items selling at .99, two for .99, three for .99.... You get the picture. Anything marked over .99 sells for .99. Some of the best buys are baby toys, party favors and party supplies, candy, spices, scrub brushes and sponges, paper goods and plastic containers. Stock is ever-changing, but there are always values. (Beware the products that look like brand names but are really clever near-misses in label!)

Pic'N'Save
75 locations; see Geographical Index
Mon.-Sat., 9-9; Sun., 10-7
Terms: MC, V, D, Check. Returns.   Parking

Pic'N'Save offers close-outs and staples at very attractive prices, including party goods, hosiery, glassware, fabric flowers, planters, foods and housewares. Wander the aisles and find specials on just about anything. A photo album I'd seen in a local department store was selling here at *one eighth* the price.

Treasure Hunt
9860 Central Av., Montclair (714) 399-0840
Mon.-Sat., 9:30-9; Sun., 10:30-7
(also in El Segundo, Norwalk, Covina, San Bernardino, Hawthorne, Paramount, Bell)
Terms: MC, V, D, Check. Returns.   Parking

They call this store an adventure in bargain hunting, and there are new treasures daily. Stock consists of close-outs, overstocks and liquidations of famous and not-so brands. Save to 70% on items like kid's clothing, canned food, cosmetic sundries, party goods and kitchenware. Stock always varies.

Discount Catalogs

Comb
(800) 328-0609
Terms: MC, V, D, SC, Check. Returns.

"The Original Authorized Liquidator," the Comb catalog is full of quality merchandise discounted 50% to 75%. There are electronics, luggage, home furnishings, appliances, linens, jewelry, toys, sporting goods and a few trinkets you're not likely to see anywhere else.

Damark International, Inc.
(800) 729-9000
Terms: MV, C, AE, D, Check. Returns.

Damark, "The Great Deal Company," is, like Comb, a mail order discount clearing house. Their mix is similar, and discounts are 50% to 75%. Damark also offers factory-serviced items at greater reductions (pieces that have been returned to a manufacturer, sometimes with no operational flaw, re-inspected, repaired if need be, and put back on the market). There is a discount card, available for $50, entitling you to 10% off purchases for one year.

Drapes and Window Treatments

Blue Chip Drapery & Blinds
2139 Stoner Av., West Los Angeles (310) 477-2421
Hours vary by location.
(also in Downey, Lomita, San Bernardino, Santa Ana, Van Nuys, and West Covina)
Terms: MC, V, Check. Returns.   Parking

Blue Chip Drapery offers all its ready-made drapes at discount prices. They come in 120 sizes, and about half of those sizes are available at even lower close-out prices. (These drapes are made out of the bolt ends of higher quality fabric, bought at low cost, and are a great value.) Check through their large selection to save up to 50% over everyday low prices. They offer a shop-at-home service for draperies and blinds, and can coordinate complete bedroom ensembles, with upholstered headboards, window treatments and pillows. They they install, and will ship for a nominal fee.

Drapery World Outlet Store
11622 Markon Dr., Garden Grove (714) 537-6275
Mon.-Sat., 9-5
Terms: MC, V, Check. Final sale.   Parking

In this showroom Drapery World sells custom drapes and window treatments

---
Custom-made drapes sold at less than half price

---

that were duplicate orders, have slight imperfections, were dyed the wrong shade, or orders that were cancelled. They are sold at prices *under half of what the original customer would have paid.* While you can get drapes cheaper, you can't get drapes of this quality at a better price anywhere. Row upon row of standard sizes are displayed, and blinds, miniblinds and other window treatments are often available if you have the magic dimensions. The colors are mainly beiges, with a few pastels, a print or two, many satins and sheers, and there are between six and twenty pair in each size. Call and see if they have what you want, or come down and browse, but remember to bring the

the measurements for *all* your windows; you never know what you might find.

Moran's Drapery Warehouse
4631 S. Huntington Dr., El Sereno (213) 221-4141
Mon.-Sat., 10-6; Sun., 10-5
Terms: MC, V, D, Check. Final sale.   Parking

Moran's has been closed for several months, since it was *hit by a tornado* (and you thought all we had to worry about was earthquakes), but will re-open September 1, 1992. They disount curtains, drapes and panels, drapery fabric bolt ends, hardware and mini-blinds. By buying discontinued and close-out stock, they pass along savings of 40% to 50%. There are parking lot sales two or three times a year, where clearance merchandise is sold at or below cost.

Stern's Discount Drapery Center
226 E. 9 St., Los Angeles (213) 622-3564
Mon.-Sat., 9-4:30
Terms: MC, V, Check. Final sale.   Street parking

Stern's sells drapery and upholstery fabrics, but they also make draperies, and sometimes they make a boo-boo, or the customer flakes out, and they wind up with custom-made drapes and no customer. So if you're in need of new drapery, check out their unclaimed stock, which sells for just about half price. If you don't find what you're looking for and you're handy with a needle, they also have a selection of low-priced close-out fabric; maybe you can whip those drapes up yourself.

Three Day Blinds
(800) 966-3DAY, EXT. 500
Tues.-Fri., 10-8; Sat. 10-5; Sun. 11-4
(40 locations; see Geographical Index)
Terms: MC, V, Check. Final sale.   Parking

Three Day Blinds sells miniblinds, verticals, wood blinds, duette and pleated shades and custom shutters by Transitions, Joanna, Bali, and Hunter Douglas; their everyday prices are low—they have a low price guarantee—and they usually run an additional special, a free upgrade on hardware or a rebate. Blinds carry a lifetime warranty.

See also
    Interior Decorating Fabrics

Dry Cleaners

Cleaners charging as little as $1 per item are popping up all over. Generally bargain basement prices do not include leather, suede, jumpsuits and other garments. I can only recommend the cleaners below with caution; *as with any new cleaner, don't try them out on your favorite outfit.*

Celebrity Cleaners
2370 S. Robertson, Los Angeles (310) 559-4395
$1.45 per garment.

The Cleaning Club
10905 Venice Blvd., Los Angeles (310) 839-9700
$1.25 per garment.

Concord Cleaners
11682 W. Olympic Blvd., West Los Angeles (310) 478-6708
$1.40 per garment.

Dress Up Cleaners
13636 Vanowen, Van Nuys (818) 988-3970
$1.50 per garment.

Empire Cleaners
1818 Victory Blvd., North Hollywood (818) 506-8036
$1.50 per garment.

Goodrich Professional Cleaners
6110 W. Pico Blvd., Los Angeles (213) 653-7175
$1.49 per garment.

Hi-Lo Laundry and Cleaners
3969 S. Sepulveda Blvd., Culver City (310) 390-6198
$1.45 per garment.

Jack's Cleaners
2465 Washington, Pasadena (818) 797-7323
$1.50 per garment.

Jasmine Cleaners, most garments $1.50
    846 N. Maclay Av., San Fernando (818) 361-1791
    9130 Reseda Blvd., Northridge (818) 349-3293
    11417 Roscoe Blvd., Panorama City (818) 891-8810
    20836 Vanowen, Canoga Park (818) 346-8234
    13304 Victory Blvd., Van Nuys (818) 901-1226
    14055 Victory Blvd., Van Nuys (818) 997-8174
    5409 Sunset Blvd., Los Angeles (213) 467-7547
    3524 Sunset Blvd., Los Angeles (213) 662-9193

$1 Cleaners, most garments $1.45
    145 S. Glendale Blvd., Glendale (818) 545-7392
    471 W. Broadway, Glendale (818) 549-1015
    539 N. Glenoaks, Burbank (818) 558-6562
    2106 Mountainview, El Monte (818) 448-0828
    6269 N. Rosemead, Temple City (818) 287-4333
    12303 E. Imperial Hwy., Norwalk (310) 929-6674
    2308 E. Colorado Blvd., Pasadena (818) 449-7134
    777 S. Arroyo Pkwy., Pasadena (818) 405-9706
    1315 S. Fair Oaks, South Pasadena (818) 441-3599

$1 Most Garments Cleaners
540 N. Azusa, W. Covina (818) 967-5075
$1 per garment.

$1.50 Most Garments Cleaners
1118 N. Azusa, Covina (818) 966-5595
$1.50 per garment.

Ritz Dry Cleaners
6022 Woodman Av., Van Nuys (818) 902-1108
$1.50 most garments.

Sprint Cleaners
103 E. 17 Street, Costa Mesa (714) 631-2745
$1.35 per garment.

Thrifty Cleaner
1385 Lake Av., Pasadena (818) 398-9533
$1.50 most garments.

World Cleaners
8107 Beverly Blvd., Los Angeles (213) 651-5505
$1.45 per garment.

Entertainment

Movie Previews

You know you can see movies for less if you go to the early show, but did you know that since you live in the movie capital of the world, you can see movies for *free*? *Before they come out*? Keep your eyes open as you pass local movie theaters and you will sometimes spot anxious looking people, clipboards in hand, scanning the crowd, in search of fodder of the appropriate demographic to dragoon into a preview. Look one in the eye and you may be asked to participate. This is studio market research, and you have to fill out a questionnaire afterwards, but it beats spending $7. (Sometimes.) I have found these people in front of the UA Cinema in old town Pasadena, and the theaters on the Santa Monica Promenade. If they ask if you work in the entertainment industry, and you tell them yes, you don't get to see the movie.

Museums

Most museums offer a day when admission charges are waived. (This policy may not apply during special exhibits.) A short list follows.

Armand Hammer Museum of Art
10899 Wilshire Blvd., Westwood (310) 443-7000
Free: last Thursday of the month, 2 to 6.

L. A. County Museum of Art
5905 Wilshire Blvd., Los Angeles (213) 857-6000
Free: second Tuesday of the month, 10 to 5.

Museum of Contemporary Art
150 S. Grand Av., Los Angeles (213) 621-2766
Free: Thursday evenings, 5 to 8.

Museum of Contemporary Art, San Diego
700 Prospect St., La Jolla (619) 454-3541
Free: Wednesday evenings, 5 to 9.

Santa Barbara Museum of Art
1130 State St., Santa Barbara (805) 963-4364
Free: Thursdays, 11 to 9.

Theater

Shakespeare Festival/LA
The Anson Ford Theater, Hollywood

Shakespeare is free for a two week run every summer (some nights they request you bring a canned good to help your fellow Angelenos), and the theater is hardly ever full. Sit back under the stars and get your Shakespeare painlessly. Bring a picnic and make a night of it.

TV Tapings

You'd be amazed at how many of your out-of-town relatives will be thrilled to find themselves in a real live television studio, watching a real live taping. The best source for tickets to television tapings is Audiences Unlimited, (818) 506-0067. If they don't have the show you want, contact the company that produces the show. If you can't figure out which that might be in the maze of end credits, call the network and they'll direct you. Get tickets in advance; the most popular shows are all but impossible to see.

Money Savers

Entertainment Publications
(310) 396-5595   *(818) 222-4233*
(714) 968-3244   *(800) 477-3234*
Terms: MC, V, Check.

Entertainment Publications puts out coupon books covering the Southern California area. The books sell for $25 to $40 and are often used as fund-raisers for charitable organizations; if you purchase one this way, a portion of the price may be tax deductible. The books used to be geared toward couples, containing two for one offers at local restaurants (fast food and dining experiences), movies, sporting events, hotels, municipal attractions, even bowling alleys. While most offers are still two for one, many restaurants have expanded the offer to half off the meal of a single diner. The books come out annually, around August or September, and coupons expire in November, a year hence. Books are available for the following areas:

    Inland Empire/Desert Communities   Orange County
    San Fernando Valley/Ventura   San Diego
    San Gabriel Valley/Pomona   South Bay/Long Beach
    West Los Angeles/Downtown Los Angeles

Entertainment Publications has also come out with coupon books for travel:
Travel American at Half Price Directory ($32.95).
National Dining and Hotel Directory ($50).
Half Price Europe ($42).
B&B Plus Directory ($12.95).
Overseas Editions for London, Amsterdam, Sweden, Denmark and Israel ($65).

On the House
(310) 392-7588
Terms: Check.

This service offers entertainment almost every night of the year, if you want it. For $125 annually you can get two tickets to a play (both off-Broadway type and larger theaters), symphony, ballet, concert, comedy club, screening, sneak preview, premier reception, benefit or cabaret *nightly*, with your choice of 25 to 40 events per week. There is a 24 hour members' hotline telling you what's available. They also offer gift certificates and group packages.

Restaurants

Elmer Dills
P. O. Box A, Hollywood, CA 90027

Restaurant critic Elmer Dills has put together a list of bargain restaurants he has enjoyed. To qualify, restaurants must offer at least 75% of their entrees at under $10. For the list, send a self-addressed, stamped business-size envelope to the above address, requesting this specific list. You might want to ask for a list of the other lists he's compiled; he's our local repository of information on travel and cuisine.

Fabric

Interior Decorating Fabric

Big Y Yardage Outlet
440 S. Main St., Santa Ana (714) 978-3970
4418 Holt Blvd., Montclair (714) 624-8541
Mon., 9:30-9; Tues.-Sat., 9:30-5:30
Terms: MC, V, Check.   Parking

If you're looking for ideas on custom window treatments, visit the Santa Ana location of Big Y. While both stores sell drapery and upholstery fabrics, the Montclair store is smaller, the bolts more precariously perched, and there isn't much room for display. These stores sell high quality drapery and upholstery fabrics, hardware and fittings. They do beautiful custom work, or will provide you with what you need to make your own. You'll find a wide assortment, good prices, and a lot of experience here to help you make the right choice.

Calico Corners
12717 Ventura Blvd., Studio City (818) 766-1120
Mon.-Sat., 10-6 (Thurs. to 7); Sun., 12-5
(also in Pasadena, Huntington Beach, Northridge, Torrance, Orange, Puente Hills)
Terms: MC, V, Check. Returns.   Parking

Calico Corners offers discounts on first quality, designer fabrics, as well as seconds at about half price. (Waverly prints are $14.95 a yard; seconds, $7.95.) Many patterns are available in seconds; if they don't have a bolt in stock they'll check the warehouse for you. If you're unsure how a print will look, leave a deposit, take a swatch back and see. They offer classes, and do custom work (bedspreads start at $99, upholstered headboards at $150). Sign the mailing list to be notified of sales, and don't forget your free yardstick.

Cutting Corners
7638 Clairemont Mesa, San Diego (619) 560-5831
Mon.-Sat., 9-5
Terms: MC, V, AE, Check.   Parking

Cutting Corners buys first quality mill ends and close-outs, passing savings along to you. There are rooms full of of beautiful upholstery and drapery fabric at discounted prices, and hundreds of fabrics to order, at a 30% discount. A large selection of lovely close-out fabrics and bolt ends were available at $10. Waverly prints began at $12.50. They also carry lace, drapery fittings, and you can take swatches home by leaving a deposit. I wandered around this store delighted by the beautiful things, and left with visions of massive reupholstering.

Decorative Fabric House **COUPON**
18085 Euclid St., Fountain Valley (714) 964-6030
Mon., 10-7; Tues.-Fri., 10:30-5; Sat., 10-5; Sun., 12-5
Terms: MC, V, D, Check. Parking

This store offers the largest selection of first quality decorative fabrics I've seen under one roof. There are the traditional Waverly prints (many at $13.95), and a large selection of imported drapery and upholstery fabrics, tapestries, velvets, more colors of moire than you can imagine, vintage type fabrics and antique linen prints, all at discount prices. Laces, 54" wide, begin at $5.95, and beautiful lace panels (53" x 93") were $20.95. They are very customer oriented here and pleasant to deal with; they will give you decorating advice, and they provide complete custom services, from bedspreads, drapes, upholstery and slipcovers to dustruffles, pillows, cornice boxes, pleated shades and window treatments. The annual parking lot sale is in June. ***The coupon entitles you to $10 off a purchase of $50 or more.***

Designer Fabric Showcase
10199 Hole Av., Riverside (714) 354-6684
Mon.-Thurs., 10-6; Fri., 10-4; Sun., 12-4
Terms: MC, V, Check. Parking

This shop is full of first quality decorator fabrics at highly competitive prices. I found Waverly prints beginning at $12.95, and a selection of drapery weaves at $2 a yard. There are a large number of sale racks, with discounts beginning at 50%, and a number of decorator prints and solids sold for $1, $2 and $3 a yard. Laces were on sale; prices began at $3.80. There are books of fabric swatches, which you can borrow for a deposit. They carry drapery fittings, and will custom-make draperies, cornice boxes and pillows.

Diamond Foam & Fabric
611 S. LaBrea Av., Los Angeles (213) 931-8148
Mon.-Fri., 9-5; Sat., 9-4
Terms: Cash and Check only. Street parking

This shop reminds me of an unfinished basement; low on ambiance, but crammed with interesting and unusual stuff, in this case, luxurious interior design fabrics, generally at prices 40% to 60% lower then elsewhere, and sometimes discounted even deeper. Fabric begins at about $10 a yard and can run as high as $90. I found a lot of European imports; unique prints and textures, from wild and bizarre to elegant and sophisticated. Unlike other fabric stores, Diamond doesn't arrange coordinated prints in the same rack; this is a place for people who know what they're looking for, and want something they're not likely to see anywhere else.

J. P. Discount Fabrics and Draperies
121 N. San Fernando Blvd., Burbank (818) 845-0862
Mon.-Sat., 9:30-5:30
Terms: MC, V, Check.   Street parking

Here the emphasis is on draperies; you can buy 106" polyester lace in an assortment of styles and shades at $16.98. They also sell fittings, and they custom-make drapes and blinds in six days. They make bedspreads and pillows, cornices, valances, swags, cascades, pleated and roller shades, vertical, mini and wooden blinds.

National Fabrics and Foam   **COUPON**
1368 N. Lake Av., Pasadena (818) 798-7337
Mon.-Sat., 9-5
Terms: MC, V, Check.   Street parking

Racks of fabrics fill this store, with aisles just big enough to browse comfortably. The inventory represents a nice variety of fabrics, and the prices are excellent. Waverly prints begin at $11.95, moire starts at $5.95 and brocades, weaves and canvas are all available. Every type of decorating fabric is in evidence, and they do custom upholstery, from boat and RV cushions to slipcovers: a chair with one loose cushion is $126; a sofa up to 8 feet with three loose cushions, $199; loveseat up to 60" with two loose cushions, $159 (fabric additional). There is also a foam room, where you can get your piece cut to size, and there are sometimes remnants for $1, $3.95 and $6.95 a yard. You can find quality fabric here for every budget. *The coupon entitles you to $5 off a purchase of $50 or more, excluding remnants.*

Off the Bolt
6812 DeSoto Av., Canoga Park (818) 999-0441
Mon.-Fri., 9-6; Sat., 10-5; Sun., 12-4
Terms: MC, V, Check.   Parking

Off the Bolt offers in-stock decorator fabrics for drapes, upholstery, slipcovers, bedspreads, and if you want, they'll custom make all those and more. Decorator fabrics here start at $5.95 a yard, including laces (45" wide), and there is a large selection of remnants beginning at $2.95.

We-R-Fabrics, Inc.
25782 Obrero Dr., Mission Viejo (714) 770-4662
Mon.-Wed., Fri., 9-6; Thurs., 9-7:30; Sat. 9-5
Terms: MC, V, Check.   *Parking*

We-R-Fabrics is an immense collection of first quality, discounted designer drapery and upholstery fabrics. Waverly prints start at $9, and there are bolts and bolts of cloth, arranged in coordinating prints and colors. Bargain shelves in back offer remnants of the same beautiful fabric, at $2.50 to $7.50. There is also a foam room, where they will cut to size. In May and November there are bolt end sales, and in February and August, $1 off sales.

Home Sewing Fabric and Notions

David Textiles
5959 Telegraph Av., City of Commerce (213) 728-3231
Mon.-Fri., 8:30-5:30; Sat.-Sun., 9-5:30
Terms: Cash only.   *Parking*

This small store behind Fabric Outlet is open to the public, and offers a large variety of fabrics at low prices. Calicos start at $2.49, rayon prints at $4.99, and remnants begin at $1.99. Leave your name to enter their annual free sewing machine drawing.

Fabric King
2270 W. Lincoln Av., Anaheim (714) 776-6200
Mon.-Sat., 9-6; Sun., 10-6
Terms: V, MC, Check. Returns.   *Parking*

Fabric King specializes in fabric and craft supplies. The front room offers craft supplies and a selection of how-to books at half price. In the warehouse-like back room is the fabric. Tables piled high offer cottons at $3.37 a yard, rayon challis at $5, lace at $1.69, and flannel at $2.69. A 6' string of maribou feathers is $7.98, in a variety of colors. (All feathers final sale.)

Fabric Lace Trims Factory Outlet
2123 S. Garey Av., Pomona (714) 465-0130
Tues.-Sun., 9:30-5:30
Terms: Cash and Check only. Final sale.   Parking

If you're looking for an orderly presentation of goods, don't come here. But if you like to pick your way through in hopes of a deal, this is a find. In stock are trims, appliques, fabric and notions, but set up without much rhyme or reason. You can find fabric by the yard if it's 45", by the pound if it's wider. There are bags of sequins (.75), sequin trim (starting at .15/yd.) lace trim and appliques (from .25). Upholstery fabric begins at $2.99 a pound and laces are $7.99 a pound, unless they're on bolts, in which case they're $2.99. And up.

Fabric Outlet
6001 Telegraph Av., City of Commerce (213) 728-1506
Mon.-Sat., 9-5:30
Terms: Cash. Final sale.   Parking

This warehouse is tremendous, and it's packed with yard goods, ribbon, notions, patterns, and a button box large enough to hide a small child. Drapery and upholstery fabrics start at $3.95, some cotton flannels were $1, cotton prints were $2.98 and calicos, $2.49. There are shelves of bargains here, and a number of tables where fabric was $1.

Fabric Warehouse
11612 W. Olympic Blvd., West Los Angeles (310) 477-7023
Mon.-Fri., 10-8; Sat., 10-6; Sun., 10-4
(also in Costa Mesa, Northridge, Valencia, and Torrance)
Terms: MC, V, AE, Check. Final sale.   Parking

There are lots of bargains at Fabric Warehouse, which sells both home decorating and personal sewing fabrics, as well as craft materials. I think the best buys are the clearance tables at the back of the store, full of odd pieces of cottons, woolens, knits and blends at $1.49/yd. Other clearance tables sell notions and lace remnants. Get on their mailing list to be informed of sales.

House of Fabrics Super Stores
1637 Lincoln Blvd., Santa Monica (310) 450-6441
Hours vary by location.
(12 additional locations; see Geographical Index)
Terms: MC, V, Check. Final sale.   Parking

These are not discount stores *per se*, but there always seems to be a sale going on, often featuring discounts of 50%. They carry fabric, notions, patterns, craft supplies of all kinds, and there is a large fabric clearance section in every store. The mailing list will notify you upcoming sales.

The Import Outlet
474 S. Arroyo Pkwy., Pasadena (818) 585-0506
Mon.-Sat., 10-6; Sun., 12-5
Terms: Cash and Check only. Final sale.   Street parking

This is not a traditional fabric store, in fact it's not a traditional any kind of store. You can buy clothes here, mainly women's but a few children's pieces, under $20. You can buy sets of china for $15, but in the back they sell fabric. Not a wide variety, but silks are $5.99/yd., cottons begin at $2, there are rayons and polyester knits at bargain prices, and there is an area of lovely remnants and unbeatable savings. You may not find everything you're looking for, but if you find something you want, you'll get it at a very good price.

Michael Levine, Inc.
920 S. Maple, Los Angeles (213) 622-6259
Mon-Fri., 9-5:30; Sat., 9-4:30
Terms: MC, V, Check. Final sale.   Street parking

This store is tremendous, it has everything you'll need from notions to patterns to every fabric you can imagine, and at a discount. One side of the store is a half price rack, but there are bargains all over, on everything from batik to swimwear fabric to fake fur to plain old cottons and wools, and many not so plain. There are tables where pieces of fabric, varying in length from one to several yards, are $1. There is fabric for every use, except home decorating; that's across the street at *917 S. Maple, Levine's Upholstery and Drapery Store*, where upholstery prints begin at $7, with a blow-out table at $2. Waverly prints were $12 a yard and poly laces were $5. There is a hocus pocus table, where astonishing bargains disappear before your very eyes.

Natural Fabric Company
10619 W. Pico Blvd., West Los Angeles (310) 475-1962
Mon.-Sat., 9:30-6
Terms: MC, V, AE, Check. Final sale.   Parking

This is a small shop packed with imported fashion fabrics, most of which are on sale. I found Liberty of London cottons at $12.98 (seen elsewhere for $18.98); a variety of silks at $6.99, designer wools, $19.99, and camel hair, originally $85, was $20. Rayons sold for $14 and $15, regularly selling for as much as $29, and Guatemalan striped cotton in a variety of colors and prints was $19.98. The stock is select, but there are some very beautiful things.

$2 Fabric Store
17013 Magnolia Av., Riverside (714) 785-5374
Mon.-Fri., 10-7; Sat., 11-6; Sun., 10-5
(also in Santa Ana, Bellflower, Lancaster, Rosemead, Rialto, San Bernardino, and Victorville)
Terms: Cash and Check only. Final sale.   Parking

In addition to rows and rows of fabric on bolts at discounts of about 50%, these stores carry a huge inventory of good-sized remnants beginning at $1.69 for cotton prints and interlock knits. Bolts feature cotton prints at $2.99, 45" muslin at $1.69, 60" laces are $2.99, and cotton upholstery fabric begins at $4.99. Broadcloth sold for $1.49 (45" width), calicos began at $1.99 and moire taffeta was $2.99. There is a half yard minimum purchase. There are notions, foam and pillow forms as well.

See also
> L. A. Trimmings and Beads
> La Petite Factorie

Discount Catalogs

Newark Dressmaker Supply
(215) 837-7500
Terms: V, MC, D. Returns.

This catalog is full of sewing and craft supplies at very reasonable prices. In addition to fabrics and notions you can find potpourri here for $2.75 a lb., silk roses at $1.20 a stem, craft ribbons, ribbon roses, wire edged ribbon at $2/yd. (1 1/2"), laces, bindings, quilting supplies, appliques and bridal crafts projects (including garlands, accessories and headpieces), doll crafts, drapery and upholstery tools, and craft books, all at great prices. There are additional discounts of 10% on orders of $50 or more, and free gifts on smaller orders.

Thai Silks
(800) 722-SILK
Terms: MC, V, AE, Check.

Thai Silks sends out several mailings a year with buys on imported silks. While prices are reasonable, they get even better in the close-out mailings, where you can save as much as 50% over everyday prices. For a small deposit they will send you samples, which include shantung, raw silk, charmeuse, peau de soie, sueded silk, pongee and others. Men's silk ties are $7.40.

Food

Baked Goods

Dolly Madison Cakes/Weber's Bakery Thrift Shops
74 locations; see Geographical Index or call (213) 849-1131
Hours vary by location.
Terms: Cash only.   Parking

Here Dolly Madison, Weber, Roman Meal, Millbrook, Springfield and Bell breads, rolls and snack foods are reduced for quick sale. Although some items are fast approaching their freshness dates, many have weeks to go and are overstocks, store returns or packages with cosmetic blemishes. Many items are marked down 50% or more. Dolly Madison snack cakes are 3/$1, Weber sandwich bread, .59, and breadsticks, $1.09. Stores also have bargain days, with an additional 10% discount. Seniors get a 10% discount daily.

Entenmann's/Orowheat Bakery Outlets
29 locations; see Geographical Index or call (213) 720-6000
Hours vary by location.
Terms: Cash only.   Parking

Selling here are Entenmann's cakes and cookies, Orowheat and Old Country breads and rolls, Boboli bread shells, and other bakery items. The stock is mainly store returns, packages not cosmetically up to snuff or incorrectly marked as to weight, and those whose freshness dates are near expiration. Entenmann's products were as much as 50% off, and other products were substantially discounted. A 10% senior citizens discount applies to all but manager's specials. On Bargain Days, Saturdays for breads, Wednesdays or Thursdays for cakes, most products are discounted 50%. Get there early on cake day; *it goes fast.*

Pioneer Bakery Retail Store
512 Rose Av., Venice (310) 392-4128
Mon.-Sat., 6:30-4
Terms: Cash only.   Street parking

Fresh, day old and store returns of Pioneer sour dough and other breads, rolls, croissants and baguettes are sold here at big savings. Twenty-four small rolls,

12 large rolls or 6 large flutes are available for $1.20 (two packages for $2), in all the varieties Pioneer makes. A sour dough loaf with olives and rosemary (yum), weighing over a pound, was .90; specialty breads like this can cost four or five times as much at a retail bakery. Store return packaged french rolls, $1.78 retail, sell here for half price. A one pound Italian sesame ring was .55 and croissants and muffins, available in the morning, range from .23 to .43.

Wonder-Hostess Thrift Bakeries
35 Locations; see Geographical Index
Hours vary by location.
Terms: Cash only.   *Parking*

These shops sell Wonder Bread and Hostess cakes store returns, often near their expiration dates. Hostess snack cakes sell for about half price; two loaves of Wonder Bread (1 1/2 lb.) are $1.17. There is an assortment of croutons, chips, breadsticks and crackers selling for a third to half off. Fill up your frequent buyer card and receive free cake or bread. (Fill it twice as fast by bringing your own bag.)

Health Foods and Vitamins

Co-opportunity Food Co-op
1530 Broadway, Santa Monica (310) 451-8502
Mon.-Sun., 9-9
Terms: Cash and Check only.   *Parking*

While not the traditional non-profit co-op, Co-opportunity offers organic, bulk, and other foods, and items found in health food stores, at prices about 5% lower. If you become a member ($100 one-time fee) you are entitled to another 5% off, and 10% off on cases of products.

Granny's Discount Natural Foods
560 S. Arroyo Pkwy., Pasadena (818) 796-8442
Mon-Fri., 9-7; Sat.-Sun., 9-6
Terms: Cash and Check only.   *Parking*

Granny's sells vitamin supplements, cosmetic sundries and health foods. Their supplements are generally discounted 20%; everything else is discounted a bit less. It's a small store, but well-stocked, with bulk, frozen and packaged foods, and hormone-free meats.

Health Food City
3645 E. Foothill Blvd., Pasadena (818) 351-8616
154-A Foothill Blvd., Monrovia (818) 303-8616
Mon.-Sat., 10-7; Sun., 10-5
Terms: MC, V ($10 min.), Check. Exchanges.   Parking

This huge health food store offers a tremendous selection of herbs, vitamins, teas and non-animal tested cosmetics, all discounted at least 10%. There is a fountain where you can get fresh smoothies.

Renee's Nutrition Center
150 S. Sepulveda Blvd., G, El Segundo (310) 615-1013
Mon.-Fri., 9-6:30; Sat., 9-5
Terms: MC, V, Check. Exchanges.   Parking

Renee's carries health foods, supplements, beauty products and homeopathic remedies, and most are discounted from 6% to 20%. Bi-weekly sales offer additional savings. The staff is friendly and knowledgeable, and will quote prices over the phone.

Venice-Ocean Park Food Co-op
839 Lincoln Blvd., Venice (213) 399-5623
Mon.-Sun., 9-9
Terms: Cash and Check only.   Parking

This small health food co-op offers one of Los Angeles' largest selections of organic produce, as well as bulk grains, nuts, pasta, flours, teas and herbs. They also carry packaged items, some sundries and cosmetics, books, baked goods, biodegradable detergents, some frozen foods, fresh deli items and juices (Juice your own wheat grass on the spot.), as well as low-sodium, non-dairy and vegetarian items, and organic coffees. Co-op members can earn discounts from 2% to 30%, but you don't have to be a member to shop here.

Produce

Farmers' Markets are a sure money-saver. Most members of the Southland Farmers Market Association are family owned farms. "By eliminating the middle man, these families are able to gain a foothold against today's hard times while you can expect an average savings of 20-30%." So says their schedule, and anyone who's shopped here will vouch for the savings. Available in some markets are flowers, baked goods, honey and olive oil. For more information, call the Association at (213) 749-9551.

Mondays
Bellflower, 10-2, Laurel & Bellflower
Colton, 10-2, Fleming Park, LaCadena & 7th
Southgate, 9-1, Southgate Park, corner of Tweedy and Walnut
West Hollywood, 9-2, 7377 Santa Monica Blvd. at Plummer Park

Tuesdays
Escondido, 4-8, Grand Av., between Bdwy. & Maple
Norwalk, 10-2, Alondra Blvd., w. of Pioneer, across from Excelsior High
Pasadena, 10-2, 363 E. Villa St.
Rialto, 5:30-8:30, Riverside Av., between Rialto and 1St.
Santa Barbara, 3-6:30 summer, 4-7:30 winter, 500 block of State St.
Torrance, 8-2, Charles H. Wilson Park, 2200 block of Crenshaw at Jefferson

Wednesdays
Escondido, 10-1, "North County CFM" Via Rancho Pkwy. & Sunset Dr.
Fullerton, 10:30-3:30, Woodcrest Park, 450 W. Orangethorpe at Richman
Los Angeles, 2-5, 1432 West Adams Blvd., St. Agnes Church
Riverside, 5-9, Downtown on 5th between Market & Orange
Santa Maria, 12-3, Target Lot, Miller St. & Betteravia Rd.
Santa Monica, 10-3, Arizona & 2 St.

Thursdays
Costa Mesa, 9-1, County Fairgrounds, 88 Fair Dr.
El Monte, 9-1, Valley Blvd. & Grenada
Mission Valley, 3-6:30, Corner of Friars & Frazee Rds.
Oxnard, 10-2, "Downtown Oxnard CFS" 7th & B Sts.
Palm Springs, 5:30-8:30, Palm Cyn. Dr. between Tahquitz Cyn. & Baristo Rd.
Pasadena, 3:30-6:30, City Hall, 100 N. Garfield
Redlands, 6-9, State St., Between Orange & 7th
Redondo Beach, End of Torrance Blvd. at Redondo Beach Pier
San Pedro, 10-2, 3 St., between Mesa & Centre
Temecula, 4-7, "Old Town"
Thousand Oaks, 5-8, Janss Mall at Wilbur Rd.
Torrance (May-Sept), 4-7, Charles H. Wilson Park, 2200 block Crenshaw at Jefferson
Upland, 5-9, 2 Av. Market between 9th & A Sts.

Fridays

Compton, 11-5, east side of Alameda at Compton
Hermosa Beach, 12-4:30, Intersection of 13th & Hermosa Av.
Highland Park, 9:30-1:30, Sycamore Grove Park,
   4600 block of N. Figueroa
Lompoc, 8:30-noon, Costa & Santa Barbara
Long Beach, 10-4, "The Promenade" between 3rd & Bdwy.
Monrovia, 3-6, Library Park at Myrtle & Lime
Riverside, 9-1, Sears lot, Arlington at Streeter
Venice, 7-11 a.m., corner of Pacific Av. & Venice Blvd.
Whittier, 9-1, 12000 block of Bailet St. Between Greenleaf
   & Comstock

Saturdays

Burbank, 8-2, 3rd St & Palm, public parking lot
Camarillo, 8:30-noon, 2220 Ventura Blvd.
Carlsbad, 1:30-4, 5600 Avineda Encinitas, San Diego
   Floral Ctr. lot
Carpinteria, 2-4, 400 block of Linden Av.
Del Mar, 1-4, City Hall lot, 10th & Caminao del Mar
Gardena, 6:30-noon, 13000 Van Ness Av., south of
   El Segundo Blvd.
Long Beach, 8-noon, Dolley's lot, Del Amo west of
   Long Beach Blvd.
Pasadena, 9-noon, Pasadena H.S., Paloma & Sierra Madre
Pomona, 7:30-11:30, Pearl at N. Garey
San Fernando Valley, 7-10 a.m. 14941 Devonshire,
   between Sepulveda and Woodman
San Marcos, 11-3, 1020 San Marcos Blvd.
Santa Barbara, 8:30-noon, Costa & Santa Barbara
Santa Monica, 9-noon, intersection of Arizona and 2 St.
Ventura, 8:30-noon, Santa Clara & Figueroa
Vista, 8-11, Escondido & Eucalyptus

Sundays

Alhambra, 9-1, Chico St. near Garfield and Main
Hollywood, 9-1, Ivar St. between Hollywood Blvd. and Selma
Ojai, 10-2, 236 W. Ojai Av., lot across from Carrows

Picking Your Own

Since so many fruits and veggies are grown here, many of us live a pleasant drive from fields of fresh produce. Some local farms offer pick your own deals, with savings over grocery store prices and adventure thrown in for free. Look on it as a fun-filled afternoon, or a way to gain empathy for farm labor.

Pine Canyon Cherry Farm
18645 Pine Cyn. Rd., Lake Hughes (805) 724-1135
Mon.-Sun., 8-5
Terms: Cash only.   Parking

Open in June, cherries this year are $1 a pound for red varieties, .80 per pound Royal Ann's and Goldens. Fruit is organically grown; bring containers.

Oak Glen Apples
Oak Glen (714) 797-6833

In September this village becomes the apple capital of Southern California, and it's not hard to reach on I-10, just about an hour east of downtown Los Angeles. The phone recording will give you directions from almost anywhere. Upon arrival, stop into a store and ask for The Oak Glen Guide, listing you-pick-em orchards and what they charge. (Either a flat fee for a ride to the orchard and all the apples you can carry back, or a per pound price.)

Prepared Foods and Groceries

Elwell Farms
2255 South Grand Av., Santa Ana (714) 546-9280
333 E. 17 St., Costa Mesa (714) 642-4311
Mon.-Fri., 9:30-5:30; Sat., 9:30-4:00
Terms: Cash and Check only.   Parking

This retail store offers a variety of prepared poultry dishes at prices far lower than frozen entrees at the market, lower still if you buy in cases. Eight ounce stuffed chicken legs (stuffed with rice and mushrooms, apple and almonds, or sage dressing) are $1.69. Chicken and beef kabobs are $1.25 (package of 10). Eight ounce stuffed chicken breasts are $2.19; boneless duck stuffed with wild rice dressing (22 oz.) is $2.99 and cornish game hens are six (10 oz.) pieces for

$14.19, or stuffed at $2.67 per (8 oz.) serving.

Golden West Meat Company
2012 Lincoln Blvd., Santa Monica (310) 392-4166
Mon.-Sat., 9-5:30
Terms: Cash only.   Parking

I pulled into this parking lot to look at a map, and began to notice a strange phenomenon. People entered this store, and every one of them came out with eggs. One carton, two, several. Golden West sells Jumbo California eggs for .99 a dozen everyday. They have a variety of meats, deli meats and sausages, and they are a full service butcher shop. Specials vary, but those eggs are always there.

LaBrea Circus
828 N. LaBrea Av., Hollywood (213) 466-7231
Mon.-Sat., 9-9; Sun., 9:30-8:30
Terms: MC, V, AE, D, Check.   Parking

This place deserves a visit as a curiosity if nothing else. From recliners to Gefilte Fish, they've got it, but not necessarily everything in between. Breads are a good buy at .89 a loaf, and there are canned goods from the sublime to the ridiculous; if you know your prices you'll spot a lot of bargains. They also have discount general merchandise, from gift wrap to books to china to linens.

Trader Joe's
610 S. Arroyo Pkwy., Pasadena (818) 568-9254
Daily, 9-9
(35 additional locations; see Geographical Index)
Terms: MC, V, AE, D, Check.   Parking

With rows of freezer cases, coffee starting at $2.99, their own line of baked goods and candy, Trader Joe's is a great place to stock up for the week. They offer their own salsa, guacamole and pesto sauce. (The latter sells for $2.19 (8 oz.), half of what you'd find it for elsewhere.) They sell standard dairy items cheaper than surrounding markets, but where they excell is in the things that pop up once and then are gone forever. A great Chardonnay for $2.99 (if you like it, buy a case before it's history), or frozen food close-outs from manufacturers who are changing their packaging, their name, their image, and need to dump perfectly good food fast. Cheeses are priced lower than elsewhere around town, as are their bread and cookies. Get on the mailing list for the monthly fearless flyer.

Van Rex Gourmet Foods, Inc.
5850 Washington Blvd., Culver City (213) 965-8094
Mon.-Fri., 10-6; Sat., 9-2
Terms: Cash and Check only.   Parking

Van Rex offers fine gourmet foods, some of which you will find nowhere else, at prices between wholesale and retail. On some items, a devoted shopper told me, they're a little cheaper then other places, on many, a lot cheaper, and they have the best caviar prices in town. In addition to the more mundane imported pasta and lavosh, Van Rex carries pastry shells, frogs legs, and all kinds of pate (including my kind, chocolate). Biscotti, selling in delis for $6.95 , is $5.75, and candy bars sold at Trader Joe's for .79 are .55 here. Product sizes go from institutional to individual. If you're a gourmet then I've just made your day; if you just have some few people over from time to time, stop in and pick up a few things: with very little effort your dinner will shine.

Candy and Nuts

Allen Wertz Candy
3070 Los Feliz Blvd., Los Feliz (213) 668-0123
Allen Wertz What's Popping
954 N. Amelia St., San Dimas (714) 592-4421
Hours vary by location.
Terms: MC,V($10 min.); Check ($5 min.).   Parking

Because this candy is made by people and not machines, sometimes pieces break, or are too big or small to fit their spots in the candy boxes, so they get sold as "misfits." One pound bags of chocolate, regular and sugar-free, selling for $10 a pound in the cases around you, sell for $3 because of their flaws. Broken pieces are also sold, priced individually. The temptation is to buy in volume: the prices, and the smells, are so good. Consider yourself warned, for all the good it may do.

Candy Factory Store
5051 Edison Av., Chino (714) 590-9777, Ext. 249
Mon.-Fri., 9:30-5
Terms: Cash and Check only.   Parking

This store features bagged, boxed and tinned chocolates and nuts; sugar-free candy, trail mix, fudge and hard candy, all at unbelievable prices. One pound bags of chocolate creams (a few pieces crushed, blemished or broken) were $2 (an $8 to $10 value). A 15 oz. bar of fudge was $2, and a three pound gift box of assorted chocolates was $7.50 ($30). A one pound box of chocolate mint truffles was $3 and a one pound bag of chocolate peanuts was $2. A gift pack of four (4 oz.) cans of roasted almonds was $2. Two-for-the-price-of-one inventory clearance sales are rare, but happen; lucky you if you hit one.

Christopher's Nut Company
15332 Calvert St., Van Nuys (818) 787-6303
Mon.-Fri., 7-5; Sat., 9-4
Terms: Cash only.   Street parking

You may be able to find some of the more mundane nuts cheaper, but for the rest, Christopher's offers nuts, seeds, dried fruits, trail mixes, spices, candies (including sugarless candy), glace fruit and dried fruit baskets and trays at reasonable prices. Smokd almonds are $3.15 (all prices are per pound), trail mix is $1.95, gummy bears are $2.50 and yogurt raisins are $2.30. Dried fruit in a 4 lb. basket is $19.95, in a 5 lb. wood tray, $24.75.

Helen Grace Chocolates
10690 Long Beach Blvd., Lynwood (213) 556-8345
Mon.-Sat., 10-5:30
Terms: MC, V, Check ($8.80 min.).   Parking

There are 10 other Helen Grace Chocolate shops in the chain, but this one is adjacent to the factory, and sells factory seconds. What's a chocolate second? Here they're pieces where the signature swirls indicating what's inside are

---
Chocolate "seconds" discounted 75%
---

indistinct, and some pieces that are crushed or broken, but still fresh, and tasty, and chocolate. The seconds come in two pound cellophane bags—you can see what you're getting even if you can't identify it—and sell for $3.95. "Perfect" candy here is $8.80 a pound, so you're saving over 75%. There are also sales after Valentine's Day, Easter and Christmas on specialty items, and if your school or non-profit organization is planning a fund-raising program, contact Helen Grace at (310) 638-8400 for candy bars at discounts of up to 45%.

Mr. MB's Wholesale Candy Outlet
22748 Ventura Blvd., Woodland Hills (818) 225-8506
Mon.-Sat. 9-5
Terms: Cash and Check only.   Parking

Mr. MB's offers a large selection of all kinds of candy, packaged in one pound bags, at prices 15% to 40% less than retail candy stores. Chocolate generally

ing elsewhere for $3.99 per pound were here at $2.99. There is also a nice variety of sugarless candy.

See also
> *Costco*
> *Fedco*
> *Pace Membership Warehouse*
> *The Price Club*
> *Smart & Final Iris*
> *99 Cents Only Stores*
> *The Lingerie Outlet (edible panties)*

Discount Catalogs

San Francisco Herb Company
(800) 622-0768
Terms: MC, V, Check, COD. Returns.

The brochure from San Francisco Herb company is a tremendous list of spice blends, herbs, dehydrated vegetables and potpourri ingredients sold by the pound, as well as fragrance oils, sprouting seeds, baking and food items, botanicals, shelled nuts, seeds and teas. Included are recipes for potpourri and sachet. Most everything listed is generally sold in much smaller volume at retail, but for at least twice the price. Compare with supermarket, even discount stores; you'll be amazed at the savings. Their minimum order is $30; orders of $200 or more are discounted an additional 10%; $500 or more, an additional 15%.

Furniture

Aaron Scott Warehouse Clearance Center
3232 Santa Monica Blvd., West Los Angeles (310) 829-4441
Mon.-Sat., 9:30-5:30; Sun., 12-5
Terms: MC, V, Check. Final sale.   *Street Parking*

Floor samples and discontinued lines of some of the finest contemporary makers of 18th century American, English and French furniture are discounted here. A Hardin solid cherry china cabinet was $2200 ($5159); a matching dining set—table, 6 chairs and leaves—was $2999 ($6136). A pine entertainment center by Lexington sold for $1099 ($2199) and Pennsylvania House oak Windsor chairs, once $445 were now $299. Their large clearance sales are held in June and December, and April is their anniversary sale. Get on the mailing list for first crack at the bargains.

Al's Furniture, Inc.
4900 Lankershim Blvd., North Hollywood (818) 766-4289
Mon.-Fri., 10-9; Sat.-Sun., 10-6
Terms: MC, V, AE, D, Check. Final sale.   *Parking*

This showroom is jumbled and crowded, but Al's guarantees the lowest prices anywhere: if you see it for less, they'll beat the price. They offer an impressive array of brand names, including Bassett, Broyhill, Stanley, Lexington, and Sealy Posturepedic, at discounts of 15% to 50%. If you see something you like elsewhere, call Al's for a price; they'll special order for you.

As Is Furniture
8585 W. Pico Blvd., Los Angeles (310) 652-1902
Thurs.-Sun., 12-5
Terms: MC, V, AE, Check. Final sale.   *Street Parking*

This is Horizon Furniture's Close-out Center, featuring a variety of discontinued, damaged and slightly soiled merchandise from this high quality furniture showroom. Most of the blemishes are correctable or not visible. The style here is modern-eclectic, and some of the pieces are unusual, most very attractive. A five piece lacquer queen bedroom set in was $999 ($2300). A lacquer armoire with wood grain lacquered doors (and a small damage inside) was $395 ($900).

Designer Bloopers
12600 Washington Blvd., Culver City   (310) 398-9396
Tues.-Sat., 10-6
Terms: MC, V, Check. Final sale.   Street parking

This space is packed with furniture, antique reproductions, lighting, rugs and art objects, all pieces designers ordered for clients, which the clients chose not to buy. These pieces are available here at prices just above the designer's cost, and while some are expensive, you'd be surprised at how inexpensive others are. Couches start at under $1,000 and some items are under $100. Stop in from time to time; stock is always changing.

Designers Clearance Center
325 N. Robertson Blvd., Los Angeles   (213) 652-9728
Mon.-Fri., 9-6; Sat., 9-4
Terms: MC, V, AE, Check. Returns.   Parking

This is the showroom for a manufacturer of custom-made, high end furniture, cabinetry and ironwork in the contemporary California style, and you can buy pieces off the floor at discounts of 10% to 80%. Available are samples, possibly decorator boo boos (e.g., the fabric turned out too light, or too dark, but for you it may be just right), and slightly soiled or damaged pieces. There are some beautiful things, and great buys. A sofa retailing for $4200 is $1500. Much of the furniture has a dramatic, one-of-a-kind look, and if the last film you saw was boring enough that you started admiring the scenery, these pieces may look familiar. Delivery is available.

Froch's Woodcraft Shop
7945 Van Nuys Blvd., Panorama City   (818) 787-3682
8659 Topanga Cyn., Canoga Park   (818) 883-4730
Mon.-Fri., 9-6; Sat., 9-5
Terms: MC, V. Final sale.   Parking

Froch's is an unfinished furniture shop, and they manufacture a good percentage of their stock, so much of the merchandise is factory direct. With the popularity of French country and Shaker styles, if you have any finishing ability (If *I* can do it....) you can have a pine country armoire from $493, or a queen pencil post bed of pine and maple for $710 ($40 additional for a canopy). Items with red dots are discontinued styles and have been further reduced. They also offer fifteen different styles of kitchen cabinets made entirely of wood. There is a mailing list for notice of upcoming sales.

Glabman's
**2250 S. Barrington Av., West Los Angeles
(310) 479-7383**
Mon.-Sat., 9:30-5:30; Sun., 12-5
(also in Costa Mesa, Torrance and Woodland Hills)
Terms: MC, V. Final sale.					Parking

Glabman's carries traditional furniture; walking into this store is like entering a decorator showroom. Glabman's doesn't advertise as a discount store, but they do have a guarantee: If you see any piece here displayed anywhere in Southern California at a cheaper price within 30 days, they'll match the price. Among the lines carried are Baker, Henredon, Karges, Karastan, Morris James, Kindel, and other fine furniture houses.

The Leather Factory
**11970 Wilshire Blvd., West Los Angeles
(310) 820-8477**
Daily, hours vary by location.
(also in Encino, Torrance, Tustin, Westminster, Corona, City of Industry, Pasadena, Fullerton, Thousand Oaks, La Mesa, and San Marcos)
Terms: MC, V, AE, D, Check. Final sale.	Parking

The emphasis here is on quality and service at a value price, which explains why this chain is expanding so rapidly. The Leather Factory manufactures sofas, convertibles, chairs, ottomans, loveseats and recliners, essentially to your specifications. There are 200 colors to chose from, a variety of grades of leather (all hides are treated with a stain resistant chemical during processing), 50 styles, from traditional to contemporary, and the style, color and grade of leather will determine your price. Couches begin at $699, and an average price is $999. If the piece is in stock you'll get almost immediate delivery, otherwise it will take three to six weeks. All furniture is produced locally, and they stand behind their product; if it starts to sag, squeak, or crack they'll send someone *out* to repair it. Every week selected styles are on sale.

Manufacturers' Clearance Warehouse
4601 S. Soto St., Los Angeles (213) 583-1836
Mon.-Sat., 10-4:30
Terms: V, MC, Check. Final sale.   Parking

This huge space is full of tables, chairs and barstools; buy one or mix and match to form a set. Formica tables start at $35 (30" round), oak at $80. A 48"x70" oak dining table with one leaf and a pedestal base was $399.95. Chairs begin at $40 and rarely go above $200. The industrial surroundings and accompanying low overhead probably account for discounts of 25% to 40%. Delivery is available in Los Angeles and Orange counties for $75.

Mark Friedman   **COUPON**
1437 4 St., Santa Monica (310) 393-2338
Mon.-Sat., 11-5; Wed.-Thurs. to 7
Terms: Cash and Check only. Final sale.   Parking

Mark Friedman calls itself a different kind of furniture store. While there is stock, including sofas, chairs, beds, lamps and tables, what's more impressive is what's *not here*, but you might have seen *elsewhere*. Mark Friedman can get you just about any current furniture piece, at a discount. And if you've found the chaise of your dreams but it's a hideous shade, you can custom order fabric from two walls of swatches. Ordering takes two to eight weeks, they require a one third deposit and once the piece comes in, pay the balance in cash and take it away, or pay by check, and wait a few days to pick it up. They are flexible, and will store merchandise for a brief period on layaway. A two piece living room set here was $1350, seen *on sale* at a better department store for $1950. They also sell AMLA approved encyclopedias at a fraction of their retail cost. ***Your coupon entitles you to a free lamp when buying a living room set for $975 or more.***

Plummer's
8876 Venice Blvd., Los Angeles (213) 837-0138
Mon.-Sat., 10-6; Sun., 11-5
(also in Pasadena, Santa Ana, Torrance, Mission Viejo, North Hollywood, and San Diego)
Terms: MC, V, Check. Final sale.   Parking

Plummer's is a chain specializing in contemporary furniture, and while not a discount store, all branches have Clearance Centers. (The Venice Blvd. location is their largest, and has the biggest Clearance Center.) Here you will find floor samples, specials and some "as is" goods at reduced prices. There are many deals to be had, but check pieces carefully. Wood bookcases, in a variety of sizes and finishes, are reduced 15% to 20%, and I found a lovely beige lacquer six drawer bureau reduced from $449 to $349. They carry couches, lamps, cabinets, dining sets, chairs and tables.

Rapport International Home Furnishings *COUPON*
435 N. La Brea, Los Angeles (213) 930-1500
Tues.-Sat., 9:30-5
Terms: MC, V, Check. Final sale.   Parking

Rapport has a selection of the most beautiful modern European furniture around. Prices are discounted 30% to 50%, many items are direct imports from Italy, and they have furniture for every room of the house, from upholstered pieces to birch and maple, marble and lacquer. A walnut sideboard with tray and side storage was $3000 ($6000); a lacquer four piece king bedroom set, platform, headboard and two end tables, was $2282 ($3800). There are less expensive pieces, queen sleepers begin around $500 and side chairs and tables are lower, but if you're a fan of Italian design, check this store out. The furniture is stunning, and you won't find it anywhere else. There are accessories and lamps as well. *The coupon entitles you to a free gift with your initial purchase.*

Sitting Pretty, Inc.
7115 Darby Av., Reseda (818) 881-3114
Mon.-Sat., 10-6; Sun., 12-5
Terms: MC, V, Check. Final sale.   Parking

Sitting Pretty has a huge selection of kitchen and dining sets, bars, stools, and a few hutches and bakers' racks. You can find a five piece set for as little as $349, as much as $2,000. Tables of wood, marble, glass, and wood and formica combinations (blended so skillfully you won't know where one ends and the other begins) are available, and you can mix and match tables and chairs. There are pieces in every decorating style and prices are competitive.

Woody's Unfinished Furniture
1817 E. Av. Q, Suite B7, Palmdale (805) 265-7410
1222 Commerce Ctr. Dr., Lancaster (805) 945-0551
Hours vary by location.
Terms: MC, V, AE, Check. Final sale.   Parking

Woody's does not sell its pine, alder and oak unfinished furniture at a discount, however unfinished furniture is cheaper then the finished variety, and Woody's will take you in back and show you what to do in order to successfully finish furniture. They'll show you how to stain; demonstrate stenciling and rag-rolling, and if you have a problem mid-project, they're there for phone support. They offer classes in furniture painting techniques, for a fee, and, if this is all making you anxious, some of the pieces are actually finished by the manufacturer. They offer quality brands, many with lifetime guarantees. Buying this kind of furniture is an easy way to match a new piece to the rest of your decor.

Rattan and Wicker

Los Feliz Rattan
428 Los Feliz Blvd., Glendale (818) 241-8893
Mon.-Sat., 12-6
Terms: MC, V, AE, Check. Final sale.   Street parking

Most items in this showroom are discounted 20% to 25%, and specials and floor samples go down from there. There is wicker and rattan for every room, as well as the patio. On a recent visit a wicker loveseat, coffee table and two side chairs was $199. A queen-size white wicker headboard was $140, a large white wicker rocker was $116. There were mirrors, dressers, dining and living room sets, bookcases and occasional tables, and a variety of fabrics for cushion upholstery.

Mastercraft Rattan & Wicker
21210 Hawthorne Blvd., Torrance (310) 316-6116
Mon.-Fri., 10-8; Sat., 10-7; Sun. 11-5
(also in Artesia, Gardena, El Toro, and Glendale)
Terms: MC, V, Check. Returns.   Parking

Mastercraft sells wicker furniture to wholesalers and other retailers, and has something to fit every budget, from high to low end. Here you can find discounts beginning at 20% on wicker and rattan, from small baskets to six piece furniture ensembles. They have chairs, sofas, tables, children's furniture, chests, lamps, hampers, and a large variety of cushion fabrics. A white wicker baby changing table was $99.99, a five piece dining set $399 and wicker wastebaskets were $5.99. They can do custom and special orders to your specifications. The Gardena store (580 W. 184 St.) is their warehouse clearance center.

Rattan Distribution Warehouse
8010 Wheatland Av., Unit I, Sun Valley (818) 504-0119
Tues.-Sun., 10-4
Terms: Cash and Check only. Final sale.   Parking

Rattan Distribution Warehouse is a direct importer of high quality rattan from the Philippines, and offers furniture for the living room and dining room, as well as bar stools and wall units. You can save as much as half here, and have your piece customized beyond the standard choice of fabrics for upholstery (they will use fabric you provide, if you choose), to actually choosing the *stain* for the rattan. Custom orders take two to three weeks, and they will deliver.

Seven Seas Rattan
2138 S. Sepulveda Blvd., West Los Angeles (310) 477-5995
Mon.-Sat., 10-6; Sun., 12-5
Terms: MC, V, Check   Parking

Seven Seas carries rattan and wicker furniture manufactured by such names as Venture, Lexington, Lang and others, at discounts starting at 25%. There is furniture for every room, from wicker chests and side tables to rattan entertainment centers, to matching sofa and loveseat combinations.

See also
Pier One Imports Clearance Center

Baby Furniture

Babyland
7134 Topanga Cyn. Blvd., Canoga Park (818) 704-7848
1782 S. La Cienega Blvd., Los Angeles (213) 836-2222
Mon.-Sat.,10-7; Sun., 12-5
Terms: MC, V, AE. Returns.   Parking

Babyland concentrates on furniture for babies and kids. A nice selection of cribs, beds, high chairs and rockers is featured, as well as pieces for older kids, with custom color accents. Discounts range from 25% to 50%.

Baby Toytown
18719 Sherman Way, Reseda (818) 881-4441
Mon.-Fri., 10-7; Sat. 10-6; Sun. 12-5
(also in City of Industry, Cerritos, Rosemead, and Upland)
Terms: MC, V, D, Check. Returns.   Parking

This store features everything for baby: cribs, playpens, strollers, high chairs, swings, and car seats, all by top manufacturers, as well as linens, diaper bags, lamps, and some young children's furniture, at prices discounted to 25%. Occasional sales and floor model clearances reduce prices further.

Carousel Baby Furniture   COUPON
1726 E. Colorado Blvd., Pasadena   (818) 792-8668
Mon.-Thurs., Sat., 9:30-6; Fri., 9:30-9:30
Terms: MC, V, Check. L. Returns.   Parking

In business for 35 years, Carousel sells everything for baby at everyday savings of 10% to 30%; specials send prices even lower. In addition to cribs, bureaus and changing tables there are folding cribs, rocking chairs, playpens, car seats, strollers, high chairs, bedding and baby clothes. There are generally some floor samples and discontinued styles of one thing or another on sale at any given time: a selection of dust ruffles and matching bumpers was on close-out on my last visit, selling for half price. There is a wide variety of merchandise in every category, and something at every price range. They have a baby shower registry and a monthly drawing in their expectant mother contest. *The coupon entitles you to $3 off your next purchase, or $10 off a purchase of $50 or more.*

Nationwide Baby Shops
1911 Lincoln Blvd., Santa Monica   (310) 452-3805
Mon.-Sat., 10-6
(also in Torrance (310) 370-6201, and West Los Angeles (310) 204-4404)
Terms: MC, V, Check. Returns.   Parking

Nationwide offers everything for baby, and many things are at substantial savings. Furniture discounts range from 15% to 35%, and there are mobiles, strollers, baby joggers, lamps, slings, bathtubs, and bedding. Most everything is somewhat marked down, but on the special sales savings can be impressive.

Sid's Discount Baby Furniture   COUPON
8338 Lincoln Blvd., Westchester   (310) 397-3903
7522 Sunset Blvd., West Hollywood   (213) 874-1787
Mon.-Thurs., Sat., 10-6; Fri., 10-7:30
Terms: MC, V, Check. Returns.   Parking

Sid's guarantees that if you find anything cheaper within 10 days of purchase, and you can document it, they'll match the price. They carry cribs, bureaus and changing tables by Simmons, Combi, Newborne, Kidsline, Baby Jogger, Graco, and Childcraft, at discounts of 10% to 20%. They also have lamps, mobiles, playpens, high chairs, crib sets, baby clothes and bottles, everything you'll need. (You supply baby.) *The coupon entitles you to your choice of either 10% off on a crib, carseat or stroller; or 15% off on a five piece baby bedding set; or $30 off any bunk bed, twinbed or race car bed (offer good on* *regular priced merchandise only).*

See also
> The Stork Shop
> Le Baby Originals
> Adray's
> Bergstrom's
> Daphna's

Beds

Americana Brass Bed Factory
6840 Vineland Av., North Hollywood (818) 985-8556
Mon.-Fri., 8-4:30; call for Saturday appt.
Terms: Cash and Check only. Final sale.   Parking

As the name implies, they make brass beds here, mainly daybeds but some head-and-footboard combinations too. A daybed without ornamentation was $89, (including link spring, two arms and back, which fits a standard twin mattress); more ornate models go to $269. Add $79 for a trundle mechanism and $69 for a canopy. A beautiful queensize headboard and footboard in an art deco style brass with white or black iron was $449 queen, $549 king. These prices reflect a 20% to 25% savings over buying through a furniture dealer.

Brass Beds Unlimited   **COUPON**
21505 Sherman Way, Canoga Park (818) 702-9999
Mon.-Sat., 10-6
Terms: MC, V, Check. Final sale.   Street parking

Brass Beds Unlimited has a large variety of brass beds, Springair and Serta mattresses, daybeds, and adjustable beds at discount prices. Everything is first quality, and styles go from plain to ornate. A white metal daybed can be purchased for $89; add two mattresses and a daybed cover and you have a trundle bed for $279. There are several floor sample brass and iron head and footboard sets, beginning at $399, and there are replicas of antique beds, with your choice of 23 colors and textures for the finish. *The coupon entitles you to a discount equivalent in value to the sales tax on your purchase.*

Electropedic Adjustable Beds
15600 Roscoe Blvd., Van Nuys (818) 847-7688
Mon.-Sat., 10-4; Sun., 12-4
(also in Burbank, Garden Grove, and Montclair)
Terms: MC, V, Check. Final sale.   Parking

If those late night commercials have you convinced you want your feet higher than your head, call these folks first. Electropedic is one of three manufacturers of adjustable beds, and selling direct to you they cut out the middleman, bringing your price down. There are three basic grades of bed and mattress, and they offer a discount for AARP members. They will deliver, at additional cost, set up the bed, and remove your old one.

Mattress Warehouse
4825 W. Rosecrans Av., Hawthorne (310) 675-5400
Mon.-Fri., 10-6; Sat.-Sun., 10-5
Terms: V, MC, D, Check. Final sale.   Parking

Beautyrest and Sealy Posturpedic mattresses are available here, at prices about 40% lower than department stores, but special buys, like when mattress cover fabrics are discontinued, or when styles change, send prices even lower. One such set, an Extra firm Beautyrest top of the line model, was being closed-out at $499 (queen). All beds come with frames; and if you already have a frame they'll give you a mattress pad. Prices include delivery, set-up, and removal of your old bed. If the item is in stock you can have it the next day.

Sit 'n Sleep   (COUPON)
3824 Culver Center, Culver City (310) 842-6859
Mon.-Fri., 10-8; Sat., 10-6; Sun., 11-5
Terms: MC, V, AE, D, Check. Exchanges.   Parking

Sit 'n Sleep offers Sealy, Serta and Simmons mattresses with a 30 day price guarantee; if you see your mattress advertised for less, they'll meet the lower price. The mattresses also come with a "30 nite sleep guarantee;" if you don't like it, exchange it for something else. The showroom has about 65 mattress sets, and if you've seen a bed elsewhere, call Sit 'n Sleep for a price. In fact, you need never come in, just place your order over the phone. Every month something else is on special, and their four major sales are on Washington's Birthday, Memorial Day, July 4th and Labor Day. Delivery charges are routinely 5% of invoice or $20 and delivery is promised within four hours. They'll also remove your old mattress. They carry a few platform and sofa beds, and a large selection of bunk beds and futons, all at discount prices. *The coupon entitles you to a sleep package valued at $180, including free local delivery, a bed frame, mattress pad, pair of pillows, as well as set up of your* new bed and removal of the old one, with purchase of a Sealy, Simmons or Serta premium mattress set.

W. J. Simmons Mattress Factory
11030 Artesia Blvd., Cerritos (310) 865-0294
Mon.-Fri., 10-7:30; Sat., 9-6; Sun., 11-5
(24 additional locations; see Geographical Index or call (800) 894-8233)
Terms: MC, V, D, Check. Final sale.   Parking

This chain sells Simmons mattresses, adjustables beds, day beds, trundle beds, brass, iron and wood beds, but the biggest savings are on the mattresses. You can save up to 40% off the retail prices of many Simmons mattresses, most of which come with a warranty. They will deliver your mattress within 2 days and take away your old one.

Discount Catalogs

Dial-A-Mattress
(800) MATTRESS
Terms: MC, V, AE, D. Final sale.

Fed up with your mattress in the middle of the night? Who you gonna call? These people are the only ones awake. They sell Sealy, Simmons or Serta mattress at discounts up to 60%, and delivery time is within one day. They'll set-up your new mattress (providing you with a heavy-duty frame), take away the old one, and have you sleeping like a baby again. Which means you'll only miss one night's sleep. (Providing someone's car alarm doesn't go off.)

Decorating Services

L.A. Design Concepts
8811 Alden Dr., Los Angeles (310) 276-2109
Mon.-Fri., 9-5. Call for appt.
Terms: MC, V, Check.   Street parking

If you want to buy at the Pacific Design Center and you're neither a designer, nor have a designer, L. A. Design Concepts may be of help. For a $20 hourly fee they will take you through the showrooms, and purchase for you, charging only an additional 20% over the wholesale cost of your purchases, less than most decorators.

Used Furniture

Budget Rents Clearance Center   CCC
6051 Telegraph Av., City of Commerce (213) 720-5020
11320 Santa Monica Blvd., West Los Angeles (310) 477-6742
Mon.-Fri., 9-5:30; Sat.-Sun., 10-4
Terms: MC, V, Check. Final sale.   Parking

Budget Rents Clearance Center sells previously rented beige, tan, grey, and blue upholstered furniture. Most fabric needs a good cleaning but seems in passable shape. Sofas began at $69, a five piece dinette set was available for $49.98, chairs were as low as $20 and wood veneer end tables were $25. Televisions were $79.99 and there were office desks from $179.99. They have payment plans.

Cort Furniture Clearance Center   CCC
5345 San Fernando Rd., Glendale (818) 244-0100
10700 Spencer St., Fountain Valley (714) 965-0500
Mon.-Fri., 9-6
Terms: MC, AE, V, Check. Final sale.   Parking

Here the selection is generally in need of a cleaning, but there are some values to be found. A fabric sofa, three cushions wide, sold for $99, a black leather three cushion sofa was $599, a matching loveseat, $499. A wrought iron and glass coffee table was $299 ($399), and a more traditional cherry stained oval coffee table was $199 ($399). There were about a dozen sofa and loveseat sets, but the inventory expands greatly during parking lot sales, held bi-monthly. Get on the mailing list to be informed of these, when the furniture Cort has rented to model homes and television and film productions comes back; most of it barely used. There are also sales around national holidays.

Leisure World Consignment Shop
23595 Moulton Pkwy., Laguna Hills (714) 770-7626
Mon.-Sat. 10-4:30
Terms: MC, V ($50 min.), Check. Final sale.   Parking

Available here are rooms full of just about anything that goes in a living room or dining room, including furniture, lamps, art, bric a brac, giftware (like Lalique, Steuben Glass and Waterford), flatware and tea services (both plate and sterling), china (ordinary and not so), and a little of everything else. The longer an item sits, the lower the price.

Outdoor Furniture

Berks
2520 Santa Monica Blvd., Santa Monica (310) 828-7447
Mon.-Sat., 9-6; Sun., 10-5
Terms: MC, V, Check. Exchanges.   Parking

COUPON

Berks carries outdoor furniture by Tricomfort, Grossflex, Samsonite and Brown Jordan, among others, in wood, wicker, wrought iron, aluminum and resin, at discounts of 20% to 40%. A Brown Jordan 48" table with four plastic webbed chairs was $699 ($1185), and a wicker chaise with upholstered cushion was $1089 ($1400). Periodic sales send prices lower. The largest sale is at the end of September, when they clear out floor samples, but you're likely to find red-tagged items all year long, as styles are discontinued, or when a special purchase has been made. There is free delivery, if you buy something in the morning you can usually have it by the afternoon. If you want to change your color scheme, they refurbish Brown Jordan furniture. *Present your coupon for a free gift with your next purchase.*

Daphna's Furniture, Inc.
2512 Santa Monica Blvd., Santa Monica (310) 453-0026
Mon.-Sat. 10-6; Sun., 10-5
(also in Encino (818) 986-1070, and Northridge (818) 886-7653)
Terms: MC, V, AE, Check. Final sale.   Parking

Daphna's sells a large variety of patio furniture. Their everyday price is generally discounted 30%, but with sales that can go as low as 70%. They

---

They sell furniture for less than other stores buy it wholesale

---

carry Winston, Meadowcraft, Kettler, and Woodard, in cast aluminum made to look like wrought iron, as well as resin and actual wrought iron. A 49" table with four swivel rockers, including cushions, was $900 ($2347). Daphna's is also a direct importer of furniture; some of their furniture comes from the same manufacturers whose products other brand names sell under their own labels, so Daphna's can *retail furniture for less than other stores can buy it wholesale*. A popular cast aluminum set—four chairs and glass-topped table—was $1400. At other stores it sells for up to $4,000. Delivery is within 24 hours. Accessories, plastic table and glassware, placemats and covers, are discounted year-round. The major sale is from November to January, and they will often have sales in summer, around Labor Day and Memorial Day. Some locations carry baby furniture and accessories, also discounted.

The Patio Place
1450 El Camino Real, Tustin (714) 731-8206
Mon.-Sat., 10-6 (closed Wed.)
(also in Santa Ana (714) 569-9242, and Palm Desert (619) 346-7272)
Terms: MC, V, AE, D, Check.   Parking

If you're looking for a good deal on resin patio furniture, look no further. The Patio Place manufactures it, and sells directly. Plastic strap chaises range from $99 to $139, with your choice of colors and four frame finishes. A five piece dining set, 36" round table and four chairs (strap or cushion seating) is $499. A five piece set featuring a 48" round table, and choice of cushion or strap seating is $599. A cast aluminium five piece set, with a wrought iron look, is $599. There are color and fabric choices to fit any taste, and if you want to change your color combination, you can replace the straps yourself. Sales are likely in September, on discontinued styles. They also sell fountains.

Barbeques and Fireplaces

Armand's Discount
9400 Venice Blvd., Culver City (310) 839-5555
Mon.-Fri., 9-5; Sat., 9-5
Terms: MC, V, AE, D, Check. Exchanges.   Street parking

At Armand's you will find PGS, Ducane, Weber, Charmglow, Arkla and other barbeques sold at discounts beginning at 10%. Periodic close-outs send prices even lower. Armand's also services barbeques, sell replacement parts, and in many instances they will assemble and deliver your grill for free.

Barbeques Galore
18922 Ventura Blvd., Tarzana (818) 345-7314
Mon.-Sat., 9:30-5:30; Sun., 11-5
(also in Costa Mesa, Riverside, Sante Fe Springs, Torrance, Escondido, San Diego and Upland)
Terms: MC, V, Check. Returns.   Parking

Here you'll find discounts from 10% to 35% on gas, liquid propane and charcoal grills. Barbeques Galore also carries a full range of barbequeing accessories, some on sale, and chips flavored with cherry, apple, hickory, and mesquite—even chips made from Jack Daniels barrels—grilling herbs and books on barbequeing.

Beverly Fireplace Shop
7533 Sunset Blvd., Hollywood (213) 874-7664
Mon.-Sat., 9-7; Sun., 10-3
Terms: MC, V, AE, Check. Final sale.   Street parking

This shop features CharBroil, Broilmaster, Ducane and Weber Barbeques at discounted prices. They also offer andirons and fireplace screens by Sunset and Pilgrim and fireplaces by Heatelitor and Marco. Fireplace screens begin at $100 and andiron sets start at $79.99.

See also
The Fan Man/The Fireplace Man
Olde Tyme Ceiling Fan Co.

Office Furniture

A.B.E. Office Furniture
3400 N. Peck Rd., ElMonte (818) 443-4223
Mon.-Fri., 8-6; Sat., 9-6
Terms: MC, V, Check. Final sale.   Parking

Here's an example of all those cliches about one person's loss being another's gain: all the recent business and bank failures benefit someone somehow; here's how they can benefit you. At A.B.E. you can buy first quality office furniture, often for a fraction of the price, because, though they do carry some

---

They pay ten to twenty cents on the dollar for office furniture, so your cost is under half the original price

---

new furniture, most of what you'll see here are used pieces, bought at ten to twenty cents on the dollar (remember those business failures?) so your cost ends up lower than half the original price for some gently used, top quality furniture. A John Widdicomb 36"x72" executive desk with a burlwood finish, $9000 new, was $3000. Wooden bookcases sold from $39.95 and steno chairs began at $49.95. There are oak stained desks with returns at $995, and upstairs are file cabinets, in not exactly pristine condition (four drawers start at $50, two drawer laterals, $150), computer work stations, and less well cared for desks and chairs. There are credenzas, tables, and tons of chairs. A.B.E. also handles copiers, time clocks, calculators and other business machines, some with warranties. Maybe you'll have better luck than the previous owners.

Cut-Rate Office Furniture
1627 S. San Pedro St., Los Angeles (213) 748-2326
Mon.-Fri., 8:30-6; Sat., 8:30-5
Terms: MC, V. Final sale.   Parking

Cut-Rate sells office furniture at a variety of pricepoints. The most cut-rate are in the Repo Center across from the main store, where metal desks begin at $29, four drawer metal file cabinets start at $40. Even a few glitzy pieces, like a dark cherry modern executive desk, was half price at $2589. In the main store the better bargain furniture is upstairs. Four drawer oak filing cabinets are $269 ($369), two drawer, $149 ($229). You can find just about anything your office might need, from folding chairs and lunchroom tables to computer and printer stands, room dividers, and every kind of seating and desk, modest metal to marble. Check out all the nooks and crannies; this is the kind of place where you don't know what's around the next corner.

Discount Desk Center
21035 Sherman Way, Canoga Park (818) 883-2112
6335 San Fernando Blvd., Burbank (818) 562-1040
Mon.-Fri., 9-6; Sat., 10-5
Terms: V, MC, Check.   Parking

You can get everything here from desks and modular office cubicles to a lone printer stand. Most of the furniture seems to be particle board, but there is a selection of wood. An oak roll top desk, 54" wide, retailing at $1854, was here for $1100; a mahogany executive desk was reduced to $1100 from $1770. There are chairs, file cabinets, sofas, everything your office needs.

See also
Staples
The Office Depot

Giftware

Arte D'Italia *COUPON*
109 S. Quarantina, Santa Barbara (805) 564-7655
Mon.-Wed., Fri., 9-12
Terms: MC, V, Check. Exchanges.   Parking

Arte D'Italia distributes Parucca majolica ceramics, made in Palermo. The pieces are one-of-a-kind, brightly colored and very appealing. While not inexpensive, you can find platters, serving dishes, bowls, centerpieces and vases here at 30% below retail prices. Seconds can be purchased at discounts of 50%, sometimes greater. Prices range from $5 to $300, but many pieces are in the $40 range. Hours are flexible; it's best to call before you come. ***The coupon entitles you to an additional 10% off your next purchase.***

Champagne Taste *COUPON*
4352 S. Sepulveda Blvd., Culver City (310) 572-6037
The 2nds Shop
1977 S. Sepulveda Blvd., West Los Angeles (310) 477-7229
Mon.-Sat., 10-5
Terms: MC, V, D, Check. Exchanges.   Parking

These two shops sell an eclectic mix of high quality manufacturers' samples, including ceramics, stoneware, planters, giftware, glass, pottery, baskets, stationary, picture frames and prints, in styles ranging from Southwest to Country, and discounts of 20% to 70%. Candles, giftwrap and party goods are also discounted. The 2nds Shop is larger, its collection of baskets and garden pottery is bigger, but check both for one-of-a-kind items at great prices. There is a mailing list for notice of periodic sales. In July The 2nds Shop holds a Parking Lot sale, where prices can be reduced another third. ***The coupon entitles you to an additional 20% discount off one purchase at either store.***

The Crafters Outlet
6445 DeSoto Av., Woodland Hills (818) 347-2900
and
Crafters City
19401 Parthenia, Northridge (818) 727-7733
Mon.-Sat., 10-7; Sun., 11-5
Terms: MC, V, Check. Final sale.   Parking

While these two stores aren't related, they carry the same type of merchandise, so if you like things home-made, be prepared to spend some time at one or both. It's a good concept: a large open space divided by aisles, where craftspeople show their wares in big and little boothes. You'll find baskets, dolls, country art, wreathes, bears, jewelry, hair accessories, painted shirts, clocks, just about anything you'd find at a craft fair, but now you don't have to wait for the fair (or worry about parking). Prices are essentially manufacturer direct. If you find pieces in here that are your style, you're going to save over gift shop prices.

Eurogift
848 N. LaCienega Blvd., #201, Los Angeles (310) 652-8850
Terms: MC, V, Check. Final sale.   Street parking

Eurogift is only open six times a year, at which time they have sales on Lalique, Baccarat and Dome crystal, Henckel knives, Mont Blanc pens, and assorted giftware, at discounts ranging from 30% to 50%. They can special order crystal at a 20% discount, with four to six week delivery. Get on their mailing list for notification of sale dates.

The Glass Garage
418 N. Robertson, Los Angeles (310) 659-5228
Mon.-Sat., 10:30-6:30
Terms: MC, V, Check. Exchanges.   Street parking

The Glass Garage sells glassware and terra cotta outdoor pots to decorators, but they also sell to the public. Discounts on terra cotta are available with a $200 minimum purchase, but there's no minimum on glassware. You won't find brand names here, but you *will* find a lot of beautiful things. The owners look for buys in high end crystal from around the world, and pass savings on to you. Discounts are generally in the 20% to 50% range, but can go deeper. They carry vases, picture frames, giftware, bar and stemware, and serving pieces, and have added a large candle section. They also sell silk and dried flowers: purchase flowers and a vase and their floral arranger will make you decorator arrangement, free of charge. Their big sale is right after Christmas.

Pier One Imports　　　　　　　　　　　　　　CCC
5711 Hollywood Blvd., Hollywood (213) 463-8854
Mon.-Fri., 10-9; Sat.-Sun., 10-7
Terms: MC, V, Check. Final sale.　　Parking

You know Pier One carries baskets, giftware and rattan furniture, but this store is special. Here they let you walk *through* the stockroom to the clearance center, where all Pier Ones send their sale merchandise to clear. Baskets are reduced, generally by another third, and there are good buys on rattan and wicker furniture, as well as serving pieces, placemats, pillows, rugs and gift wrap. Wicker furniture, depending on its condition, was reduced by at least a third, frequently more: a curved-back love seat, marked "as is" but without noticeable damage, was $64.98 ($200), a matching side table was $51.98 ($80).

The Pottery Barn Clearance Store　　　　　　CCC
Fashion Valley Mall, San Diego (619) 296-8014
Mon.-Fri., 10-9; Sat., 10-7; Sun., 11-5
Terms: MC, V, AE, D, Check. Exchanges.　　Parking

While this is a retail outlet for The Pottery Barn chain, the back of the store is the final clearance location for Southern California stores, and additional markdowns are taken. You'll find linen (a wall of placemats and coordinating napkins, from silks to woven cottons, selling at half price, $2 to $5), glassware (large emerald and sapphire bowls, nappies, and vases reduced 33%); and whimsical ceramics (Italian "plum" pitchers at half price). There was a smattering of candlesticks, chargers, Italian country china, mugs, a little of everything. Reductions were generally a third to half off.

Santa Barbara Ceramic Design Studio Outlet Stores
428 E. Haley St., Santa Barbara (805) 966-3883　　**COUPON**
1691 Copenhagen Dr., Solvang (805) 686-5770
Mon.-Sat., 9:30-5:30; Sun., 11-5
Terms: MC, V, Check. Final sale.　　Street parking

The Santa Barbara Ceramic Design Studio creates ceramic clocks, picture frames, mirror frames, address tiles, vases, platters and trivets, generally selling in better department stores and upscale catalogs. Here you can purchase the same goods, sometimes with all but imperceptible flaws, at prices ranging from 30% to 75% below retail. Clocks with ceramic faces, offered in catalogs at up to $80, are here for $27.50. Ceramic trivets are $16 and $9.50, and ceramic picture frames range in price from $12.50 to $16.75, a saving of about 50%. Fiori Ware, brightly decorated ceramic pieces which are dishwasher, microwave and ovenproof, were available in several wild patterns. A large pitcher was $44; a serving bowl, $62; a platter, $47; about half price. There is also a "Good Deal" rack, where items are further reduced. *The coupon entitles you to 10% off any purchase of Santa Barbara Ceramic Studio ceramics.*

Tuesday Morning
1005 S. Glendora, West Covina (818) 962-5177
Mon.-Sat., 9:30-6 (Thurs. to 9); Sun., 12-6 (6 months/yr)
(also in Rolling Hills, Montclair, Irvine, Huntington Beach, Mission Viejo, Cathedral City and Anaheim)
Terms: MC, V, Check. Returns.   Parking

You never know what's going to show up at Tuesday Morning. This is a liquidator of first quality famous maker close-outs, sold at no less than 50% off, often up to 80%. There's giftware: picture frames in all styles (an 8x10 brass frame was reduced from $40 to $11.99, a ceramic 5x7 reduced from $10 to $2.99), crystal, ceramics, candles, stationary; generally an assortment of party goods. Linens are a good bet, often by the best of designers (a Laura Ashley queen sheet set was $39.99, half price). Baskets, sachets and scented drawer liners make this a great spot to go with your holiday gift list. This store is never the same twice; it's the kind of place that a bargain hunter will visit periodically, just to make sure she hasn't missed anything. There is a mailing list to let you know when they're open. (They call these "sales events"; there are six of them annually. They open for two months, then they're closed for a month, open again for six weeks, close for six weeks.) If you're not on the mailing list, call before coming; they may be on vacation.

Discount Catalogs

Tuesday Morning Close-Out Gift Catalog
(800) 999-7061
Terms: MC, V, D. Returns.

In case you can't come to Tuesday Mornings, an abbreviated version can come to you. Offered are a selection of linens, gifts, home furnishings, crystal and tabletop items, kitchenware, luggage, toys and accessories for children, at discounts ranging from 30% to 80%. The catalog also lists when their "Sales events" are, i.e., when local retail stores are open.

Hobbies

Discount Train Warehouse
777 W. Imperial Hwy., Brea (714) 255-0185
Mon.-Fri., 11:30-7:30; Sat., 11-5; Sun., 12-4
Terms: MC, V, AE, Check. Exchanges.　　　　Parking

There are many ways to save at Discount Train Warehouse, which carries everything for the model train enthusiast. Varying sale specials reduce some items as much as 50%; there's a sale table in the back; and they've got an incentive called Bonus Bucks. For each purchase you get Bucks, and when you've accumulated $100 worth, you get $15 in store credit. Bonus Bucks are no good on Wednesdays, because that's the day that mail order pricing is offered in the store, and prices on most things go down. Get on the mailing list for information on their model train swap meets, held twice a year.

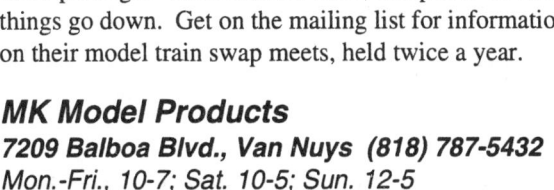

MK Model Products
7209 Balboa Blvd., Van Nuys (818) 787-5432
Mon.-Fri., 10-7; Sat. 10-5; Sun. 12-5
Terms: MC, V, AE, D, Check. Final sale.　　　Parking

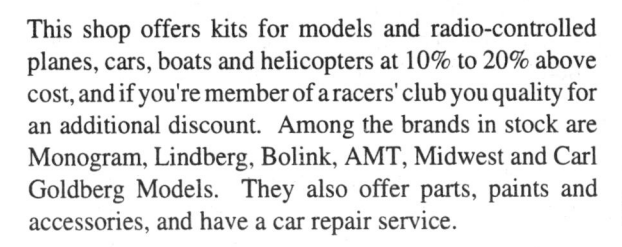

This shop offers kits for models and radio-controlled planes, cars, boats and helicopters at 10% to 20% above cost, and if you're member of a racers' club you quality for an additional discount. Among the brands in stock are Monogram, Lindberg, Bolink, AMT, Midwest and Carl Goldberg Models. They also offer parts, paints and accessories, and have a car repair service.

The Train Shack, Inc.
1030 N. Hollywood Way, Burbank (818) 842-3330
Mon.-Fri., 10-7; Sat., 9:30-6; Sun. 11-5
Terms: MC, V, AE, Check. Exchanges.   Parking

This shop features Brio, Lionel, and L.G.B. trains and cars, and all kinds of accessories to make model railroading a seemingly viable alternative to reality. The prices here are 10% to 25% below manufacturers' suggested list (books are not discounted); with occasional sales and promotions, discounts go even deeper.

Discount Catalogs

Direct Safety Company
(800) 528-7405
Terms: MC, V, Check. Returns.

Direct Safety offers products hobbyists can use to avoid dire consequences while pursuing leisure-time enjoyment. Here you will find masks, air filtration systems, goggles of varying kinds and other protective gear, very competitively priced.

Orion Telescope Center
(800) 443-1001
Terms: MC, V, Check. Returns.

The Orion catalog is full of telescopes, from simple to computer controlled, as well as binoculars, eyepieces, spotting scopes, mounts, tripods, filters, accessories for astrophotography and astronomy books, software and videos, many discounted as much as 50%. The Preferred Customer Sale page offers prices reduced to an additional 20%. There is also information on how to choose the telescope that best fits your needs.

Housewares

Avery Restaurant Supply
905 E. 2 St., Los Angeles (213) 624-7832
Mon.-Fri., 8-5; Sat., 8-1
Terms: MC, V, Check. Returns.   Street parking

If all your cookware comes from late night tv offers and it suits you just fine, Avery isn't for you. This is a place for the serious cook, not just the institutional cook. Here you can find pots and pans, from tiny to tremendous, platters, serving pieces, china, baking equipment, knives, gadgets and utensils, discounted 20% to 25%. They also feature Wolf's professional ranges.

Corning Revere Factory Store
The Citadel, City of Commerce (213) 725-3155
Hours vary by location.
(also in Cabazon, Barstow, Ontario, and San Ysidro)
Terms: MC, V, Check. Returns.   Parking

Corning Revere offers 20% discounts on Corningware sets, 30% off open stock Correlle, (more if you purchase twelve or more pieces of an item) and a 20% discount on discontinued Corningware patterns and styles. You can find open stock on all Corningware patterns, in more sizes and shapes then most stores carry. Revere Stainless Steel cookware is available; the greatest discounts are on damages: an 8" saucepan is $13.99; with a cosmetic damage, difficult to find, the cost is $8.99. There are also specials throughout the store: a Crown Corning Giftware one quart Thermal Server was $13.99; a set of four Pyrex mixing bowls in bright colors, $12.99. They will ship for a nominal fee.

Famous Brands Housewares Outlet
Lake Elsinore Outlet Ctr. (714) 245-4078
San Diego Factory Outlet Ctr. (619) 690-0420
Hours vary by location.
Terms: MC, V, D, Check. Returns.   Parking

This is the outlet for Lechters, featuring everything your kitchen will ever need, and some useful things for the rest of the house. Prices on some items are below Lechters everyday low prices. You can always find kitchen gadgets, pot holders, dish towels, pots, picture frames, closet and bath accessories, storage containers, glassware and china. Just about everything in housewares, at a better price than just about anywhere else.

Lechters
Topanga Plaza, Canoga Park (818) 340-7335
Hours vary by location.
(also in Huntington Beach, Westminster, Lakewood, Northridge, Sherman Oaks, West Los Angeles, West Covina, and Arcadia)
Terms: MC, V, AE, D, Check. Returns.   Parking

The Lechters chain sells everything for the home (see Famous Brands Outlet, above).   Something is always on sale beyond the normal markdowns (bakeware often around the holidays).

Libbey Glass Factory Outlet Store
200 Old Ranch Rd., City of Industry (714) 595-1375
Mon.-Sat., 9-4:30
Terms: MC, V, Check. Exchanges.   Parking

If you want some country air and a good deal on glassware, this is the place. Stock includes Libbey glassware and giftware at discounted prices. On my last visit I found lead crystal wine glasses for $3.48, highballs and old fashioneds for $2.98. Juice glasses were as low as .82, and there were a few styles at three for the price of one. Glass plates, glasses, goblets and champagne flutes in cobalt blue or black glass were reasonably priced: plates at $2.54; four (14 oz.) glasses at $7.97, and four champagnes at $7.65. Glasses coordinated to Caleca's Italian country china were $9.95 a set (4), but many four piece sets were under $5. Some modern glass platters, clear lines and geometric shapes, were $15.95. There is a sale area in back, where glass dinner plates start at .85.

Discount Catalogs

Tapestry
(800) 833-9333
Terms: MC, V, AE, CB, D. Returns

Tapestry is a catalog of stylishly designed items for the home, from furniture to linen, rugs to pool chairs, china to planters. You would find this kind of merchandise in other catalogs at two and three times the price. There is often a section in back of merchandise reduced to $10.

Jewelry

The Diamond Mine Co.
(213) 933-GEMS
Mon.-Fri., 10-6, by appointment
Terms: MC, V, AE, CB, DC, D, Check. Street parking

The Diamond Mine is an importer and manufacturer of jewelry, and can offer you savings of up to 300% over other retail jewelers. They can show you pieces in any quality of stone, from investment grade on down, diamonds and other gemstones, and offer many high quality pieces within your price range.

Grafstein & Co.
Santa Ana (714) 835-6100
Hours by appointment.
Terms: MC, V, AE, D, Check. Returns. Parking

Grafstein is one of the oldest and largest discounters in the fine jewelry business. They sell wholesale to jewelers and recently began selling to the public. Discounts range from 20% to 60% on new and pre-owned European watches, including Rolex, Cartier and Patek Phillipe (new watches have a lifetime warranty), lab certified diamonds and pearls, gemstones and estate jewelry. They ask that you comparison shop first; see them when you're ready to buy. Before making an appointment, call for their brochure, explaining their services in depth. You will hear the longest voicemail message ever, but it's all information. Grafstein takes trade-ins, they purchase jewelry, carry discounted designer pieces, and can manufacture from your design.

Jewelry Exchange
2017 S. Main, Santa Ana (714) 557-4200
3683 N. Midway, San Diego (619) 224-0500
Mon.-Sat., 10-5:30
Terms: MC, V, AE, D, Check. Parking

The Jewelry Exchange offers fine jewelry factory direct, and guarantees that the retail appraised value will be at least double the purchase price on anything they stock. One carat diamond earrings are available at $399; three ct. diamond tennis bracelets, $999. They carry jewelry for men and women, and guarantee the lowest prices.

Rubenfeld Kennedy Estate Jewelry `COUPON`
California Jewelry Mart, Los Angeles (213) 627-8118
By appointment only.
Terms: MC, V, AE, D, Check.   *Street parking*

If you love older jewelry and you don't want to pay top dollar, try Rubenfeld Kennedy. These two women buy the bankrupt stock of other jewelers (and a lot of them seem to be going under lately), as well as buying from estate sales, and pass the savings along to you. Since their overhead is so low, you wind up purchasing jewelry at one quarter to one half its appraised value. If shopping for diamonds, they'll make sure you know the cut, clarity and color of pieces you are considering. They also supply written appraisals. *The coupon entitles you to 10% off your next purchase.*

Steven & Co. Jewelers
437 A N. Bedford Dr., Beverly Hills (310) 274-8336
Mon.-Fri., 10-5
Terms: MC, V, AE, D, Check.   *Street parking*

Steven & Co. sells fine jewelry at 10% to 20% above cost. Among the names they carry are Cartier, Rolex and Movado watches (the Movado Museum Watch is discounted 30%). You can purchase gold and precious stones; they also buy jewelry, will appraise yours, and can reset or redesign pieces.

St. Vincent's Jewelry Center
7th St. and Broadway, Los Angeles (213) 629-2124
Mon.-Sat., 10-6
Terms: MC, V, Check.   *Parking*

St. Vincent's Jewelry Center is made up of three buildings, 650 S. Hill St., 640 S. Hill St., and 639-659 S. Broadway, housing over 400 retailers selling gold and precious stones at 40% to 70% below retail. Here you'll find vendors who repair jewelry, design jewelry around your stones, or sell loose stones. They validate parking, and the Broadway location is open on Sunday, from 10-6.

Costume Jewelry

The Bead Gallery   *COUPON*
1571 Barry Av., West Los Angeles (310) 820-9606
1809 Manhattan Beach Blvd., Manhattan Beach (310) 372-3136
Mon.-Sat., 10-6
Terms: Cash and Check only. Final sale.   Parking

This store offers a large selection of costume jewelry and hair ornaments. Prices range from $6 to $15 for earrings and bracelets of rhinestones, *faux* pearls and stones selling for at least twice the price in department stores. Hair ornaments range from simple to intricate designs on barrettes, as well as clips, headbands and scrunchies, at $1 to $6. They also carry beads and findings for hobbyists. *Save 10% on your next purchase with the coupon.*

Collector's Eye
21435 Sherman Way, Canoga Park (818) 347-9343
Mon.-Sat., 10-6
Terms: MC, V ($25 min.), Check. Final sale.   Street Parking

Short of haunting estate sales yourself, the Collector's Eye may be the cheapest way to find quality vintage costume jewelry. There is a huge selection, from the 1890's on (each piece is marked with its decade), of rhinestones, *faux* pearls, bakelite and other goodies, arranged by color. Prices are reasonable, generally less than what you'd pay at a department store for a quality piece, and the finds more interesting. Check purchases carefully, some may be missing a few stones. I found earrings from $12 (a lot of flashy clip earrings); bracelets, broaches and necklaces from about $20.

The Costume Jewelry Mart
918 Santee St., Los Angeles (213) 623-8817
Mon.-Fri., 10-5:30; Sat., 10-6; Sun., 11-5
Terms: Check and Cash only. Final sale.   Street parking

With over 35,000 dozen pieces of jewelry at .50 to $2, no wonder The Costume Jewelry Mart has to close it's doors from time to time to keep the crowds out. You would find the same jewelry selling in the fun jewelry sections of department stores, at several times what you can get it for here.

K. T. Fashion
934 S. Los Angeles St., Los Angeles (213) 622-2457
Mon.-Sat., 9-5:45; Sun., 11-5
Terms: MC, V, Check. Final sale. Street parking

This part of South Los Angeles St. is the wholesale costume jewelry and hair accessory stretch, but K.T.'s seems more geared to the retail buyer. They have a large selection of jewelry at prices from 25% to 75% below retail, and they stock some lovely pewter picture frames in a back corner, at very reasonable prices.

Kriegers
1606 Gower St., Hollywood (213) 461-9463
Mon.-Sat., 12-6 (closed Wed.)
Terms: MC, V, Check. Final sale. Street parking

Kriegers offers all kinds of collectibles and vintage clothing, but the thing I like best is the huge collection of costume jewelry. You can see some in the display cases at the front counter, but that's the tip of the iceberg. Tell them what you're looking for—by color and type—and they'll produce tray after tray of earrings, broaches and odds and ends to sort through. The prices are good, the selection endless.

Reckless Women
421 Ocean Front Walk, Venice (310) 396-8402
Mon.-Sun., 11-5
Terms: MC, V, D, AE, Check. Exchanges. Street parking

Reckless Women is a little store full of earrings, bracelets, necklaces, hair accessories, scarves and pins. The majority of earrings are $1.50, hair scrunchies start at $1. Jewelry continues up in price to moderately expensive, unique pieces, at less than full retail.

Rossi D'Italia   **COUPON**
8413 Beverly Blvd., Los Angeles (213) 658-8967
Mon.-Fri., 9-5:30; Sat., 10-4
Terms: MC, V, Check. Exchanges. Street parking

Rossi D'Italia is a wholesaler and manufacturer of fine jewelry that allows the public to browse and shop their showroom, at 25% off marked prices. One can buy beautiful pieces here, and sometimes wind up paying as little as half the price you would find them for in better department stores. There is a nice selection: mainly earrings, some bracelets, chains and necklaces. Prices range from a few dollars to about $75. There is also a small selection of hair accessories. Make sure you see all of the shop: behind one of the main displays is a sale area with even greater buys. Call or stop in to get on the mailing list for notification of sales. Generally there is a sale during holiday time, but things are discounted all the time here, so keep checking in. *The couopn entitles you to save an additional 10% on one purchase.*

> **Estate Sales are often advertised in the classified section of the newspaper. Pick up estate jewelry where the pros do.**

Light Fixtures

Castle Chandelier & Lighting Co., Inc.
12311 Sherman Way, North Hollywood (818) 982-0825
Mon.-Thurs., Sat., 9-6; Fri., 9-8; Sun., 11-5
(also in Studio City, Canoga Park, Glendale, Torrance, and West Covina)
Terms: MC, V, Check. Final sale.   Parking

Castle Chandeliers manufactures many of the products they sell, and there is a tremendous variety of lamps, chandeliers, landscape and outdoor lighting here. All lamps are discounted, prices averaging 20% below other stores. There are ceiling fans, sconces, track lighting, some modern and halogen pieces, and a large variety of ornate lamps and chandeliers.

Discount Lighting Outlet
5359 Valley Blvd., Los Angeles (213) 223-2301
18045 E. Gale Av., City of Industry (818) 854-6410
Mon.-Sun., 10-6
Terms: MC, V, Check. Exchanges.   Parking

Discount Lighting offers a variety of first quality lamps in discontinued styles, some factory overruns, and some factory reconditioned lamps. While they do have some ceramic, porcelain and brass-tone traditional styles (at prices beginning at $2.99), what you'll find the most of here are halogen torchieres and desk lamps. Prices for these begin at $19.99 (including the bulb). They also carry a large selection of lamp shades, beginning at $4.50.

Dynasty Classics Factory Outlet
22333 S. Wilmington, Carson (310) 549-5172
Thurs.-Sat.,10-5; Sun., 10-4
Terms: MC, V. Check. Final sale.   Parking

Directly across from the Arco refinery is the Dynasty Classics factory, manufacturing lamps, Christmas lights, ceiling and free-standing fans. The outlet sells these products at a fraction of what you'd find them for elsewhere. Halogen desks lamps were as low as $27.99, brass torchieres with glass domes began at $59.99; halogen torchieres began at $45.99. Small ginger jar lamps were $9.99, and a brass piano lamp was $19.99. Outdoor coachlights were $19.99 and interior ceiling fixtures, $9.99. Ceiling fans, in a variety of styles, ranged from $45 to $65, with a 52" brass model with light package at $49.99. Hand-painted wooden Christmas ornaments (24) were $19.99; brass and ceramic ornaments were similarly priced. A string of 100 indoor/outdoor lights was $12.99.

Lamps Factory Outlet
17424 Beach Blvd., Huntington Beach (714) 847-8100
Mon.-Fri., 10-9; Sat., 10-6; Sun., 11-5
Terms: MC, V, AE, Check. Returns.   Parking

This store carries contemporary and traditional floor lamps, hanging lamps, chandeliers, sconces, trac lighting, table and desk lamps, at discounts ranging from 20% to 50%. They also carry a good selection of lampshades, at competitive prices.

Lamps Plus
2012 S. Bundy Dr., West Los Angeles (310) 820-7567
Mon.-Fri., 10-9; Sat.-Sun., 10-6
(20 additional locations; see Geographical Index)
Terms: MC, V, AE, Check. Returns.   Parking

Lamps Plus offers factory direct prices on a wide range of fixtures, crystal chandeliers to bedside lamps and everything in between, at discounts from 20% to 40%, and there are many models with "Sale" tags at even greater reductions. They also carry a ceiling fans.

Lamps Plus Factory Outlet   CCC
20244 Plummer St., Chatsworth (818) 886-7705
Mon-Sat., 10-6; Sun., 11-6
Terms: MC, V, Check. Final sale.   Parking

Here you'll find overstocks and discontinued merchandise from the Lamps Plus chain, as well as seconds and factory reconditioned products. Torchieres begin at $19.99, and there are some halogen pieces in the mix. They also sell ceiling fans, which begin at $29.99.

Sanders House of Lights
576 S. Fair Oaks Av., Pasadena (818) 796-1705
Mon.-Sat., 10-6; Sun., 12-5
Terms: MC, V, Check. Returns.   Parking

Sanders manufactures lighting products and sells them direct. Most of the fixtures have "Sale" tags all the time, reflecting 25% to 50% savings, and include outdoor home and garden lighting, bath and kitchen fixtures, chandeliers, sconces, lamps and fans at substantial savings. There is also a large collection of beautiful, hand-made reproduction Tiffany shades.

Uni-Lite
1510 N. State College Blvd., Anaheim (714) 991-0710
Mon., Fri., 9-9; Tues.-Thurs., 9-6; Sat., 10-5
Terms: MC, V, D, Check. Returns.   Parking

You can find all manner of lighting here, indoor and outdoor, by manufacturers such as Stiffel, Harris Industries, Casual Lamps, Rainbow Lighting and more. There are a number of ways to save money at Uni-lite. There's always a sale, where up to a third of the stock is reduced, and sale items change monthly. If you want something not on sale you can save, too; buy three items within 60 days; hold on to your receipts and get a 10% refund on any lamp not purchased on sale.

Discount Catalogs

Golden Valley Lighting
(800) 735-3377
Terms: MC, V, Check. Final sale.

Golden Valley offers discounts of up to 50% on first quality lamps from over 200 lighting manufacturers. You go window shopping, find the lamp you want, call Golden Valley with the manufacturer, model number, color and finish, and they give you a price. They require a 50% deposit at time of order, and your lamp will be sent when the balance is paid. They are open Mon-Fri., 10-6 and Sat., 11-1, Eastern Time.

Ceiling Fans

Beverly Hills Fan Company Factory Outlet
6035 De Soto Av., Woodland Hills (818) 992-5562
Tues.-Sat., 10-5
Terms: MC, V, Check. Final sale.   Parking

This showroom contains a number of discontinued ceiling fans, some at unbelievably low prices. A 42" fan—five blades, three speeds, reversible—was $29.99; a 52" model, $39.99. Get 'em while they last, which may not be long, since these fans *retail* at $160 to $200 (i.e., you're price is considerably under cost). Colors vary, and once these specials are gone there will be other styles to replace them, but probably not at such deep discounts, since Beverly Hills recently opened this store and is trying to build up a clientele. Discontinued merchandise will sell here at about half price.

The Fan Man/The Fireplace Man   **COUPON**
11239 183 St., Cerritos (310) 865-6666
Mon.-Fri., 10-9; Sat., 10-6; Sun., 11-5
Terms: MC, V, Check. L. Final sale.   *Parking*

Here ceiling fans by Hunter, Casablanca and Emerson are discounted 30% to 50%, sometimes more. Fans are available in a variety of styles, sizes and finishes, with and without light kits. You can also find a selection of fan lights, as well as other ceiling fan paraphernalia, and discounted fireplace accessories (screens, baskets and andirons, in all price ranges), mantles and wood stoves. *The Fan Man coupon entitles you to $10 off a Hunter Fan, or $15 off a Casablanca Fan, or $25 off an Emerson Fan, one coupon per item. The Fireplace Man coupon entitles you to 10% off one purchase, one coupon per item.*

Old Tyme Ceiling Fan Company   **COUPON**
22743 Ventura Blvd., Woodland Hills (818) 888-8176
Mon.-Fri., 10:30-6; Sat., 10:30-5:30; Sun., 12-4
Terms: MC, V, Check. Exchanges.   *Street parking*

Hunter, Casablanca and Emerson Ceiling Fans are sold here at discounts beginning at 40%, and specific styles are further discounted with coupons in the Valley edition of Saturday's *Los Angeles Times*, saving up to $30 more. There are lighting kits, and shades for fan lights are available in a number of styles, including some lovely French glass, deco looks and traditionals. They also carry fireplace accessories from Dagan Industries and Sunset Frame Screens, many of which are discounted 50% and more. Andirons are discounted 35% to 60%, and firewood baskets begin at $15. *The coupon entitles you to an additional discount of $10 off a Hunter Fan, $15 off a Casablanca Fan, or $25 off an Emerson Fan. One coupon per item.*

See also
    Dynasty Classics Factory Outlet

Linens

A Bedtime Story
COUPON
9035 Venice Blvd., Los Angeles (310) 815-8115
Mon.-Fri., 9-6:30; Sat., Sun., 11-7
Terms: Cash and Check only.   Parking

This is the factory outlet for Table Manners placemats and napkins, and 100% Pure, a line of all cotton sheets. Available are throw pillows, placemats ($2.99), napkins ($1.99), bed linen (including baby linen) and shower curtains. The current line is priced comparably to the better linen chains mentioned in this section, but discontinued patterns are reduced about 40% (six or seven times a year, each time they come out with new styles). The linens are unusual, from bold contemporary prints to subtle, romantic and traditional looks. Included in the reduced mix are occasional samples or one-of-a-kinds, but if you find a sheet and can't find a duvet cover or pillow cases to go with it, and if they still have the fabric at the factory, they'll make one up for you. It'll take two to three weeks, and even though it's been custom-made, it's yours at the reduced price. *Use the coupon for a 10% discount on one purchase of non-sale items.*

Al Greenwood's Bedspread Kingdom
7250 Pacific Coast Hwy., Long Beach (310) 498-9277
8468 State St., Southgate (213) 566-9393
Mon.-Thurs., Sat., 10-5:30; Fri.,10-7; Sun.,12-5
Terms: MC, V, Check. L. Exchanges.   Parking

This store is a little overwhelming, but bargain hunters' blood will race at the sight of all the bins, and that visceral sense of a deal approaching. The main store is a block long, stuffed with bedspreads, comforters, sheets, pillows, shams, curtains, table cloths and towels. Quilted bedspreads in a variety of prints and solids begin at $14.95, twin; $19.95, full; $24.95, queen; and $29.95, king. Add $10 for first quality comforters, which range up to $300. Comforter sets, including shams and in some cases dust ruffles, start at $49.99. Satin sheets were $5 to $15, satin dust ruffles were $10, and I found a queen size Laura Ashley irregular comforter for $99.99; a matching queen sheet set was $54.95. (Other top brands were in evidence, though not in packaging that identified them as such.) There are aisles of curtains, cushions and chair pads, and they do custom work.

Anna's Linens
10970 Jefferson Blvd., Culver City   (310) 398-5175
Mon.-Fri., 10-8; Sat., 10-7; Sun., 11-6
(40 additional locations; see Geographical Index)
Terms: MC, V, Check. Returns.   Parking

A little lower on the price scale than Strouds or Bed, Bath and Beyond, Anna's offers a good selection of bath, bed and drapery goods. Floor length poly lace panels were $15 ($30); chintz chair pads, $3.99; Dan River, Fieldcrest and Springmaid sheet sets, in poly/cotton blends, $29.99, queen, and Signature sheet sets were $18.99, queen. Comforter sets in a variety of styles were $59.95, twin; $99.95, queen. Placemats and napkins were $1 and Cannon cotton bath towels were $4.99. Anna's has a new sale every two weeks, and a lowest price guarantee; they'll beat any advertised price, excluding clearance and special order items, by 10%.

Bed, Bath and Beyond
19836 Ventura Blvd., Woodland Hills (818) 702-9301
Mon.-Fri., 9:30-9; Sat., 9:30-7; Sun., 9:30-6
(also in West Los Angeles, Huntington Beach, Studio City, Redondo Beach, and San Diego)
Terms: MC, V, AE, Check. Returns.   Parking

This store is hard to categorize—"beyond" doesn't do it justice—it's filled with everything for your home, at discounts of 10% to 60%. There are storage bins for closets and offices and kitchens, there are housewares, china, stemware, cookware, cutlery, linen (ranging from Waverly, Croscill, Eileen West and Laura Ashley, to solid sets at $16.99, twin; $34.99, full; $44.99, queen; and $54.99, king), blankets, comforters, and a kids' department with sheets, towels and dinnerware imprinted with the merchandised character of the minute. One stop shopping for your entire home.

Bedspread Creations   **COUPON**
14054 E. Firestone Blvd., Santa Fe Springs   (213) 802-7938
Mon.-Fri., 9-6; Sat., 10-5
Terms: MC, V, AE, D, Check. Final sale.   Parking

Bedspread Creations sells bedspreads, comforters and daybed sets, as well as dust ruffles, curtains, shades and blinds. They can finish your bedroom with a custom look, and for much less then you might expect. There are a number of spreads on the racks: some are manufactured by other suppliers, offered at discounts of 30% to 50%, (kings as low as $49.95), but many are made by Bedspread Creations, and going with one of their custom sets can save you 30% to 70% over what you'd pay for a better ensemble elsewhere. A queen custom spread costs $100 in labor plus twelve yards of fabric (check with them once you've found your fabric: they may be able to get it cheaper); a dust ruffle is $50 labor plus fabric. Decorators are on hand to assist you. *The coupon entitles you to 5% off a purchase of $25 or more.*

The Bedspread Warehouse
6949 Topanga Canyon Blvd., Canoga Park   (818) 887-4347
Mon.-Sat., 10-6
Terms: MC, V, AE, Check. Returns.   Parking

While Bedspread Warehouse offers a large variety of household goods, linens, bath items and pillows at discount prices, their biggest business is custom bedspreads. They've been doing custom work for 24 years and produce high quality work at great value. A sampling can be found along the back wall at $99 (values to $399). They also carry most better names in linen, at savings of 30% to 75%. There are curtains, day-bed sets and bed-in-a-bag sets, and decorator pillows start at $2.99. They can special order anything a department store carries, and they'll quote prices over the phone.

Custom Quilt and Craft Co.
(310) 829-7701

With the resurgence of country style, quilts are becoming more popular than ever. You can buy mass-produced quilts almost anywhere, but if you want a hand-made quilt, in your choice of color and pattern, Valerie Roach will make one for you. You'll be paying the same price as the boutiques do for her quilts, essentially wholesale. Pricing varies by size and difficulty of pattern. Twins can begin at $225, a patchwork queen can run $400, but prices depend on what you want. Valerie also makes balloon shades, dust ruffles and shams to go with your quilt, as well as nursery bedding (baby quilts are $90), hand-made teddy bears, fabric albums, and seasonal gift items.

Dana Bedspreads
1408 S. E St., San Bernardino   (714) 432-1100
Mon.-Fri., 11-7; Sat., 10-6
(also in La Mesa, City of Industry, and Fountain Valley)
Terms: MC, V, AE, Check. GC. Returns.   Parking

Dana manufactures bedspreads, and has over 4,000 spreads, comforters and daybed covers in stock. They will also custom make spreads, dust ruffles, curtains, draperies and pillows. The labor cost to make a comforter ranges from $120, king, to $80, twin, plus fabric. However, in the showroom there are plenty of bedspreads and comforters Dana has manufactured, and since they sell direct, prices are 30% to 50% cheaper than these spreads would be, if you could find this quality and variety elsewhere. You can order dust ruffles, curtains, shams, and pillows, or whatever else you may want them to make up, in the same fabric as your comforter or spread, including furniture. They offer 18 different styles of custom upholstered headboards, 4 styles of upholstered bed, 30 styles of chairs and ottomans, and 18 styles of chaises.

Dana Bedspreads Clearance Store   CCC
263 East Highland Av., San Bernardino (714) 881-2345
Mon.-Fri., 10-9; Sat., 10-7; Sun., 11-6
Terms: MC, V, AE, Check. GC. Final sale.   Parking

The merchandise here is mainly bedspreads and comforters, in discontinued fabrics, which means you can't have coordinating pieces made. Prices are slightly lower then the rest of the chain.

Down Comforter Warehouse
10060 Ventura Blvd., Woodland Hills (818) 716-1602
Mon.-Sat., 10-7; Sun., 11-6
(also The Home Shop in Culver City, Santa Ana, West Los Angeles and Huntington Park)
Terms: MC, V, Check. Returns.   Parking

From the back parking lot it looks like Ralph's swallowed this place up and forgot to take down the sign. But don't be fooled. Once you enter this shop (through Ralph's) you are surrounded by high quality linen at very competitive prices. Down comforters begin at $69, twin; $79, full/queen; and $89, king. The great prices extend to 100% cotton sheets, which begin at $14.99 (twin) and go to $32.99 (full). You will also find sale comforters, pillows, towels and coordinating accessories.

Fieldcrest/Cannon Outlet Store
Factory Merchants of Barstow (619) 253-3591
San Diego Factory Outlet Ctr. (619) 662-4620
Hours vary by location.
Terms: MC, V, Check. Exchanges.   Parking

This shop offers a variety of bed and bath products at savings comparable to other linen stores. What this has that the others don't is institutional towel bundles, so if you have need for white cotton/poly towels in multiples of 6 bath ($21.99), 12 hand ($16.99), or 24 wash cloths ($14.99), you'll find them here.

The Linen Club
The Citadel, City of Commerce (213) 721-2444
Mon.-Sat., 9-8; Sun. 10-6
Terms: MC, V, Check. Exchanges.   Parking

This is a comparatively small store, but if you're looking for a Laura Ashley queen sheet set but wince at the $140 price tag, here you'll find it for $89.95. They also have a variety of placemats from $2 to $3, napkins from $1 to $2, and Fieldcrest Encore pima cotton towels, $6.95 bath, $4.95 hand, $2.95 wash. Bath accessories, pillows, comforters and small woven rugs are also available.

Mr. Satin, Inc.
2236 Barrington, West Los Angeles (213) 879-3353
Mon.-Fri., 8:30-4; Sat., 12-5
Terms: Cash and Check only. Final sale.   Street parking

Mr. Satin is a manufacturer of satin sheets, and in this small store off the factory they sells seconds of their sheets, comforters, shams, dust ruffles and boudoir pillows, generally available in six to eight colors, discounted 30% to 40%. Sheet sets range from twin at $49 to king at $80.50, and comforters range from $60 to $105. In addition to their everyday low prices, there is always something on close-out, further reduced.

Royal Bedspreads
22414 S. Normandie Av., Torrance (310) 320-4909
Mon.-Fri., 9-6; Sat., 9:30-5
Terms: Cash and Check only. Exchanges.   Parking

Royal Bedspreads manufactures bedspreads and comforters and can offer you one of their ready-made spreads, or a spread or comforter made to your specifications. The outer office is piled with swatch books. Enter the showroom, so full of spreads and comforters it's hard to get around, and let them show off some of their beautiful workmanship. I drooled over a hand-knotted comforter in a Waverly print at $350 (queen); shams were $45. Bedspreads start at $79, and they do custom drapes.

Scandia Down Outlet Store   CCC
Mission Valley Center, San Diego (619) 692-9186
Mon.-Fri., 10-9; Sat., 10-7; Sun., 11-5
Terms: MC, V, AE, Check. Final sale.   Parking

Here you can find seconds and discontinued styles of the sumptuous linens and comforters of Scandia Down. All merchandise is generally a third or more off, and comforters are available in a variety of weights. A queen 39.5 oz. down style was $228 ($380), which was mid-price range. Feather pillows are also available, from $21 for a queen ($35), to $177 for a king size, with a higher grade of feathers. They also carry a small inventory of linens. While cotton predominates, I found a set of silk sheets patterned with small flowers that I'm still dreaming about: original retail $575; here $230.

Strouds
10830 Santa Monica Blvd., Los Angeles (310) 470-7606
Hours vary by location.
(25 additional locations; see Geographic Index)
Terms: MC, V, AE, D, Check. Returns.   Parking

This chain offers savings in high quality linens of all kinds, as well as bath and tabletop accessories. Flannel sheet sets sold for $19.99 twin ($52); and queen sheet sets from Springmaid were $34.99, half off the regular store price. They have a wide selection of Waverly, Croscill, Laura Ashley, Eileen West and other designer comforters, sheet sets and towels, at discounts ranging from 25% to 60%. There are also Palais Royal French cotton linens, discounted but still pricey. They carry pillows, blankets, tablecloths, napkins and placemats, shower curtains, bath rugs, you name it, they have it. Their large clearance sales are in January and June. As if these bargains weren't enough, Strouds also four Clearance Centers!

Strouds Clearance Centers   CCC
3733 E. Foothill Blvd., Pasadena (818) 351-9605
Mon.-Fri., 10-8; Sat., 10-6; Sun., 12-5
(also in Torrance, West Los Angeles, and Downey)
Terms: MC, V, AE, D, Check. L. Returns.   Parking

These four stores are packed with discontinued merchandise and special purchases, and although comforters are here and dust ruffles over there, with a little searching you may be able to put together a lovely bedroom or bath at a very affordable price. Towels are as low as $3.99, bath, going up to $7.99. Irregular print comforters are $19.99, twin ($65); full/ queen, $24.99 ($100); and California king, $29.99 ($125). There are bed-in-a-bag sets, duvet covers, bed and decorative pillows, placemats and napkins (an eight piece set of embroidered cotton placemats and napkins was $4.99). Most prices are lower than Strouds regular stores. Of course, the level of order is lower than Stroud's as well; this place requires a little patience, but your efforts will be well rewarded.

Three D Bed & Bath
330 S. La Cienega, Los Angeles (213) 657-8450
Mon.-Fri., 10-9; Sat.-Sun. 10-6
(15 additional locations; see Geographical Index)
Terms: MC, V, D, AE, Check. Returns.   Parking

A full range of bed and bath products by top of the line designers are available here at discounts of 30% to 60%. You will find sheets, comforters, dust ruffles, shams, blankets, towels, pillows, bath accessories, and table top linen. 3D also carries picture frames, pillows, glassware, housewares, silk flowers, a little of everything. Their major sale is in January.

Welcome Home
The Citadel, City of Commerce (213) 722-7802
Hours vary by location.
(also in Cabazon, Ontario, Barstow, Lake Elsinore and San Ysidro)
Terms: MC, V, AE, D, Check. Returns.   Parking

This store offers more than linens, but it was the prices on linens that caught my eye. If your taste is traditional, country, even Victorian, many pieces will fit with your decor. Cotton napkins are 2/$1, and placemats are $1. Afghans are $19.99, quilts are $59.99, and various antimacassars, ladies' handkerchiefs and table cloths are discounted as well. Picture frames are marked down 25%, and potpourri (6 oz.) in several scents, is $2.99 ($8). There is also a small selection of ladies' stationary, discounted 10% to 20%, and beautiful wreaths and sprays of dried flowers.

West Point Pepperell Mill Store
Desert Hills Factory Stores at Cabazon (714) 849-0644
Mon.-Sun., 9-8
Terms: MC, V, Check. Exchanges.   Parking

This large store features West Point Pepperell goods, ranging from towels and sheets to lace table runners and placemats, at savings of 20% to 45%. Three piece towel sets were $11.97, and individual sheets began at $3.99, twin; and $9.99, king. Some towels were sold "by the pound" at $4.99, but a bath towel weighed in at $4.19: you may be better off choosing from the greater range of colors available off the shelves at the same price.

See also
> **Regal Rents Sale**
> **Leading Designer Outlet**

Baby Linen

Le Baby Originals
9840 Indiana Av., #3, Riverside (714) 352-0340
Tues.-Fri., 9:30-5:30
Terms: MC, V, AE, Check. Final sale.   Parking

Le Baby manufactures baby linen, and since the factory is right here, if you find something you like you can have it customized: change the color, the lace, take away a ruffle here, add one there. There are several styles available, most consist of a headboard piece, bumper, pillow, dust ruffle, sheet and comforter, and prices range from $110 to $185, about half what you would find these selling for in better baby stores and catalogs. Diaper stackers are available in most patterns for $24, high chair covers are $25, and rocking chair pillows, $35. Cradle sets (headboard piece, bumper, sheet and comforter) are $45 to $55. There is a baby shower registry, and while you're there, check the prices on their cribs, cradles, strollers, mobiles and high chairs. Le Baby sells at the Orange County Marketplace on Saturdays and Sundays.

NoJo Factory Outlet Store
22942 Arroyo Vista, Rancho Santa Margarita (714) 858-9496
Mon.-Sat., 10-5
Terms: MC, V, Check. Final sale.   Parking

Selling infant bedding and bedroom accessories, this large, cheery store will overwhelm you with the volume and variety of merchandise, down to fabric and trim, at discount prices. Stock consists of one-of-a-kind samples, discontinued merchandise and irregulars of crib and cradle bedding, lamps, curtains, wall hangings, carseat covers, diaper bags and kids' bedding in cotton and blends. The pricing works out to 48% of retail (*of* retail, not *off* retail), less if what you've chosen is on special. Cradle bumpers begin at $4.80, and crib bumpers at $8, going up to $35. Comforters start at $14.40, but a Battenberg lace keepsake comforter was $62. Baby slings were $23.90, stroller covers $19.50, car seat covers $21.50 and high chair covers, $14.50 (I saw each of these items priced at $32 at a *discount* baby store.) There were three piece crib sets (comforter, sheet and bumper) for $40, and some specials featured a comforter, headboard bumper, dust ruffle and sheet set for $39.95 (the comforter alone *wholesaled* for $52). Children's bedding consists of comforters and pillow shams in a bright assortment of prints at $45. There is a baby shower registry. Worth a trip.

Discount Catalogs

The Company Store
(800) 323-8000
Terms: MC, V, AE, D, Check. Returns.

The Company Store sells down comforters, pieced quilts, woven bedspreads, comforter cover sets, flannel sheets and mattress pads, but the down products are factory direct and often great buys. There are many choices of color, style, and desired warmth level, as well as copious explanations of grades of down, and how to choose the best comforter for you.

Domestications
(800) 782-7722
Terms: MC, V, AE, D, DC, CB. Returns.

Domestications offers coordinated linen for bed, bath or kitchen, plus accessories, rugs, and curtains at discounted prices. Among the best buys are the linen sets: sheets, pillowcases, comforter and dust ruffle cost less than what you might pay for a comforter alone elsewhere. While they carry brand names like Dan River, Bill Blass, and J.P. Stevens, many of their beautiful bedroom ensembles are knock-offs of designer looks. Comforters are often on sale for $29.99 (any size), and sheet sets range from $9.99 to $29.99.

Merryland by Marilyn
(818) 780-5999
Terms: Cash and Check only. Final sale.

Call for a brochure of Marilyn's whimsical crib bumpers and nursery coordinates. All pieces are sold separately, but a set (bumper, quilt, pillow, sheet and dust ruffle) will run around $150. She also offers coordinated diaper stackers, wall hangings, and fabric yardage on some patterns.

Mother Harts
P. O. Box 4229, Boynton Beach, FL 33424-4229 (407) 738-5866
Terms: MC, V, Check. GC. Returns.

Mother Harts offers natural products for the home. Untreated, undyed, unbleached 100% cotton sheets start $15.80, twin, to $32.80, king. Crib sheets are $9.80. They also carry untreated percale sheets, unbleached and untreated blankets, towels, flannel sheets, down comforters, duvet covers, infant clothing and bedding, and irregular 100% cotton infant underwear at savings of close to 50%.

Luggage

American Tourister Factory Store
Desert Hills Factory Stores at Cabazon   (714) 849-1177
Mon.-Sun., 9-8
Terms: V, MC, Check. Returns.   Parking

This shop features luggage, attache cases and travel accessories by American Tourister. Most merchandise is first quality but seconds do show up and are clearly marked. Because this is the factory outlet your savings are generally 68% off manufacturers' suggested retail. There are leather pieces, and hardsided and softsided cases and sets in tapestry, canvas, fabric and vinyl; many styles have wheels. There is usually a set on special, and a clearance rack with a dozen or so bags. They will quote prices over the phone.

California Luggage
18110 Euclid St., Fountain Valley (714) 540-5878
Mon.-Sat., 10-6
Terms MC, V, Check. Final sale.   Parking

California Luggage carries travel accessories, attache and brief cases, sport bags, garment bags, trunks and sets of luggage at savings up to 50%. They carry all the major brands, including Hartman, Delsey, Andiamo, Lark, Samsonite, Haliburton and High Sierra. Most merchandise is first quality, but some is not, and it is in the seconds and irregulars that you will find some amazing bargains. Luggage and accessories that are *never* discounted in first quality turn up here, but check to make sure you can live with the flaw or irregularity. Stock keeps changing, so stop in often to check it out, or tell them what you're looking for and they'll call you if one comes in.

Hartmann Luggage Outlet
Factory Merchants of Barstow (619) 253-7668
Mon-Sat., 9-8
Terms: MC, V, Check. Exchanges.   Parking

There's something about leather luggage that reminds me of George Bailey and big dreams. Of course, he wanted a battered old suitcase, which you'd be hard-pressed to find here. What you will find are seconds, irregulars and discontinued stock of luggage, attache cases, purses and small leathergoods at prices discounted about 40%. Much of the merchandise is leather, so check for scratches, unless you're looking for a battered suitcase too. A 29" leather pullman with rigid sides was $495 ($825), the 24" companion case was $375 ($625). A 29" canvas pullman was $155, half price, and a canvas four-suiter garment bag was $267, also half off. Leather attache cases were $315 ($525) and there were a few Crouch & Fitzgerald bags.

H. Savinar Luggage Company
6931 Topanga Cyn. Blvd., Canoga Park (818) 703-1313
4625 W. Washington Blvd., Venice (310) 938-2501
Mon.-Sat., 10-6; Sun., 10-4
Terms: MC, V, Check. Exchanges.　　　　Parking

At Savinar there is a huge selection of luggage, attache and briefcases, artist's portfolios, small leather goods, backpacks, and travel accessories by such manufacturers as Hartmann, Haliburton, Delsey, Lark, Ventura, Boyt, Andiamo, Filofax, and DayRunner. Most brands are discounted at least 20%, many 50% or more. Every product comes with a one year warranty against manufacturers' defects, and many have a lifetime guarantee. Savinar generally does its own repairs; they will special order, and they ship anywhere. They also have a toll free number: (800) 877-8683.

LAX Luggage
2233 S. Sepulveda Blvd., West Los Angeles (310) 478-2661
Mon.-Sat., 10-6; Sun., 11-5
(also in Tarzana (818) 343-4422, and Los Angeles (310) 417-2307)
Terms: MC, V, Check. Returns.　　　　Parking

These three stores carry a large variety of luggage and small leather goods, mainly discounted 20%, but some pieces are marked down as much as 50%. They carry most major brands, including Hartman, Tumi, Lark, Pegasus, Haliburton, Skyway, Samsonite and Filofax. There is a selection of travel products discounted 20%.

Luggage 4 Less　　　　　　　　　　　　　(COUPON)
5144 Lankershim Blvd., North Hollywood (818) 760-1360
Mon.-Sat., 9-5:30
Terms: MC, V, AE, Check. Returns.　　　　Parking

Luggage 4 Less offers buys on most major brands of luggage, including Tumi, Boyt, Samsonite, Skyway, French and more. Their discounts range from 20% down to cost when they get specials buys. They not only offer luggage, but a selection of briefcases, wallets, small leather goods and pens. They usually have year-end and summer-end sales, and they have a repair shop on the premises, so if you have any problem with a purchase it can be repaired and returned quickly. Most brands carry warranties, from two years to a lifetime. *The coupon entitles you to 10% off any ticketed price.*

Luggage For Less
17850 Newhope St., Fountain Valley (714) 434-6401
Mon.-Fri., 10-6; Sat., 10-6; Sun., 11-5
Terms: MC, V, AE, D, Check. Returns.   Parking

This large store offers discounts of 20% to 50% on small leather goods, fine writing instruments, and luggage lines such as Delsey, Samsonite, Verdi, Skyway, Florentine, Bill Blass and Seward trunks, as well as leather luggage and attache cases. The styles include hard and soft-sided luggage, tapestries, leathers, vinyls, complete sets and individual pieces.

Luggage Outlet
17775 Main St., Santa Ana (714) 250-0774
Mon.-Fri., 9-6; Sat., 10-5; Sun., 11-5
Terms: MC, V, AE, DC, CB, Check. Exchanges. Parking

Located across from the John Wayne Airport, this shop carries all major brands of luggage. Their everyday prices are discounted 20% to 50%, and sometimes more, when they can pass a manufacturer's special on to you. In addition to luggage they also discount attache cases, business cases, travel accessories and small leather goods.

Olympic Luggage
210 W. 6 St., Los Angeles (213) 489-7982
Mon.-Sat.,10-6
Terms: MC, V, AE, Check. Final sale.   Street parking

All major brands of luggage, including Samsonite, Delsy, Tumi, Ventura, Skyway and Lark are sold here for up to half off. They also discount travel accessories, luggage carts, dual voltage small electrics, Seiko travel clocks, small leathers, briefcases, wallets, backpacks and organizers.

Marine Supplies

American Rubber & Supply Co.
15849 Stagg St., Van Nuys (818) 782-8234
Mon.-Fri., 9-5:30; Sat. by appt.
Terms: Cash and Check only.   Final sale.   Parking

American Rubber & Supply can outfit you with boots, rainwear, and other rubber products and do it far more cheaply than sporting goods stores. Heavy yellow hooded rainsuits, with bib overalls, are $27.50; vinyl rain ponchos begin at $5.95 and nylon waterproof rain suits are $42.95. A rain slicker with hood is $24.95, without, $19.95. They carry all manner of rubber products, including bungee cords, tarps, aprons and gloves.

Catalogs

E&B Discount Marine
(800) 553-5007
Terms: MC, V, AE, D, Check. Returns.

E&B Discount Marine puts out several catalogs yearly, full of buys on boating supplies. They will not be undersold, and throughout their catalogs special value items are highlighted. Some mailings come with coupons, saving you up to 10% more. They offer electronics, boat covers, paints, sanitation needs, seating, flotation devices, inflatable boats and water sports items, at discounts of up to 55%.

Goldberg's Marine
(800) BOATING
Terms: MC, V, AE, D. Returns.

Goldberg's, "Where thousands of boaters save millions of dollars," lists over 300 pages of boating gear and accessories in their catalog, and promises not to be undersold. They carry the latest marine products, from rescue equipment to computer-cut boat lettering (and every marine graphic known to any old salt), and the standard electronics, paints and varnishes, hardware, teak accessories, bilge pumps, engine accessories, anchors, radar, galley gear, flotation, first aid and water sports paraphernalia. Discounts go as high as 50%.

West Marine
(800) 538-0775
Terms: MC, V, Check. GC. Returns.

West Marine not only sells every conceivable boating accessory, down to hardware (need a marine screw?), discounted up to 40%, but on the products they manufacture discounts go even deeper. They offer electronics, first aid paraphernalia, flotation devices, chart accessories, scopes and compasses, books and videos, food preparation accessories, marine sanitation, paints and clothing and accessories. A master catalog is published annually, with updates.

Medical and Optical Needs

Medical

Alan's Medical Products
840 N. Main, Orange (714) 639-8222
Mon.-Fri., 8-5
Terms: MC, V, Check, some insurance plans.   Parking

Alan's sells, rents and customizes wheelchairs, and also offers hospital beds, walking aids, and all kinds of medical hardware. They guarantee the lowest prices; bring them a written estimate of anyone else's and they'll beat it. They offer cash discounts, and they not only sell but buy and exchange equipment. They have some used equipment in stock. Get on their mailing list for monthly specials.

Family Practice Center of UCLA
200 Medical Plaza, Westwood (310) 825-9111
Mon.-Sun., 7-9
Terms: MC, V, AE, D, Checks.   Parking

The Family Practice Center gives Hepatitis-B shots for $75 per injection. These shots are not covered by most insurance plans (Why should they pay for preventative health care?), but if you are a sexually active adult you should know that epidemiologists believe Hepatitis-B is spreading faster than AIDS, it can be as deadly, and it is completely preventable.

Immune Testing Center Medical Group
7951 Beverly Blvd., Los Angeles (213) 653-8571
Mon.-Fri., 9-6
Terms: Cash and Check only.   Street Parking

Here you can get an HIV test for $40; testing is performed by a federal and state licensed clinical laboratory, offering complete confidentiality and anonymity. You get your results within 48 hours.

Optical

Complete Eye Care
12328 Washington Pl., Mar Vista (310) 390-2432
Mon.-Sat., 10-6
Terms: MC, V, AE, Check.   Street parking

Here glasses start at $30 a pair, bi-focals at $49.

Pacific Eyes & T's
2649 Vista Way, #1, Oceanside (619) 722-9099
Hours vary by location.
(12 additional locations; see Geographical Index)
Terms: MC, V, Check. Final sale.   Parking

Pacific Eyes & T's discounts many of their sunglasses as much as 50%. They carry Ray-Bans, Vuarnet, Serengeti, Solarshields, some convincing knock-offs of designer brands, and a large selection of cycling sunglasses. There is a low price guarantee; bring them a competitor's ad and they'll sell you the same item for 5% less. They run frequent coupons in local newspapers.

Discount Catalogs

Bruce Medical Supply
(800) 225-8446
Terms: MC, V, Check. Returns.

The Bruce catalog has diabetes monitoring equipment and ostomy supplies, as well as general medical supplies and equipment, including canes, walkers and wheelchairs, dressings and antiseptic cleansers. They quote prices over the phone.

Contact Lens Replacement Center
(516) 491-7763
Terms: Check. Returns.

The Contact Lens replacement Center guarantees the lowest prices, and will generally ship replacement lenses in one to three days. Discounts of up to 60% are available on all brands including Bausch & Lomb, Allergan Hydrop, Ciba

Vision, Coopervision, Occular Science, Sunsoft and others; in soft lenses, Daily and Extended Wear, clear and colors. Next Day Air service is offered. They also discount Ray-Ban sunglasses.

Hidalgo
(800) 786-2021
Terms: MC, V, D, AE, CB, DC. Returns.

Hidalgo manufactures eye glass frames, offering savings of up to 50%. Styles are current and are made of titanium, metal, graphite, and various kinds of plastic. In case you're worried about ordering prescription glasses by mail, they provide how-to information, and give you lots of choices, including tinted, gradient, or polarized lenses. They also carry Ray-Bans.

Medi-Mail, Inc.
(800) 331-1458
Terms: MC, V, Check.

Medi-Mail will fill your prescriptions quickly, efficiently, and cheaply, offering discounts of up to 75% on some items, and an additional discount of 20% off generic drugs if you are a member of one of many organizations qualifying for a group rate (including AARP); check when you call, the list of qualifying organizations is lengthy. Minimum order is $2.50. Shipping is free. Call for a quote on your next prescription.

Rhodes Hearing
(618) 564-2026
Terms: Check. Exchanges.

Rhodes offers hearing aids at less than 50% of what you'd pay for comparable models elsewhere. There are also hearing aid accessories, and they will repair any hearing aid for $95, with a six month warranty. For a $35 non-refundable deposit you can try any item for 45 days.

Sunglasses U.S.A.
(800) USA-RAYS
Terms: MC, V. Returns.

Sunglasses U.S.A. carries Ray-Bans at 33% below retail. They offer every imaginable style, with a variety of lens colors. Additionally, there are lines by other designers on rotating special. All products are made by Bausch & Lomb.

Musical Instruments

Betnun Music *COUPON*
403 N. Larchmont Blvd., Los Angeles (213) 464-7468
Mon.-Sat., 10:30-6; Sun., 12-4
Terms: MC, V, AE, D, Check. L. Exchanges.   Street parking

Betnun deals in all kinds of instruments, including keyboards, woodwinds, and electronic instruments. They carry everything but full-sized acoustic pianos, and have a large selection saxes and guitars, including possibly the best selection of Gibson guitars, and the Les Paul line, in the area. They also carry hard to find instruments, used instruments, and may take your old instrument in trade if they happen to need what you're offering. New instruments are discounted up to 25%. They also rent instruments, and repair them. Their two major sale times are summer and Christmas. *The coupon entitles you to 10% off one purchase, cash sales only.*

The Piano Outlet *COUPON*
551 N. Azusa Av., West Covina (818) 858-6100
Mon.-Fri., 10-8; Sat., 10-6; Sun., 12-6
Terms: MC, V, Check. Financing.   Parking

The Piano Outlet has a large selection of pianos, organs and keyboards, mostly new but some used, often at prices 55% below retail. Among the pianos are Weber, Young Chang, Yamaha, and Brentwood; a model retailing for $3,695 was selling here for $1,496. Some are showroom models, others bankrupt stock, never used but rechecked by the factory anyway. Most come with a ten year warranty. A few pieces may have a scratch here or there, so check carefully. The Piano Outlet will rent you a new piano, they have a rent-to-buy option where your rental fee goes to the purchase price, they take trade-ins, give music lessons and sell sheet music. In late May or early June, they run a sale of pianos used by the University of LaVerne during the previous school year. These pianos have been well-maintained, are fully warrantied, and can be bought at prices 15% to 20% below *discounted* new piano prices at The Piano Outlet. *The coupon entitles you to a free piano lamp of your choice (value to $200) with the purchase of any new piano.*

West L. A. Music
11345 Santa Monica Blvd., West Los Angeles (310) 477-1945
Mon.-Fri., 11-7; Sat., 10-6
Terms: MC, V, AE, Check. Exchanges.   Parking

West L. A. Music carries guitars, keyboards and drums, and all the paraphernalia and accessories that go with them (with the exception of sheet music, there's some but not much of that), as well as speakers, microphones, synthesizers, recording equipment, mixers, music software, everything for the studio. Their prices are generally the lowest around, but should you manage to find an item elsewhere for less, they'll refund the difference.

Discount Catalogs

Carvin
(800) 854-2235
Terms: MC, V, Checks. Returns.

Carvin manufactures mixers, equalizers, amps, microphones, cables, loudspeakers, sound systems, guitars, guitar parts, guitar amps, and speaker parts, and sells them directly to you at discount prices. Generally discounts run 40% to 50%, but if they are having a sale you can save up to 70%. All products have a one year warranty (guitars, two years), and there is a technical service department to answer your questions.

Interstate Music Supply
(800) 982-BAND
Terms: MC, V, Checks. Returns.

Interstate Music Supply has varying sales and close-outs where you can routinely save 50%, often much more, on everything from snare drums to bass guitars to Renaissance trumpets, and the accessories that go with them. They also sell microphones and sound systems.

Office Supplies and Equipment

Office Supplies

The Office Depot
1355 W. 109 St., Gardena (310) 538-8045
Mon.-Fri, 8-8; Sat., 9-5; Sun, 11-5
(13 additional locations; see Geographical Index)
Terms: MC, V, Check. Returns.   Parking

You can buy everything for the office here, from pens to computers, desks to paper cutters to paper clips, and discounts range from 30% to 75%. They take orders by phone or fax, 24 hours a day, seven days a week. The stores are huge and staffed with pleasant people, ready to help. They deliver, for a fee, and will special order anything they don't carry at a 25% discount, generally available the next business day. Take home a catalog.

Staples
1830 S. LaCienega Blvd., Los Angeles (310) 287-3950
Mon.-Fri., 7-7; Sat., 9-6; Sun. 11-5
(25 additional locations; see Geographical Index)
Terms: MC, V, AE, D, Check. Returns. Parking

Staples is a membership buying store, but membership is free. You don't have to join, but might as well, because if you don't, you'll pay 5% more. Staples guarantees to meet the lowest prices you can find. They sell everything from computers to, well, staples, at discounts averaging 50%. Special orders are 25% off list price and they guarantee delivery within three days. There is a free delivery service on all purchases of $150 or more. You can order by fax, they offer extended service plans for business machines, the option of saving more through purchasing bulk packs, and they feature products made of recycled material. Call for a catalog: (800) 333-3330.

See also
> Checks in the Mail
> The Typebox

Office Machines

Action Copiers
8105 Orion Av., Van Nuys (800) 325-2590
Mon.-Fri., 9-5; Sat., 9-12
Terms: MC, V, Check. Final sale.   Parking

Action Copiers sells new copiers at up to half price, but they also sell repossessed copiers that have been factory serviced. These sell for as low as 20% of their original price, and come with a 90 day warranty. There are service

---
Copiers as low as 20% of their original price
---

contracts available on all machines, new and used. There are usually over 200 machines in the store at any one time, but models vary. If you buy a copier from Action they will sell you copier supplies, generally at 10% over cost. They also discount new fax machines. Most of the clientele are retailers; buy at the same prices they do.

Dyna-tek
14525 Valleyview, Suite F, Santa Fe Springs (310) 802-8120
Mon.-Fri., 9-5; Sat., 9-2
Terms: MC, V, AE, Check. Final sale.   Parking

Dyna-tek sells faxes machines, copiers and color monitors that are bankruptcy repossessions. They are all reconditioned, some models come with a one year parts warranty and a 30 days labor warranty, on other models this is available at an additional charge. You can save a lot of money by going this route. A Ricoh Laser Fax that retailed for $10,995 was selling here for $795.

See also
> A.B.E. Office Furniture

Discount Catalogs

Fax City
(800) 426-6499
Terms: MC, V, AE, Check. Returns.

Fax City stocks fax machines, paper and supplies, and discounts can range to 50%. Among the brands they carry are Brother, Canon, Epson, Minolta, Panasonic, Ricoh, Sanyo, Sharp and Toshiba. They will send a price list, or if you have a model in mind, call for a quote. They also offer specials on fax paper.

Torres Ribbon Company
(714) 796-5559
Terms: Cash or Check. Returns.

Torres specializes in ribbons and toner cartridges for printers, laser printers and copiers. You can buy new ribbons, or save money by having your old ones re-inked. They do not sell toner cartridges, but will refill your old ones (they say cartridges can be refilled two or three times before giving up the ghost).

Viking Office Products
(800) 421-1222
Terms: V, MC, Check. Returns.

Viking offers a catalog full of great deals on office products, with discounts up to 78%. I found printer ribbons here at about half the price of other *discount* stores; you had to buy in a minimum quantity, and they were an off-brand, but the savings were substantial. There is free delivery on orders of $25 or more, and your merchandise arrives the next day. (Remember this next time you need a carton of computer paper. They will bring it to your door.) Each catalog offers new specials and gifts with purchase. Their store in downtown Los Angeles is at 13809 S. Figueroa.

Adventurous?
Your local newspaper lists auctions where office and other equipment is sold for pennies on the dollar

Outlet Malls

Outlet Malls are made up of stores operated by nationwide manufacturers, selling discontinued first quality merchandise, some seconds and irregulars, at discounted prices. Before the advent of these malls one had to travel widely to find this kind of diversity in discount shopping, and while you won't find everything, **discounts of 20% to 90% are available daily on brand names**, from clothing and sporting goods to china and toys. Generally out in the middle of nowhere, the malls offer manufacturers low overhead while giving the consumer quality merchandise at close to wholesale prices.

Some bargain shoppers aren't that impressed on visiting an outlet mall for the first time. They can do better then 20% off at just about any department store, several times a season, during sales. But outlet malls offer the convenience of many discount retailers in one location, discounts everyday, and they too have sales, where markdowns are taken off *already discounted prices*. First quality merchandise can be reduced as much as 90% during these sales.

There are a few things to remember when planning a trip to these malls. Firstly, despite the trees and the orange groves and the birds of paradise, Southern California is still a desert. When you get to Barstow or Cabazon, this will be quite apparent, so a hat, sunscreen, frequent hydration, and comfortable shoes will make the outing more pleasant. And with the number of stores (up to 50), it's wise to do some advance planning. Decide which ones are important to see and go to them first, because at the big malls there isn't time to see everything and get home the same day. If you aren't sure about a store, walk in, let the merchandise register, and if it's not to your taste walk out. Immediately. A bargain isn't a bargain if it isn't you, and with so much to look at and so many good deals to be had, on one of these trips time can be your most precious commodity.

What follows is a list of Southern California outlet malls and the stores included in them. Some of these stores are reviewed in the body of this book. Those that are not were not left out because they didn't offer good value, but because of space constraints.

Outletbound, (800) 336-8853, can give you information on outlet malls across the country. On request, they'll send you information on malls in specific areas, so you can save money wherever you go.

Factory Merchants of Barstow
2837 Lenwood Rd., Barstow (619) 253-7342
Lenwood Rd. exit of the 15 Freeway
Mon.-Sun., 9-8

This mall is located between Los Angeles and Las Vegas, and it's closed Thanksgiving and Christmas. If you call they'll send you a brochure describing the layout and listing the merchants. They include:

ACA Joe	Johnston & Murphy
Adolfo II	Kitchen Collection
Aileen	Leading Designer Outlet
Anne Klein	Leather Loft
Banister Outlet	Leggoons Sportswear
Barbizon Outlet	L'eggs/Hanes/Bali
Bass Outlet	Lenox
Big Dogs Sportswear	Levi's Outlet
Black & Decker	London Fog Outlet
Book Warehouse	Oneida
Boot Factory, The	Oshkosh B'Gosh
Bruce Alan Bags	The Paper Outlet
Bugle Boy	Polly Flinders Childrenswear
Capezio Shoes	Rawlings Sporting Goods
Coach Value Store	Reebok
Corning Revere Factory Store	The Ribbon Outlet
Designer Brands Accessories	Robert Scott & David Brooks
Eagle's Eye	Royal Doulton
Evan-Picone/Gant	Sergio Tacchini
Fieldcrest Cannon	Skyr
Fragrance World	Socks Galore & More
General Housewares	Swank
Gitano Outlet	Toys Unlimited
Hanes Activewear	Van Heusen
Izod Monet	Wallet Works, The
John Henry & Friends	Welcome Home

The restaurant here, Lunch Break, is small; the menu not much beyond a few sandwiches, chips, coffee, soda and ice cream.

On the way out on 15 you'll pass the Roy Rogers and Dale Evans Museum in Victorville. Roy is rumored to stop in and greet guests on mornings he's in town, so you might want to stop here first. You can see good old Trigger anytime (as long as you enter before 3:30). This actually *is* his final resting place. If you continue on towards Las Vegas, the Calico Ghost Town, remnants of a real ghost town, is another attraction just off 15 past Barstow.

The Citadel
5675 E. Telegraph Rd., City of Commerce (213) 888-1220
Washington exit of the 5 Freeway
Mon-Sat., 9-8; Sun., 10-6

The Citadel is nine miles south of downtown Los Angeles and 13 miles from Orange County, in an old tire factory resembling an Ancient Near Eastern Temple. The Citadel contains:

Aileen	Joan and David Shoes
Ann Taylor Clearance Center	Kitchen Collection
Bijoux Medici	L. Bates Contemporary Clothes
Book Warehouse	Leather Loft
Capezio Shoe	Linen Club
Corning Revere Factory Store	Max Studio
Crisa Factory Stores	Multiples Modular Knits
Designer Labels for Less	Nathan J Children's Wear
Designer Labels for Men	Paper Outlet, The
Designers Own	Paul Jardin Outlet
Designs by Desre	Perry Ellis Shoes
Direction Menswear	Politix
Eddie Bauer Outlet Store	Prestige Fragrance & Cosmetics
Firenze Factory Outlet Store	Prime Time
Francine Browner Outlet	Sbicca Shoes Factory Outlet
Full Size Fashions	Socks Galore
Gap Outlet, The	Star Baby
Gitano Outlet	Toy Liquidators
Harve Bernard	United Colors of Benetton
Hawaiian Cotton	Welcome Home
In 2 Shape	Whims/Sarah Coventry

There is an outdoor dining area; choose from Johnny Rockets, Sbarro, Taipan Express, Steve's Ice Cream, Heidi's Frogen Yozurt, David's Cookies, and Subway Sandwiches.

To order additional copies of this book, please see the last page

Desert Hills Factory Stores
48650 Seminole Rd., Cabazon (714) 849-6641
Fields Road exit of the 10 Freeway
Mon.-Sun., 9-8

The stores currently in the Cabazon Outlet Mall are:

Adolfo II	Joan and David Shoes
Adrienne Vittadini	John Henry
Aileen	Johnston Fashions for Children
Albert Nipon	Jones New York
American Tourister	Kitchen Collection
Anne Klein	Leather Loft
Barbizon Lingerie	Maidenform
Bass Shoes	Nike Factory Store
Capezio Shoes	Oneida Silver
Corning Revere Factory Store	Paper Outlet, The
Designer Brands Accessories	Patagonia
Designer's Own/Nancy Johnson	Perry Ellis Shoes
Duffel	Pfaltzgraff Stoneware
Eddie Bauer Outlet Store	Ribbon Outlet, The
Esprit	Robert Scott & David Brooks
Evan Picone/Gant	Royal Doulton
Famous Footwear	Socks Galore
Full Size Fashions	SpaGear
Geoffrey Beene	Tanner
Gitano Outlet	Toy Liquidators
Gorham	Van Heusen
Guess?	Wallet Works, The
Harve Bernard	Welcome Home
Hawaiian Cotton	West Point Pepperell
He-Ro Group Outlet	The Wicker Factory

There is a food court here, offering corndogs, Chinese food, croissant sandwiches, pastry and Mexican food.

An attraction for young kids is the Dinosaur Truck Stop, on 10 on the way to Cabazon. Can't recommend the food because I've never stopped (in too much of a hurry to get to those bargains), but the dinosaurs *do* look inviting.

Lake Elsinore Outlet Center
17600 Collier Av., Lake Elsinore (714) 245-3767
Central Av. exit off the 15 Freeway
Mon.-Sat., 10-9; Sun., 11-6

The Lake Elsinore Outlet Center includes the following manufacturers:

Adolfo II	Leslie Fay Manufac. Outlet
American Tourister	Liz Claiborne
Bass Shoe	London Fog Outlet
Cape Isle Knitters	Maidenform
Chicago Cutlery, Etc.	Marika
Cole Haan	Nathan J Outlet
Crisa Factory Store	Nike Factory Store
Famous Brands Houseware	The North Face
Geoffrey Beene	Oneida Factory Store
Hang Ten Outlet	Perfumania
He-Ro Group Outlet	Sbicca Shoes Factory Outlet
I.B. Diffusion	Socks Galore
i.e.	Van Heusen
JH Collectibles	Wallet Works
Jones NY Factory Store	Welcome Home
Leather Loft	West & Co.
L'Eggs/Hanes/Bali	Whims/Sarah Coventry Outlet

At this point food service consists of a popcorn cart, and a coffee wagon with sandwiches, muffins and pastries. There are candy vending machines near the restrooms.

Plaza Continental Factory Stores
3700 E. Inland Empire Blvd., Ontario (714) 980-6231
Haven Av. exit of the 10 Freeway
Mon-Sat., 10-9; Sun., 10-6

Plaza Continental Factory Stores offers the following outlets:

Adolfo II	Hathaway Factory Outlet
Aileen	In 2 Shape/Designer's Own
Book Warehouse	Leather Loft
Capezio Shoes	Olga/Warners Factory Outlet
Converse Factory Outlet	Prestige Fragrance & Cosmetics
Corning Revere Factory Store	Sbicca Shoes Factory Outlet
Crisa Factory Stores	Welcome Home
Gitano Outlet	Whims/Sarah Coventry

There are *real* restaurants in and alongside this mall, as well as a coffee and popcorn cart for snacks.

San Diego Factory Outlet Center
4498 Camino de la Plaza, San Ysidro (619) 690-2999
Camino de la Plaza exit of the 5 Freeway
Mon-Fri., 10-8; Sat., 10-7; Sun., 10-6

Here you will find the following manufacturer's outlets:

Accessorize Fashions Jewelry Outlet	Izod/Gant
Adolfo II	Leather Loft
Aileen	Levi's Factory Outlet
Banister 40 Brand Outlet	Maidenform
Bass Shoe Factory Outlet	Marika
Black & Decker Factory Outlet	Mikasa Factory Store
Book Warehouse	Multiples Modular Knits
Corning Revere Factory Store	Nike Factory Store
Designer Accessories Outlet	PFC Fragrance & Cosmetics
Eddie Bauer Factory Store	Polly Flinders Childrenswear
Famous Brands Housewares Outlet	Ribbon Outlet, The
Fieldcrest Cannon	Star Baby
Firenze Factory Outlet Store	Toy Liquidators
G&G Nintendo-Sega Outlet	Van Heusen Factory Store
Georgiou	Wallet Works, The
Gitano Factory Store	Welcome Home

There is a restaurant here, Filippi's, as well as a post office.

This is the last U. S. exit on the freeway, so sightseeing from here might include Tijuana.

More Outlet Malls

Two factory outlet malls are being planned for the Gorman area, and malls in Pismo Beach, Camarillo, Brea and Palmdale are soon to be opened.

Paint and Wallpaper

Mann Brothers Paints & Lacquer
757 N. La Brea Av., Los Angeles (213) 936-5168
Mon.-Fri., 7-5; Sat., 8-3
Terms: MC, V, Cash, Check. Returns.		Parking

Mann Brothers does most of its business with the film studios, but this is a secret do-it-yourselfer's haven. They not only carry a large variety of paints and stains, they will share their expertise on using them. If you're interesting in marbelizing, sponge painting, antiquing, woodgraining or aging walls, floors or furniture, come on in; materials will be discounted 15% to 18%, and advice is free. Should you run into a disaster mid-job, during business hours, call them and they'll tell you how to get out of it. Their delivery area is large, and delivery is free on orders $100 or more. They'll soon have a color matching computer. Their toll free number is (800) 245-MANN.

Painters' Warehouse
11941 Exposition Blvd., West Los Angeles (310) 820-3336
Mon.-Fri., 7-5; Sat., 8-5
Terms: MC, V. Final sale.		Parking

Painters Warehouse carries Spectra-tone paints, and sells them at a 20% to 33% discount. Their vinyl acrylic flat, in factory formulated colors, is $9.95 a gallon ($15). To blend colors, the cost increases by $2. The store is stocked with brushes, varnish, spackle, everything a painter needs, all discounted.

Scotch Paint
555 W. 189 St., Gardena (310) 329-1259
Mon.-Fri., 7-5; Sat., 8-12
(also in Lancaster (805) 945-8080, and Rancho California (714) 694-9498)
Terms: MC, V, AE, D, Check. Returns.		Parking

Scotch Paint manufactures gloss enamel, acrylic stain, and a variety of primers, paints and lacquers, and sells them in one and five gallon cans, factory direct. They also sell paint related items: brushes, rollers, furniture stripper, caulking, putty, wallpaper remover, glazing compound and wood stain. All items are discounted 10% to 20%. In a high volume order, delivery is free.

The Wallpaper Bin
8969 Tampa Av., Northridge (818) 886-1291
4255 E. Main St., Ventura (805) 642-6422
Mon.-Sat., 10-6
Terms: MC, V, Check. Final sale.   Parking

This store is full of high quality wallpaper and borders, mainly discontinued patterns and over-stocks, at discounts beginning at 55%, and sometimes going as high as 80%. Papers that once retailed for $18.95 routinely sell at $7.95; those once selling for $24.95 and $27.95 (and an occasional much more expensive pattern) are $8.95. Borders are available from $6.99, and many of the papers are pre-pasted and vinyl coated. There are specials in the back of the store, often two rolls for $10.

Wallpapers To Go
18851 Ventura Blvd., Tarzana (818) 996-6063
Mon.-Sat., 10-6; Thurs. to 8; Sun., 12-5
(11 additional locations; see Geographical Index)
Terms: MC, V. Returns.   Parking

About half the stock here is discounted at any one time. Markdowns range from 15% to 35%; wallpaper rolls are priced from $13 to $18; and you can take a roll home to see how it looks in your room. There are close-out bins of borders at $1.99, and wallpaper at additional discounts of 50%. There are three major sales annually: Spring, Summer and Fall.

Discount Catalogs

Post Wallcovering Distributors, Inc.
(800) 521-0650
Terms: MC, V, Check.

Post claims to beat any price on wallpaper and major brands of window blinds. Because they're out of state there is no sales tax, and they pay freight. They're merchandise is first quality and they will quote you a price over the phone, if you give them the name of the book, style, and retail price.

Other services operating the same way are:
  Action Discount Wallpaper Company (800) 972-7691
  Ameritone Paint (800) 548-1036
  Direct Discount Wallcoverings (800) 523-5070

Party and Paper Goods

Alin Party Supply
4929 Woodruff, Lakewood (310) 925-5501
Mon.-Fri., 9-9; Sat., 9-6; Sun., 9-5
(also in Downey, Fountain Valley, and Riverside)
Terms: MC, V, Check. Exchanges. Parking

This huge party store sells everything for a bash. "Happy Birthday" balloons in a variety of names—never mine— were $1.69 a dozen; balloons by the gross were $11.99. Plastic utensils were .99 a dozen, and matching 9" plates (50) were $3.09. Fifty luncheon napkins were $2.49, and a matching plastic table cover (54" x 108") was $1.59. In the close-out corner everything is 50% off.

Herman's Party Supplies
2547 Pacific Coast Hwy., Torrance (310) 530-7735
3220 Industry Dr., Signal Hill (310) 597-0838
Mon.-Fri., 10-7; Sat., 10-5:30; Sun., 11-4
Terms: MC, V, AE, Check. Exchanges. Parking

Herman's offers a variety of party supplies, gift wrap and decorations at discounts of about 10%. There is a 50% off section, where dinner napkins (40) were $1.30, 7 oz. hot cups (25) were $1.85 and 10 1/2" plates (8) were $1.85, and a kid's birthday registry; register your child, and he or she gets a card on their birthday, asking them to come in for their free gift and balloons!

The Paper Outlet
Factory Merchants of Barstow (619) 253-5584
Desert Hills Factory Stores at Cabazon (714) 849-4771
Hours vary by location.
Terms: V, MC, Check. Exchanges. Parking

This is one of my favorite places to save money. Wrapping paper is $3.97 a pound (approximately 40 square feet, enough to wrap 20 shirt boxes). There are lots of patterns to choose from, and bows (10 for $1.05) and ribbon (curling ribbon, 300 yds., $1.79) to go with them. Tissue paper, gift boxes, and a selection of party goods, all at discount prices round out the wares. Dinner napkins were $1.79 a pound and cocktail napkins, $2.29 a pound (97-99 napkins to a pound). Color coordinated party goods are at competitive prices, and from time to time they have close-outs.

Parties-N-Us
25782 Obrero, Mission Viejo   (714) 770-6244
Mon.-Fri., 9-6; Sat., 9-5; Sun., 10-4
Terms: MC, V ($20 min.), Check. Returns.   Parking

The regular prices here are discounted 10%, but they've decided to go roll back prices to the '80's; you can find a pack of 50 beverage napkins for $2.21, 50 luncheon napkins for $3.03, 7" and 9" plates (24) for $2.30 and $3.38 respectively. There is a clearance section at half price, with a selection of cups, plates and napkins. The store also offers balloons, plastic tableware, tablecloths, cards, wrapping paper and ribbon. There is a senior citizens discount of 10% on Mondays, but this does not apply to clearance goods.

Party Corner Discount Party Center
11422 Laurel Cyn. Blvd., Mission Hills   (818) 365-6909
Mon.-Thurs., 10-6; Fri., 10-7; Sat., 9-6; Sun., 11-4
Terms: MC, V, D, AE, Check. Exchanges.   Parking

This store is tremendous, and full of decorations, balloons, costumes, wrapping paper, favors and pinatas. There is a choice of papergoods for every conceivable occasion. Plates (25) were $2.84 in the 9" size, in the 7" size, $1.97; luncheon napkins (50) were $2.50, and beverage napkins were $1.87. Nine ounce hot cups (24) were $2.37, and a plastic table cover was $1.67 (54"x108"). Matching plastic utensils (12) were .97. They also carry gift wrap, ribbons, and offer 25% off printed wedding invitations. There is a large close-out table of party goods at half price.

Party World
11910 Pico Blvd., West Los Angeles   (310) 473-8822
Mon.-Fri., 10-7; Sat., 9:30-5:30
(18 additional locations; see Geographical Index)
Terms: MC, V, Check. Returns.   Parking

Party World offers lots of choices in party goods, at competitive prices. Eight ounce hot drink cups (24) were $2.79, matching beverage napkins (50), $1.80. Plastic coated plates (24) in the 9" size were $3.09 (24); 7" plates were $1.99. There is a 15% discount on cases. They also have a close-out section, where all items are reduced 50%. They carry gift wrap, cellophane, ribbons and bows, pre-printed invitations, centerpieces and cards.

Standard Brands
3020 Wilshire Blvd., Santa Monica   (310) 828-0022
Mon.-Fri., 10-5; Sat., 10-4
Terms: MC, V, Check. Final sale.   Parking

A bouquet of 12 helium balloons is $5.88, possibly the lowest price in the city. They also sell discounted party goods.

Boxes, Moving and Mailing Supplies

Box City
10775 W. Pico Blvd., West Los Angeles   (310) 474-5144
Mon.-Sat., 9-6; Sun., 11-4
(also in North Hollywood, Van Nuys and Valencia)
Terms: MC, V, D, AE, Check.   Parking

Box City sells over 200 sizes of boxes, cushioning material and shipping supplies; they also gift wrap and ship. On moving boxes, they are consistently cheaper than Bekins, 28% to 40%.

Pickwick Paper Products
1791 Placentia Av., Costa Mesa   (714) 548-5591
Mon.-Fri., 8-5
Terms: MC, V, Check. Final sale.   Parking

This moving and packaging supply wholesaler sells to the public. The more you buy, the lower the price. They carry mailing bags, boxes, peanuts, bubblepack and other moving supplies.

Wholesale Paper Houses

With home computers and sophisticated printers making more of us desk-top artists and publishers, wholesale paper houses are a money-saving alternative to stationers. The following companies sell to individuals.

Kelly Paper
1405 Sunkist St., Anaheim   (714) 758-0936
Mon.-Fri., 8-5; Sat., 9-1
(17 additional locations; see Geographical Index)
Terms: Cash and Check only. Returns w/rstg.   Parking

Kirk Paper
11800 W. Olympic Blvd., West Los Angeles (310) 478-4026
Mon.-Fri., 7:30-5; Sat., 8-4
(12 additional locations; see Geographical Index)
Terms: V, MC, Check. Returns.　　　　　　　Parking

Business and Personal Checks

Checks in the Mail
P. O. Box 7802, Irwindale, CA 91706 (800) 733-4433
Terms: Check.

Checks in the Mail prints checks cheaper than the bank. Two hundred personal checks, are $4.95, first order, $6.95, re-order; 400 checks, the best buy, are $11.50. They also offer duplicate, business and computer checks.

Printing

The Typebox   COUPON
1604 Vista del Mar, Hollywood (213) 464-2463
Mon.-Fri., 9-5; Sat., 10-2
Terms: Cash and Check only.　　　　　　　Parking

Here you'll find quality printing at discounted prices. They do everything from business and social stationary to business cards, resumes, zed cards, newsletters, invitations, flyers, graphic design, veloxes, stats, typesetting, mailing lists, and posters, all at low prices. During their promotions, their prices are *the lowest in the country.* The service is friendly and the staff is full of advice on

---

Promotional specials feature the lowest printing prices in the country

---

how to do your job well and cost effectively at the same time. They periodically liquidate office supplies and other goods at ridiculously low prices. Ask if anything's on close-out. ***The coupon entitles you to 10% off on your next purchase (not including promotional specials).***

Pet and Equestrian Supplies

If you're interested in getting a cat or dog, your local Humane Society has lots of them ready to be adopted. Cost is minimal; pay for the license and vaccinations, and give a homeless pet a home.

Alan's Acquarium
845 Lincoln Blvd., Venice (310) 399-5464
Mon.-Fri., 11-8; Sat.-Sun., 10-6
Terms: MC, V, AE, D, Check. Exchanges.   Street parking

This is a two level pet shop selling acquariums, fish, tarantulas, reptiles, snakes, birds, rodents, chameleons and fishing bait, as well as everyday pet supplies, all at discount prices. Premium pet food specials vary; I found Science Diet, Canine Maintenance (40 lbs.), at $27.95, and Feline (20 lbs.), at $22.95.

Barbara and Carolyn's Quality Tack
735 Windy Dr., Newberry Park (805) 498-7675
Mon-Sat., 10-6; Sun., 12-5
Terms: MC, V, Check. Exchanges.   Parking

This shop carries new and used tack and saddles, both Western and English. While new merchandise is sold at retail prices, if you can find what you need among the used equipment, you'll save 20% to 60% over original prices. Blemishes are noted on all items, and they do not accept anything not structurally sound. There are occasional sales, the largest in October and April, where even used merchandise is reduced.

Bracken Bird Farm
10797 New Jersey St., Redlands (714) 792-5735
Wed.-Mon., 9-5
Terms: MC, V, Check. Final sale.   Parking

Bracken breeds birds (try saying that three times fast), and sells them to retail pet stores, but you can buy here, factory direct, so to speak, at lower prices. They carry many popular breeds, including parakeets, baby parrots, and love birds. There are occasional specials, when they're overstocked with a particular breed, but these are not generally advertised. In addition to being a good deal, this is a nice family outing, with some suprises of nature.

C&C Pet Supermarket
20920 Sherman Way, Canoga Park   (818) 348-3018
Mon.-Fri., 9:30-6; Sat., 9-5; Sun., 11-5
Terms: MC, V, Check. Exchanges.   Parking

This tremendous store promises to beat any lower verifiable price on pet food. They carry everything your pet needs, at discount prices. There are cages, beds and furniture, doggy doors, medical and grooming needs, bulk biscuits and birdseed as well as cans, cases and sacks of food. Some items are on special as you stroll around the store, and there is a mailing list to be kept apprised of future sales. A low cost vaccination clinic is offered weekly.

Collar and Leash
8615 Beverly Blvd., West Hollywood   (800) 640-PETT
Mon.-Sat., 9-9; Sun., 11-7
Terms: V, MC, Check. Exchanges.   Parking

Food, medical supplies, vitamins and accessories for dogs and cats, as well as bird and small animal supplies are here at discount prices, but pets must be on a leash to browse. Monthly specials on varying high quality foods are featured. I found Science Diet Canine Maintenance (40 lb.), at $19.99; Feline (20 lb.), $24.99. They also discount shampoos, furniture, collars and leashes. Low cost vaccination clinics are held periodically. Watch out for the black cat lounging in the feline food aisle.

Consolidated Pet Foods
1840 14 St., Santa Monica   (310) 393-9393
Mon.-Fri., 8-5; Sat., 8:30-12:30
Terms: Check and Cash only.   Parking

Consolidated offers competitive prices on premium pet foods, and they also deliver, for free, from Oxnard to San Juan Capistrano, a bonus if you want the

---
Free delivery from Oxnard to San Juan Capistrano
---

savings those huge sacks can offer, but aren't able to get them from the car to the house. Consolidated has also created their own foods for a variety of special diets. Ask about new customer discounts.

Discount Pet Center
3840 Midway, Culver City (310) 202-1115
Mon.-Fri., 10-7; Sat., 10-5
Terms: MC, V, AE, D, Check. Exchanges.   Parking

COUPON

Discount Pet Center carries a complete line of pet foods and supplies at about a third off, but will match any lower price. They also sell rodents and a lot of exotic birds—which you'll find perched around the store. If you're having a problem with your animal talk to them; advice is included in the service. They have a flea product sale during flea season, and offer low cost vaccination clinics. ***The coupon entitles you to 10% off one purchase.***

Discount Pet Food
17641 Vanowen, Van Nuys (818) 996-2066
Mon., 10-7; Tues.-Fri., 10-6; Sat., 10-5
Terms: MC, V, Check. Exchanges.   Parking

This tremendous store sells everything for all kinds of pets at a discount, from grooming needs to furniture, medications, toys, and bulk chewies. A premium pet food is always on special, and they provide a low cost vaccination clinic.

Discount Tropical Fish
561 W. La Habra Blvd., La Habra (310) 691-2037
Mon-Fri., 10-9; Sat-Sun., 10-8
Terms: MC, V, D, Check. Final sale.   Parking

If you're a fish lover, get on this mailing list. Coupons for discounts of up to 25% on products, and up to $5 off on purchases of fish, are sent out monthly. They carry many breeds, from guppies to koi, with almost everything in between, and there are different fish on sale each month. The mailings will give you the rundown.

Pet and Equestrian Thrift Store
13317 Ventura Blvd., Unit F, Sherman Oaks (818) 986-3541
Sat.-Sun., 1-5
Terms: Cash only. Final sale.   Parking

This store benefits the Equine Project, a charity dedicated to education and rehabilitation of physically handicapped young adults. It's staffed by volunteers (if you'd like to be one, give a call), and sells used animal equipment. Available are pet and animal accessories, including bird cages, acquariums, some furniture, tack and saddles. You may not realize that your pets' old bowls or collars are recyclable. Here they'll go to a good cause, and contributions are tax deductible. They also take goods on consignment.

Pet Nutrition Center
831 1/2 E. Valley Blvd., San Gabriel (818) 284-8211
Mon.-Fri., 9-7; Sat., 9-6
Terms: V, MC, AE, Check. Exchanges.   Street Parking

Pet Nutrition Center has numbered among its clients the K-9 Corps, and if it's good enough for our dogs in blue.... Premium pet foods are often on special; NutroMax Canine (40 lb.) was $28.20; Feline (20 lb.), $24.30. Delivery is free in the San Gabriel valley on orders of 100 lbs. or more. They carry a full line of discount pet supplies including 35 different brands of shampoo. If your pet isn't doing so well, come in and talk to Stan; he's been in the business for twelve years and may be able to suggest some nutritional changes that will perk that pooch or kitty, or whatever, right up.

Pet Supply
18549 Brookhurst, Fountain Valley (714) 964-5585
Mon.-Fri., 10-8; Sat., 10-6; Sun., 11-5
Terms: MC, V, AE, D, Check. Exchanges.   Parking

Pet Supply sells everything for all kinds of pets, and at as much as 50% less than surrounding stores. They will special order items they don't carry, also at a discount, but this is the kind of store where you can find oddball things others don't stock.

Steinberg's Discount Tack & Feed   **COUPON**
2929 W. Edinger Av., Santa Ana (714) 557-1180
Mon-Fri., 9:30-5:30; Sat., 9:30-5
Terms: MC, V, Check.   Parking

For English and Western equipment, English clothing, feed, and just about anything having to do with a horse, come to Steinberg's. Their prices are below everyon else's by about 10%, and if you can stand bedlam, the first week of

---
People journey from neighboring countries to this sale

November is their 20% off everything sale. In addition to your savings everyone gets a little gift at the checkout (Like some nice hoof oil?), and bigger gifts (say, a saddle) are randomly given away. Come prepared to stand in line; people travel from *neighboring countries* to this sale, which is as close to wholesale as this stuff gets. Steinberg's also offers a full line of pet products: foods, furniture, grooming and medical needs, at substantial discounts all year round. *The coupon entitles you to 10% off the purchase of any brand of dog food not on special.*

Veterinary

Animal Birth Control
1950 Pacific Coast Hwy., Lomita (310) 539-3112
(also West Los Angeles (310) 559-3313, and Palm Springs (619) 343-3697)
Terms: Cash and Check only.   Parking

Here they provide same day service for neutering pets. Male cats can be altered for $20, female cats spayed for $30; the cost for altering dogs ranges from $35 to $75, depending on size.

Holiday Humane Society, Inc.
7301 Fulton Av., North Hollywood (818) 765-8196
Tues.-Sat., 8-5
Terms: Cash and Check only.   Parking

Holiday will spay dogs for as low as $35, and neuter them for as low as $30. Cats are spayed for as low as $20, and neutered for $10. There are additional charges if pets are pregnant or in heat.

Low Cost Spay and Neuter
2407 E. Orangethorpe, Fullerton (714) 525-1331
Mon.-Fri., 8-7; Sat., 8-4
Terms: Cash and Check only.   Parking

Here you can have your cat or small dog neutered for $30; cost for dogs varies by size, and generally doesn't go higher than $75.

Pet Vaccine Services
(800) 336-4228
Terms: MC, V, D, Check.

Pet Vaccine Services travels to local pet stores, giving low cost vaccinations. Rabies shots are $4; Parvo, $6; a four-in-one cat package, $36. Call to find out when they'll be in your neighborhood.

VCA Animal Hospital West
2106 S. Sepulveda Blvd., West Los Angeles (310) 477-6735
VCA Robertson Blvd. Animal Hospital
656 N. Robertson Blvd., W. Hollywood (310) 659-2260
Hours vary by location.
Terms: MC, V, Check.   Parking

Low cost pet vaccination clinics are available on alternating Saturdays. Rabies shots are $5; a puppy vaccination package of DHLP-Parvo, Corona Bordetella and deworming for round worms is $24; a kitten vaccination package of FVRCP, deworming for roundworms and Feline Leukemia is $20. There are vaccination packages for older animals.

Discount Catalogs

Kennel Vet
(800) 782-0627
Terms: MC, V, AE, D, Check. Returns.

Kennel Vet offers vaccines, flea and tick products, vitamins and health needs, cages, crates, and grooming supplies for dogs, cats and horses, at discounts of up to 70%. The catalog is packed with pet necessities, from chewies, bones and toys to sprays to keep animals away from furniture (or your shoes). There is also a selection of books about various breeds, books on training and obedience, even dog psychology.

Pet Warehouse
(800) 443-1160
Terms: MC, V, D, Check. Returns.

Pet Warehouse offers food, medical and grooming supplies, pet carriers, exercise pens and furniture for dogs, cats, birds and fish, as well as well balanced meals for reptiles and rodents, a great variety of acquarium supplies, and books on pets and pet care, at discounts ranging to 50%.

R. C. Steele Wholesale Pet Supplies
(800) 872-3773
Terms: MC, V. Returns.

R. C. Steels has separate catalogs for cat care, dog care, acquariums, bird and grooming catalogs. Most items are discounted 50%, with close-outs as low as 70% off. Offered are beds, books and videos, grooming supplies, crates, cages, collars, foods, dental and nutritional products, deodorizers, feeders, flea repellent, toys and treats. If you want something you don't see in the catalog, ask; they may be able to get it for you.

Plants, Planters, Flowers

Botanical Gardens Plant Sales

The Los Angeles Arboretum
301 N. Baldwin Av., Arcadia (818) 821-3222
Held annually in May.
Terms: Cash and Check only. Admission $3.   Parking

The Arboretum holds its annual plant sale, the Baldwin Bonanza, every May. Sold are an array of plants propagated from specimens proven hardy for our area, as well as some never seen here before. There are also duplicates of arboretum orchids. If it's not too hot these are beautiful grounds to stroll, but don't feed the peacocks.

South Coast Botanic Gardens
26300 Crenshaw Blvd., Palos Verdes Peninsula (310) 544-1847
Held annually in May.
Terms: Cash and Check only.   Parking

The Fiesta de Flores Annual Plant Sale is held in May, and here you can find plants raised by the Botanic Garden and surrounding nurseries, from miniatures to trees, from $1 to $35. The variety of plants and bushes runs the gamut from cacti to orchids to annuals. The Native Plant Society sells drought resistant plants, and home and garden manufacturers display their products. There is food, entertainment and lectures. The sale runs two days.

Plants and Planters

C. E. Jones Ceramics
1881 S. Hoover St., Gardena (310) 323-7754
Mon.-Sat., 10-4:30
Terms: MC, V, AE. Final sale.   Parking

This is a large pottery yard, with a sizeable selection of terra cotta seconds. A

4" standard pot was .23; a 6" pot, .45 (Home Depot carried the same pot at .69). An 18" standard pot (15" high) was $17.05; a 10" Roman window box was $3.30, on up to $25.55 for a 24" box, with three sizes in between. There is a large inventory, and frequent specials are offered on seconds. The imperfections aren't noticeable, and you'd pay twice as much at a nursery.

Mainly Seconds, Pottery, Plants and Things
12144 Magnolia Blvd., North Hollywood (818) 985-4499
Mon.-Fri., 9-9; Sat., 9-6
(also in Buena Park (714) 994-0540, and Costa Mesa (714) 548-7710)
Terms: MC, V, Check. Returns.   Parking

This store is chock full of good things. There are tiny plants at tiny prices, and cacti in 6" pots are $4.99, half what you see them for elsewhere. Large, healthy plants in pots and hanging baskets are available at $6.99. Everything here is discounted, including gardening books, planters and pots (terra cotta, ceramic and copper), baskets (painted, decorated and natural), artificial and dried flowers, wreaths and other forms for making arrangements, candles and ribbon. Periodically sales are held on giftware, ceramics and picture frames bought at close-out prices. The savings are passed on to you, and can be as high as 80%. You never know what will show up, or, unfortunately, when.

Nursery Liquidators
1500 S. State College Blvd., Anaheim (714) 533-4065
Mon.-Sun., 10-5; Closed Wed.
Terms: MC, V ($20 min.). Final sale.   Parking

Shrubs and trees are the real values at this nursery, where one gallon plants, trees and shrubs are generally $2.95, two gallon pots go for $5.95, five gallon pots are $9.95 and seven gallon pots are $19.95. Most 15 gallon trees and shrubs are $29.95, a $60 to $90 value.

Palm City Indoor and Outdoor Plants
12204 Pico Blvd., West Los Angeles (310) 826-1232
Daily 10-6; closed Wed.
Terms: Cash only. Final sale.   Street Parking

Palm city is a small space crammed with greenery. Three foot palm and ficus trees sell for $9.99. Four foot orchids are $29, and potted plants and trees in the six foot range sell for $45. There are a few small house plants, but most of the space is taken up with larger plants and trees.

Pottery and Floral World

COUPON

3352 San Fernando Rd., Glendale (213) 254-5281
Mon.-Sun., 9-7
Terms: MC, V, AE, Check. Returns.   Parking

This is a huge, wonderful place, two places really, a warehouse full of garden pottery, planters and vases, next to a warehouse full of dried and fabric flowers, ribbons, seasonal and Christmas decorations and wreath and craft-making supplies, and all at very good prices. There are frequent half price sales on pottery, and within the floral portion of the world there are many clearance bins and stands. Some of the fabric flowers look incredibly lifelike and there are more types and combinations than I've seen anywhere. This store deserves a visit if you decorate with any of these things; the number and variety of baskets, vases, ceramics and florals is overwhelming. Whatever you're looking for, it's here. *The coupon entitles you to 10% off your next purchase.*

The Pottery Store

10761 Venice Blvd., Venice (310) 558-3124
Mon.-Sun., 9-5:30
Terms: MC, V, Check. Returns.   Street parking

This large outdoor store specializes in pottery seconds. Beautifully painted ceramic flower pots ranged from $1 to $8; small unglazed ocher and tan pots with desert scenes (nice for cacti) were $1. There were ceramic planters and vases of every description starting at $3. The seconds extended to terra cotta pots, which were quite a bit cheaper than at garden centers. There is a selection of plants at $1.50, and gift plants, potted in a ceramic container (in animal and seashell shapes) were about $10. (Or buy a planter for $3, a plant for $1.50, add some soil, a bow, and ... viola!)

San Gabriel Nursery and Florist

632 S. San Gabriel Blvd., San Gabriel (818) 286-0787
Mon.-Sun. 8-5:30
Terms: MC, V, D, Check. Returns.   Parking

This is not a discount nursery, although there is always something on sale, but this place is notable for the variety of plants, flowers, spices, vegetables, climbers, hanging baskets, bulbs, annuals, trees and topiary you can't find anywhere else, and some of their everyday prices *beat discount store sale prices.* The big annual sale is in the spring, when it seems that one quarter of the stock has been reduced. A trip here during the sale is not only good for your wallet, it's good for your soul. Get on their mailing list to receive their gardener's newsletter, telling you what new plants are in. This is a beautiful place in which to wander.

Sig's Pottery and Nursery
17825 Devonshire, Northridge (818) 368-5171
Mon.-Sat., 9-6; Sun., 9:30-6
Terms: MC, V, Check. Final sale.   Parking

Sig's carries a large variety of plants and pots, but of special interest is their wall of pottery seconds. These are ceramic glazed pots, selling for one third to half what you might pay elsewhere. Six inch ceramic pots with bottom lips were $3.19; in the 8" size, $9.99. Some of the plants were good values as well: a one gallon cyclamen sold for $3.99, cacti and succulents in 8" pots were $16.99 and up, three gallon ficus benjaminica were $15.99.

Valley Wholesale Nursery
9350 Laurel Cyn. Blvd., Pacoima (818) 767-7351
Mon.-Sat., 7:30-4:30
Terms: Cash only. Final sale.   Parking

This nursery is strictly self-service, and since no prices are marked, you find what you want, and come back and ask the price of the guy in the office. Since he has all the prices in his head you can probably call for quotes. There is a wide variety of plants, trees, flowers, bulbs, shrubs and annuals here. Five gallon azaleas were $9.75, 5 gallon camellias, $11.50; five gallon ficus benjaminica, $13.50; 5 gallon bird of paradise, $10.50. There are a variety of fruit trees; 15 gallon apple trees were $45, plum, walnut and olive trees were $40. This is a great place to be in a light rain.

See also
The 2nds Shop /Champagne Taste
Tuesday Morning

Flowers

American Flower Exchange
754 Wall St., Los Angeles (213) 627-2482
Mon.-Fri., 6-4
Terms: Cash only.   Street parking

This is the wholesale flower market, but you don't have to be a retailer to get wholesale prices. Some dealers will sell to individuals at prices 50% below retail and lower. Pay parking for the flower market is at 752 Maple; you can enter the market through the parking structure.

Arturo's Flowers
1261 N. LaBrea, Hollywood (213) 876-6482
8101 Beverly Blvd., Los Angeles (213) 655-0140
Mon.-Sat., 8-9; Sun., 8-8
Terms: MC, V, Check. Final sale.   Parking

Arturo's offers long-stemmed roses beginning at $25 a dozen and going up to $49.50 (they start at $50 everywhere else). They charge for delivery, beginning at $7.50, generally not higher than $12.50. There are plant specials, varying with the time of the year. (Remember, prices go up everywhere around February 14th.)

Something Special Flowers
14303 Ventura Blvd., Sherman Oaks (800) 544-2619
Sat., 9-7
Terms: Cash. Final sale.   Parking

Something Special is trying something different. On Saturdays they're offering as close to wholesale prices as you can get short of *schlepping* to the flower market. Examples of the specials, depending on season, are bunches of daffodils (10) for $3, and Iris (10) for $7.

Stewart Orchids
3838 S. Sepulveda Blvd., Culver City (310) 390-2574
3376 Foothill Rd., Carpinteria (805) 684-5448
Hours vary by location.
Terms: MC, V, Check.   Parking

Stewarts sells orchids, and during the year they hold several sales, where you can save 25% to 50%. Sales are generally held in January, April, May and August; there is a mailing list to let you know just when.

Garden Tools

See
    Black & Decker Outlet
    Sears Outlet
    Penney's Catalog Outlet Store
    Mongtomery Ward Outlet

Pool Supplies

J. B. Sebrell Co.
365 S. Central, Los Angeles (213) 625-2648
Mon.-Fri., 9-5:30; Sat., 9-5; Sun., 10-3
Terms: MC, V, Check.   Parking

Here you will find equipment for spas and swimming pools, both in and above ground, as well as chemicals, filters, vacuums, brushes and cleaning supplies, toys and accessories. They take trade-ins on equipment, and buy and sell used equipment. Their discounts range from 20% to 40%. Get on their mailing list for catalogs

Standard Pool
7223 Santa Monica Blvd., Hollywood (213) 851-7665
Mon.-Fri., 7-6; Sat., 8-6
Terms: AE, Check. Exchanges.   Parking

Standard Pool Supply was recommended to me by a number of pool supply wholesalers; this is the place the pool guys go when they need something, and Standard Pool sells to individuals as well. Their discounts range from 20% to 50% and they carry chemicals, filters, cleaning equipment, everything for a pool or spa.

Records and CDs

Aron's Record Shop
1150 N. Highland, Hollywood (213) 469-4700
Mon.-Thurs., 10-10; Fri., Sat., 10-12; Sun., 11-8
Terms: MC, V, D, AE. Trade. Exchanges.   Parking

Aron's carries new and older merchandise, used albums, CDs and tapes as well as imports and small labels. They take albums, CDs and tapes in trade.

CD Banzai
6250 W. Third St., West Hollywood (213) 653-0800
Mon.-Thurs., Sun., 12-6; Fri.-Sat., 12-10
Terms: MC, V, Check. Trade. Final sale.   Street parking

CD Banzai not only sells used and new CDs, they buy used CDs, paying $2.50 to $4, cash; more in credit. Used CDs sell from .49 to $9. They carry all kinds of music, and specialize in European and Japanese contemporary music that's hard to find.

Compact Disc Count
10741 W. Pico Blvd., West Los Angeles 475-4122
Mon.-Sun., 10-10
Terms: MC, V, AE, Check. Trade. Final sale.   Parking

Compact Disc Count buys and sells used and new CDs. They will buy your used CDs for up to $6 in credit, $5 cash. Used CDs sell from $7.99 to $9.99.

Disc-Connection   **COUPON**
10970 W. Pico Blvd., West Los Angeles (310) 208-7211
Mon.-Sat., 11-7; Fri. to 9
Terms: MC, V, AE, D, Check. Trade. Exchanges.   Parking

Disc-Connection discounts everything they sell, and their prices seem to be about as low as you're going to find on current CDs and tapes. They specialize in movie and show soundtracks, but carry an eclectic assortment of music, as well as books and magazines. They will purchase your old LPs and cassettes for cash or credit. ***The coupon entitles you to $1 off all new and used CDs, excluding sale items.***

Platter Puss Records
2204 Lincoln Blvd., Santa Monica (310) 396-2528
Mon.-Sat., 10-9; Sun., 11-7
Terms: MC, V, Checks. Final sale.   Street parking

Platter Puss buys and sell used CDs, beginning at $2 (they pay $1 to $5) and they have a listening booth. They also carry new CDs, and have monthly sales.

Record Surplus
8913 Sunset Blvd., West Hollywood (213) 659-9994
Mon.-Thurs., 11-9; Fri.-Sat., 11-10; Sun., 11-7
(also in West Los Angeles, Costa Mesa and Sherman Oaks)
Terms: MC, V, Check. Trade. Final sale.   Street parking

Record Surplus buys and and sells used CDs, which sell for a top price of $8.78. They pay up to $5 for used CDs, more in store credit.

Rhino Records
1720 Westwood Blvd., Westwood (310) 474-8685
Mon.-Fri., 10-11; Sat.-Sun., 10-12
Terms: MC, V, AE, Checks. Trade. Final sale. Street parking

Rhino buys, sells and trades new and used tapes, records and CDs, they have frequent parking lot sales, and bonus sales are held the first full weekend of every month.   Used CDs begin at $3.99, and you can listen before buying. They have a selection of books and videos, and they will special order.

Rockaway Records
2390 N. Glendale Blvd., Los Angeles (213) 664-3232
Mon.-Sun., 10-9:30
Terms: MC, V, Check. Trade. Final sale.   Street parking

Rockaway will buy your used CDs for up to $5 in cash, and more in credit. They sell used CDs from $1.99 to $8.99, and carry a new merchandise.

Tower Records Outlet   CCC
14621 Ventura Blvd., Sherman Oaks (818) 783-8810
Daily, 10-10
Terms: MC, V, Check. Exchanges.   Street Parking

This store offers the last of Tower Records records, lps and 45s, and a selection of cassette tapes from .25 up. CDs begin at .99, and videotapes start at $4.95. The videos have been viewed, the records are being phased out, and the CDs are overstocks, older merchandise or used.

Shoes

Men's Shoes

Converse Factory Outlet
18555 Main, Huntington Beach (714) 375-7456
Plaza Continental Factory Stores, Ontario (714) 986-0444
Hours vary by location.
Terms: MC, V, Check. Returns.   Parking

Sales here vary, but you can count on finding the lowest prices on everything Converse makes. On a recent visit the Conquest Athletic Leather basketball shoe, retailing at $74.95, was on sale for $24.99. Irregular Converse All Stars, in assorted colors, were as low as $9.99; first quality, $24.99 ($31.95). Kids Converse All Star high tops were $14.99 ($29.95).

Michael's
3747 Wilshire Blvd., Los Angeles (213) 387-6123
Mon.-Fri., 10-9; Sat., 10-6; Sun., 11-6
(also in West Los Angeles, Encino, Agoura Hills, Torrance, Santa Ana and Fullerton)
Terms: MC, V, Check. Returns.   Parking

Top quality men's shoes are sold at low prices at this chain, from the old reliable penny loafer to Italian slip-ons. Everything is discounted, but when Michael's gets low on stock in a particular style, it goes into a "$39.99 or 3 pair for $100", or " $79.98 or two for $150" sale. The brands are impressive: Bruno Magli, Johnston and Murphy, Rockport, Nunn Bush. A beautiful Bruno Magli suede sport oxford was $80 ($195); a Johnston & Murphy tassle loafer was $99.98 ($145), and French Shriner Wing-tip oxfords with manmade soles were $59.98 (three pairs of $59.98 shoes were $150).

Michael's Outlet   CCC
20930 Ventura Blvd., Woodland Hills (818) 716-8875
Mon.-Fri., 10-9; Sat., 10-6; Sun., 11-6
Terms: MC, V, Check. Exchanges.   Street parking

This is Michael's chainwide clearance center, full of inventory left over from the other stores, at even better prices. Conservative work shoes are plentiful, as are casual and sport shoes. Boxes of shoes are stacked on tables by price ($39.98 tables, going up, in $10 increments, to $99.98 tables), but the two dozen or so shoes on top of the boxes are not necessarily representative of what you'll find on the sale table. This is treasure-hunt shopping: check inside all boxes in your size. Among the brands I found were Nunn Bush, Johnston & Murphy, French Shriner, Freeman, Dexter, Rockport, Brass Boot and Topsider.

Work Boot Warehouse
21608 Sherman Way, Canoga Park (818) 703-8498
Mon-Fri., 9:30-6:30; Sat., 9-6; Sun., 11-5
Terms: MC, V, AE. Returns.   Street parking

Work Boot Warehouse is a factory outlet for such brands as Timberland, Hi-Tec, Coleman, Wolverine, Thorogood and Chippewa. In addition to work boots, they feature footwear for hunting, hiking and fishing, and will give you advice on what sort of shoe best fits your requirements. You can expect to save 10% to 20% here, and among their hundred or so styles you'll probably find what you need. A new addition is Dr. Martens.

See also
Eddy's for Men
Paul Jardin

Women's Shoes

Clayton Shoes
2800 Hayden Av., Culver City (310) 836-0765
20942 S. Normandie Av., Gardena (310) 212-0765
Mon.-Sat., 10-5:30: Sun., 11-5
Terms: MC, V, AE, D, Check. L. Exchanges.   Parking

Discounts of 15% to 25% on shoes and boots (to size 12) by Jazz, Nickels, Glacee, Capparos, Impo and Nina, as well as handbags, hats and hosiery, are always available at Clayton Shoes. Sometimes half the store is full of bargain racks where shoes are marked down an additional 25% to 50%. There is a mailing list to be apprised of special sales.

Joan and David
The Citadel, City of Commerce (213) 722-5844
Desert Hills Factory Stores at Cabazon (714) 922-2237
Hours vary by location.
Terms: MC, V, Check. Final sale.   Parking

Women's high fashion shoes can be found at these stores, with reductions starting at 30%. I found a pair of leather pumps for $85 ($192), metallic mesh sandals were $159 ($210) and a beautiful pair of Calvin Klein riding boots was $299 ($450).

Ladies Shoe Outlet
5470-B Moreno St., Montclair (714) 985-0105
Mon.-Sat. 10-6; Sun., 12-5
Terms: MC, V, Check. Exchanges.   Parking

All the goods in this store are 50% off the lowest marked price, which makes most pairs $25 and under. There are a good number of narrows and a few wides in the selection, which includes Red Cross, Life Stride, Caressa, John Weitz, Mushrooms and Beene Bag shoes. About half the inventory is one-of-a-kinds, on the rest there was some stock. Among the latter were Dolce satin pumps, suitable for dying.

Le Petit Jean   COUPON
368 N. Beverly Dr., Beverly Hills (310) 858-3843
Mon.-Sat., 10-6; Fri., 10-7
Terms: MC, V, AE, Check. Exchanges.   Parking

Le Petit Jean is not a discount store, but they offer their own label all leather women's pumps for $55. There are high and low heeled styles, and for an all leather shoe it's a steal. But it gets better: there are usually a number of styles on sale at $35. If you like a shoe but it doesn't quite fit, they'll obligingly stretch it, or put in an inner sole, or do whatever it takes to make that shoe yours. *The coupon entitles you to 10% off your next purchase of non-sale merchandise.*

Mosquitoes
9532 Brighton Way, Beverly Hills (310) 858-0129
Mon.-Sat., 10-6
Terms: MC, V, AE, Check. Exchanges.   Street parking

Adjacent to Stephane Kelian, where you can buy Miss Maud, Isaye Mikaye and Stephane Kelian shoes at $200 to $500, is Mosquitoes, the somewhat less pricey division of the outfit. Mosquitoes carries sale shoes from next door, typically at half price, in addition to the Mosquito line, made in Italy and Spain, priced in the $100 to $200 range, and generally displaying a lot more flair than department store shoes in that price range. During sales you can pick up Mosquitoes for as low as two pair for $99.

Patrini Shoes   CCC
2 E. Main St., Alhambra (818) 281-2088
Mon.-Fri., 10-9; Sat., 10-8; Sun., 11-6
Terms: AE, MC, D, V. Final sale.   Parking

Much of this store is Patrini's clearance center, where shoes sell for discounts of an additional 10% to 50% off their lowest prices.

Perry Ellis Shoes
The Citadel, City of Commerce (213) 274-3864
Desert Hills Factory Stores at Cabazon (714) 922-9204
Hours vary by location.
Terms: MC, V, Check. Exchanges.   Parking

You can find many styles here by the popular designer, and at great values. On my last visit all pumps were selling for $59.99 (to $185). Flats that had retailed for up to $110 were $49.99. There was a $19.99 "last chance" table (values to $150), and waterproof knee-high boots in a pallette of bright colors were $19.99. There were more narrow sizes then not, but plenty of stock in medium widths.

Sacha of London Outlet   CCC
1731 Wilshire Blvd., Santa Monica (310) 828-9557
Mon.-Fri., 10-9; Sat., 10-6; Sun., 12-6
Terms: MC, V, Check. Final sale.   Street Parking

How good a deal you'll get here seems to be pure luck. The day I walked in everything was 60% off the lowest marked price (discounts can range from 25% to 80%), which translated to a pair of brown suede, sling-back, open-toed

---

The day I walked in everything was 60% off the lowest marked price

---

wedgies, originally selling for $88, now $10! A white leather low cut shoe boot was $35.20, a hot pink suede sling-back high heel was $18.50. There was also a half price sale on handbags: a natural leather briefcase with shoulder strap was $34.50, and a black leather backpack was $63. Occasionally the store features a small selection of men's styles.

Samples Only, Inc.
19590 Ventura Blvd., Tarzana (818) 881-8621
Mon.-Sat., 9:30-5:30; Sun., 12-5
Terms: MC, V, Check. Exchanges.   Parking

As the name implies, Samples Only is full of sample shoes, sizes 4 through 7, and since each is a sample, there is only one pair. Among the brands are Bruno Magli, Charles Jordan, Ellen Tracy, Petra and Joyce, all at substantial savings. There is also a small selection of high fashion sample handbags, also discounted. Twice a year, usually in June and December, they hold sales, where (for cash) you can take an additional 30% to 50% off.

Sample Shoes Unlimited
1255 2 St., Santa Monica (310) 394-0026
Mon.-Sat., 10-5 and by appt.
Terms: MC,V,Check. Exchanges.   Street parking

This store specializes in sample shoes in sizes 5 to 6, has one pair of each style, and guarantees that if you find the same shoe for the same price or less, they'll give it to you. Most stock is priced 40% to 60% below retail, and they feature

---
If you find the same shoe for less, they'll give it to you

Van Eli, Sesto Meucci, Amalfi, Evan Picone, Bandalino, and Papagallo, among others. An Evan Picone flat, here $55, sold in a Robinson's catalog for $108. I found a beautiful pair of aubergine Italian leather boots selling for $95 (almost worth trying to squeeze in that size 9 tootsie). If you can't get here during business hours, call and schedule an appointment: they'll open the store Friday and Saturday nights just for you.

Shoe Crazy
150 S. Sepulveda Blvd., El Segundo (213) 414-0700
Mon.-Fri., 10-6; Sat., 10-5
Terms: MC, V, Check. Exchanges.   Parking

Shoe Crazy features shoes by Caparros, Jasmin, Chilis, Impo, Nina and others at substantial savings. Most shoes are $15 to $25, a small selection at higher prices; boots are in the $40 range.

Shoes by Shirley
17037 Ventura Blvd., Encino (818) 788-1195
Tues.-Sat., 9-5, and by appt.
Terms: MC, V, AE, Check. Returns.　　　Street parking

Shirley's features nothing over $29.99, with a $10 sale corner in back. A sampling of the brands she carries are Cobbies, Jasmin, Amalfi, Bandolino, Golo, Impo, Selby, Magdeseans and Caparros. She specializes in narrow widths, and carries from AAAA to medium (no wides). She also offers a selection of purses discounted 25%, and some boutique clothing items, also discounted. Often at discount stores, customer service goes out the window. Not here. Shoppers made point of telling me how great Shirley is to deal with.

West & Co. Shoes
Lake Elsinore Outlet Ctr. (714) 245-4070
Mon.-Sat., 10-9; Sun., 11-6
Terms: MC, V, Check. GC. Final sale.　　　Parking

This is the outlet for 9 West Shoes, and most styles begin at discounts of 30%. Leather pumps originally retailing for $56 were $39.97, suede open-toed pumps were $42.97 ($62); an ankle boot was $54.92 ($78) and there was a bargain shelf, where $50 pumps were $14.97.

See also
Bullocks Outlet
Millie's Shoes and Bags

Shoes for Men, Women and Children

Adler Shoes
860 Los Angeles St., Los Angeles (213) 689-1469
Mon.-Sat., 9:30-5:30; Sun., 11-5
Terms: MC, V, Check. Final sale.　　　Street parking

This place *looks like* a discount shoe store, full of racks at clearance prices. Dr. Martens Air Ware Oxfords and boots were $89.99 ($110). Jasmin pumps were $15 to $25, and a Mootsies Tootsies Oxford was $39 ($50). The mens' department is as extensive as the women's. A Buffaloland Moccasin was $29 ($75), Zodiac suede oxfords were half price at $49, and Black Hawk ankle lace up boots, suede or leather, were $29 ($55).

Bankruptcy Liquidators of America
2129 S. Barrington Av., West Los Angeles (310) 473-3931
Mon.-Sat., 10-6
Terms: MC, V, Check. Exchanges.   Parking

The huge inventory is made up of bankruptcies and buy-outs from store and factory closings, so not all merchandise is first quality. In stock are men's and women's dress and athletic shoes, and some men's clothing. Women's boots in varying styles were $29.99 (two for $50); shoes were $15, and included such brands as Bandolino, Jasmin, and City Limits. Men's shoes, at $90 (two for $150), had labels like Bruno Magli and Mario Bruni; and there were men's sale racks at $59.99 (two for $100). There was a large stock of name brand athletic shoes: lo-tops at $20; hi-tops, $30. Among the menswear were some great looking Hunt Club leather bomber jackets at $59 (two for $100, a buy for twins). Wool gabardine slacks were $50 and suits began at $99. There is a mailing list to be apprised of sales.

Bass Factory Outlet
Factory Merchants of Barstow (619) 253-2188
Hours vary by location.
(also in Cabazon, Lake Elsinore and San Ysidro)
Terms: MC,V, Check. Returns.   Parking

The Bass outlet features a large selection of women's and men's shoes at discounts beginning at 20%. Weejuns were $54.99, a savings of 26%, and TopSiders were $29.99, 40% below retail. Women's all leather sling-back flats were $36.99, discounted 26%, and there were $19.99 sale specials in the back of the store.

Boot Factory
Factory Merchants of Barstow (619) 253-4940
Mon.-Sun., 8-9
Terms: MC, V, Check. Returns.   Parking

This store is packed with flashy boots at great prices. Inventory is made up of irregulars and discontinued styles of Code West and Laredo Boots for men, women and kids, in a variety of colors and hides, starting at $39. There is also a selection of Minnetonka Moccasins. Get on their mailing list for notification of sales, and enter the monthly drawing to win free boots.

Capezio Factory Outlet Store
The Citadel, City of Commerce (213) 724-7723
Hours vary by location.
(also in Cabazon, Barstow and Ontario)
Terms: MC, V, AE, D, DC, Check. Returns. Parking

Here brands such as Capezio, Pappagallo, Liz Claiborne, Aerosole, Evan Picone, Easy Spirits, U. S. Sports, Reebok, French Shriner, Deerstags, Dexter, Florsheim, and Sperry Topsiders are discounted 15% to 40%. Most women's shoes had manmade soles, but a few styles did feature leather soles; many of the better men's shoes were all leather.

Cole Haan
Lake Elsinore Outlet Ctr. (714) 674-7164
Mon.-Sat., 10-9; Sun., 11-6
Terms: MC, V, AE, Check. Returns. Parking

This looks like anything but an outlet: you sit on carved wooden armchairs to try on beautiful shoes, which are discontinued styles, overruns, past sale merchandise, and occasional seconds of the Cole Haan line. There are shoes for the entire family at savings of about 40%. A men's crocodile loafer, originally $425, was $240; a woman's woven leather boot, originally $365, was $236; women's pumps and loafers, originally $195, were $130; and men's wing-tip oxfords, originally $245, were $160. Children's penny loafers, originally $84, were $56. There is also a selection of bags and belts. Your biggest problem will be that each pair you pick up you'll want a little more than the one you lusted for moments ago.

Del Rey Tennis Shoes Warehouse
10971 Currier Rd., Walnut (714) 594-4832
Mon.-Fri.,10-8; Sat.,10-7; Sun.10-6
(also in Rancho Cucomonga (714) 989-3328, and Corona (714) 278-8819)
Terms: MC, V, Check. Exchanges. Parking

This store carries athletic shoes for the whole family, as well as a selection of men's everyday and dress shoes. Prices are $10 to $30 under retail on most items, but if they're discontinuing a style the price falls dramatically, sometimes below 50%. Weeboks start at $21.99, men's Nike Pumps at $79. A woman's Reebok High Top Freestyle was $44.99, and men's Nunn Bush shoes range in price from $22.99 to $44.99. Coupons are given with some sales, for savings on your next purchase.

Famous Footwear
8150 Mira Mesa, San Diego (619) 271-5720
Mon.-Fri., 9:30-9; Sat., 9:30-6; Sun., 11-5
(also in Cabazon, Escondido, Palm Desert, Palm Springs, and Poway)
Terms: MC, V, Check. Returns.   Parking

Famous Footwear offers discounts of 20% to 33%, sometimes dropping to 50%, on shoes for the whole family. Among the brands are Reebok, Nunn Bush, French Shriner, Dexter, Impo, Esprit, Sam & Libby, Lifestride, Naturalizer, Mushrooms, Playskool, Jumping Jacks and Mootsies. If you find two pair you like on their sale racks, the second pair is half price.

Foster's Shoes
8765 W. Pico Blvd., Los Angeles (310) 278-9335
Mon.-Sat., 9:30-6; Sun., 11-5
Terms: MC, V, Check. Exchanges.   Parking

Foster's carries a large selection of Bally shoes at discounts of 25% to 50%. They also carry Sesto Meucci, Charles David, Xavier Danaud, Garolini, Nunn Bush and Johnston and Murphy. There is also a selection of men's clothing; Courreges suits were $279 ($375), and an Adolfo silk sport jacket was reduced from $235 to $139. There is a mailing list for notification of special sales.

Johnston & Murphy Outlet
Factory Merchants of Barstow (619) 253-5920
Mon.-Sun., 9-8
Terms: MC, V, AE, Check. Final sale.   Parking

A variety of men's better leather shoes, including golf shoes, are sold here at discounts of 30% to 40%. A pair of men's black wingtip oxfords were $168 ($225), and loafers were $99.50 ($165). Women's shoes are coming.

Kinney Shoes Outlet   CCC
2603 S. Bristol, Santa Ana (714) 545-6836
Mon.-Sat., 10-9; Sun., 10-6
Terms: MC, V, AE, D, Check. Returns.   Parking

This is the Kinney Shoes Clearance Center, and here shoes received from the chains' many stores are marked down an additional 30%. There are shoes for men, women and kids, in casual, athletic and formal styles. In January and July they have their major sales, where everything is marked down 60%.

Reebok Factory Store
Factory Merchants of Barstow (619) 253-5866
Mon.-Sun., 9-8
Terms: MC, V, Check. Final sale.　　　　Parking

This store has men's, women's, kids' and infants' Reeboks at discounts starting at 20%, but there's a catch: the shoes are blemished. Often it's hard to see where. In addition to the regular markdown, there are several specials each month, and a sale table where adult low-tops are $24.95, high-tops $29.95; kids shoes (0-8) are $17.95, and (8-6) $21.95; pumps were $69 for adult high-top; $59 adult low-top; and $49 for junior sizes. Also available are Rockports at discounts of 25%, and some athletic clothing.

The Shoe Club
17860 Newhope St., Fountain Valley (714) 662-4444
Mon.-Fri., 10-9; Sat., Sun., 10-6
Terms: MC, V, AE, D, Check. Returns.　　　Parking

Another in the line of lowest price athletic shoe stores, The Shoe Club's prices are competitive with the lowest. They offer Reeboks, Adidas, Rockport, K-Swiss, Avia, Ellesse, as well as a selection of men's dress and women's uniform shoes at value prices. Women's Reebok High-Top Free Styles were $43.95, boy's Reebok Basketball Pump II were $59.99, girls' Reebok Princesses were $29.99 and Converse Hi-Tops were $23.99. Dr. Martens were $79.99 and Nursemates loafers were $42.99. There are a number of discontinued styles at deeper discounts.

Shoes Here
10951 Sherman Way, Sun Valley (818) 765-5030
Mon.-Fri., 9:30-9; Sat., 9:30-6; Sun., 9:30-6:30
Terms: MC, V, Check. Returns.　　　Parking

This store carries mens and women's shoes, athletic shoes for the whole family and some children's shoes, at discounts ranging from 25% to 40%. There is a back wall of women's shoes at $14.90, and bins of sandals and huaraches at $5.90. On the men's side there is a large selection of Florsheims at $59.90 (two for $100). They carry Dr. Martens, Jazz, Impo, Van Eli, Bandolino, Jasmin, all the major sports shoes, Nunn Bush, Bally, Oleg Casini, and many others. There is a mailing list to be apprised of sales.

Standard Shoes Clearance Center   CCC
12345 Hawthorne Blvd., Hawthorne (213) 772-4712
Mon.-Fri., 10-7; Sat., 10-6; Sun., 11-5
Terms: MC, V, Check. Returns.   Street parking

This is where Standard Shoes go to retire. Men's, women's and some youth shoes, featuring such brands as Reebok, L. A. Gear, Mootsie's Tootsies, Jacques Cohen Espadrilles, Keds, Stanley Blacker, Sam and Libby's, Candies, and Pierre Cardin are a fraction of what is available, with reductions beginning at half off the original price. There is a selection of men's and women's duty shoes, from $12.25 to $19.75. Handbags are discounted 50% to 75%. The store is self service, and there are occasional sales, advertised in the *Los Angeles Times*, when shoes are often $7.50, two for $10.

Thieves Market
12241 Wilshire Blvd., West Los Angeles (310) 820-4288
Mon.-Sat., 10-9; Sun., 11-5
(also in Studio City, Torrance, Costa Mesa, Fullerton, Northridge, Glendale, Los Angeles, San Dimas, Los Alamitos, and El Toro)
Terms: MC, V, AE, Check. Returns.   Parking

Thieves Market has the biggest selection of discounted western boots you're likely to see, and a smattering of leather jackets, belts, belt buckles and hats. If you don't see what you want let them know, they'll note your request and if something like it comes in they'll call. They have two big sales annually, January and August, where at least half the store is further marked down. Justin Buffalo boots were $179 ($225); a smooth quill ostrich boot was $200 ($300); lizard and embroidered leather boots were $149 ($329) and sea bass (no joke) was $80.

Top To Top
2313 Wilshire Blvd., Santa Monica (310) 829-7030
4724 1/4 Admiralty Way, Marina Del Rey (310) 821-6111
Mon.-Sat., 10-8; Sun., 10-6
Terms: MC, V, Check. Final sale.   Parking

Top to Top guarantees it will meet anyone's price in athletic shoes. It offers Nike, Reebok, Avia, Brooks, New Balance, Asics, Saucony, K-Swiss, and Ellesse shoes at prices below other discounters. There's a mailing list for notice of their two annual sales, May and October, and often a $10 coupon in local papers.

Van's Factory Outlet
1212 S. Bristol, Santa Ana (714) 957-6130
Mon.-Fri., 10-8; Sat.-Sun., 10-6
Terms: MC, V, AE, D, Check. Final sale.   Parking

On the walls of this store are shoes that sell for full retail price, but taking up the center, and most of the store, are racks of "sale" shoes, discounted to 40%, irregulars and seconds of Van's canvas, suede and leather casuals. Kids' and infants' shoes don't go over $14, and sell regularly for up to $27.99; women's canvas shoes go up to $15, and leather and suede shoes to $20; men's canvas shoes are priced up to $20 and suede and leather shoes up to $25. The ceiling for youth shoes is $18 canvas; $25, leather and suede.

Warehouse Shoe Sale
4935 McConnell Av., #7, Culver City (310) 827-8024
Hours vary by location.
(also in Huntington Beach, Compton, Oxnard, Los Angeles and Santa Ana)
Terms: MC, V, Check. Exchanges.   Parking

This is a store for the whole family. Athletic shoes are discounted 20% to 40%; an assortment of shoes and boots for women ranged from $15 to $45; men's shoes began at about $29. There are work boots, canvas slip-ons, sneakers and kids' shoes, as well as a selection of sweats and sport clothes.

See also
Nana Outlet
Pillers of Eagle Rock
Nordstrom Rack
Shirley's Shoes & Bags

Discount Catalogs

Justin Discount Boots
(800) 677-BOOT
Terms: V, MC, GC, COD. Returns.

Justin sells boots, western headwear, belts, shirts and jeans, but the best priced items are the ones they manufacture. There are boots for kids, youth, men and women, at savings from 15% to 25%. Boots are available in a variety of skins.

Sporting Goods and Athletic Wear

Foot Locker Outlet
115 Lincoln Blvd., Venice (310) 450-8178
1775 Artesia Blvd., Manhattan Beach (310) 376-7277
Mon.-Fri., 10-9; Sat., 10-7; Sun., 11-6
Terms: MC, V, Check. Returns.   Parking

These stores offer name brand athletic shoes at discounts of 30% to 50%. Since the merchandise is discontinued, don't expect to find all sizes in all styles. They also stock marked down sports clothing. On a recent visit I found Lycra Nike leggings, regularly on sale at Foot Locker for $15.90, here $7.90; a men's Nike nylon jumpsuit was $49.95 ($140); a Lakers windbreaker, $11.95 ($40).

The Golf Exchange
830 S. Olive, Los Angeles (213) 622-0403
Mon.-Fri., 9-5; Sat., 9-4
Terms: MC, V, Check. Final sale.   Street parking

The Golf Exchange sells golf clubs, shoes and golfing accessories at discounts of 20% to 40%. You'll find used clubs and equipment in the *eighth room back* of this seemingly unending store; the first seven are full of new, discounted merchandise.

H&H Jobbing Company
840 S. Los Angeles St., Los Angeles (213) 627-6861
Mon.-Sat., 9-5
Terms: MC, V, Check. Final sale.   Street parking

This ski and tennis outlet features clothing for men, women and children by top manufacturers. You'll find everything from parkas and jumpsuits to sweatsuits, sweaters and shirts, all at a discount. Much of the ski clothing, according to store tags, originally retailed around $400. Pieces were marked down several times, and by February most jumpsuits were going for $149, and down to as low as $50. Ski pants were $49, down from $149, many adult jackets were in the $149 range, and kids' jackets and jumpsuits were around $49. There is a wide selection of manufacturers, colors and styles.

Love Tennis
4134 Lincoln Blvd., Marina del Rey (310) 390-6177
Mon.-Fri., 10-6; Sat., 9:30-5:30; Sun., 12-4
Terms: V, MC, Check. Exchanges.   Parking

Love Tennis is not a discount store, but there's always something on sale here. It features everything for the tennis buff: clothing for men and women, racquets, balls, shoes and accessories. They have a large sale in February where almost everything is reduced.

Manufacturer's Sports Outlet
1134 Chapala St., Santa Barbara (805) 965-6652
Mon.-Sat., 10-6; Sun., 12-5
Terms: MC, V, D, Check. Final sale.   Street parking

Manufacturer's Sports Outlet sells Hind and Danskin athletic wear for working out, cycling and swimming. There are first quality pieces at retail prices, but also a stock of Hind seconds and close-out merchandise, which is reduced. Men's running shorts were $6 to $11; women's running shorts were $10 and up; men's bikini swimsuits ranged from $7 to $14, women's suits began at $14; cycling shorts were $17. There are insulated suits, sweats, workout tights and accessories; seconds are available in most styles.

Nevada Bob's Golf and Tennis
131 W. Katella Av., Anaheim (714) 520-0687
Mon.-Fri.,10-10; Sat., 10-9; Sun., 10-8
(also in Canoga Park, City of Industry, Costa Mesa, Laguna Hills, Los Alamitos, Montclair, Pasadena, Riverside, Torrance and West Los Angeles)
Terms: MC, V, AE, CB, Check. L. Returns.   Parking

This chain features a huge selection of golf clubs, accessories, clothing and shoes for men and women, as well as books and videotapes, and a somewhat smaller selection of tennis clothing, equipment and accessories, many at sale prices. Books and videos are always discounted 20%, and there is a large variety of sale items in each store. On a recent visit a Pima H R Putter was $39.99 ($49.99) and a dozen Spalding Eagle Golf Balls were $8.99 ($11.99). Varying golf club sets were discounted 20%, and most shoes were 10% to 20% off retail. Tennis racquets were discounted 15% to 45%. There is a mailing list for notification of upcoming sales.

Nike Factory Store
Desert Hills Factory Stores at Cabazon (714) 849-0466
Mon.-Sun., 10-8
(also in Lake Elsinore (714) 245-5665, and San Ysidro (619) 428-8849)
Terms: MC, V, AE, Check, GC.   Exchanges.   Parking

Clothing and shoes from prior seasons, blemishes and samples are sold here at discounted prices. There are $10-and-under racks of blemished shoes, where I found women's white leather low-tops and men's red leather high-tops. (I couldn't find the blemishes.) Most other athletic shoes were discounted 25% to 35% and featured shoes for all sports. While shoes are clearly the big draw,

---
Racks of shoes at $10 and under
---

there is also sport clothing. A man's sweat suit, originally $120, was $85; a woman's, $85 ($145); a child's, $35 ($50). An Aqua Gear neoprene shorty was $35 ($130), and men's biking shorts were $30 ($60).

The North Face
Lake Elsinore Outlet Ctr. (714) 245-2038
Mon.-Sat., 10-9; Sun., 11-6
Terms: MC, V, Check. Final sale.   Parking

The North Face manufactures high quality outerwear, sleeping bags, backpacks and tents, and at their outlet you'll find a large, well-organized shop offering savings of 30% to 70% on apparel, and 20% to 40% on equipment. Merchandise is discontinued stock, seconds and special make-ups, and does not carry the North Face lifetime warranty. A Dragonfly tent was $150 ($220); and a polarguard sleeping bag (good to zero degrees) was $135 ($196). There was a tremendous selection of backpacks, tents, parkas and outerwear. March is when all skiwear is reduced *an additional* 40%, and they have an end of season clearance sale in August.

Oshman's Warehouse Outlet   CCC
9th and Hill Sts., Los Angeles (213) 624-2233
Mon.-Sat., 9-6; Sun., 11-5
Terms: V, MC, D, Check. Exchanges.   Street parking

Oshman's Outlet carries discontinued and surplus merchandise from the chain's 200 stores, as well as special purchases, close-outs and factory samples. Merchandise is ever-changing and values are tremendous. I found an Impex Easy Stepper, retailing originally for $199, at $80, water skis at $50, wet suits were $129, and Arnold Palmer Golf Bags were $35. There were a variety of tennis racquets reduced to 75%. Name brand athletic shoes took up the back corner, selling at $19.96 (women's) and $19.96 and $24.96 (men's). A Coleman sleeping bag was $29.96, and a Sevylor two person pool and beach boat kit, including two oars and pump, was $39.96. A Quartz River two room tent was $99.96 ($169.99), but it was hard to make out that second room. Skiwear was an additional 70% off the lowest marked price (just after ski season), which made for some incredible bargains: women's Ossi overalls, originally $69.99, were $10.50. Thermal underwear was $3 and Tyrola ski pants were $21 ($100). Swimwear was also discounted; Speedo women's suits were $19.96 ($47.97), and men's Tri-Fit trunks were $8 ($28). Casual and sport clothing was generally marked down twice and now some percentage off. Goods arrive daily. One hour validated parking with minimum purchase.

P. F. McMullin Co.
1530 E. Edinger, Suite 8 & 9, Santa Ana (714) 547-7479
Mon.-Fri., 10-9; Sat., 10-6; Sun., 12-6 (Aug-Apr)
Terms: MC, V, Check, L. Exchanges.   Parking

P. F. McMullin has been selling ski clothing and accessories for men, women, and young adults for 26 years. They carry top American and European brands at discounts beginning at 30% and going down from there. Inventory includes down jackets, powder jackets, jumpsuits, windpants, insulated pants, stretch pants, thermal underwear, hats, gloves, liners, sweaters and turtlenecks. All merchandise is first quality, high style and well-constructed. The store is closed May, June, and July, and at its merchandise peak in November.

Pace Cyclewear Factory Store
15422 Assembly Ln., Huntington Beach (714) 892-0435
Mon.-Fri., 8-5; Sat., 8-2
Terms: MC, V($20 min.), Check. Final sale.   Parking

In this large showroom of cycling shorts, jerseys and jackets, there are a few sample racks of buys. Racing jackets sold for $20, shorts for $15 (to $45), jerseys for $10 ($40), and tops for $5. Kids' jerseys were $10, shorts, $15. The goods are samples, store returns, irregulars and damages, so check carefully.

Patagonia
Desert Hills Factory Stores at Cabazon (714) 922-9838
Mon.-Sun., 9-8
Terms: MC, V, Check. Final sale.   Parking

Here you can buy discontinued first and second quality pieces of the upscale outdoorwear manufactured by Patagonia. (The first quality clothing sells mainly through their mail order catalog.) There is clothing for the entire family, at savings of 25% to 50%. A child's anorak was $28 ($36) and a baby's print coverall was $19.50 ($32.50). An adult's down vest was $69 ($145), and an insulated anorak, $89.50 ($130).

Play it Again Sports
10814 Jefferson Blvd., Culver City (310) 287-2237
Tues.-Fri., 10-8; Sat., 10-7; Sun., 12-6
Terms: MC, V, Check. Final sale.　　Parking

This sporting goods shop offers new equipment for all sports at competitive prices, as well as recycled high quality sporting goods. They buy, sell and trade equipment for hockey, golf, skiing, baseball, football, scuba and watersports, tennis, camping, skating, biking, soccer, weight training, fishing, and anything else you can think of. The store is large and the assortment (including shoes, clothing and protective gear), ever-changing. *(This is a franchise operation. Other Play it Again Sports locations are at 6705 Telephone Rd., Ventura, (805) 644-4948; and 9969 Mira Mesa Blvd., San Diego (619) 695-3030.)*

Plaza Golf
2521 Pacific Coast Hwy., Torrance (310) 534-3346
Mon.-Fri., 10-7; Sat., 10-6; Sun., 11-5
Terms: MC, V, AE, Check. Returns.　　Parking

This store is crammed to bursting with golf equipment, most of it on sale. As you open the door you're greeted by a pile of club sets selling at or below cost. (A set originally selling for $456 was $249.95.) Nike Golf shoes were $94.95 and $89.95, and Footjoys ranged from $68 to 147.95 ($185). Titleist Perma Grip gloves were $12.95 and Top Flite Plus II balls were $17.99 a dozen.

Rawlings Sporting Goods
Factory Merchants of Barstow (619) 253-5610
Mon.-Sun., 9-8
Terms: MC, V, Check. Exchanges.　　Parking

Rawlings carries a huge range of MLB and NFL licensed apparel (including kids' size uniforms) but the big draw is Rawlings sporting goods at discounts as high as 60%, with frequent sales sending prices even lower. Catcher's mitts begin at $7.99, and go to $150. There are footballs, basketballs, golf clubs and accessories, bats and protective gear. Some goods are cosmetically blemished (e.g., the leather color is uneven), but these flaws will not affect performance.

Real Cheap Sports
36 W. Santa Clara St., Ventura   (805) 648-3803
Mon.-Sat., 10-6; Sun., 11-5
Terms: MC, V, Check. Exchanges.   Street parking

Real Cheap Sports features outdoor clothing by Patagonia for climbing, backpacking, kayaking and other activies. Stock is mainly over-runs, closeouts and seconds, and you save from 30% to 65%. A white water stretch dry top was $79 ($195), and a paddling jacket was $39 ($80). A toddler's insulated jacket was $79.50 ($115), matching pants were $62.50 ($92). Adult insulated jackets were $89 ($231). There were gloves, hats, shorts and shirts, and an Irish wool crew was $48 ($140). A great place to stock up on the outdoorsy look, even if it's just for sitting by the fire.

Skis, Etc.
12625 Harbor Blvd., Garden Grove   (714) 636-3753
Mon.-Fri., 10-9; Sat., 9-6; Sun., 11-5 (Aug-Apr)
Terms: MC, V, D, AE, Check. Final sale.   Parking

Skis, Etc. sells everything adults and children need for downhill skiing at discounts beginning at 20%. Sales three times a year send prices even lower. Brand names vary, depending on where they can get the best deals. The Ski Swap and Sale, generally in October, enables you to buy or sell used ski equipment and clothing.

Snea Kee Feet
16100 Crenshaw Blvd., Gardena   (310) 329-6519
Mon.-Sat., 10-7; Sun., 10-5
Terms: MC, V, Check. Exchanges.   Parking

This is an athletic outlet offering name brand shoes and work out clothes at discount prices. Everything is reduced, but some items are drastically reduced, like the outside tables full of Nike, Reebok, L.A. Gear and other shoes as low as $10. Women's Reeboks, retailing for $44, were here for $20, and men's Nike Quantum Force low basketball shoes, retailing at $53, were $19.90. These are often discontinued styles, so not all sizes are available. Sweats, running clothes and tees round out the inventory.

The Sporting Outlet
31654 Rancho Viejo Rd., San Juan Capistrano   (714) 248-5175
Mon.-Fri., 10-6; Sat., 10-5
Terms: MC, V, Check. Final sale.   Parking

The Sporting Outlet is a consignment sporting goods store selling gently used sporting goods. You'll pay about half the original retail price, and they carry equipment for everything, from golf and tennis to wind-surfing, scuba, skiing and horseback riding. Bicycles come and go, and there is always weight-training paraphernalia; the day I stopped in a multi-station gym was $3,000.

Sportmart
1919 S. Sepulveda Blvd., West Los Angeles (310) 312-9600
Mon.-Sat., 9:30-9:30; Sun., 10-7
(also in Riverside, Cerritos, Fullerton, Huntington Beach, West Covina, Costa Mesa, San Bernardino, Glendale, Northridge, and Redondo Beach)
Terms: MC, V, Check. Returns.   Parking

Here sporting goods, accessories and apparel are discounted 18% to 42% every day. During sales prices fall from there. They carry athletic wear for every sport, as well as a full line of apparel imprinted with the name of your favorite team. The athletic shoe department is tremendous, and equipment ranging from bench presses to bowling balls to bikes to bass lures is plentiful. Everything for your sport is here, at a discount. If they don't have it they'll special order it, and they'll meet anyone's lower price.

Sports Again   **COUPON**
19942 Ventura Blvd., Woodland Hills (818) 888-9728
Mon.-Fri., 10-6; Sat. 10-5; Sun., 11-3
Terms: MC, V, Check. Final sale.   Parking

Sports Again sells recycled sporting and exercise equipment, as well as some new equipment close-outs. It's hard to say what will be there at any give time. On my last visit I found a number of new Proteus exercise machines, discounted 35%, as well as a number of exercise bikes which were, well, recycled. There were new fishing poles, recycled skates and weights, some wetsuits, a little of this and a little of that. They also take merchandise on consignment, so if you're getting into a new sport or getting out of an old one, check this place out. *The coupon entitles you to 10% off your next purchase.*

Sports Spectacular
8859 West Pico Blvd., Los Angeles (310) 275-5453
Mon.-Sat., 10-6:30; Sun., 11-5
Terms: MC, V, Check. Final sale.   Parking

Carrying a full line of sweats, athletic wear and athletic shoes, Sports Spectacular's prices begin at 20% below retail. A sale clothing rack, and varying shoe specials as styles are discontinued, offer lower prices. Air Jordan's sold here for $109, and Reebok women's high top free styles were $49.95. Keds, which range for $24 to $27 elsewhere, here were $19. They also carry a large variety of team jackets.

Tiffany's Toys
3280 Motor Av., Los Angeles (213) 838-TOYS
Mon.-Fri., 9-7; Sat., 9-6; Sun., 11-5
Terms: MC, V, AE, Check. Final sale.   Parking

Tiffany's Toys offers exercise equipment, both used and new, at prices 30% to 70% below what the equipment origninally retailed for. New equipment is covered by manufacturer's warranty; used equipment has a 30 day warranty. There are multi-purpose weight machines here, but what the store seems full of are Life Cycles, Stairmasters and treadmills. Most are used, and I was surprised to learn that the same type of Life Cycle I use in the gym retails for $2395, and I could purchase a used version for $495 to $795.

Walter Keller Golf & Tennis
2138 Westwood Blvd., West Los Angeles (310) 474-1547
Mon.-Fri., 10-7; Sat., 10-6; Sun., 11-5
Terms: MC, V, AE, DC, Check. Returns.   Parking

Walter Keller's offers everything for golf and tennis, including instruction, club fitting, a golf and tennis pro shop, 105 models of irons, and shoes from size 5D to 15D, at prices well below retail. There are sales all over this store, from clothing and balls to racquets and clubs. Tennis items are routinely marked down 25% to 50%.

See also
Eddie Bauer Factory Outlet
Olga/Warner's Factory Outlet

Discount Catalogs

Bart's Watersports Catalog
(800) 348-501
Terms: MC, V, AE, D. Returns.

Barts sells wetsuits, drysuits, gloves, booties, hoods, knee protectors, socks, swimwear, waterskis, harnesses, skiboards, knee boards, boat covers, life vests and marine accessories. Many items are close-outs, with savings up to 70%. They also offer quantity discounts: at $600 you get an additional 5% off, plus free shipping; at $1200, an extra 7.5% off.

Berry Scuba
(800) 621-6019
Terms: MC, V, AE, D. Returns.

Berry Scuba carries everything a scuba diver needs—they claim to have more product lines than anyone else—and they will beat any advertised deal. Their catalog routinely features merchandise at discounts up to 60%. On dive packages you can save as much as 50%, on regulators as much as 33%.

Cabela's
(800) 237-4444
Terms: MC, V, AE, D, GC. Returns.

Cabela's is the world's foremost outfitter of hunting, fishing and outdoor gear, and in their catalog they offer clothing, equipment and accessories, at discounts of up to 30%.

Camp-mor
(800) 526-4784
Terms: MC, V, AE, D, Check. Returns.

The Camp-mor catalog is full of camping equipment, packs, shoes, and clothing for outdoor activities, much of which is on close-out, offering you savings of as much as 50%. Non-profit groups get an additional 10% discount.

Overton's
(800) 334-6541
Terms: MC, V, AE, D. Returns.

Overton's Water Sports Catalog guarantees that if you find anything at a lower price in any other catalog, they'll refund you the difference plus 10%. They offer marine accessories, and equipment and clothing for every water sport.

Road Runner Sports
(800) 551-5558
Terms: MC, V, AE, D, Check. Returns.

The bulk of the offerings in the Road Runner catalog is, naturally enough, running paraphernalia, but there are also pages of values for those involved in hiking, walking, volleyball, cross-training, aerobics, basketball, soccer, swimming and biking, and a huge variety of athletic shoes, many of which are discounted to 30%.

Sailboard Warehouse, Inc.
(800) 992-SAIL
Terms: MC, V, AE, D. L. GC. Returns.

Here you'll find sailboards and accessories up to 35% below retail. Complete boards sell from $258, and rig packages from $299. There are wetsuits, drysuits, fins, accessories, hardware and sails. On some items you can earn Bonus Bucks, incentives you can turn into equipment rentals, sailboarding vacations, or further discounts on items in the Bonus Buck Section of the catalog.

Exercise and Dance Wear

Alitta Factory Outlet
602 Colorado Av., Santa Monica (310) 396-0123
Mon.-Sat., 10-6; Sun., 12-5
Terms: AE, Check. Exchanges.   Parking

COUPON

Alitta manufactures fitness wear for men and women and on the racks you'll find distinctive pieces made of Spandex, cotton and Lycra, and Supplex (a new synthetic that wicks water away from the skin). The styling is attractive and unusual, with dramatic contrasting panels of color. Leggings are $19.95 ($35), catsuits (or trisuits, suitable for any or all of the triathalon sports of swimming, biking or running) are $19.95 ($56), leotards with Supplex are $25 ($40), and there is a selection of shorts in weights of Lycra varying according to the sport for which you intend to use them. Alitta also manufactures tops, bra tops and bikinis. There is a $5 clearance bin, and other additional sale items throughout the store. ***Save 10% on your next purchase with the coupon.***

Apparel Warehouse
6010 Yolanda St., Tarzana (818) 344-3224
Shelly's Discount Aerobic and Dancewear
2089 Westwood Blvd., Westwood (310) 475-1400
Mon.-Fri., 10-6; Sat., 10-5
Terms: MC, V, Check. Exchanges.   Parking

These two shops discount many lines of dancewear, including Body Image, Softouch, Baryshnikov, Gilda Marx, and Flextard. Cotton/poly/Lycra leggings are $10.99 (3/$30), leotards are $12.99 (3/$35) and $15.99 (3/$45). There is also a selection of Spandex. They carry sizes up to 4X in adults, and also feature maternity dancewear, children's dancewear, shoes, socks and accessories. Its gets busy here come Halloween, because they offer a wide assortment of low-cost costume options, many based on a leotard and tights. They have a frequent buyer program: purchase $100 worth of merchandise and get your choice of $15.99 leotards free.

Marika
Lake Elsinore Outlet Ctr. (714) 245-5545
San Diego Factory Outlet Ctr. (619) 690-5177
Hours vary by location.
Terms: MC, V, Check. Final sale.   Parking

The factory outlet for this popular brand of dancewear and activewear is bright with patterns and vibrant solids. In addition to the Marika line, you'll find some Baryshnikov dance wear, and Jazzercise for girls. There are also leotards, jumpsuits and some knit sportswear in maternity sizes. Most pieces are discounted 40%. Nylon blend warm-up suits in a range of bright colors were $45 ($75), leotards were $16.99 ($28) and unitards were $23.99 ($40). Girls' leotards were $12.99 ($21), and a maternity jumpsuit was $45 ($85).

Move It
308 Rosecrans Av., Manhattan Beach (310) 545-6455
Tues., Fri., 11-6; Wed.-Thurs., 11-7; Sat., 10-6; Sun., 11-5
Terms: V, MC, Check. Returns.   Street Parking

Move It is the outlet for L. A. Movers casual and exercise wear for women and girls, toddler sizes on up. The garments are first quality, generally blends of cotton, poly and Lycra, and prices are 30% to 50% lower than department stores. There are multi-purchase discounts: buy three items within the same price category and get an additional 20% to 30% off. Women's snap crotch body suits are $16.99, leggings are $14.99, bike shorts are $13.99, leotards are mainly $16.99, and ankle length unitards are $24.99. There is usually a $10 and under clearance rack, as well as a children's sale rack. There is a mailing list, for notification of sales. August is their anniversary, there's like to be a sale then.

SpaGear
Desert Hills Factory Stores at Cabazon (714) 922-9600
Mon.-Sun., 9-8
Terms: V, MC, AE, Checks. Exchanges.   Parking

This is an outlet for LaCosta sport and resortwear; some spa beauty treatments are available as well. All merchandise is first quality and you'll find bathing suits, leotards and leggings at savings of 25% to 45%. Terry-lined cotton print robes were $89 ($128); the La Costa white terry robe with gold insignia on the back was $39. There were sale racks of swimsuits at $9 and $19. Stock up on calming milk bath, ordinarily $25, now $18.75: after a day browsing the outlet mall you may need it.

Step In Time
27601 Forbes Rd., #38, Laguna Niguel (714) 582-2974
Mon.-Fri., 10-6; Sat., 10-5
Terms: Cash and Check only. Exchanges.   Parking

Step in Time features dancewear, leggings, leotards, and dance shoes for girls and women, at prices beginning at 15% off retail, and plummeting to way below 50% when you start sorting through the bargain box, where dance wear sells for $5. The store also offers a large assortment of costumes, and Dena, the proprietress, is a designer who specializes in custom uniforms for groups and teams at reasonable prices.

See also
Fresh Peaches Swimwear

Know the difference between a sale and a clearance? A second and an irregular? Check the Introduction

Tools

AAA Wholesale Tool and Supply
17309 Roscoe Blvd., Northridge (818) 99601800
Mon.-Fri., 8-6; Sat., 9-5; Sun., 10-4
Terms: MC, V, Check. Returns. Parking

If you're looking for a mundane drill or router you'll find them competitively priced here, but where AAA shines is in exotic tools, pieces most hardware stores don't commonly carry. They carry power and hand tools by Amana, Freud, Jepson, Makita, Ryobi, Milwaukee, Bosch, Porter Cable and Delta, discounted up to 40%. Most are American-made.

Black & Decker/DeWalt
14920 Victory Blvd., Van Nuys (818) 787-5531
Mon.-Fri., 8-5; Sat., 10-3
(also in Anaheim, Riverside, and Long Beach)
Terms: MC, V, Check. Returns. Parking

Factory reconditioned and blemished product (generally in freight damaged cartons) are sold at discounts of 10% to 20%. These are mainly professional quality tools, and range from drills to routers to saws to automotive vacuums. They also carry lawn and garden tools, and everything is covered by the same warranty as all Black & Decker products, two years on consumer lawn and garden, and professional tools, one year on everything else.

Black & Decker Factory Store
Factory Merchants of Barstow (619) 253-5042
San Diego Factory Outlet Ctr. (619) 428-7743
Mon.-Sun., 9-8
Terms: MC, V, D, Check. Returns. Parking

Here you can find Black & Decker tools for home, car, lawn and garden, as well as small appliances, at discounts of 10% to 40%. The best buys are in the white cartons; these units did not pass quality control checks the first time and were returned to be repaired; the problem--perhaps as small as a missing knob--corrected, they went through quality control again, passed, and are sold in the Factory Store at reduced prices. They carry the Black & Decker two year warranty and can be serviced by any authorized dealer anywhere. The bargains range from a Quik Finish Palm Sander at $22.99 to a 12" yard trimmer at

$40.99; a 3/8" variable speed drill at $49.99 to a 13" hedge trimmer at $23.99. An 8 gallon wet/dry shop vac was $75.99; hand mixers were $15.99.

Pacific Supply Company
1331 S. Vermont, Los Angeles (213) 384-3101
Mon.-Fri., 8-4
Terms: Cash and Check only. Final sale.   Street parking

Pacific Supply sells power tools at contractors discounts. Savings can run from 20% to 35%. They carry Makita, Milwaukee Electric, AEF, Bosch, Porter-Cable, Black and Decker, Skil and Master Power.

Tool Power   **COUPON**
2836 Santa Monica Blvd., Santa Monica (310) 453-2012
Mon.-Fri., 7-6:30; Sat., 8-5; Sun., 11-4
Terms: MC, V, Check. Exchanges.   Parking

Calling themselves "Santa Monica's Quality Tool Store," Tool Power sells professional quality tools at prices 10% to 15% below what you'd find them for at a lumber yard. They feature Bosch, Makita, Hitachi, Milwaukee Electric and Porter-Cable, and specialize in hard to find tools. They will special order, also at a discount, and they match any advertised price. ***The coupon entitles you to $5 off a purchase of $100 or more.***

Tool Shack
229 S. Glendale Av., Glendale (818) 956-1144
Mon.-Fri., 8-5; Sat., 9-5
Terms: MV, V, AE, D, Check. Exchanges.   Parking

The Tool Shack carries name brand, professional quality hand tools, power tools and precision tools for plumbing, electric, carpentry and mechanical, at discounts from 10% to 50%. Prices are even lower during monthly sales.

Discount Catalogs

Tools on Sale
(800) 328-0457
Terms: V, MC, D, Check. Returns.

Here you'll find all major brands of high quality contractors' tools at discounts of up to 50%. They offer just about everything; the catalog is 416 pages of tool and accessory bargains.

Toys and Games

AAA Billiard & Barstool Gallery
557 N. Azusa Av., West Covina (818) 915-8390
6326 Laurel Cyn. Blvd., North Hollywood (818) 762-2040
Mon.-Fri., 9-6; Sat., 9-5; Sun., 11-5
Terms: MC, V, AE, Check. Exchanges.   Parking

This showroom offers billiard, poker and bumper pool tables, barstools, and game room supplies. Prices begin at about 10% below retail, and go as low as 25% off. Styles are varied; I even found one with a wooden cover, enabling your pool table to masquerade in the dining room. They also sell cues, cases, and accessories.

G&G Nintendo-Sega Outlet
San Diego Factory Outlet Ctr. (619) 690-2355
Mon-Fri., 10-8; Sat., 10-7; Sun., 10-6
Terms: MC, V, D, Check. Exchanges.   Parking

Here the current stock of Sega, Nintendo and Genesis games are discounted $3 to $10; there are generally about 40 new games available at any one time, all fist quality, factory warrantied.

Game City   COUPON
14341 Ventura Blvd., Sherman Oaks (818) 986-3500
Mon.-Sat., 10-8; Sun., 12-8
Terms: MC, V, D, Check. Final sale.   Parking

Game City offers Nintendo, Super Nintendo and Genesis video games at prices $2 to $15 lower than other stores, averaging about $6 lower. They rent video games, and buy and sell used games and systems, which they sell for as low as half the original price. Everything comes with a 90 day manufacturer's warranty, and Game City gives you a 15 day exchange period. Used games have been tested to insure soundness. ***The coupon entitles you to $5 off any new game, or a free game rental.***

Game Dude
12104 Sherman Way, North Hollywood (818) 764-2442
Mon.-Sat., 9-7; Sun., 10-6
Terms: MC, V, D, AE. Final sale.　　　　Parking

Game Dude buys, sells and rents video games. You can buy new games here, but you'll save money if you buy them used. Prices vary depending on demand, but you can save 15% to 20% this way (games range from $5 to $30). You can also make some cash when the video addict gets tired of one game and moves on to the next. You must be 18 or over to sell games.

Golden West Billiards
21260 Deering Ct., Canoga Park (818) 888-2300
301 S. Robertson Blvd., Beverly Hills (310) 659-9487
Hours vary by location.
Terms: MC, V, GC, L, Check. Exchanges.　　Parking

Calling themselves "the ultimate game room stores," these outlets offer you a 15% discount on their many styles of pool and billiard tables. Starting at about $1200 and going up to $42,000, billiard tables come in a variety of woods and finishes, and in styles ranging from Victorian to Craftsman to Danish Modern. They also sell poker tables, bar stools, bumper pool tables, and gaming accessories, from poker chips to roulette wheels; and recover and repair pool tables.

Intelliplay
14425 Ventura Blvd., Sherman Oaks (818) 906-2133
Mon-Sat., 10-6
Terms: MC, V, Check. Exchanges.　　　Parking

At Intelliplay they believe you shouldn't have to mortgage your house to provide toys for your kids. Full of "intelligent toys for growing minds," this shop does not call itself a discount store, but sells high quality toys at prices far lower than the other stores that carry them. Hand puppets selling here at $13.95 were $17.95 elsewhere; wooden dinosaur skeleton models, elsewhere up to $17.95, were $3.95 to $6.95. There are toy demonstrations for all skill and age levels. Tell them the child's age, and what you want to spend; they'll make suggestions.

L. E. C. World Traders
8150 Sunland Blvd., Sun Valley (818) 768-6126
Mon.-Fri., 9-5; Sat., 9-5
Terms: MC, V, Checks. Final sale.   Parking

This store offers discounts of 40% to 50% on all kinds toys, domestic and many foreign, if you have one of their discount cards. To get one all you have to do is ask. Among the brands you'll find are Mattel, Little Tikes, Lego, Duplo, Tyco, Revell models, and PlaySkool. There are stuffed animals of all sizes and tons of small toys and items suitable for party favors beginning at .05. The store is literally packed with toy items, so you probably want to leave the kids home. In several cases it was cheaper to buy here than at the major toy chains.

Toys R'Us
11136 Jefferson Blvd., Culver City (310) 398-5775
Mon.-Sat., 9:30-9:30; Sun., 10-7
(35 additional locations; see Geographical Index)
Terms: MC, V, AE, D, Check.   Parking

It's the world's biggest toystore, and if you're popping in anytime in December, do yourself a favor and take aspirin first. Actually, that might be a good idea whenever you go. Toys R'Us carries toys and games for infants on up, bicycles, sporting goods, video games, hobby and craft equipment and a selection of baby furniture and needs, and claims lowest prices anywhere. They are always busy, they have a low price guarantee, and I have yet to find a toy store with as much stock. There are occasional clearances sales, where toys are reduced by as much as 90% off.

20/20 Video Rentals
3000 S. Sepulveda Blvd., West Los Angeles (310) 836-2020
Sun.-Thurs., 10-10; Fri.-Sat., 10-11
Terms: MC, V, Exchanges.   Parking

Some branches of 20/20 Videos are selling previously rented video games, starting at $9.95. The games are generally not older than two years, and can be exchanged if defective within seven days. Prices range to $20.

The Wholesale Toy District is the 600 block of S. Wall Street, in Los Angeles. Many stores will sell to individuals

Travel Values

Automobile Club of Southern California, A. A. A.
87 locations; see Geographical Index
Mon.-Fri., 9-5
Terms: MC, V, Check.   Parking

AAA is one of the best travel bargains in Southern California. Membership is $38 a year (a second membership within the household is $16). Beyond emergency road service and domestic travel planning services (with unlimited maps and tour books), there are free travelers' checks (for cash), and no more hassles with the DMV: conduct all business at the friendly and far less crowded AAA desk. Stop in monthly for the "Travel Saver," a newsletter of bargains on attractions, sporting events, lodgings, campgrounds, and travel. *The Auto Club News* lists additional tour packages open to club members.

Flight Coordinators
1150 Yale St., #8, Santa Monica (310) 453-1396
Mon.-Fri., 9-5:30; Sat., 11-3
Terms: MC, V, AE, Check. Exchanges. Street parking

Check with Flight Coordinators on your next trip, particularly if it's on short notice; bargain prices are available on flights the next day. (Now you can be impetuous and thrifty at the same time.) All prices quoted are for cash. You can give them a check if your departure is three weeks or more away, and some fares are refundable, at an extra charge.

Spur of the Moment Cruises
411 N. Harbor Blvd., San Pedro 90731 (310) 521-1060
Mon.-Fri., 9-6
Terms: MC, V, Check. Final sale.   Parking

Spur of the Moment represents cruise lines, and offers you big savings if you can go, well, at the spur of the moment. (A few weeks before sailing, companies discount unsold space.) Cruises are from all ports, and many packages include airfare and hotel. Send a self-addressed, stamped envelope for this month's availability list, a dozen envelopes for a year's worth. A sampling can be heard on their recorded message.

Thomas Cook
425 N. Bedford Dr., Beverly Hills (310) 274-9176
Mon.-Fri., 9-5; Sat., 10-4
(also in Sherman Oaks, Los Angeles, Long Beach, Torrance, San Diego, Glendale, Orange, Costa Mesa and Newport Beach)
Terms: Cash, Cashier's Check and U. S. Travelers Checks.

Thomas Cook provides free Thomas Cook Traveler's Checks, and Travelers Checks written in ten foreign currencies.

Ticket Bazaar Info Line
(900) 844-TIXX
24 Hour information line

This service matches travelers with tickets who can't make their flights with those wishing to fly, but not at full fare. Prices are negotiable. Tell the computer where you want to go, then browse the entries. This is a 900 service, so there is a charge: $1.95 for the first minute, .35 each additional.

See also
Entertainment Books

> *Get a better exchange rate abroad by charging purchases on a credit card*

Magazines

Best Fares Magazine
(800) 635-3033
Terms: MC, V, AE, D, Check.

For $58 you can subscribe to *Best Fares*, a 60 page monthly that keeps you abreast of airline, hotel and car rental promotions, shows you how to save money with split and hidden city fares, tells you the *secret words* needed to qualify for special airline savings (you thought all you had to be was an alert consumer), and informs you of un-promoted fares and discounts. With each subscription you get travel coupons, a discount hotel directory, information on cruise bargains, and you are eligible for the Best Fares travel club, offering a 5% to 7% rebate with each ticket.

Uniforms

Glamour Uniform Shop
COUPON
4951 W. Sunset Blvd., Hollywood (213) 666-2122
Owl Uniforms
984 W. Vernon, Los Angeles (213) 233-1830
Mon.-Fri., 10-6; Sat., 10-5
Terms: MC, V, AE, D. Exchanges.   Street parking

Here you will find uniforms for medical, restaurant and beauty professions, in regular, petite and large sizes, discounted 20% to 40%. Shoes, including Nursemaids, SAS and Soft Spots, are also discounted. There are periodic sales where prices are further reduced. ***The coupon entitles you to 10% off one purchase of non-sale merchandise.***

Hollywood Cedars Uniforms, Inc.
1303 N. Vermont Av., Los Angeles (213) 661-7649
Mon.-Sat., 9-6:30
Terms: MC, V, Check. GC. Exchanges.   Street parking

Half the merchandise in this store seems to be on sale at any one time. The stock consists of medical, restaurant, beautician and security guard uniforms, as well as hosiery, footwear and accessories. There are always a few featured shoe styles on sale, as well as a the buy two and get $10 back offer. Uniforms are available to size 46, men; 16 1/2, women. They also carry maternity uniforms.

Nadine of California Uniforms
18552 Sherman Way, Reseda (818) 343-7554
Mon.-Fri., 9:30-5; Sat., 11-3
Terms: MC, V, Check. Exchanges.   Parking

Nadine offers a full line of uniforms for hospital, restaurant, industrial and security workers, and all at discounts of 15% to 20% (lab coats start at $18.95). They have their own line of industrial shirts, pants and coveralls, and stock security uniform accessories, as well as waitress, nurse and industrial shoes.

Uniforms West, Inc.
22930 Hawthorne Blvd., Torrance   (310) 375-6211
Mon.-Sat., 10-6
Terms: V, MC, D, Check. Returns.   Parking

This store features uniforms for medical and restaurant workers at prices 10% to 20% below department store retail, and they carry up to size 52. In addition to regular discounts, there are sale items in the front of the store, and all maternity medical uniforms are discounted 50%. Nurse Mate Pantyhose are usually buy-one-get-one-free. Big sales are generally around November-December and July-August, but call to be sure.

See also
   J.C. Penney Outlet Store

For free updates, don't forget to fill out and mail the Reader Response Card on the last page of this book

Warehouse Buying Clubs and Wholesale Grocers

Warehouse Buying Clubs

Costco
Fedco
Pace Membership Warehouse
The Price Club

These warehouses are a shopper's delight; if you know your prices you can save a fortune, though not everything is cheaper then elsewhere. Everything *is* under one roof, from TVs and computers to office needs, shampoo to tires to tennis shoes, automotive and pet needs to dishes and clothes, bestsellers to food products (prepared and baked goods, produce, meats and liquor stock), including the one gallon jar of Best Foods mayonnaise large enough to drown a Pekinese. All carry essentially the same merchandise mix, and products are in large sizes, geared to families. If you're single, you'll have to go in with a friend on perishables (nobody can eat *that much* fresh broccoli). As for the rest, eventually you'll use up that case of t.p.

These stores also offer fleet car buying. Tell them the car you're looking for, with all the extras you've chosen, they locate such a car, negotiate for you, and come back to you with a price, which can be as low as $500 over dealer invoice.

Many of these stores aren't open to everyone. Fedco's eligibility requirements (similar to those of Costco and The Price Club) are that you be a California resident and one of the following:
- **-a Federal, State or Local government employee**
- **-a member of an approved credit union**
- **-a Social Security or Disability recipient**
- **-an active or retired member of the armed forces, including the National Guard**
- **-a veteran of the U.S. armed forces including National Guard**
- **-a school or college employee, or full-time student**

- an employee of a hospital, dental or medical facility
- an employee of a firm that does primary business with Federal, State or Local governments
- a bank or savings and loan employee
- an employee of insurance company, nonprofit corporation or public utility

Before committing to a store with a membership fee, go in and browse to make sure there are buys for you. You may be impressed by the price on a dozen cans of tuna, but if you like it in oil and they sell it in water.... You like ziti, they sell macaroni..... Oil, water ... ziti, macaroni.... You get the idea.

Costco
Mon.-Fri., 11-8:30; Sat, 9:30-6; Sun., 10-5
Locations in Canoga Park, City of Industry, Garden Grove, Hawthorne, Laguna Niguel, Lancaster, Riverside, San Bernardino, Van Nuys, Victorville, Tustin, and Lawndale
Terms: Cash and Check only.   Parking

You can join Costco in one of two ways: you must either be a member of a credit union, a banking club or other recognized organization (see above), and your membership fee is $30, or, if you have your own business, you qualify for a gold card, and your membership fee is $25. Fees are annual and membership entitles you to one card for yourself and one for your spouse. Gold card holders also get an extra hour to shop, 10 to 11 a.m. weekdays. Costco has good buys on tires, and unlike other warehouses, their bakery will decorate sheet cakes for your occasion. An 8 lb. cake is $12.99.

Fedco
Mon.-Fri., 10-8; Sat.-Sun., 10-6
Locations in Escondido, Los Angeles, National City, San Bernardino, Van Nuys, Cerritos, Costa Mesa, Ontario and Pasadena.
Terms: Check, SC.   Parking

The lifetime membership fee at Fedco is $10 and your can join if you fit into any of the classifications above. Fedco carries seemingly everything, with good buys on televisions and video products, and they guarantee the lowest prices on Goodyear tires. Here you can buy foods in portions suitable for less than a small army; they actually sell some things in a quantity of *one*. If you feel the need to say "Charge it," apply for a Fedco charge.

Pace Membership Warehouse
Mon.-Fri., 9-9; Sat., 9-6:30; Sun., 9-6
Locations in Gardena, San Bernardino, Chino, Fullerton, San Fernando, ElMonte, Woodland Hills, Downey, Fountain Valley, Montclair, Stanton, Irvine, City of Industry, and Southgate
Terms: Check and Cash only.   Parking

Anyone with a Drivers License and $25 can join Pace, but you can shop here if you're not a member, paying 4% over members' prices. You can use a credit card, but there is a $5 fee *per use*.

The Price Club
Mon.-Sat., 11-8:30
Locations in Corona, Northridge, Yorba Linda, San Juan Capistrano, Alhambra, San Diego, Fullerton, Chula Vista, Colton, Norwalk, Fountain Valley, Azusa, Burbank, Inglewood, Oxnard, Pomona, and Signal Hill.
Terms: Check and Cash only.   Parking

In order to join you must be a member of a credit union, a banking club or other recognized organization (membership fee, $30), or have your own business (membership fee, $25). Fees are annual. Most Price Clubs offer a snack bar outside, with truly great fat free frozen yogurt.

Wholesale Grocers

Smart & Final Iris
Over 120 locations; see Geographical Index
Hours vary by location.
Terms: Cash and Check only.   Parking

The democratic alternative to the warehouse club, where there is no membership fee or hierarchy by color of card, Smart & Final has its roots in supplying the institutional user, so some products can't be found in consumer oriented stores. Though smaller than the buying clubs, Smart & Final offers substantial discounts on food, cleaning supplies and paper goods. If you don't see what you're looking for in the store, check out their catalog, which features additional cleaning and food service items you can order, at a discount.

Sale Calendar

The following listings reflect when these stores have had sales in previous years, or when some retailers plan to have them in the future. Be sure to sign the mailing list of any retailer whose sales you don't want to miss. Sales by stores or companies not reviewed in this book also list address and phone number. When stores have multiple sales noted, address information will be in the first mention. Dates are approximations; call well in advance for exact sale dates. If you have a favorite sale I've overlooked, let me know.

January

Aaron Scott Furniture Warehouse Clearance Sale

Almost & Perfect English China Sale

Arkraft Annual Clearance Sale
3375 E. Hill St., Long Beach (310) 597-1359
Their entire stock of Chinese furniture and accessories goes on sale once a year.

Bally Semi-Annual Sale
Beverly Hills, South Coast Plaza, San Diego

Brooks Brothers Winter Clearance Sale
Los Angeles, Century City, Newport Beach. 35% to 50% off.

C&R Semi-Annual Sale

Crazy Ladies and Friends
1606 Santa Monica Blvd., Santa Monica (310) 828-3122
Crazy Ladies sells quilting cottons and blends, and the first of the year they have their only sale, where the more you buy, the more you save.

Europa,The Suit Club End of Season Sale

For Kids Only Sale

Geary's Anniversary Sale
351 N. Beverly Dr., Beverly Hills (310) 273-4743
Savings of up to 60% on china, crystal and fine tabletop items.

Hollywood Cedars Uniforms Annual Clearance Sale

Horizon Showroom of Contemporary Furniture January Clearance Sale
8600 W. Pico Blvd., Los Angeles (310) 652-4933

Kinney Shoe Outlet Sale

Kreiss Annual Inventory Clearance
8619 Melrose Av., Los Angeles (213) 657-3991
(also in La Jolla, Laguna Niguel and Rancho Mirage)
Kreiss manufactures high end California contemporary furniture. Sales are generally on floor models and discontinued styles.

Lanz II Outlet Sale

Lisa Norman Lingerie Sale
1334 Montana Av., Santa Monica (310) 451-2026
(also in Brentwood and West Hollywood)
Lisa Norman sells some of the prettiest lingerie around, and in mid-January, running until inventory is gone, there is a big sale on winter stock. Men: Note the proximity of this sale to Valentine's Day.

Nordstroms Semi-Annual Men's Sale

Rick Pallack Semi-Annual Sale

Robinson's Warehouse Sale
Downtown Los Angeles and Pasadena locations.

Strouds Semi-Annual Sale and Clearance

Talbot's Semi-Annual Sale
All locations. 50% to 60% off.

Thieves Market Semi-Annual Sale

3D Bed and Bath Sale

W. J. Simmons Mattress Factory January Clearance

February

Bachelor Auction
Boys Clubs of L. A. (213) 221-9111
Wanna buy a man?

Brooks Brothers Presidents Day Values
20% to 25% off.

David Orgell Warehouse Sale
(213) 272-3355
$2,000,000 inventory clearance, featuring bargains of up to 90% off on china, crystal, silverplate, silver holloware, sterling and stainless. Call store for location.

Esther's Full Fashions Sale

Firenze Factory Outlet Sale

Fresh Peaches Swim and Dance Wear Sale

Pacific Design Center Semi-Annual Home Furnishings Sample Sale
8687 Melrose Av., West Hollywood (Parking entrance, San Vicente Blvd.)
$1 admission
Available here are rugs, chairs, tables, sofas, lamps, accessories and other furniture pieces that are discontinued models and floor samples. Generally cash and checks.

Sit 'n Sleep Washington's Birthday Sale

We-R-Fabric $1 Off Sale.

March

Book Again Anniversary Two for One Sale

California Kids Sale

Junior League of Long Beach Rummage Sale

Junior League of Los Angeles Rummage Sale

Regal Rents Sale

San Gabriel Nursery Spring Sale

Shore Shop Spring Preview Sale

April

Aaron Scott Furniture Anniversary Sale

Barbara & Carolyn's Quality Tack Semi-Annual Sale

Talbot's Spring Sale

W. J. Simmons Spring Clearance Sale

May

A-16 Once a Year Sale
11161 W. Pico Blvd., West Los Angeles (310) 473-4574
 High quality used rental camping and hiking gear, and discontinued, one-of-a-kind, and irregular merchandise. Save 40% to 70% on names like Patagonia, Black Diamond, Marmot, Eagle Creek, Lowe Aline Systems, Sierra Designs and more.

Artemide & Ron Rezek Annual Warehouse Sale
West Los Angeles (310) 837-0179
This is a warehouse sale of lighting and accessories, and samples and seconds of modern furniture pieces. Included are the Artemide, Ron Rezek, Luce Plan, Ve Art and Sidecar lines, and Tizio, Tolomeo and Orbis halogen lamps.

Baldwin Bonanza Plant Sale, Los Angeles Arboretum

Blueprint Semi-Annual Parking Lot Sale
8366 Beverly Blvd., Los Angeles (213) 653-2439
Blueprint sells modern and contemporary furniture.

Europa, The Suit Club End of Season Sale

Fiesta De Flores Annual Plant Sale, South Coast Botanic Garden

Laykin et Cie at I. Magnin Annual Sale of Estate and Contemporary Jewelry
Beverly Hills
This sale features savings of 30% to 50% off regular prices.

Pacific Design Center American Society of Interior Designers Home Furnishings Sample Sale

Piano Outlet sale of used pianos at the University of La Verne

Saks Fifth Avenue Spring Sale

Sit 'n Sleep Memorial Day Sale

Top 2 Top Sale

We-R-Fabrics Bolt End Sale

June

The Annual Great Beverly Hills Garage Sale

Carushka Bodywear Close-Out Sale
13940 Ventura Blvd., Sherman Oaks (818) 788-7938

David Orgell Summer Sale
320 N. Rodeo Dr., Beverly Hills (213) 272-3355
Save up to 75% on Reed & Barton, International, Towle and Wallace silver.

Decorative Fabric House Annual Parking Lot Sale

European Natural Leather Bags Sale

Home Comfort Center Pre-season Sale
18419 Vanowen, Reseda (818) 345-9557
Home air conditioning and heating products.

Ikea Once a Year Sale
600 N. San Fernando Blvd., Burbank (818) 842-4532
Also in Fontana, City of Industry.

Marlene Gaines Handbags Semi-Annual Storewide Sale

Mikasa Factory Store Annual Sale

Nordstrom's Semi-Annual Men's Sale

101 North Corp. Retail Store
6856 Valjean Av., Van Nuys (818) 909-0111
This is a liquidator for a number of sportswear lines for men, women, boys and girls, and they are open essentially for sales only. Call for information on additional sale dates, or get on the mailing list by calling or writing.

Radio Shack Nationwide Tent Sale
Discontinued items must go to make way for new models at all locations. You will find savings of 13% to 60%; all stores participate. Not all merchandise available at all stores.

Robertson Crafts Open House and Sale

Rodeo Drive Boutiques End of Season Clearance Sales
This applies to many of the designer boutiques on Rodeo Drive, as well as their counterparts in La Jolla, South Coast Plaza, wherever else they are located in Southern California.

Samples Only Sale

Stats Annual Half Price Sale
120 S. Raymond Av., Pasadena (818) 795-9308
(also in Capistrano Beach, Redondo Beach, and Whittier)
Stats sells wreath forms, dried and silk flowers and greens for crafts projects, and during this annual sale all silk flowers are half price. this does not include silk greens, plants or trees. Sale is generally in late June or early July.

Strouds Semi-Annual Sale and Clearance

Stuart Scott Showrooms Sale
405 N. Robertson Blvd., Los Angeles (310) 274-6169
Stuart Scott has lovely decorator fabrics, on sale once a year. Prices start at $10 a yard.

Talbots Semi-Annual Sale

Wallpapers to Go Annual Waverly Sale

July

Bullock's Pre-Season Sale

Champagne Taste /The 2nds Shop Parking Lot Sale

Florsheim Shoes Clearance Sale
All Locations

For Kids Only Sale

Graphaids Summer Sale

H. Savinar Luggage Clearance Sale

H. G. Daniels Annual Parking Lot Sale and Warehouse Clearance
2543 W. 6 St., Los Angeles (213) 387-1211
Fine and graphic artists' supplies.

Krause's Sofa Factory Semi-Annual Sale

Rick Pallack Semi-Annual Sale

Nordstrom's Anniversary Sale

Robinson's Warehouse Sale

Sacks SFO Summer Sale

Shore Shop Sale

Sit 'n Sleep July 4th Sale

Talbot's Semi-Annual Sale

W. J. Simmons July Mattress Sale

August

Book Again Semi-Annual Sale

Bristol Bay End of Summer Home Furniture Factory Anniversary Sale
17359 Gale Av., City of Industry (818) 854-179
Furniture for the bedroom, dining room, office, wall units and upholstered furniture.

David Orgell Summer Sale

Esther's Full Fashions Sale

Ethan Allen Summer Sale

Firenze Factory Outlet Sale

Georgette Klinger Annual Sale
312 N. Rodeo Dr., Beverly Hills (310) 274-6347
Annual sale of skin care products and services.

Harpers End of Season Sale

Luggage 4 Less End of Summer Sale

Move It Factory Outlet Sale

The North Face End of Season Clearance Sale

Oshman's Pre-Season Ski Sale

Pacific Design Center Semi-Annual Sale

Rick Pallack Once a Year Warehouse Sale
Reductions to 75%.

Stats Annual Half Price Sale
All silk plants, foliage and trees are reduced.

Thieves Market Semi-Annual Sale

We-R-Fabric $1 Off Sale

September

Berk's Outdoor Furniture Floor Sample Sale

Bristol Bay Home Furniture Factory Anniversary Sale

Brooks Brothers Special Values for Fall

California Kids Back to School Sale

Europa, The Suit Club End of Season Sale

House of Farbrics Superstores Anniversary Sale

Kreiss End of Summer Clearance Sale

Nordstrom's Fall Sale

The Patio Place Sale

Robertson Crafts Open House and Sale

Shore Shop Back to School Sale

Sit 'n Sleep Labor Day Sale

Stats End of Summer Patio Furniture Blowout

October

Bally Anniversary Sale

Barbara & Carolyn's Quality Tack Semi-Annual Sale

David Orgell Clearance Sale

I. Magnin Women's Fall Shoe and Handbag Sale

Robinson's Fall Sale

Saks Fifth Avenue Columbus Day Sale

Sierra Madre Library Annual Book Sale
(818) 355-7186
There are intermittent sales during the year, but this is the big one, lasting four days.

Talbots Finds for Fall Sale

Top to Top Semi-Annual Sale

Wallpapers to Go Semi-Annual Home Sale

November

Blue Print Semi-Annual Parking Lot Sale

Daphna's Outdoor Furniture Sale

Gucci Fall Clearance
Beverly Hills, Costa Mesa

The Lingerie Outlet Sale

Robertsons Thanksgiving Weekend Sale

St. John Knits Annual Sale
Irvine (714) 863-1171
Call for information. Cash only.

Steinberg's Discount Tack & Feed Annual 20% off Everything Sale

We-R-Fabric Bolt End Sale

December

Aaron Scott Furniture Clearance Sale

Betnun Music Sale

Country Elegance
10144 Riverside Dr., Toluca Lake (818) 985-8968
The first Saturday of December, 10-4. Bridal gowns and eveningwear parking lot sale of excess inventory. No dressing rooms. MC, V, Cash.

General Wax and Candle Company Pre-Christmas Sale

Glass Garage Annual Sale

Graphaids Christmas Sale

Harpers End of Season Sale

Luggage 4 Less Year-end Sale

Marlene Gaines Handbag Sale

Nordstrom's Semi-Annual Men's Sale

101 North Corp. Christmas Sale

Rossi D'Italia Sale

Samples Only Sale

Stat's After Christmas Sale
Seasonal goods are available, and people line up hours before the doors open (check to find out just how early this year).

Woody's Unfinished Furniture 10% off Sale

Any sales I've overlooked?
Please let me know.
Shopping Secrets of Southern California
P. O. Box 24447
Los Angeles, CA 90024-0447

Alphabetical Index 297

Alphabetical Index of Stores

A
A.A.A., 281
AAA Billiard and Barstool Gallery, 278
AAA Wholesale Tool and Supply, 276
ABC Premiums, 14
A.B.E. Office Furniture, 185
ACA Joe, 227
A Bedtime Story, 204
A Star is Worn, 90
Aaron Bros. Art Mart, 18
Aaron Scott Clear. Ctr., 171
Academy Award Clothing, 69
Accessorize Jewelry, 231
Acres of Books, 30
Action Copiers, 224
Adler Shoes, 257
Adolfo II, 227
Adray's, 22
Adrienne Vittadini Outlet, 99
Aileen Stores, 99
Air Conditioning Exchange, 36
Alandales, 69
Alan's Acquarium, 238
Alan's Medical, 218
Albee's Appliances, 14
Albert Nipon Outlet, 99
Algert Appliances, 15
Al Greenwood's Bedspread Kingdom, 204
Alin Party Goods, 234
Alitta Factory Outlet, 273
Allen Wertz Candies, 168
All That Jazz Outlet, 100
All Together, 100
Almost & Perfect English China, 55
Alpine Automotive, 50
Al's Furniture, 171
Americana Brass Bed Factory, 179
American Flower Exchange, 247
American Rubber & Supply, 216
American Tourister, 213
Animal Birth Control, 242
Anna's Linens, 205
Anne Klein Outlet, 100
Ann Taylor Outlet, 100
Annual Beverly Hills Garage Sale, 53
Antique Exchange, 6
Antique Guild's Showcase Gallery, 6
Antique Palace Mall, 6
Antique Warehouse, 7
Apparel Designer Zone, 76
Apparel Warehouse, 273
Arco Smog Pros, 50
Armand Hammer Museum of Art, 151
Armand's Discount, 184
Aron's Records, 250
Arrow Shirts, 78
Arte D'Italia, 87
Art Glass Doors, 36
Art Store, 18
Art Supply Warehouse, 18
Arthur John's, 101
Arturo's Flowers, 248
As Is Furniture, 171
Atlantis Discount Swim, 94
Auto Parts Club, 48
Avery Rest. Supply, 193
Azita J, 101
Aztec Appliances, 15

B
Baby Guess, 62
Babyland, 177
Baby Toytown, 177
Back Door Boutique, 101
Bag Lady, 1
Bagnall Camera Show, 10
Bailey's Men's Resale, 76
Bankruptcy Liquidators, 258
Banister Shoe Outlet, 227
Barbara & Carolyn's Quality Tack, 238
Barbeques Galore, 184
Barbizon Outlet, 122
Bargain Books, 31
Barrett's Appliances, 15
Bass Shoe Outlet, 258
Bead Gallery, 197
Bed, Bath & Beyond, 205
Bedspread Creations, 205
Bedspread Whse., 206
Bel Air Camera, 40
Beno's, 78
Bergstroms, 62
Berk's, 183
Best of Times Antiques, 7
Betnun Music, 221
Betty's Large Sizes, 129
Beverly Fireplace Shop, 185
Beverly Hills Fan Co., 203
Beverly Hills Library, 34
Beverly Hills Hosiery, 123
Bev's Crafts and Lace, 135
Big, Bad and Beautiful, 130
Big City Woman Resale, 132
Big Dogs Sportswear, 78
Big Fella Warehouse, 69
Big Y Yardage Outlet, 154
Bijoux Medici, 1
Bizarre Bazaar, 102
Black & Decker/DeWalt, 276
Black & Decker Factory Store, 276
Black & White Wholesalers, 102
Blue Chip Draperies, 147
Blue Moon Exchange, 94
Bodhi Tree Used Books, 31
Book Again, 31
Bookie Joint, 32
Bookstar, 29
Book Warehouse, 29
Boot Factory, 258
Boston Stores Clear. Ctr., 138
Box City, 236
Bracken Bird Farm, 238
Brand Bookstore, 33
Brass Beds Unlimited, 179
Brides of California, 116
Broadway Antique Mall, 7
Broadway Clear. Ctr., 138
Bruce Alan Bags, 227
Budget Rents Clear. Ctr., 182
Bugle Boy Outlet, 79
Builders Discount, 39
Bullocks Grand Finale, 139

C
C&C Pet Supermarket, 239
C&R Clothiers, 70
CD Banzai, 250
C. E. Jones Ceramics, 244
C.W. Design, 63
Calico Corners, 154
California Fit, 79
California Kids, 63
California Luggage, 213
California Mart Sales, 79
California Wholesale Tile, 44
Candy Factory Outlet, 168
Cape Isle Knitters, 230
Capezio Outlet, 259
Capital Auto Parts, 49
Carl's Pocketbook Exchange, 33
Caroline's Designer Resale, 116
Carousel Baby Furniture, 178
Carpet Club, 42
Carpetland Mills, 42
Carpet Showcase, 43
Castle Chandeliers, 200
Celebrity Cleaners, 149
Cellular Fantasy Phones, 52
Cellular Wholesalers, 52
Center for Independent Living Sale, 53
Champagne Taste, 187
Cheep Lace, 135
Chic Lingerie Outlet, 123
Chicago Cutlery, 230
Children's Exchange, 67
Children's Orchard, 67
Christine's Place, 67
Christopher's Nut Co., 169
Citadel, The, 228
City of L.A. Salvage, 17
Clayton's Shoes, 253
Cleaning Club, 149
Cliff's Books, 32
Clothestime Outlet, 102
Clothing Factory, 103
Coach Value Store, 2
Cole Haan, 259
Cole of California Outlet, 94
Collar & Leash, 239
Colleagues Glamour Sale, 53
Collectibles, 103
Collector's Eye, 197
Compact Disc Count, 250
Compagnia Della Moda, 70
Complete Eye Care, 219
Comp USA, 133
Computer Show & Sale, 133
Concord Cleaners, 149
Consolidated Pet Foods, 239

298 Shopping Secrets of Southern California

Contempo Casuals Outlet, 103
Contractors Warehouse, 39
Converse Outlet, 252
Co-opportunity Food Co-op, 162
Corning Revere Outlet, 193
Cort Furniture Clear. Ctr., 182
Costco, 286
Costume Jewelry Mart, 197
Country Antique Fair Mall, 7
Covercraft Outlet Store, 48
Crafters City, 188
Crafters Outlet, 188
Crisa Factory Store, 228
Crown Books, 29
Crystal Factory, The, 55
Crystal Sonics, 22
Culver Carpet Center, 43
Custom Quilt & Craft, 206
Cut-Rate Office Furniture, 186
Cutting Corners, 154

D
DAK Outlet, 22
Damone, 104
Dana Bedspreads, 206
Dana Bedspreads Clear. Ctr., 207
Dan Howard's Maternity Factory, 127
Dansk Outlet, 55
Daphna's Outdoor Furniture, 183
David Textiles, 157
Dawn's Discount Lace II, 135
Deco Brass, 36
Decorative Fabric Whse., 155
Deja Vu, 120
Del Rey Tennis Shoes Whse., 259
Desert Hills Factory Stores, 229
Designer/Brands, 227
Designer Consigner, 116
Designer Fabric Showcase, 155
Designer Labels for Less, 80
Designer Labels for Less Whse., 80
Designer Labels for Men, 228
Designer's Bloopers, 172
Designer's Clear. Ctr., 172
Designers Own, 228
Designs by Desre, 228
Diamond Foam and Fabric, 185
Diamond Mine, 195
Direction Menswear, 228
Disc Connection, 250
Discount Bridal Services, 117
Discount Desk Center, 186
Discount Lighting Outlet, 200
Discount Pet Center, 240

Discount Pet Food, 240
Discount Reader Books, 30
Discount Sales Stores, 23
Discount Tile Center, 45
Discount Train Whse,, 192
Discount Tropical Fish, 240
Dolly Madison Bakery, 161
Dorman Winthrop, 70
Down Comforter Whse., 207
Drapery World Outlet, 147
Dressed Up, 104
Dress Up Cleaners, 149
Duffel, 229
Dutton's Books, 33
Dynasty Classics Outlet, 200
Dyna-tek, 224

E
Eagle's Eye, 227
Eddie Bauer Outlet, 80
Eddy's For Men, 71
Egghead Software Clear. Ctr., 134
El Cajon Antique Mart, 7
Electropedic Adjustable Beds, 80
Elwell Farms, 166
Empire Cleaners, 149
English China House, 56
Entenmanns/Orowheat Bakery, 161
Entertainment Publications, 152
Esprit, 104
Esther's Full Fashions, 130
Evan Picone/Gant Outlet, 81
Eurogift, 188
Europa, The Suit Club, 71
European Leather Natural Bags, 2
Everything but Water, 95
Everything for Kids, 67

F
Fabric Barn, 136
Fabric King, 157
Fabric Lace Trims Factory Outlet, 158
Fabric Outlet, 158
Fabric Warehouse, 158
Factory Bridal Imports, 117
Factory Merchants of Barstow, 227
Fallbrook Handbag Outlet, 2
Family Practice Center of UCLA, 218
Famous Brands Housewares 193
Famous Footwear, 260
Fan/Fireplace Man, 203
Fantastic Sportswear, 105
Farmers' Markets, 164
Fashion West, 2
Fedco, 286
Fellini Leather, 91
Fence Factory, 37
Fieldcrest/Cannon, 207
Fiesta De Flores Plant Sale, 244

Firenze Factory Outlet, 91
$5 Clothing Store, 105
Flap Happy Kids, 63
Flax Art Supplies, 19
Flight Coordinators, 281
Foot Locker Outlet, 264
For Kids Only, 63
Foster's Shoes, 260
Four Day Tire Stores, 48
Francine Browner Outlet, 228
Frank's Highland Park Camera, 40
Freestyle, 41
Fresh Peaches, 95
Friedman's, 16
Froch's Woodcraft Shop, 172
Frontier Village Antiques, 7
Full Size Fashions, 130

G
G&G Nintendo-Sega, 278
Galaxy of Gowns, 117
Game City, 278
Game Dude, 279
Gap Outlet, The, 81
General Housewares, 227
General Wax & Candle, 56
Geoffrey Beene Outlet, 71
Georgiou, 231
Gigi Shoppe, 105
Gino Robair Beauty College, 27
Gitano Outlet, 81
Glabman's, 173
Glamour Uniform Shop, 283
Glass Garage, 188
Glendale Antique Show, 13
Gloves by Hammer, 5
Golden Frame, 20
Golden West Billiards, 279
Golden West Meat Co., 167
Golf Exchange, The, 264
Goodrich Cleaners, 149
Gorham, 229
Grafstein & Co., 195
Granny's Disc. Natural Foods, 162
Graphaids, 19
Guess Outlet, 82

H
H&H Jobbing Co., 264
H. Savinar Luggage, 213
Hacienda Brides Intl., 118
Hairmasters University, 28
Half Price House, 121
Handbag Hangup, 3
Hanes Activewear, 227
Hang Ten Outlet, 64
Harbor Antique Mall, 8
Harpers, 106
Harris & Frank Outlet, 72
Hartmann Luggage, 213
Harve Bernard, 228
Hathaway Outlet, 72
Hawaiian Cotton, 228
Health Food City, 163
Heidi's Whse. Outlet, 106
Helen Grace Chocolates, 169

Alphabetical Index 299

Herman's Party Supplies, 234
He-Ro Group Outlet, 122
Hi-Lo Cleaners, 149
Hit or Miss, 106
Holiday Humane Soc., 242
Hollywood Cedars Uniforms, 283
Home Base, 39
Home Shop, 207
Hosiery Depot, 123
House of Fabrics, 158
Hub Caps, 49
Hunter's Books, 30

I

I. B. Diffusion, 230
i.e., 230
Ibex Apparel, 118
Immune Testing Ctr., 218
Import Outlet, 159
Intelliplay, 280
Intermoda Exchange, 82
In 2 Shape, 228
Irish Crystal Co., 56
It's a Wrap, 90
Izod/Monet, 227
Izod/Gant, 231

J

J. B. Sebrell Co., 249
J. C. Penney Outlet, 140
JH Collectibles, 107
J. P. Discount Fabrics, 156
Jackeez & Nicolz, 107
Jack's Cleaners, 149
Jasmine Cleaners, 150
Jay Jacobs, 107
Jean Star's Apparel, 115
Jenkins Products, 43
Jerry Piller's, 82
Jess/Maddox, 107
Jewelry Exchange, 195
Joan & David, 254
Joan Geddes Sportswear, 108
John Anthony Apparel, 83
John Fulmer Outlet, 64
John Henry & Friends, 227
Johnston & Murphy, 260
Johnston Fashions for Children, 229
Jones NY Outlet, 229
Judy's Outlet, 108
Junior League of Long Beach Sale, 54
Junior League of Los Angeles Sale, 54

K

K-Mart, 144
K. T. Fashion, 198
Kelly Paper, 236
Kids Cottage, 68
Kids Double Time, 68
Kids for Less, 64
Kids Mart, 65
Kids R'Us, 65
Kids Store, 68
Kids Stuff, 68
King Richard's Antique Mall, 8

Kinney Shoe Outlet, 260
Kirk Paper, 237
Kirkpatrick Sales, 95
Kitchen & Bath Clear. Ctr., 37
Kitchen & Bath Specialists, 37
Kitchen Collection, 227
Kitchen Warehouse, 38
Kriegers, 198

L

L.A.C.M.A., 151
L.A. Design Concepts, 181
L. A. Trimmings, 119
L. A. Tronics, 23
LAX Luggage, 214
L.E.C. World Traders, 280
L. Bates Clothing, 228
La Brea Circus, 167
Lace and Scents, 124
Ladies' Shoe Outlet, 254
Lake Elsinore Outlet Center, 230
Lakenor Auto Salvage, 49
Lamps Factory Outlet, 201
Lamps Plus, 201
Lamps Plus Outlet, 201
Lanz II, 108
La Petite Factorie, 109
Laura M. Sportswear, 109
Leading Designer Outlet, 83
Leather Factory, 173
Leather Loft, 92
Leather to the Limit, 92
Le Baby Originals, 211
Lechters, 194
Leggoons Sportswear, 227
L'Eggs/Bali/Hanes, 124
Le Club Handbag Co., 3
Leisure World Consignment Shop, 182
Lenox Factory Store, 57
Le Petit Jean, 254
Leslie Fay Outlet, 109
Levi's Outlet, 83
Libbey Glass Outlet, 194
Liberty Carpet, 44
Lila's Discount Boutique, 110
Lillie Rubin Outlet, 110
Lincoln Antique Mall, 8
Lincoln Appliances, 16
Linen Club, 208
Lingerie for Less, 124
Lingerie Outlet, 125
Liquidation Club, 84
Little Folks, 65
Little Ones Reruns, 68
Little Orphan Overalls, 68
Liz Claiborne Outlet, 110
Loehmann's, 111
London Fog Outlet, 84
Long Beach Flea Mkt., 11
Lora's Perfumes, 26
Lore Lingerie Factory, 125
Los Angeles Arboretum, 244
Los Feliz Rattan, 176
Love Tennis, 265
Low Cost Spay/Neuter, 242
Luggage 4 Less, 214
Luggage For Less, 215

Luggage Outlet, 215
Luna Garcia, 57

M

M. Fredric Outlet, 111
MK Model Products, 191
Maidenform, 125
Mainly Seconds, 245
Make Room for Baby, 68
Mann Brothers Paint, 232
Manufacturer's Clearance Whse., 174
Manufacturer's Sports Outlet, 265
Marika, 274
Marinello Beauty School, 28
Mark Friedman Furniture, 174
Marlene Gaines Handbags, 4
Marlow's Books, 32
Marshall's, 144
Marv's Auto, 50
Mastercraft Rattan/Wicker, 176
Maternity Ltd., 128
Mattress Warehouse, 180
Max Levine & Son, 72
Max Studio, 111
May Co. Clothing Clear. Ctr., 140
May Co. Home Clear. Ctr., 140
Men's Wearhouse, 72
Mercedes Designer Resale, 116
Michael Levine, 159
Michael's Art Store, 19
Michael's Shoes, 252
Michael's Shoes Outlet, 252
Mickey's Auto Sales & Leasing, 46
Mikasa Factory Store, 57
Millie's Bags and Shoes, 4
Miller's Outpost Clear. Ctr., 85
Modern Woman, 131
Mom's the Word, 128
Mona's Custom Tailors, 73
Montgomery Ward Clear. Ctr., 141
Moran Drapery Whse., 148
Morrie's, 112
Mosquitoes, 254
Mother Goose Garment Exchange, 68
Move It, 274
Movies, Free, 151
Mr. MB's Candy, 169
Mr. Satin, 208
Multi-Factory Outlet, 112
Multiples Modular Knits, 112
Munn's, 58
Museum of Contemporary Art, 151
My Secret Place, 132

N

Nadine of CA Uniforms, 283
NaNa Outlet, 85
Nathan J Children's Wear Outlet, 228

300   Shopping Secrets of Southern California

National Auto Brokers, 46
National Fabrics & Foam, 156
Nationwide Baby Shops, 178
Nationwide Auctioneers, 47
Natural Fabric Co., 159
Nevada Bob's Golf & Tennis, 265
Nike Factory Store, 266
99 Cents Only Stores, 145
Ninth Street Outlet, 85
NoJo Outlet Store, 211
Nordstrom's Rack, 141
North Face, The, 266
Nursery Liquidators, 245

O
Oak Glen Apples, 166
Office Depot, 223
Off The Bolt, 156
Old Tyme Ceiling Fan Co., 203
Olde Towne Pomona Antique Mall, 8
Olga/Warner's Outlet, 126
Olympic Luggage, 215
Once Read Books, 32
$1 Cleaners, 150
$1 Most Garments Cleaners, 150
$1.50 Most Garments Cleaners, 150
Oneida Factory Store, 227
On the House, 153
Orange County Swap Meet, 12
Oshkosh B'Gosh Outlet, 65
Oshman's Outlet, 266
Outlet, The, 113
Owl Uniforms, 285

P
PCH Clothing, 74
PFC Fragrance, 231
P. F. McMullin Co., 267
P. J. London, 116
P. S. Plus Sizes, 131
PTS Leather Whse., 92
Pace Cyclewear., 267
Pace Membership Whse., 287
Pacific Airbrush, 20
Pacific Eyes & T's, 219
Pacific Sales, 16
Pacific Supply Co., 277
Painters' Warehouse, 232
Palm City, 245
Panel-it, The Kitchen Store, 38
Paperback Trader, 34
Paper Outlet, 234
Parties-N-Us, 235
Party Corner, 235
Party World, 235
Pasadena Antique Ctr., 9
Pasadena City College Flea Mkt., 11
Past Perfect, 116
Patagonia, 267
Patio Place, 184
Patrini Shoes, 255
Paul Jardin Outlet, 73

Penny Pinchers, 9
Perfumania, 230
Perfume City, 26
Perfume West, 16
Perry Ellis Shoes, 255
Pet and Equestrian Thrift Store, 240
Pet Nutrition Center, 241
Pet Supply, 241
Pet Vaccine Services, 242
Pfaltzgraff Stoneware, 58
Piano Outlet, 221
Pickwick Antique Show, 13
Pickwick Paper Products, 236
Pic'N' Save, 146
Pier One Clear. Ctr., 189
Piller's of Eagle Rock, 86
Pine Canyon Cherries, 66
Pioneer Bakery, 161
Place & Co., The, 115
Platter Puss Records, 251
Play It Again Sports, 268
Plaza Continental Factory Stores, 230
Plaza Golf, 268
Plummers, 174
Politix Outlet Store, 74
Polly Flinders Children's Wear, 227
Pomona Car Show, 50
Pottery and Floral World, 246
Pottery Barn Clear. Ctr., 189
Pottery Ranch, 58
Pottery Shack, 59
Pottery Store, 246
Prestige Fragrances, 26
Price Club, 287
Price-Less Bridals, 118
Prima Beauty Center, 27
Prime Time, 228
Priscilla's Bridal, 118

R
Rapport Intl. Home Furnishings, 175
Rattan Distribution Whse., 76
Rawling's Outlet, 268
Real Cheap Sports, 269
Reckless Women, 198
Record Surplus, 251
Recycled Rags, 116
Reebok Factory Store, 261
Regal Rents Sale, 59
Remy Leather, 93
Renee's Nutrition Ctr., 162
Rhino Records, 251
Ribbon Outlet, 227
Ricci Clothestique, 113
Richard's Beauty College, 28
Rick Pallak, 74
Ritz Dry Cleaners, 150
Roadium, The, 12
Robbins Antique Mart, 9
Robe Outlet, 126
Robert Scott David Brooks Outlet, 227
Robertson's, 136
Robinsons Clear. Ctr., 142
Rockaway Records, 251

Roger Stuart Clothes, 75
Rose Bowl Flea Market, 11
Rosenman Associates, 75
Ross Dress For Less, 145
Rossi D'Italia, 198
Royal Bedspreads, 208
Royal Doulton Direct, 60
Royal Mode, 75
Rubenfeld Kennedy Estate Jewelry, 196

S
Sacha of London Outlet, 255
Sacks SFO, 86
Sacks SFO Kids, 66
St. Vincent's Jewelry Ctr., 196
Saka's Outlet, 113
Samples Only, Inc., 256
Sample Shoes Unlimited, 256
Samy's Camera, 41
San Diego Factory Outlet Ctr., 231
San Gabriel Nursery, 246
Santa Barbara Ceramic Design Outlet, 157
Santa Barbara Museum of Art, 152
Santa Margarita Auction Barn, 10
Santa Monica Antiques, 9
Sanders House of Lights, 202
Sara Designers Outlet, 142
Saugus Swap Meet, 12
Sbicca Shoes, 228
Scandia Down Outlet, 208
Scotch Paints, 232
Sear's Outlet, 143
Second Heaven Bridal Resale, 121
Second Look Bridal Resale, 121
2nds Shop, 187
See Me Color, 86
Sergio Tacchini, 227
Seven Seas Rattan, 177
Seventh Avenue West, 114
Sewing Machine Whse., 17
Shakespeare Festival, 152
Sharper Image Outlet, 24
Shelly's Dancewear, 273
Sherman Oaks Antiques, 9
Shipley's, 87
Shirley's Shoes and Handbags, 4
Shirts Mart, 97
Shoe Club, 261
Shoe Crazy, 256
Shoes by Shirley, 256
Shoes Here, 261
Shore Shop, 87
Sid's Discount Baby Furniture, 178
Sig's Pottery and Nursery, 247
Sit 'n Sleep, 180
Sitting Pretty, Inc., 175
Skis, Etc., 269
Smart & Final Iris, 289
Snea Kee Feet, 269

Alphabetical Index

Socks Galore and More, 227
Something Special Flowers, 248
South Coast Botanic Garden, 244
Southland Farmers' Market Assn., 163
SpaGear, 275
Speaker City, U.S.A., 24
Sporting Outlet, 269
Sportmart, 270
Sports Again, 270
Sports Spectacular, 270
Sprint Cleaners, 150
Spur of the Moment Cruises, 281
Standard Brands Paper, 236
Standard Pool, 249
Standard Shoes, 262
Staples, 223
Star Baby, 66
Star Wares on Main, 90
Steinberg's Discount Tack & Feed, 241
Step in Time, 275
Stern's Discount Drapery Ctr., 148
Steven & Co. Jewelers, 196
Steven Craig Wholesale Clothiers, 75
Stewart Orchids, 248
Stork Club Resale Maternity, 129
Stork Club II, 129
Stork Shop, 66
Stroud's, 209
Stroud's's Clear. Ctr., 209
St. Vincent's Jewelry Ctr., 196
Studio Wardrobe, 90
Super Yarn Mart, 136
Susie's Deals, 114
Sutter Place, 109
Swank, 227
Sweats 'N Surf, 97

T
T.J. Maxx, 145
T&R Antiques, 10
T-Shirt Warehouse, 92
T-Shirt Wholesale Mart, 98
T-Shirts Mart, 98
T-Shirts Warehouse, 98
T-Shirts Wholesale Whse., 98
Tanner, 229
Thel's, 87
Thieve's Market, 262
Thomas Cook, 282
3D Bed and Bath, 210
3 Day Blinds, 148
Thrifty Cleaners, 150
Ticket Bazaar Info Line, 282
Tiffany's Toys, 271
Tile Importers, 44
Time-Off Apparel, 96
Tool Power, 277
Tool Shack, 278
Top to Top, 262
Tower Records Outlet, 251
Town Fair Bazaar, 54
Toy Liquidators, 229
Toys 'R Us, 281
Toys Unlimited, 227
Trader Joe's, 167
Train Shack, 191
Treasure House, 60
Treasure Hunt, 146
Treasure Mart, 10
20/20 Video Rentals, 280
$2 Fabric Store, 160
Tuesday Mornings, 190
TV Tapings, 152
Typebox, The, 237

U
Uniforms West, Inc., 283
Uni-Lite, 202
United Colors of Benetton, 88

V
VCA Animal Hospitals, 242
Valley Book City, 34
Valley Indoor Swap Meet, 13
Valley Indoor Swap Meet Pomona, 13
Valley Wholesale Nursery, 247
Van Heusen Outlet, 88
Van Rex Gourmet Foods, 168
Van's Factory Outlet, 263
Venice Beach Embroidery, 88
Venice-Ocean Beach Co-op, 163
Vidal Sassoon Beauty School, 28

W
W. J. Simmons Mattress Factory, 181
Wallet Works, 227
Wallpaper Bin, 233
Wallpapers To Go, 233
Walter Keller Golf & Tennis, 271
Warehouse Outlet, 89
Warehouse Shoe Sales, 263
Weber-Milbrook Bakery, 162
Welcome Home, 210
We-R-Fabrics, 157
Wesco Auto Parts, 49
West & Co. Outlet, 257
Westchester Faire Antique Mall, 10
Westlake Antique Ctr., 10
West L. A. Music, 222
West Point Pepperell, 210
Wet Seal Clear. Ctr., 114
Whim's/Sarah Coventry, 228
Wholesale Leather Apparel, 92
Wicker Factory, 229
Wilson's House of Suede & Leather Outlet, 93
Wonder-Hostess Bakery, 162
Woodland Hills Indoor Swap Meet, 13
Woody's Unfinished Furniture, 175
Work Boot Warehouse, 253
World Cleaners, 150

Y
Young Seconds, 68

Z
Zachary All, 76
Zeig Smog, 50

Index of Discount Catalogs and Other Sources

ABC Vacuum Cleaner Whse., 17
Action Discount Wallpaper Co., 233
Ameritone Paint, 233
Art Supply Whse., 21
Barnes & Noble, 35
Barrons, 61
Bart's Watersports, 271
Berry Scuba, 272
Best Fares Magazine, 282
Bosom Buddies, 128
Bridal Bargains, 120
Bruce Medical Supply, 219
Cabela's, 272
Camp-mor, 272
Carvin, 222
Chadwicks' of Boston, 115
Checks in the Mail, 237
Comb, 146
Company Store, The, 212
Computer Shopper, 133
Contact Lens Replacement Ctr., 219
Consumer Reports Auto Price Service, 46
Cos-Tom Picture Framing, 21
Crutchfield, 24
Daedalus Books, 35
Damark International, 146
Daniel Smith, 21
Deerskin Place, The, 93
Dial-A-Mattress, 181
Dills, Elmer, 153
Direct Discount Wall Coverings, 233
Direct Safety Co., 192
Domestications, 212
E&B Discount Marine, 216
Edward R. Hamilton, 35
Entertainment Publications, 152
Euro-Tire, 51
Fax City, 225
Finals, The, 96
47th Street Photo, 134
Goldberg's Marine, 217
Golden Valley Lighting, 202
Grand Finale, 143
Hidalgo, 220
Home-Sew, 136
Huntington Clothiers , 76
Interstate Music Supply, 222

J&R Music World, 24
Johnson's Carpets, 45
Justin Discount Boots, 263
Kennel Vet, 243
Lands' End, 89
Medi-Mail, 220
Merryland by Marilyn, 212
Midas China & Silver, 61
Mother Harts, 212
Mother's Place, 129
National Wholesale Co., 127
Nat Schwartz & Co., 61
Newark Dressmaking, 160
Orion Telescope, 192
Overton's, 272
Parrish, Darrell, 51
  The Car Buyer's Art
  Lease Cars
  Used Cars
Pet Warehouse, 243
Petticoat Express, 119
Post Wallcovering Distributors, 233
R. C. Steele Wholesale Pet Supplies, 243
Renovator's Supply, 38
Rhodes Hearing, 220
Road Runner Sports, 272
Sailboard Warehouse, 272
San Francisco Herb Co., 170
Showcase of Savings, 127
Silver Queen, The, 61
Sunglasses U. S. A., 220
Tapestry, 194
Thai Silks, 160
Tools on Sale, 278
Torres Ribbon Co., 225
Tuesday Morning Gift Catalog, 190
Viking Office Products, 225
Warehouse Carpets, 45
West Marine, 217
Wholesale Tape & Supply, 24
Wintersilks, 89

GEOGRAPHICAL INDEX

AGOURA
Designer Labels for Less, 80
Fence Factory, 37
Michael's Shoes, 252
Entenmann's/Oroweat Bakery, 161

ALHAMBRA
A.A.A., 281
Anna's Linens, 205
Farmers' Market, 164
$5 Clothing Store, 105
Four Day Tire Stores, 48
House of Fabrics, 158
Kids Mart, 65
P. S. Plus Sizes, 131
Patrini Shoes, 255
Pic'N'Save, 146
Price Club, 289
Staples, 233
Susie's Deals, 114
W. J. Simmons Mattress Factory, 181
Weber Millbrook Bakery, 162

ANAHEIM
A.A.A., 281
Aaron Bros. Art Mart, 18
Auto Parts Club, 48
Bergstroms, 62
Black & Decker/Dewalt, 276
C&R Clothiers, 70
California Wholesale Tile, 44
Crown Books, 29
Discount Sales Stores, 23
Dolly Madison Bakery, 161
Entenmann's/Oroweat Bakery, 161
Fabric King, 157
$5 Clothing Store, 105
Four Day Tire Stores, 48
Kelly Paper, 236
Kirk Paper, 237
Lincoln Antique Mall, 8
Nevada Bob's Golf & Tennis, 265
Nursery Liquidators, 245
P. S. Plus Sizes, 131
Pacific Airbrush, 20
Shipley's, 87
Smart & Final Iris, 287
Staples, 223
Susie's Deals, 114
3D Bed & Bath, 210
Tile Importers, 44
Toys 'R Us, 280
Tuesday Morning, 190
Uni-Lite, 202
W. J. Simmons Mattress Factory, 181
Wholesale Leather Apparel, 92

ARCADIA
Aaron Bros. Art Mart, 18
Crown Books, 29
Discount Sales Stores, 23
Lechters, 194
Loehmann's, 111
Los Angeles Arboretum, 244
99 Cents Only Stores, 145
Pic'N'Save, 146
P.S. Plus Sizes, 131
3 Day Blinds, 148
Wallpapers To Go, 233

ARTESIA
A.A.A., 281
Lamps Plus, 201
Mastercraft Rattan and Wicker, 176
Weber-Milbrook Bakery, 162

AZUSA
A.A.A., 281
Kids Mart, 65
99 Cents Only Stores, 145
Price Club, 287
Wonder-Hostess Bakery, 162

BALDWIN PARK
Anna's Linens, 205
$5 Clothing Store, 105

BARSTOW
ACA Joe, 227
Adolfo II, 227
Aileen Stores, 99
Anne Klein Outlet, 100
Banister Shoe Outlet, 227
Barbizon Outlet, 122
Bass Factory Outlet, 258
Big Dogs Sportswear, 78
Black & Decker Factory Store, 276
Book Warehouse, 29
Boot Factory, 258
Bruce Alan Bags, 227
Bugle Boy Outlet, 79
Capezio Outlet, 259
Coach Value Store, 2
Corning Revere Outlet, 193
Designer Brands Accessories, 227
Eagle's Eye, 227
Evan Picone/Gant, 81
Fieldcrest/Cannon, 207
General Housewares, 227
Gitano Outlet, 81
Hanes Activewear, 227
Hartmann Luggage Outlet, 213
Izod/Monet, 227
John Henry & Friends, 227
Johnston & Murphy Outlet, 260
Kitchen Collection, 227
Leading Designer Outlet, 83
Leather Loft, 92
Leggoons Sportswear, 227
L'Eggs/Hanes/Bali Outlet, 124
Lenox Factory Store, 57
Levi's Outlet, 83
London Fog Outlet, 84
Oneida Factory Store, 227
Oshkosh B'Gosh Outlet, 65
Paper Outlet, 234
Polly Flinders Outlet, 227
Rawlings Outlet, 268
Reebok Outlet, 261
Ribbon Outlet, 227
Robert Scott & David Brooks, 227
Royal Doulton Direct, 60
Sergio Tacchini, 227
Skyr, 227
Smart & Final Iris, 287
Socks Galore & More, 227
Swank, 227
Toys Unlimited, 227
Van Heusen, 88
Wallet Works, 227
Weber-Milbrook Bakery, 162
Welcome Home, 210

BELL
99 Cents Only Stores, 145
Smart & Final Iris, 287
Toys 'R Us, 280
Treasure Hunt, 60
Weber Milbrook Bakery, 162

BELLFLOWER
Farmers' Market, 164
Smart & Final Iris, 287
Staples, 223
$2 Fabric Store, 160

BEVERLY HILLS
Annual Beverly Hills Garage Sale, 53
Bijoux Medici, 1
Crown Books, 29
Friends of the Library Sale, 34
Golden West Billiards, 279
Le Petit Jean, 254
Mosquitoes, 254
Steven & Co. Jewelers, 196
Thomas Cook, 282

BREA
Bookstar, 29
C&R Clothiers, 70
Crown Books, 29
Discount Train Whse., 192
Hit or Miss, 106
Lamps Plus, 201
Marshalls, 144
Strouds, 209
3 Day Blinds, 148
T. J. Maxx, 145
Toys 'R Us, 180

BRENTWOOD
Crown Books, 29

Dutton's Bookstore, 33
Lora's Perfumes, 26
P. J. London, 116

BUENA PARK
Bagnall Camera Show, 10
Computer Marketplace Show, 133
Crystal Factory, 55
K-Mart, 144
Kids Mart, 65
Mainly Seconds, 245
Marinello Beauty School, 26
May Co. Clothing Clear. Ctr., 140
Modern Woman, 131
Montgomery Ward Clear. Ctr., 141
Pacific Sales, 16
Pic'N'Save, 146
Smart & Final Iris, 187
Super Yarn Mart, 136
Susie's Deals, 114
T. J. Maxx, 145
T-Shirt Warehouse, 98
Weber Milbrook Bakery, 162
Wesco Auto Parts, 49

BURBANK
A.A.A., 281
Crown Books, 29
Designer Labels for Less, 80
Discount Desk Center, 186
Discount Sales Store, 23
Dutton's Bookstore, 29
Electropedic Adjustable Beds, 80
Farmers' Market, 165
Gigi Shoppe, 105
J. P. Discount Fabrics, 156
K-Mart, 144
Kids Cottage, 68
Kids Mart, 65
$1 Cleaners, 150
Party World, 235
Pickwick, The, 13
Pic'N'Save, 146
Price Club, 287
Robe Outlet, 126
Sacks SFO, 86
Sacks SFO Kids, 66
Smart & Final Iris, 287
Speaker City U.S.A., 24
3 Day Blinds, 48
Toys 'R Us, 280
Train Shack, 191
Wilson's House of Suede & Leather Outlet, 93

CABAZON
Adolfo II, 229
Adrienne Vittadini Outlet, 99
Aileen Stores, 99
Albert Nipon Outlet, 99
American Tourister Outlet, 213
Anne Klein Outlet, 100
Arrow Shirts, 78
Barbizon Outlet, 122
Bass Factory Outlet, 258
Capezio Factory Outlet, 259

Corning/Revere Outlet, 193
Designer Brands Accessories, 229
Designer's Own/Nancy Johnson, 229
Duffel, 229
Eddie Bauer Outlet, 80
Esprit, 104
Evan Picone/Gant Outlet, 81
Famous Footwear, 260
Full Size Fashions, 130
Geoffrey Beene Outlet, 71
Gitano Outlet, 81
Gorham, 229
Guess Outlet, 82
Harve Bernard, 229
Hawaiian Cotton, 229
He-Ro Group, 122
Joan and David, 254
John Henry, 229
Johnston Fashion for Children, 229
Jones NY, 229
Kitchen Collection, 229
Leather Loft, 92
Maidenform, 125
Nike Factory Store, 266
Oneida Silver, 229
Paper Outlet, 234
Patagonia, 267
Perry Ellis Shoes, 255
Pfaltzgraff Stoneware, 58
Ribbon Outlet, 229
Robert Scott & David Brooks, 229
Royal Doulton Direct, 60
Socks Galore, 229
SpaGear, 275
Tanner, 229
Toy Liquidators, 229
Van Heusen Outlet, 88
Wallet Works, 229
Welcome Home, 210
West Point Pepperell, 210
Wicker Factory, 229

CAMARILLO
Crown Books, 29
Kids Mart, 65
Pic'N'Save, 146
3 Day Blinds, 148
Wonder-Hostess Bakery, 162

CANOGA PARK
Anna's Linens, 205
Adray's, 22
Babyland, 177
Bedspread Whse., 206
Beverly Hills Fan Co. Outlet, 203
Brass Beds Unlimited, 179
C&C Pet Supermarket, 239
Castle Chandeliers, 200
Collector's Eye, 197
Costco, 286
DAK Outlet Store, 22
Discount Desk Center, 186
Entenmann's/Oroweat Bakery, 161
Fallbrook Handbag Outlet, 2

$5 Clothing Store, 105
Four Day Tire Stores, 48
Froch's Woodcraft Shop, 172
Golden West Billiards, 279
H. Savinar Luggage, 213
Home Base, 39
J. C. Penney Outlet, 140
Jasmine Cleaners, 150
Joan Geddes Sportswear, 108
Kids Mart, 65
Lechters, 194
Marshalls, 144
Nevada Bob's Golf & Tennis, 265
99 Cents Only Stores, 145
Off the Bolt, 156
Pic'N'Save, 146
Super Yarn Mart, 136
Sweats & Surf, 97
T. J. Maxx, 145
W. J. Simmons Mattress Factory, 181
Work Boot Warehouse, 253

CARLSBAD
Smart & Final Iris, 287

CARPINTERIA
Stewart Orchids, 248

CARSON
Algert Appliances, 15
Anna's Linens, 205
Discount Sales Stores, 23
Dynasty Classics Outlet, 200
$5 Clothing Store, 105
Kids Mart, 65
Kids R'Us, 65
Mikasa Factory Store, 57
Modern Woman, 131
Smart & Final Iris, 287
Toys 'R Us, 280

CATHEDRAL CITY
Aaron Bros. Art Mart, 18
Bag Lady, 1
Lila's Women's Discount Boutique, 110
Shirley's Shoes & Handbags, 4
Smart & Final Iris, 287
Tuesday Morning, 190
Weber Milbrook Bakery, 162

CENTURY CITY
A.A.A., 281
Hit or Miss, 106
Star Baby, 66

CERRITOS
Aaron Bros. Art Mart, 18
Baby Toytown, 177
C&R Clothiers, 70
Dan Howard's Maternity Factory, 127
Fan/Fireplace Man, 203
Fedco, 286
Kelly Paper, 236

Geographical Index   305

Kids R'Us, 65
Pic'N'Save, 146
Sportmart, 270
T. J. Maxx, 145
Toys 'R Us, 280
W. J. Simmons Mattress Factory, 181

CHATSWORTH
Builders Discount, 39
Covercraft Outlet, 48
Kelly Paper, 236
Kirk Paper, 237
Lace and Scents, 124
Lamps Plus Outlet, 201
Marshalls, 144
Pic'N'Save, 146
Ross Dress For Less, 145
3 Day Blinds, 148
Wonder-Hostess Bakery, 162

CHINO
A.A.A., 281
Aaron Bros. Art Mart, 18
Candy Factory Store, 168
Designer Labels for Less, 80
$5 Clothing Store, 105
Kids Mart, 65
Nordstrom Rack, 141
Pace Membership Whse., 287
Pic'N'Save, 146
Staples, 223
T. J. Maxx, 145
3D Bed & Bath, 210
3 Day Blinds, 148

CHULA VISTA
A.A.A., 281
Entenmann's/Oroweat Bakery, 161
Price Club, 287
Smart & Final Iris, 287
Super Yarn Mart, 136
Toys 'R Us, 280

CITY OF COMMERCE
Aileen Stores, 99
Ann Taylor Outlet, 100
Bijoux Medici, 1
Book Warehouse, 29
Budget Rents Clear. Ctr., 182
Capezio Outlet, 259
Cole of California Outlet, 94
Corning/Revere Outlet, 193
David Textiles, 157
Designer Labels for Less, 80
Designer Labels for Men, 228
Designers Own, 228
Designs by Desre, 228
Direction Menswear, 228
Eddie Bauer Outlet, 80
Fabric Outlet, 158
Firenze Factory Outlet, 91
$5 Clothing Stores, 105
Francine Browner Outlet, 228
Full Size Fashions, 130

Gap Outlet, 81
Gitano Outlet, 81
Harve Bernard, 228
Hawaiian Cotton, 228
In 2 Shape, 228
Joan and David, 254
John Fulmer Outlet, 64
Kids Mart, 65
Kitchen Collection, 228
L. Bates Clothing, 228
Leather Loft, 92
Linen Club, 208
Max Studio, 111
Multiples Modular Knits, 112
Nathan J Children's Wear, 228
Paul Jardin Outlet, 73
Perry Ellis Shoes, 255
Politix Outlet, 74
Prestige Fragrances, 26
Prime Time, 228
Sbicca Shoes Outlet, 228
Smart & Final Iris, 287
Socks Galore, 228
Star Baby, 66
Toy Liquidators, 228
United Colors of Benetton, 88
Welcome Home, 210
Whims/Sarah Coventry, 228

CITY OF INDUSTRY
Baby Toytown, 177
Cheep Lace, 135
Comp USA, 133
Costco, 286
Dana Bedspreads, 206
Discount Lighting Outlet, 200
Home Base, 39
Leather Factory, 173
Libbey Glass Outlet, 194
Nationwide Commercial Auctioneers, 47
Nevada Bob's Golf & Tennis, 265
Pace Membership Whse., 287
Pacific Sales, 16
Party World, 235
Shirts Mart, 97
Staples, 223
T-Shirt Wholesale Mart, 98

COLTON
Price Club, 287

COMPTON
Anna's Linens, 205
Warehouse Shoe Sale, 263
Weber Milbrook Bakery, 162

CORONA
Anna's Linens, 205
Del Rey Tennis Shoes Whse., 259
Discount Sales Stores, 23
Kids Mart, 65
Leather Factory, 173
Pic'N'Save, 146
Price Club, 287

Smart & Final Iris, 287
T. J. Maxx, 145
W. J. Simmons Mattress Factory, 181
Wonder-Hostess Bakery, 162

CORONA DEL MAR
Recycled Rags, 116
Young Seconds, 68

COSTA MESA
A.A.A., 281
Aaron Bros. Art Mart, 18
Barbeques Galore, 184
Bergstroms, 62
C&R Clothiers, 70
Crown Books, 29
Dawn's Discount Lace, 135
Elwell Farms, 166
Fabric Warehouse, 158
Fedco, 286
Glabman's, 173
K-Mart, 144
Kids Mart, 65
Lingerie for Less, 124
Mainly Seconds Pottery, 245
Marshalls, 144
Nevada Bob's Golf & Tennis, 265
Olga/Warner's Outlet, 126
Orange County Swap Meet, 12
Pacific Eyes & T's, 219
Pickwick Paper Products, 236
Record Surplus, 251
Shipley's, 87
Smart & Final Iris, 287
Sportmart, 270
Sprint Cleaners, 150
Strouds, 209
Susie's Deals, 114
Thieves Market, 262
Thomas Cook, 282
Toys 'R US, 280
W. J. Simmons Mattress Factory, 181
Wonder-Hostess Bakery, 162

COVINA
A.A.A., 281
Anna's Linens, 205
Discount Sales Stores, 23
K-Mart, 144
Kids R'Us, 65
Marinello Beauty School, 28
$1.50 Most Garments Cleaners, 150
Pic'N'Save, 146
Staples, 223
Toys 'R Us, 180
Treasure Hunt, 146
Weber Milbrook Bakery, 162
Wesco Auto Parts, 29

CUDAHY
Anna's Linens, 205
Clothestime Outlet, 102
Pic'N'Save, 146

CULVER CITY
A.A.A., 281
Anna's Linens, 205
Armand's Discount, 184
Bookstar, 29
C&R Clothiers, 70
Champagne Taste, 187
Clayton Shoes, 253
Comp USA, 133
Crown Books, 29
Culver Carpet Center, 43
Designer Bloopers, 172
Designer Labels for Less, 80
Discount Pet Center, 240
Dolly Madison Bakery, 161
Entenmanns/Oroweat Bakery, 161
Fellini Leather, 91
$5 Clothing Store, 105
Graphaids, 19
Handbag Hang-up, 3
Harpers, 106
Hi-Lo Cleaners, 149
Home Shop, 207
Hub Caps, 49
Kids Mart, 65
Kids R'Us, 65
Kirkpatrick Sales, 95
Panel It, 38
Pic'N'Save, 146
Play it Again Sports, 268
Regal Rents Sale, 59
Ross Dress for Less, 145
Sacks SFO, 86
Sit 'N Sleep, 180
Stewart Orchids, 248
T. J. Maxx, 145
Thel's, 87
Toys 'R Us, 280
Trader Joe's, 167
Van Rex Gourmet Foods, 168
Warehouse Shoe Sale, 263

CYPRESS
Crown Books, 29
Dolly Madison Bakery, 161
$5 Clothing Store, 105
Kids Mart, 65
Lingerie for Less, 124
Staples, 223
Wonder-Hostess Bakery, 161

DANA POINT
Pacific Eyes & T's, 219

DEL MAR
Farmers' Market, 164

DOWNEY
A.A.A., 281
Alin Party Supplies, 234
Blue Chip Drapery, 147
C&R Clothiers, 70
Crown Books, 29
Kids Mart, 65
Marinello Beauty School, 28
Pace Membership Whse., 287
Pic'N'Save, 146

Strouds, 209
Strouds Clear. Ctr., 209
3 Day Blinds, 148

DUARTE
Pic'N'Save, 146
Staples, 223

EAGLE ROCK
Factory Bridal Imports, 117
Pillers of Eagle Rock, 86
Trader Joe's, 167

EL CAJON
Apparel Designer Zone, 76
Auto Parts Club, 28
El Cajon Antique Mart, 7
Entenmann's/Oroweat Bakery, 161
Kids Mart, 65
Pic'N'Save, 146
Smart & Final Iris, 287
Stork Club Resale Maternity, 129
Wonder-Hostess Bakery, 162

EL MONTE
A.A.A., 281
A.B.E. Office Furniture, 185
Dolly Madison Bakery, 161
$5 Clothing Store, 105
Home Base, 39
Kelly Paper, 236
Kids Mart, 65
Kirk Paper, 237
$1 Cleaners, 150
Outlet, The, 113
Pace Membership Whse., 287
Smart & Final Iris, 287
Weber-Milbrook Bakery, 162
Wesco Auto Parts, 49

EL SEGUNDO
Renee's Nutrition Ctr., 162
Shoe Crazy, 256
Treasure Hunt, 146

EL SERENO
Moran Drapery Whse., 148

EL TORO
Aaron Bros. Art Mart, 18
C&R Clothiers, 70
Children's Orchard, 68
Crown Books, 29
Entenmann's/Oroweat Bakery, 161
House of Fabrics, 158
Kids Mart, 65
Mastercraft Rattan and Wicker, 176
Office Depot, 223
Smart & Final Iris, 287
Thieves Market, 262

ENCINITAS
Crown Books, 29
Kids Mart, 65
L. A. Tronics, 23
Pacific Eyes & T's, 219

ENCINO
C&R Clothiers, 70
Daphna's, 183
Designer Labels for Less, 80
Friedman's, 16
Harpers, 106
Leather Factory, 173
Michael's Shoes, 252
Shoes by Shirley, 256
Trader Joe's, 167

ESCONDIDO
A.A.A., 281
Barbeques Galore, 184
Entenmann's/Oroweat Bakery, 161
Famous Footwear, 260
Fedco, 286
Kelly Paper, 236
Kids Mart, 65
Pic'N'Save, 146
Smart & Final Iris, 287
Stork Club II, 129
T. J. Maxx, 145
Toys 'R Us, 280
Weber-Milbrook Bakery, 162
Wonder-Hostess Bakery, 162

FONTANA
$5 Clothing Store, 105
Kids Mart, 65
Pic'N'Save, 146
Smart & Final Iris, 287
Toys 'R Us, 180
Wonder-Hostess Bakery, 162

FOUNTAIN VALLEY
Alin Party Supply, 234
Anna's Linens, 205
Auto Parts Club, 48
California Luggage, 213
Comp USA, 133
Cort Furniture Clear. Ctr., 182
Crown Books, 29
Dana Bedspreads, 206
Decorative Fabric House, 155
Hit or Miss, 106
Home Base, 39
Luggage for Less, 214
Office Depot, 223
Pace Membership Whse., 287
Pet Supply, 241
Price Club, 287
Shoe Club, 261
Staples, 223
Super Yarn Mart, 136
T. J. Maxx, 145
3D Bed & Bath, 210

FULLERTON
A.A.A., 281
Aaron Bros. Art Mart, 18
Anna's Linens, 205
Art Store, 17

Geographical Index

$5 Clothing Store, 105
Harbor Antique Mall, 8
Home Base, 39
K-Mart, 144
Kids Mart, 65
Leather Factory, 173
Low Cost Spay & Neuter, 242
Michael's Shoes, 252
Modern Woman, 131
Pace Membership Whse., 287
Party World, 235
Price Club, 287
Sportmart, 270
Staples, 223
Thieves Market, 262
Toys 'R Us, 280
Wonder-Hostess Bakery, 162

GARDENA
A.A.A., 281
C. E. Jones Ceramics, 244
Capital Auto Parts, 49
Carl's Pocketbook Exchange, 33
Clayton's Shoes, 253
Electropedic Adjustable Beds, 80
Farmers' Market, 164
Home Base, 39
Kelly Paper, 236
Kirk Paper, 237
Liquidation Club, 85
Mastercraft Rattan and Wicker, 176
Office Depot, 223
Pace Membership Whse., 287
Pic'N'Save, 146
Scotch Paint, 232
Snea Kee Feet, 269
Wonder-Hostess Bakery, 162

GARDEN GROVE
A.A.A., 281
Anna's Linens, 205
Costco, 286
Drapery World Outlet, 147
$5 Clothing Store, 105
Four Day Tire Stores, 48
Half Price House, 121
Hit or Miss, 106
Kids Mart, 65
Montgomery Ward Clear. Ctr., 141
Newport Antique Mall, 8
99 Cents Only Stores, 145
Pic'N'Save, 146
Skis, Etc., 269
Smart & Final Iris, 287
Susie's Deals, 114
T. J. Maxx, 145

GLENDALE
A.A.A., 281
Aaron Bros. Art Mart, 18
Air Conditioning Exchange, 36
Bergstroms, 62
Brand Bookshop, 33

C&R Clothiers, 70
Castle Chandelier, 200
Cort Furniture Clear. Ctr., 182
Crystal Sonics, 22
Designer Labels for Less, 80
Glendale Show, 13
House of Fabrics, 158
Kirk Paper, 237
K-Mart, 144
Lamps Plus, 201
Little Folks, 65
Los Feliz Rattan, 176
Mastercraft Rattan and Wicker, 176
Max Studio, 111
Munns, 58
Office Depot, 223
$1 Cleaners, 150
Party World, 235
Pottery & Floral World, 246
Smart & Final Iris, 287
Sportmart, 270
Strouds, 209
Super Crown, 29
Thieves Market, 262
Thomas Cook, 282
Tool Shack, 278
Weber Milbrook Bakery, 162
Wonder-Hostess Bakery, 162

GOLETA
Blue Moon Exchange, 94
Fence Factory, 37

GRANADA HILLS
Crown Books, 29
$5 Clothing Store, 105
Hit or Miss, 106
Kids Mart, 65
Marinello Beauty School, 28
Marshalls, 144
Pic'N'Save, 146
Susie's Deals, 114
T. J. Maxx, 145
Trader Joe's, 167

GRAND TERRACE
Mother Goose Garment Exchange, 68

GROSSMONT
Bullocks Grand Finale, 139
Pacific Eyes & T's, 219
Strouds, 209

HAWTHORNE
Bookstar, 29
Costco, 286
Dolly Madison Bakery, 161
Entenmann's/Oroweat Bakery, 161
Fellini Leather, 91
House of Fabrics, 158
Kids Mart, 65
Mattress Warehouse, 180
99 Cents Only Store, 145
Pacific Eyes & T's, 219
Standard Shoes Clear. Ctr., 262

3 Day Blinds, 148
Toys 'R Us, 280
Treasure Hunt, 146

HEMET
A.A.A., 281
Kids Mart, 65
Pic'N'Save, 146
Smart & Final Iris, 287
3 Day Blinds, 148

HERMOSA BEACH
Aaron Bros. Art Mart, 18
Farmers' Market, 164

HIGHLAND PARK
Anna's Linens, 205

HOLLYWOOD
A.A.A., 281
Aaron Bros. Art Mart, 18
Anna's Linens, 205
Aron's Record Shop, 250
Arturo's Flowers, 248
Beverly Fireplace Shop, 185
C&R Clothiers, 70
Crown Books, 29
Farmers' Market, 164
$5 Clothing Store, 105
Glamour Uniform Shop, 283
Kids Mart, 65
Kriegers, 198
La Brea Circus, 167
Michael's Art Store, 19
Office Depot, 223
Pic'N'Save, 146
Pier One Imports Clear. Ctr, 189
Ross Dress for Less, 145
Sacks SFO, 86
Sacks SFO Kids, 66
Shakespeare Festival L. A., 152
Standard Pool, 262
Susie's Deals, 114
TV Tapings, 152
Typebox, The, 237

HUNTINGTON BEACH
A.A.A., 281
Aaron Bros. Art Mart, 18
Arthur John's, 101
Bed, Bath & Beyond, 205
Calico Corners, 154
Christine's Place, 68
Contempo Casuals Outlet, 103
Converse Outlet, 252
Crown Books, 29
Discount Sales Stores, 23
Four Day Tire Stores, 48
Kids Mart, 65
Kids R'Us, 65
Lamps Factory Outlet, 201
$5 Clothing Store, 105
L. A. Tronics, 23
Lamps Plus, 201
Lechters, 194
Little Ones Reruns, 68
Lingerie for Less, 124
Loehmann's, 111
Marshalls, 144

308 Shopping Secrets of Southern California

My Secret Place, 132
Pace Cyclewear, 267
Party World, 235
Pic'N'Save, 146
Robe Outlet, 126
Sears Outlet, 143
Shore Shop, 87
Smart & Final Iris, 287
Sportmart, 270
Staples, 223
Strouds, 209
Susie's Deals, 114
Sutter Place, 109
3 Day Blinds, 148
Toys 'R Us, 280
Trader Joe's, 167
Tuesday Mornings, 190
W. J. Simmons Mattress Factory, 181
Warehouse Shoe Sale, 263
Weber Milbrook Bakery, 162

HUNTINGTON PARK
Home Shop, 207

INDIO
A.A.A., 281
Dolly Madison Bakery, 161
Pic'N'Save, 146
Smart & Final Iris, 287
Wonder-Hostess Bakery, 162

INGLEWOOD
A.A.A., 29
Anna's Linens, 205
Home Base, 39
House of Fabrics, 158
Marinello Beauty School, 23
Office Depot, 223
Pic'N'Save, 146
Price Club, 287
Smart & Final Iris, 287
Weber-Milbrook Bakery, 162
Wonder-Hostess Bakery, 162

IRVINE
Aaron Bros. Art Mart, 18
Bergstroms, 62
Crown Books, 29
Four Day Tire Stores, 48
Hit or Miss, 106
Home Base, 39
Kids Mart, 65
Kirk Paper, 237
Lingerie for Less, 124
Pace Membership Whse., 287
Pacific Eyes & T's, 219
Pacific Sales, 16
Staples, 223
Susie's Deals, 114
3D Bed and Bath, 210
Trader Joe's, 167
Tuesday Mornings, 190
W. J. Simmons Mattress Factory, 181

LA CANADA
Kids Mart, 65

Pic'N'Save, 146

LA CRESCENTA
Crown Books, 29

LAGUNA BEACH
Crown Books, 29
Pacific Eyes & T's, 219
Pottery Shack, 59

LAGUNA HILLS
A.A.A., 281
Entenmann's/Oroweat Bakery, 161
Lamps Plus, 201
Leisure World Consignment Shop, 182
National Auto Brokers, 46
Nevada Bob's Golf & Tennis, 265
Marshalls, 144
P. S. Plus Sizes, 131
Strouds, 209
T. J. Maxx, 145
Trader Joe's, 167
W. J. Simmons Mattress Factory, 181

LAGUNA NIGUEL
Children's Orchard, 68
Costco, 286
Home Base, 39
Lingerie for Less, 124
Loehmann's, 111
Step in Time, 275
Strouds, 209
Super Crown, 29
T.J. Maxx, 145
3D Bed & Bath, 210

LA HABRA
A.A.A., 281
Aaron Bros. Art Mart, 18
C&R Clothiers, 70
Contractors Warehouse, 39
Discount Tropical Fish, 240
Four Day Tire Stores, 48
Pic'N'Save, 146
Sears Outlet, 143
Smart & Final Iris, 287
Super Yarn Mart, 136
Susie's Deals, 114
T. J. Maxx, 145
W. J. Simmons Mattress Factory, 181
Wonder-Hostess Bakery, 162

LA JOLLA
Aaron Brothers Art Mart, 18
Apparel Designer Zone, 76
Designer Consigner, 116
Hunter's Books, 30
Lillie Rubin Outlet, 110
Museum of Contemporary Art, 151
Pacific Eyes & T's, 219
Strouds, 209

LAKE ELSINORE
Adolfo II, 230
American Tourister, 213
Bass Factory Store, 258

Cape Isle Knitters, 230
Chicago Cutlery, 230
Cole Haan, 259
Corning/Revere Outlet, 193
Crisa Factory Store, 230
Famous Brands Housewares, 193
Geoffrey Beene Outlet, 71
He-Ro Group Outlet, 122
JH Collectibles Outlet, 107
Jones NY Outlet, 230
Leather Loft, 92
L'Eggs/Hanes/Bali Outlet, 124
Leslie Fay Outlet, 109
Liz Claiborne, 110
London Fog Outlet, 84
Maidenform, 125
Marika, 274
Nathan J Outlet, 230
Nike Factory Store, 266
North Face, 266
Oneida Factory Store, 230
Perfumania, 230
Sbicca Shoes Outlet, 230
Socks Galore, 230
Van Heusen Outlet, 88
Wallet Works, 230
Welcome Home, 210
West & Co. Shoes, 257
Whims/Sarah Coventry, 230

LAKE FOREST
Treasure House, 60
Wonder-Hostess Bakery, 162

LAKEWOOD
Aaron Bros. Art Mart, 18
Adray's, 22
Alin Party Supply, 234
Bullocks Grand Finale, 139
C&R Clothiers, 70
Crown Books, 29
Designer Labels for Less, 80
$5 Clothing Store, 105
Hit or Miss, 106
House of Fabrics, 158
Kelly Paper, 236
Lechters, 194
Marinello Beauty School, 28
Marshalls, 144
Once Read Books, 32
P. S. Plus Sizes, 131
Party World, 235
Shipley's, 87
Strouds, 209
Super Yarn Mart, 136
Susie's Deals, 114
3 Day Blinds, 248

LA MESA
A.A.A., 281
Aaron Bros. Art Mart, 18
Bookstar, 29
Dana Bedspreads, 206
Kelly Paper, 236
Kids Mart, 65
Lamps Plus, 201
Leather Factory, 173

Geographical Index

Pic'N'Save, 146
Super Yarn Mart, 136
Toys 'R Us, 280

LA MIRADA
Hit or Miss, 106
Kids Mart, 65
Kids R'Us, 65
99 Cents Only Stores, 145
Pic'N'Save, 146
Staples, 223
Toys 'R Us, 280

LANCASTER
A.A.A., 218
Aaron Bros. Art Mart, 18
Anna's Linens, 205
Big, Bad & Beautiful, 130
Costco, 286
Entenmann's/Oroweat Bakery, 161
K-Mart, 144
Kids Mart, 65
Marshalls, 145
Modern Woman, 131
Pic'N'Save, 146
Scotch Paint, 232
Smart & Final Iris, 287
3 Day Blinds, 148
$2 Fabric Store, 160
Toys 'R Us, 280
Weber Milbrook Bakery, 162
Wonder-Hostess Bakery, 162
Woody's Unfinished Furniture, 175

LA PUENTE
Aaron Bros. Art Mart, 18
Clothestime Outlet, 102
99 Cents Only Stores, 145
Pic'N'Save, 146
Wonder-Hostess Bakery, 162

LA VERNE
Aaron Bros. Art Mart, 18
Cole of California Outlet, 94
Kids Mart, 65

LAWNDALE
Costco, 286
99 Cents Only Stores, 145
W. J. Simmons Mattress Factory, 181

LEMON GROVE
Broadway Antique Mall, 7
Smart & Final Iris, 287
Weber Milbrook Bakery, 162

LOMA LINDA
Super Yarn Mart, 136

LOMITA
Animal Birth Control, 242
Blue Chip Drapery, 147
Pic'N'Save, 146
Weber Milbrook Thrift Bakery, 162

LONG BEACH
A.A.A., 281
Acres of Books, 30
Al Greenwood's Bedspread Kingdom, 204
Anna's Linens, 205
Auto Parts Club, 48
Black & Decker/DeWalt, 276
C&R Clothiers, 70
Crown Books, 29
Dolly Madison Bakery, 161
Fabric Barn, 136
Four Day Tire Stores, 48
Friedman's 16
House of Fabrics, 158
Junior League of Long Beach Sale, 54
K-Mart, 144
Kids Mart, 65
Kirk Paper, 237
Long Beach Flea Mkt., 11
Marshalls, 144
Mona's Custom Tailors, 73
PTS Leather Whse., 92
Pacific Eyes & T's, 219
Pic'N'Save, 146
Second Heaven Bridal Resale, 121
Shipley's, 87
Smart & Final Iris, 287
Susie's Deals, 114
T. J. Maxx, 145
Thomas Cook, 282
3 Day Blinds, 48
Trader Joe's, 167
Weber Milbrook Bakery, 162

LOS ALAMITOS
Entenmann's/Oroweat Bakery, 161
Designer Labels for Less, 80
Nevada Bob's Golf & Tennis, 265
PCH Factory Outlet, 74
Shipley's, 87
Thieves Market, 262

LOS ANGELES
A.A.A., 281
A Bedtime Story, 204
ABC Premiums, 14
Aaron Bros. Art Mart, 18
Academy Award Clothes, 69
Adler Shoes, 257
Adray's, 22
Albee's Discount Appliances, 12
All that Jazz Factory Outlet, 100
All Together, 100
American Flower Exchange, 247
Animal Birth Control, 242
Anna's Linens, 205
Antique Guild Showcase Gallery, 6
Art Store, 18
Arturo's Flowers, 101
As Is Furniture, 171

Avery Rest. Supply, 193
Baby Guess, 62
Babyland, 177
Beno's, 78
Betnun Music, 221
Betty's Large Sizes, 129
Beverly Hills Hosiery, 123
Black & White Wholesalers, 102
Bodhi Tree Used Books, 31
Bookstar, 29
Builders Discount, 39
C&R Clothiers, 70
California Mart Sales, 79
Celebrity Cleaners, 149
Cleaning Club, 149
Collectibles, 103
Costume Jewelry Mart, 197
Crown Books, 29
Cut-Rate Office Furniture, 186
Damone, 104
Designer Labels for Less, 80
Designers Clear. Ctr., 172
Diamond Foam and Fabric, 185
Diamond Mine Co., 195
Discount Lighting Outlet, 200
Discount Tile Center, 45
Dutton's Bookstore, 33
Eddy's for Men, 71
Entenmann's/Oroweat Bakery, 161
Eurogift, 188
Fantastic Sportswear, 105
Farmers' Market, 164
Fedco, 286
Foster's Shoes, 260
Four Day Tire Stores, 48
Frank's Highland Park Camera, 20
Freestyle, 41
Glass Garage, 188
Gloves by Hammer, 5
Golf Exchange, 264
Goodrich Cleaners, 149
Guess Outlet, 82
H&H Jobbing Co., 264
Hacienda Brides Intl., 118
Hollywood Cedars Uniforms, 283
Ibex Apparel, 118
Immune Testing Center, 218
Intermoda Exchange, 82
J. B. Sebrell, 249
Jasmine Cleaners, 150
Judy's Outlet, 108
Junior League of L.A. Sale, 54
K-Mart, 144
K. T. Fashion, 198
Kelly Paper, 236
Kids Mart, 65
Kirk Paper, 237
Kitchen Warehouse, 38
L. A. C. M. A., 151
L. A. Trimmings, 119
LAX Luggage, 214
Lamps Plus, 201
Lanz II, 108

Le Club Handbag Co., 3
Liberty Carpet, 44
Lingerie for Less, 124
Little Folks, 65
Loehmann's, 111
Mann Brothers Paints & Lacquer, 232
Manufacturers' Clearance Whse., 174
Max Levine & Son, 72
Max Studio, 111
May Co. Clothing Clear. Ctr., 140
Mercedes Designer Resale, 116
Michael Levine Inc., 159
Millie's Bags & Shoes, 4
Modern Woman, 131
Morrie's, 112
Museum of Contemporary Art, 151
NaNa Outlet, 85
99 Cents Only Stores, 145
Office Depot, 223
Olga/Warners Outlet, 126
Olympic Luggage, 215
Oshman's Outlet, 266
Outlet, The, 113
Owl Uniforms, 285
Pacific Supply Co., 277
Pic'N'Save, 146
Place & Co., The, 115
Rapports Intl. Home Furnishings, 175
Remy Leather, 93
Ricci Clothestique, 113
Robe Outlet, 126
Robinsons Clear. Ctr., 142
Rockaway Records, 251
Roger Stuart Clothes, 75
Rosenman & Associates, 75
Rossi D'Italia, 198
Royal Mode, 75
Rubenfeld Kennedy Estate Jewelry, 196
St. Vincent's Jewelry Ctr., 196
Samy's Camera, 41
Shakespeare Festival L.A., 152
Sharper Image Outlet, 24
Smart & Final Iris, 287
Sports Spectacular, 270
Staples, 223
Star is Worn, A, 90
Stern's Discount Draperies, 148
Stork Shop, 66
Strouds, 209
Super Yarn Mart, 136
3D Bed & Bath, 210
Thieves Market, 262
Thomas Cook, 282
Tiffany's Toys, 271
Town Fair Bazaar, 54
Toys 'R Us, 280
W. J. Simmons Mattress Factory, 181
Wallpapers to Go, 233
Warehouse Shoe Sale, 263
Weber Milbrook Bakery, 162

Westchester Faire Antique Mall, 10
World Cleaners, 150
Zachary All, 76

LOS FELIZ
Allen Wertz Candy, 168

LYNWOOD
Anna's Linens, 205
Helen Grace Chocolate, 169
Smart & Final Iris, 287

MALIBU
Crown Books, 29

MANHATTAN BEACH
A.A.A., 218
Bead Gallery, 197
Foot Locker Outlet, 264
Four Day Tire Stores, 48
Kids Mart, 65
Move It, 274
Super Crown, 29
3D Bed & Bath, 210
Trader Joe's, 167

MARINA DEL REY
Bookstar, 29
Cellular Wholesalers, 52
Crown Books, 29
Designer Labels for Less, 80
Europa, The Suit Club, 71
Kelly Paper, 236
Love Tennis, 265
3 Day Blinds, 48
Top-to-Top, 262

MAR VISTA
Complete Eye Care, 219

MIRA MESA
Apparel Designer Zone, 76
Famous Footwear, 260
Men's Wearhouse, 72
Pic'N'Save, 146
Smart & Final Iris, 287

MISSION HILLS
C&R Clothiers, 70
Party Corner Discount Party Ctr., 235

MISSION VALLEY
Farmers' Market, 164

MISSION VIEJO
Children's Exchange, 68
Crown Books, 29
Parties-N-Us, 235
Party World, 235
Plummer's, 174
Tuesday Morning, 190
We-R-Fabrics, 157
Weber-Milbrook Bakery, 161

MONROVIA
A.A.A., 281
Crown Books, 29
Farmers' Market, 164

Health Food City, 163
Pottery Ranch, 58
Smart & Final Iris, 287

MONTCLAIR
Aaron Bros. Art Mart, 18
Big Y Yardage Outlet, 154
California Fit, 79
Electropedic Adjustable Beds, 80
Entenmann's/Oroweat Bakery, 161
Home Base, 39
Kelly Paper, 236
Kids Mart, 65
Kirk Paper, 237
Ladies Shoes Outlet, 254
La Petite Factorie, 109
Marinello Beauty School, 28
Marshalls, 144
Modern Woman, 131
Nevada Bob's Golf & Tennis, 265
P.S. Plus Sizes, 131
Pace Membership Whse., 287
Paul Jardin Outlet, 73
Robe Outlet, 236
Strouds, 209
3 Day Blinds, 48
Treasure Hunt, 126
Tuesday Mornings, 190
Wallpapers To Go, 233

MONTEBELLO
A.A.A., 281
Anna's Linens, 205
Entenmann's/Oroweat Bakery, 161
Kids Mart, 65
Modern Woman, 131
99 Cents Only Stores, 145
Susie's Deals, 114

MONTEREY PARK
C&R Clothiers, 70
Kids Mart, 65

MORENO VALLEY
Home Base, 39
Modern Woman, 133
Pic'N'Save, 146
3 Day Blinds, 48
Toys 'R Us, 280
Wonder-Hostess Bakery, 162

MURIETTA
Smart & Final Iris, 287
3 Day Blinds, 48
Toys 'R Us, 280

NATIONAL CITY
Fedco, 286
Pic'N'Save, 146
Smart & Final Iris, 287

NEWBERRY PARK
Barbara & Carolyn's Quality Tack, 238

NEWPORT BEACH
A.A.A., 281

Art Store, 18
C&R Clothiers, 70
Crown Books, 29
Four Day Tire Stores, 48
Thomas Cook, 282

NORTH HILLS
Carpet Club, 42

NORTH HOLLYWOOD
AAA Billiard & Barstool Gallery, 278
Al's Furniture, 171
Americana Brass Bed Factory, 179
Art Glass Doors, 36
Big Fella Whse. Store, 69
Bizarre Bazaar, 102
Box City, 236
Builders Discount, 39
C&R Clothiers, 70
Castle Chandeliers, 200
Dolly Madison Bakery, 161
Dorman Winthrop, 70
Dutton's Bookstore, 29
Empire Cleaners, 149
Four Day Tire Stores, 48
Game Dude, 279
General Wax & Candle, 56
Harris & Frank Outlet, 72
Holiday Humane Society, 242
Home Base, 39
Kelly Paper, 236
Kids Mart, 65
Kitchen & Bath Clear. Ctr., 37
Lamps Plus, 201
Luggage 4 Less, 215
Mainly Seconds, 245
99 Cents Only Stores, 145
Paul Jardin Outlet, 73
Pic'N'Save, 146
Plummer's, 174
Robe Outlet, 126
Smart & Final Iris, 287
Staples, 223
Super Yarn Mart, 136
T-Shirts Wholesale Whse., 98
Valley Book City, 34
W. J. Simmons Mattress Factory, 181
Weber Milbrook Bakery, 162
Zeig Smog, 50

NORTHRIDGE
A.A.A., 281
AAA Wholesale Tool and Supply, 276
Aaron Bros. Art Mart, 18
Builders Discount, 39
C&R Clothiers, 70
Calico Corners, 154
Carpet Showcase, 43
Cole of California Outlet, 94
Crown Books, 29
Crafter's City, 188
Daphna's, 183
Dolly Madison Bakery, 161
Fabric Warehouse, 158
$5 Clothing Store, 105

Hosiery Depot, 123
Jasmine Cleaners, 150
Kids Mart, 65
Lamps Plus, 201
Laura M Contemporary Sportswear, 109
Lechters 194
Lingerie for Less, 124
Little Folks, 65
Marinello Beauty School, 28
Marshalls, 144
Multi-Factory Outlet, 112
Party World, 235
Priscilla's Bridal, 118
Price Club, 287
Robertson's, 136
Ross Dress for Less, 145
Sig's Pottery & Nursery, 247
Sportmart, 270
Steven Craig Wholesale Clothiers, 75
Thieves Market, 262
W. J.Simmons Mattress Factory, 181
Wallpaper Bin, 233

NORWALK
A.A.A., 281
Anna's Linens, 205
$5 Clothing Store, 105
Home Base, 39
Kids Mart, 65
Montgomery Ward Clear. Ctr., 141
99 Cents Only Stores, 145
$1 Cleaners, 150
Sears Outlet, 143
Smart & Final Iris, 287
Staples, 223
Treasure Hunt, 146

OCEANSIDE
A.A.A., 281
Entenmann's/Oroweat Bakery, 161
Kids Mart, 65
Lamps Plus, 201
Loehmann's, 111
Pacific Eyes & T's, 219
Pic'N'Save, 146
Strouds, 209
Toys 'R Us, 180
Weber Milbrook Bakery, 162
Wonder-Hostess Bakery, 162

ONTARIO
Adolfo II, 230
Aileen Stores, 99
Book Warehouse, 29
C&R Clothiers, 70
Capezio Outlet, 259
Converse Outlet, 252
Corning/Revere Outlet, 193
Crisa, 230
Fedco, 286
Four Day Tire Stores, 48
Gitano Outlet, 81
Hathaway Outlet, 72
In 2 Shape/Designers Own, 230
K-Mart, 144

Kids for Less, 64
Leather Loft, 92
99 Cents Only Stores, 145
Olga/Warners Outlet, 126
Outlet, The, 113
Prestige Fragrances, 26
Richard's Beauty College, 28
Sbicca Shoes Outlet, 230
Smart & Final Iris, 287
Toys 'R Us, 180
Weber Milbrook Bakery, 162
Welcome Home, 210
Whims/Sarah Coventry, 230
Wonder-Hostess Bakery, 162

ORANGE
Aaron Bros. Art Mart, 18
Alan's Medical Products, 218
C&R Clothiers, 70
Calico Corners, 154
Crown Books, 29
Dawn's Discount Lace II, 135
Entenmann's/Oroweat Bakery, 161
Friedman's, 16
K-Mart, 144
Kids Mart, 65
Lamps Plus, 201
Party World, 235
Pic'N'Save, 146
Shipleys, 87
Smart & Final Iris, 287
Staples, 223
Strouds, 209
Susie's Deals, 114
T. J. Maxx, 145
Thomas Cook, 282
W. J. Simmons Mattress Factory, 181
Weber Milbrook Bakery, 162
Wet Seal Clearance Store, 114

OXNARD
Dolly Madison Bakery, 161
Entenmann's/Oroweat Bakery, 161
Hathaway Outlet, 72
Kids Mart, 65
Marshalls, 144
Party World, 235
Pic'N'Save, 146
Price Club, 287
Smart & Final Iris, 287
Super Yarn Mart, 136
T. J. Maxx, 167
T-Shirts Warehouse, 98
3D Bed and Bath, 210
3 Day Blinds, 48
Warehouse Shoe Sale, 263

PACIFIC BEACH
Alpine Automotive, 50
Apparel Designer Zone, 76
Pacific Eyes & T's, 219

PACIFIC PALISADES
Crown Books, 29

PACOIMA
Four Day Tire Stores, 48
Pic'N' Save, 146
Smart & Final Iris, 287
Valley Wholesale Nursery, 247

PALMDALE
Dolly Madison Bakery, 161
Kids Mart, 65
K-Mart, 144
3 Day Blinds, 48
Wonder-HostessBakery, 161
Woody's Unfinished Furniture, 175

PALM DESERT
Crown Books, 29
Designer Labels for Less, 80
Famous Footwear, 260
Marshalls, 145
Patio Place, 184

PALM SPRINGS
A.A.A., 281
Animal Birth Control, 242
Crown Books, 29
Dansk Outlet, 55
Entenmann's/Oroweat Bakery, 161
Famous Footwear, 260
K-Mart, 144
Loehmann's, 111
Mikasa Factory Store, 57
Tuesday Mornings, 190

PALOS VERDES
Crown Books, 29

PANORAMA CITY
Antique Palace Mall, 6
Broadway Clear. Ctr., 138
Entenmann's/Oroweat Bakery, 161
Froch's Woodcraft Shop, 172
Jasmine Cleaners, 150
Little Folks, 65
May Co. Home Clear. Ctr., 140
Ninety-nine Cents Only Stores, 145
P. S. Plus Sizes, 131
Valley Indoor Swap Meet, 13

PARAMOUNT
Dolly Madison Bakery, 161
99 Cents Only Stores, 145
Treasure Hunt, 146

PASADENA
A.A.A., 281
Art Store, 18
Bailey's Men's Resale, 76
C&R Clothiers, 70
Calico Corners, 154

Carousel Baby Furniture, 178
Cliff's Books, 32
Crown Books, 29
Fedco, 286
$5 Clothing Store, 105
Four Day Tire Stores, 48
Friedman's, 16
Granny's Discount Natural Foods, 162
Health Food City, 163
House of Fabrics, 158
Hunter's Books, 30
Import Outlet, 159
Jack's Cleaners, 149
Jerry Pillers, 82
Kids Mart, 65
L. A. Tronics, 23
Lamps Plus, 201
Leather Factory, 173
Little Orphan Overalls, 68
Marshalls, 144
Modern Woman, 131
National Fabrics & Foam, 156
Nevada Bob's Golf & Tennis, 265
99 Cents Only Stores, 145
Office Depot, 223
$1 Cleaners, 150
Party World, 235
Pasadena Antique Ctr., 9
Pasadena City College Flea Mkt., 11
Plummer's, 174
Rose Bowl Flea Mkt., 11
Sanders House of Lights, 202
Smart & Final Iris, 287
Staples, 223
Strouds, 209
Strouds Clear. Ctr., 209
Susie's Deals, 114
3D Bed & Bath, 210
3 Day Blinds, 48
Thrifty Cleaner, 150
Trader Joe's 167
W. J. Simmons Mattress Factory, 181

PLACENTIA
California Kids, 63
Shipley's, 87
Strouds, 209
Weber Milbrook Bakery, 162

POMONA
Anna's Linens, 205
Boston Stores Clear. Ctr., 138
Computer Marketplace Show, 133
Contractors Warehouse, 39
Dolly Madison Bakery, 161
Fabric Lace Trims Factory Outlet, 158
Olde Towne Pomona Antique Mall, 8
Pomona Car Show, 50
Price Club, 287

Robbins Antique Mart, 9
Smart & Final Iris, 287
Super Yarn Mart, 136
Susie's Deals, 114
Valley Indoor Swap Meet of Pomona, 13
Wonder-Hostess Bakery, 162

POWAY
Famous Footwear, 260

PUENTE HILLS
C&R Clothiers, 70
Calico Corners, 154
Crown Books, 29
Lamps Plus, 201
Marshalls, 144
Strouds, 209
3 Day Blinds, 48
Toys 'R Us, 180
W. J. Simmons Mattress Facotry, 181

RANCHO CALIFORNIA
Scotch Paint, 232

RANCHO CUCAMONGA
Anna's Linens, 205
California Kids, 63
Del Rey Tennis Shoes Whse., 259
$5 Clothing Store, 105
Fresh Peaches Swimwear, 95
Kids Mart, 65
Pic'N'Save, 146
Smart & Final Iris, 287
3 Day Blinds, 48

RANCHO MIRAGE
Fashion West, 2
7th Avenue West, 114
Shirley's Shoes & Handbags, 4
Strouds, 209
W. J. Simmons Mattress Factory, 181

RANCHO PALOS VERDES
South Coast Botanic Gardens, 244
Trader Joe's, 167

RANCHO SANTA MARGARITA
NoJo Factory Outlet Store, 211

REDLANDS
A.A.A., 281
Aaron Bros. Art Mart, 18
Bracken Bird Farm, 238
Kids Mart, 65
Smart & Final Iris, 287
Trader Joe's, 167

REDONDO BEACH
Auto Parts Club, 48
Bed, Bath & Beyond, 205
C&R Clothiers, 70
Chic Lingerie Outlet, 123

Crown Books, 29
Farmers' Market, 164
Pic'N'Save, 146
Smart & Final Iris, 287
Sportmart, 270
Trader Joe's, 167

RESEDA
Baby Toytown, 177
Bev's Crafts and Lace, 135
Big, Bad & Beautiful, 130
Bookie Joint, 32
Carpetland Mills, 42
Clothing Factory, 103
Computer Marketplace Show, 133
$5 Clothing Store, 105
For Kids Only, 63
House of Fabrics, 158
Judy's Outlet, 108
Kids Mart, 65
Loehmann's, 111
Marinello Beauty School, 28
Marshalls, 144
Nadine of CA Uniforms, 283
99 Cents Only Stores, 145
Sara Designer's Outlet, 142
Sitting Pretty, 175

RIALTO
Anna's Linens, 205
Clothestime Outlet, 102
Contempo Casuals Outlet, 103
Entenmann's/Oroweat Bakery, 161
Farmers' Market, 164
Kids Mart, 65
$2 Fabric Store, 160

RIVERSIDE
A.A.A., 281
Aaron Bros. Art Mart, 18
Alin Party Supply, 234
Anna's Linens, 205
Barbeques Galore, 184
Black & Decker/DeWalt, 276
Costco, 286
Designer Fabric Showcase, 155
Dolly Madison Bakery, 161
Entenmanns/Oroweat Bakery, 161
$5 Clothing Store, 105
Four Day Tire Stores, 48
Gino Robair Beauty College, 27
Home Base, 39
K-Mart, 144
Kelly Paper, 236
Kids Mart, 65
Lamps Plus, 201
Le Baby Originals, 211
Marshalls, 144
Nevada Bob's Golf & Tennis, 265
Party World, 235
Pic'N'Save, 146
Smart & Final Iris, 287
Sportmart, 270
Staples, 233
Strouds, 209

3 Day Blinds, 48
Toys 'R' Us, 280
$2 Fabric Store, 160
Wonder-Hostess Bakery, 162

ROLLING HILLS
Aaron Bros. Art Mart, 18
Crown Books, 29
T. J. Maxx, 167
Tuesday Morning, 190

ROSEMEAD
Baby Toytown, 177
Entenmann's/Oroweat Bakery, 161
Pic'N'Save, 146
Toys 'R Us, 280
Trader Joe's, 167
$2 Fabric Store, 160

ROWLAND HEIGHTS
Four Day Tire Stores, 48
Kids Mart, 65
Pic'N'Save, 146
P. S. Plus Sizes, 131
Wesco Auto Parts, 49

SAN BERNARDINO
A.A.A., 281
Anna's Linens, 205
Blue Chip Drapery, 147
Costco, 286
Dana Bedspreads, 206
Dana Bedspreads Clear. Ctr., 207
Fedco, 286
Four Day Tire Stores, 48
Hairmasters University, 28
Home Base, 39
Kelly Paper, 236
Kids Mart, 65
K-Mart, 144
Lamps Plus, 201
Marinello Beauty School, 28
Marshalls, 144
Millers Outpost Clear. Ctr., 144
Office Depot, 223
Pace Membership Whse., 287
Pic'N'Save, 146
Smart & Final Iris, 287
Sportmart, 270
Staples, 223
Susie's Deals, 114
T-Shirts Mart, 98
3 Day Blinds, 148
$2 Fabric Store, 160
Toys R'Us, 280
Treasure Hunt, 146
W. J. Simmons Mattress Factory, 181
Wallpapers To Go, 233
Weber-Milbrook Bakery, 162
Wonder-Hostess Bakery, 162

SAN CLEMENTE
Aaron Bros. Art Mart, 18
Crown Books, 29

SAN DIEGO
A.A.A., 281
Alpine Automotive, 50
Auto Parts Club, 48
Aztec Appliances, 15
Barbeques Galore, 184
Bed, Bath & Beyond, 205
Big City Woman Resale, 132
Bookstar, 29
Comp USA, 133
Crown Books, 29
Cutting Corners, 154
Dan Howard's Maternity Factory, 127
Designer Labels for Less, 80
Dolly Madison Bakery, 161
Entenmann's/Oroweat Bakery, 161
Famous Footwear, 260
Four Day Tire Stores, 48
Jewelry Exchange, 195
K-Mart, 144
Kelly Paper, 236
Kids Mart, 65
Kirk Paper, 237
Lamps Plus, 201
Marinello Beauty School, 28
Marshalls, 144
Men's Wearhouse, 72
Modern Woman, 131
Museum of Contemporary Art, 151
Nordstroms Rack, 141
Pacific Eyes & T's, 219
Play it Again Sports, 268
Plummers, 174
Pottery Barn Clearance Store, 189
Price Club, 276
Ross Dress for Less, 145
Scandia Down Outlet, 208
Sears Outlet, 143
Smart & Final Iris, 287
Susie's Deals, 114
T. J. Maxx, 145
T&R Antiques Whse., 10
Thomas Cook, 282
3D Bed & Bath, 210
W. J. Simmons Mattress Factory, 181
Wallpapers To Go, 222
Wonder-Hostess Bakery, 162

SAN DIMAS
Allen Wertz What's Popping, 168
Crown Books, 29
Frontier Village Antique Mall, 7
Hit or Miss, 106
Kids Mart, 65
Lingerie for Less, 124
T. J. Maxx, 167
Thieves Market, 262
3 Day Blinds, 148

SAN FERNANDO
A.A.A., 281
Jasmine Cleaners, 150
Pace Membership Whse., 287

Warehouse Outlet, 89
Weber Milbrook Bakery, 162

SAN GABRIEL
A.A.A., 281
Europa, The Suit Club, 71
Hacienda Brides Intl., 118
Jenkins Products, 43
Pet Nutrition Center, 241
San Gabriel Nursery & Florist, 246
Smart & Final Iris, 287

SAN JUAN CAPISTRANO
Crown Books, 29
Marshalls, 144
Price Club, 287
Sporting Outlet, 269
W. J. Simmons Mattress Factory, 181

SAN MARCOS
Leather Factory, 173
Wallpapers To Go, 233

SAN PEDRO
A.A.A., 281
Best of Times Antiques, 7
Crown Books, 29
$5 Clothing Store, 105
Smart & Final Iris, 287
Spur of the Moment Cruises, 281

SANTA ANA
A.A.A., 281
Anna's Linens, 204
Big Y Yardage Outlet, 154
Blue Chip Drapery, 147
Dan Howard's Maternity Factory, 126
Designer Labels for Less Whse., 80
Elwell Farms, 166
$5 Clothing Store, 105
Four Day Tire Stores, 48
Grafstein & Co., 195
Hacienda Brides Intl., 118
Home Base, 39
Home Shop, 207
Jewelry Exchange, 195
Kelly Paper, 236
Kids Mart, 65
Kids R'Us, 65
Kinney Shoe Outlet, 260
Kirk Paper, 237
Lingerie for Less, 124
Luggage Outlet. 215
Marinello Beauty School, 28
Maternity Ltd., 128
Michael's Shoes, 252
Montgomery Ward Clear. Ctr., 141
Nordstroms Rack, 141
Office Depot, 223
P. F. McMullin Co., 267
P. S. Plus Sizes, 131
Patio Place, 184
Pic'N'Save, 146
Plummer's, 174
Smart & Final Iris, 287
Staples, 223

Steinberg's Discount Tack & Feed, 241
Strouds, 209
Susie's Deals, 114
3D Bed & Bath, 210
Trader Joe's, 167
$2 Fabric Store, 160
Van's Factory Outlet, 263
Warehouse Shoe Sale, 263
Weber Milbrook Bakery, 162
Wesco Auto Parts, 48
Wonder-Hostess Bakery, 162

SANTA BARBARA
A.A.A., 281
Aaron Brothers Art Mart, 18
Arte D'Italia, 87
Bagnall Camera Show, 10
Big Dogs Sportswear Outlet, 78
Crown Books, 29
Entenmann's/Oroweat Bakery, 161
Firenze Factory Outlet, 91
Kids Mart, 65
Manufacturers Sports Outlet, 265
Marshalls, 144
Santa Barbara Ceramic Design Outlet Store, 157
Santa Barbara Museum of Art, 152
Smart & Final Iris, 287
Super Yarn Mart, 136
Susie's Deals, 114
3 Day Blinds, 148
Weber Milbrook Bakery, 162

SANTA CLARA
Auto Parts Club, 48
Smart & Final Iris, 287

SANTA FE SPRINGS
Anna's Linens, 205
Barbeques Galore, 184
Bedspread Creations, 205
Dyna-Tek, 224
Kids Mart, 65
Lakenor Auto Salvage, 49
T-Shirt Warehouse, 92

SANTA MARGARITA
Santa Margarita Auction Barn, 10

SANTA MARIA
A.A.A., 182
Farmers' Market, 164
Fence Factory, 37
Kids Mart, 65
Marshalls, 144
Smart & Final Iris, 287

SANTA MONICA
A.A.A., 281
Aaron Bros. Art Mart, 18
Aaron Scott Clear. Ctr., 171
Alitta Factory Outlet, 273
Barrett's Appliances, 15
Berks, 183

Bookstar, 29
Center for Independent Living Rummage Sale, 53
Colleagues Sale, 53
Consolidated Pet Foods, 239
Co-opportunity Food Co-op, 162
Crown Books, 29
Daphna's, 183
Farmers' Market, 164
Flight Coordinators, 281
Golden West Meat Co., 167
House of Fabrics, 158
John Anthony Apparel, 83
Junior League of L. A. Sale, 54
Kelly Paper, 236
Kids Mart, 65
Lincoln Appliances, 16
Mark Friedman, 174
Marlow's Books, 32
Nationwide Baby Shops, 178
99 Cents Only Stores, 145
Paperback Trader, 34
Platter Puss Records, 251
Sacha of London Outlet, 255
Sample Shoes Unlimited, 256
Santa Monica Antique Mkt., 9
Standard Brands, 236
Strouds, 209
Super Yarn Mart, 136
3 Day Blinds, 148
Tool Power, 277
Top-to-Top, 262
Vidal Sassoon Beauty School, 28

SAN YSIDRO
Accessorize Jewelry Outlet, 231
Adolfo II, 231
Aileen Factory Store, 99
Banister Outlet, 231
Bass Shoe Outlet, 258
Black & Decker Outlet, 276
Book Warehouse, 29
Corning/Revere Outlet, 193
Designer Brands Accessories Outlet, 231
Eddie Bauer Outlet, 80
Famous Brands Housewares Outlet, 193
Fieldcrest Cannon, 207
Firenze Factory Outlet, 91
G&G Nintendo-Sega Outlet, 278
Georgiou, 231
Gitano Factory Store, 81
Izod/Gant, 231
Leather Loft, 92
Levi's Factory Outlet, 83
Maidenform Outlet, 125
Marika, 274
Mikasa Factory Store, 57
Multiples Factory Outlet, 112
Nike Factory Store, 266

PFC Fragrance Outlet, 231
Polly Flinders, 231
Ribbon Outlet, 231
Star Baby, 66
Toy Liquidators Outlet, 231
Van Heusen Outlet, 88
Wallet Works Outlet, 231
Welcome Home, 210

SAUGUS
A.A.A., 281
Country Antique Fair Mall, 7
Saugus Swap Meet, 12

SEAL BEACH
Shore Shop, 87

SEPULVEDA
Kids' Store, 68

SHERMAN OAKS
Almost & Perfect English China, 55
Game City, 278
House of Fabrics, 158
Intelliplay, 279
Jay Jacobs Outlet, 107
Jean Star's Apparel, 115
Lechters, 194
Lingerie for Less, 124
Little Folks, 65
Pacific Eyes & T's, 219
Pet and Equestrian Thrift Shop, 240
Record Surplus, 251
Rick Pallack, 74
Sherman Oaks Antique Mall, 9
Something Special Flowers, 248
Thomas Cook, 282
Tower Records Outlet, 251
Trader Joe's, 167

SIGNAL HILL
Herman's Party Supplies, 234
Price Club, 287

SIMI VALLEY
A.A.A., 182
Anna's Linens, 205
Big, Bad & Beautiful, 130
Builders Discount, 39
Crown Books, 29
Galaxy of Gowns, 117
Home Base, 39
Kids Mart, 65
Penny Pinchers, 9
Pic'N'Save, 146
Sears Outlet, 143
See Me Color, 86
Smart & Final Iris, 287
Susie's Deals, 114
3 Day Blinds, 248
Weber Milbrook Bakery, 162
Wonder-Hostess Bakery, 162

SOLANO BEACH
A.A.A., 281

Antique Warehouse, 7
Designer Labels for Less, 80

SOLVANG
Santa Barbara Ceramic Design Studio Outlet, 157

SOUTHGATE
Al Greenwood's Bedspread Kingdom, 204
Farmers' Market, 164
$5 Clothing Store, 105
Pace Membership Whse., 287
Wonder-Hostess Bakery, 162

SOUTH PASADENA
Crown Books, 29
Entenmann's/Oroweat Bakery, 161
Hang Ten Outlet, 64
Mom's the Word, 128
$1 Cleaners, 150
Trader Joe's, 167

STANTON
Home Base, 39
99 Cents Only Stores, 145
Pace Membership Whse., 287
Wonder-Hostess Bakery, 162

STUDIO CITY
Aaron Bros. Art Mart, 18
Bed, Bath & Beyond, 205
Bookstar, 29
Calico Corners, 154
Castle Chandeliers, 200
European Natural Leather Bags, 2
Past Perfect, 116
Perfume City, 26
Strouds, 209
Thieves Market, 262
3 Day Blinds, 148
Wallpapers to Go, 233

SUN VALLEY
$5 Clothing Store, 105
L.E.C. World Traders, 280
Marv's Auto, 50
Pic'N'Save, 146
Rattan Distribution Whse., 176
Shoes Here, 261
T-Shirts Whse., 98

SYLMAR
Kid's Mart, 65

TARZANA
Aaron Bros. Art Mart, 18
Apparel Warehouse, 273
Barbeques Galore, 184
C. W. Designs, 63
Crown Books, 29
Deco Brass, 36
Designer Labels for Less, 80

Dressed Up, 104
Esther's Full Fashions, 130
Everything for Kids, 67
Kids Double Time, 68
Kids Stuff, 68
LAX Luggage, 214
Lingerie for Less, 124
Lora's, 26
Marlene Gaines Handbags, 4
Ross Dress for less, 145
Sacks SFO, 86
Samples Only, 256
Super Yarn Mart, 136
Time-Off Apparel, 96
Wallpapers to Go, 233

TEMECULA
Anna's Linens, 205
T. J. Maxx, 145

TEMPLE CITY
A.A.A., 281
C&R Clothiers, 70
$5 CLothing Store, 104
K-Mart, 144
99 Cents Only Stores, 145
$1 Cleaners, 150
T. J. Maxx, 167

THOUSAND OAKS
A.A.A., 281
Aaron Bros. Art Mart, 18
Crown Books, 29
Harpers, 106
Irish Crystal Co., 56
Kids Mart, 65
Leather Factory, 194
Lingerie for Less, 124
Marshalls, 144
Outlet, The, 113
Party World, 235
Smart & Final Iris, 287
Strouds, 209
Susie's Deals, 114
3 Day Blinds, 148
Toys 'R Us, 280

TORRANCE
A.A.A., 281
Aaron Bros. Art Mart, 18
Adray's, 22
Anna's Linens, 205
Barbeques Galore, 184
Book Again, 31
Bookstar, 29
Brides of California, 116
C&R Clothiers, 70
Calico Corners, 154
Caroline's Designer Resale, 116
Castle Chandeliers, 200
Comp USA, 133
Dan Howard's Maternity Factory, 127
Designer Labels for Less, 80
Entenmann's/Oroweat Bakery, 161
Everything for Kids, 67
Fabric Warehouse, 158
$5 Clothing Store, 105
Glabman's, 173

Herman's Party Supplies, 234
Kids Double Time, 68
Kids Mart, 65
Kids R'Us, 65
Kids Stuff, 68
L.A. Tronics, 23
Lamps Plus, 201
Leather Factory, 173
Lingerie for Less, 124
Marshalls, 144
Mastercraft Rattan and Wicker, 176
Michael's Shoes, 252
Modern Woman, 131
Nationwide Baby Shops, 178
Nevada Bob's Golf & Tennis, 265
Office Depot, 223
Olga/Warners Outlet, 126
P. S. Plus Sizes, 131
Pacific Sales, 16
Party World, 235
Pic'N'Save, 146
Plaza Golf, 268
Plummer's, 174
Roadium, The, 12
Robe Outlet, 126
Ross Dress for Less, 125
Royal Bedspreads, 208
Smart & Final Iris, 287
Staples, 223
Strouds, 209
Strouds Clear. Ctr., 209
Super Yarn Mart, 136
Thieves Market, 262
Thomas Cook, 282
3D Bed & Bath, 210
3 Day Blinds, 148
Toys 'R Us, 280
Uniforms West Inc., 283
Weber Milbrook Bakery, 162
W. J. Simmons Mattress Factory, 181

TUSTIN
Atlantis Discount Swim, 94
Back Door Boutique, 101
Bookstar, 29
C&R Clothiers, 70
Children's Orchard, 67
Costco, 286
Crown Books, 29
Four Day Tire Stores, 48
$5 Clothing Store, 105
Hit or Miss, 106
Kids Mart, 65
Kids R'Us, 65
Leather Factory, 173
Marshalls, 144
Patio Place, 184
Second Look Bridal Resale, 121
Shipley's, 87
T. J. Maxx, 145
3D Bed & Bath, 210
Toys R' Us, 280

UNIVERSAL CITY
Art Store, 13

UPLAND
A.A.A., 281
Baby Toytown, 177
Barbeques Galore, 184
Crown Books, 29
Discount Sales Stores, 23
$5 Clothing Store, 105
Hit or Miss, 106
Kids for Less, 64
Lamps Plus, 201
Ninth Street Outlet, 85
Party World, 235
Pic'N'Save, 287
Sears Outlet, 143
Staples, 223
Stork CLub II, 129
T. J. Maxx, 145
W. J. Simmons Mattress Factory, 181
Wonder-Hostess Bakery, 162

VALENCIA
A.A.A., 281
Box City, 236
Fabric Warehouse, 158
House of Fabrics, 158
Kids Mart, 65

VAN NUYS
A.A.A., 281
Action Copiers, 224
Adray's, 22
American Rubber & Supply, 216
Bargain Books, 31
Black & Decker/DeWalt, 276
Blue Chip Drapery, 147
Box City, 236
Christopher's Nut Co., 169
Costco, 286
Discount Pet Food, 240
Dress Up Cleaners, 149
Electropedic Adjustable Beds, 80
Fedco, 286
Heidi's Warehouse Fashion Outlet, 106
Jasmine Cleaners, 150
Kids 'R Us, 65
Kirk Paper, 237
Kitchen and Bath Specialists, 37

VENTURA
Blue Moon Exchange, 94
Real Cheap Sports, 269

WALNUT
Del Rey Tennis Shoes Whse., 259

WESTCHESTER
Dawn's Discount Lace II, 135
Discount Reader, 30
Flax Art Supplies, 19
99 Cents Only Stores, 146
Sid's Discount Baby Furniture, 178
Trader Joe's, 167

WEST COVINA
AAA Billiard & Barstool Gallery, 278
Aaron Bros. Art Mart, 18
Blue Chip Drapery, 147
C&R Clothiers, 80
Castle Chandeliers, 200
K-Mart, 144
Kids Mart, 65
Lamps Plus, 201
Lechters, 194
Marinello Beauty School, 28
Marshalls, 144
May Co. Home Clear. Ctr., 140
$1 Most Garments Cleaners, 150
Party World, 235
Piano Outlet, 221
Pic'N'Save, 146
Smart & Final Iris, 297
Sportmart, 270
Super Yarn Mart, 136
Susie's Deals, 114
T. J. Maxx, 145
Trader Joe's, 167
Tuesday Morning, 190
W. J. Simmons Mattress Factory, 181
Wesco Auto Parts, 49

WEST HILLS
Carpet Club, 42
L. A. Tronics, 23
Paul Jardin Outlet, 73
Price-Less Bridals, 118
Sewing Machine Whse., 17

WEST HOLLYWOOD
Bookstar, 29
CD Banzai, 250
Collar & Leash, 239
Farmers' Market, 164
For Kids Only, 63
Kids R'Us, 65
Leather to the Limit, 92
Record Surplus, 251
Ross Dress for Less, 145
Sacks SFO, 86
Saka's Outlet, 113
Sid's Discount Baby Furniture, 178
VCA Animal Hospitals, 242

WESTLAKE VILLAGE
Compagnia Della Moda, 70
Trader Joe's, 167
Westlake Antique Ctr., 10

WEST LOS ANGELES
Aaron Scott Clear. Ctr., 171
Adray's, 22
Alandales, 69
Animal Birth Control, 242
Art Store, 18
Azita J, 101
Bankruptcy Liquidators, 258
Bead Gallery, 197
Bed, Bath & Beyond, 205
Bergstroms, 62

Geographical Index

Blue Chip Drapery, 147
Box City, 236
Budget Rents Clear. Ctr., 182
C&R Clothiers, 70
Cellular Fantasy, 52
Children's Exchange, 67
Compact Disc Count, 250
Concord Cleaners, 149
Crown Books, 29
Disc Connection, 250
Discount Sales Store, 23
Dorman Winthrop, 70
Egghead Discount Software Clear. Ctr., 134
Europa, The Suit Club, 71
Everything but Water, 95
Fabric Warehouse, 158
Four Day Tire Stores, 48
$5 Clothing Store, 105
Flap Happy Kids, 63
Flax Art Supplies, 19
Glabman's, 173
Graphaids, 19
Home Shop, 207
Jess/Maddox Clear. Ctr., 107
Kids R'Us, 65
Kirk Paper, 237
L. A. Tronics, 23
LAX Luggage, 214
Lamps Plus, 201
Leather Factory, 173
Lechters, 194
Le Petit Jean, 254
Lingerie for Less, 124
M. Fredric Outlet Store, 111
Michael's Shoes, 252
Mr. Satin, 208
Nationwide Baby Shops, 178
Natural Fabric Co., 159
Nevada Bob's Golf & Tennis, 265
99 Cents Only Stores, 146
Office Depot, 223
Painters' Warehouse, 232
Palm City Plants, 245
Party World, 235
Record Surplus, 251
Robe Outlet, 126
Sacks SFO, 86
2nds Shop, 187
Seven Seas Rattan, 177
Smart & Final Iris, 287
Sportmart, 270
Staples, 223
Strouds, 209
Strouds Clear. Ctr., 209
Thieves Market, 262
3 Day Blinds, 148
Toys 'R Us, 280
20/20 Video Rentals, 280
VCA Animal Hospital, 242
W. J. Simmons Mattress Factory, 281
Wallpapers to Go, 233
Walter Keller Golf & Tennis, 271
West L. A. Music, 222

WESTMINSTER
Art Supply Whse., 18
C&R Clothiers, 79
Dorman Winthrop, 79
Golden Frame, 20
Hit or Miss, 106
Leather Factory, 173
Lechters, 194
Pic'N'Save, 146
3D Bed & Bath, 210

WESTWOOD
Aaron Bros. Art Mart, 18
Armand Hammer Museum, of Art, 151
Bel Air Camera, 40
Crown Books, 29
European Natural Leather Bags, 2
Everything but Water, 95
Family Practice Center of UCLA, 218
Perfumes West, 16
Prima Beauty Center, 27
Rhino Records, 251
Ross Dress For Less, 145
Shelly's Discount Aerobic & Dancewear, 273

WHITTIER
A.A.A., 281
Anna's Linens, 205
Crown Books, 29
Four Day Tire Stores, 48
King Richards Antique Mall, 8
Marinello Beauty School, 28
99 Cents Only Stores, 146
Pic'N'Save, 147
Smart & Final Iris, 287
3 Day Blinds, 148
T. J. Maxx, 145
Trader Joe's, 167
Weber Milbrook Thrift Bakeries, 162

WILMINGTON
Smart & Final Iris, 287

WOODLAND HILLS
A.A.A., 281
Bed, Bath & Beyond, 205
Beverly Hills Fan Co. Outlet, 203
Bookstar, 29
C&R Clothiers, 70
Crafter's Outlet, 188
Crown Books, 29
Dan Howard's Maternity Factory, 127
Designer Labels for Less, 80
Down Comforter Whse., 207
English China House, 56
Europa, The Suit Club, 71
Glabman's, 173
Harpers, 106
Jackeez & Nicolz, 107
Michael's Shoes Outlet, 252
Mr. MB's Candy Outlet, 169
Nordstroms Rack, 141
Office Depot, 223
Old Tyme Ceiling Fan Co., 203
Party World, 235
Sports Again, 270
Susie's Deals, 114
3D Bed & Bath, 210
3 Day Blinds, 148
Toys 'R Us
Woodland Hills Indoor Swap Meet, 13

YORBA LINDA
Crown Books, 29
Price Club, 287

YUCAIPA
Antique Exchange, 6

YUCCA VALLEY
Pic'N'Save, 287

Index of Chainwide Clearance Centers

Ann Taylor Outlet, 100
Boston Stores Clearance Center, 138
Broadway Clearance Center, The, 138
Bullock's Gran Finale, 139
California Fit, The, 79
Clothestime Outlet, 102
Contempo Casuals Outlet, 103
Dana Bedspread Clearance Store, 207
Designer Labels for Less Clearance Center, 80
Egghead Discount Software Clearance Store, 134
Everything But Water, 95
Gitano Outlet, 81
J. C. Penney Catalog Outlet Store, 140
Jay Jacobs Clearance Store, 107
Jess/Maddox, 107
Judy's Outlet, 108
Kinney Shoes Outlet, 260
Kitchen and Bath Clearance Center, 37
Lamps Plus Factory Outlet, 201
Lanz II Outlet, 109
Lillie Rubin Outlet, 110
M. Fredric Outlet Store, 111
May Company Clothing Clearance Center, The, 140
May Company Home Clearance Center, The, 140
Michael's Outlet, 252
Millers Outpost Clearance Center, 85
Modern Woman, 131
Montgomery Ward Clearance Center, 141
Nordstrom's Rack, 141
Oshman's Warehouse Outlet, 266
Patrini Shoes, 255
Paul Jardin Outlet, 73
Pier One Imports, 189
Politix Outlet Store, 74

Pottery Barn Clearance Store, 189
Robinson's Clearance Center, 142
Sacha of London Outlet, 255
Scandia Down Outlet Store, 208
Sear's Outlet, 143
Sharper Image Outlet, 23
Standard Shoes Clearance Center, 262
Stroud's Clearance Centers, 209
Tower Records Outlet, 251
Wet Seal Clearance Store, 114
Wilson's House of Suede and Leather Outlet, 93

Shopping Secrets of Southern California	Shopping Secrets of Southern California
A Bedtime Story	**Bag Lady**
Air Conditioning Exchange	**Bagnall Camera Show and Sale**
Alitta Factory Outlet	**Bailey's Men's Resale**
Arte D'Italia	**Barrett's Appliances**

5% off One Purchase Some items may be excluded from this offer. Expires 12/31/95.	**10% off One Purchase (non-sale items only)** Some items may be excluded from this offer. Expires 12/31/95.
One Free Admission Some items may be excluded from this offer. Expires 12/31/95.	**10% off One Purchase** Some items may be excluded from this offer. Expires 12/31/95.
10% off One Purchase Some items may be excluded from this offer. Expires 12/31/95.	**10% off One Purchase** Some items may be excluded from this offer. Expires 12/31/95.
Free Delivery within Delivery Area Some items may be excluded from this offer. Expires 12/31/95.	**10% off One Purchase** Some items may be excluded from this offer. Expires 12/31/95.

Shopping Secrets of Southern California	Shopping Secrets of Southern California
The Bead Gallery	**Black and White Wholesalers**
Shopping Secrets of Southern California	Shopping Secrets of Southern California
Bedspread Creations	**Brass Beds Unlimited**
Shopping Secrets of Southern California	Shopping Secrets of Southern California
Berk's	**Carousel Baby Furniture**
Shopping Secrets of Southern California	Shopping Secrets of Southern California
Betnun Music	**The Carpet Club**

10% off One Purchase Some items may be excluded from this offer. Expires 12/31/95.	**10% off One Purchase** Some items may be excluded from this offer. Expires 12/31/95.
Discount equal to the amount of Sales Tax, on one Purchase Some items may be excluded from this offer. Expires 12/31/95.	**5% off one Purchase of $25 or more** Some items may be excluded from this offer. Expires 12/31/95.
$3 off one Purchase, or $10 off a purchaseof $50 or more Some items may be excluded from this offer. Expires 12/31/95.	**Free Gift with Purchase** Some items may be excluded from this offer. Expires 12/31/95.
$50 off a Purchase of $500; $100 off a purchase of $1,000; or $200 off a $5,000 or more purchase Some items may be excluded from this offer. Expires 12/31/95.	**10% off one Purchase. Cash sales only.** Some items may be excluded from this offer. Expires 12/31/95.

Shopping Secrets of Southern California	Shopping Secrets of Southern California
Carpetland Mills	**Decorative Fabric House**
Shopping Secrets of Southern California	Shopping Secrets of Southern California
Champagne Taste or The 2nds Shop	**Designer Labels for Less**
Shopping Secrets of Southern California	Shopping Secrets of Southern California
Covercraft Outlet Store	**Disc Connection**
Shopping Secrets of Southern California	Shopping Secrets of Southern California
Dawn's Discount Lace II	**Discount Pet Center**

$10 off a Purchase of $50 or more

Some items may be excluded from this offer.
Expires 12/31/95.

$100 off a purchase of $1,000 or more

Some items may be excluded from this offer.
Expires 12/31/95.

10% off One Purchase
(all but marked down merchandise)

Some items may be excluded from this offer.
Expires 12/31/95.

20% off One Purchase

Some items may be excluded from this offer.
Expires 12/31/95.

$1 off new or used CD's
(excluding sale items)

Some items may be excluded from this offer.
Expires 12/31/95.

10% off One Purchase

Some items may be excluded from this offer.
Expires 12/31/95.

10% off One Purchase

Some items may be excluded from this offer.
Expires 12/31/95.

10% off One Purchase

Some items may be excluded from this offer.
Expires 12/31/95.

Shopping Secrets of Southern California	Shopping Secrets of Southern California
Discount Tile Center	**The Fireplace Man**
Shopping Secrets of Southern California	Shopping Secrets of Southern California
Europa, The Suit Club	**Fresh Peaches Swimwear**
Shopping Secrets of Southern California	Shopping Secrets of Southern California
The Fan Man	**Game City**
Shopping Secrets of Southern California	Shopping Secrets of Southern California
Firenze Factory Outlet	**Glamour or Owl Uniforms**

10% off One Purchase (one item per coupon) Some items may be excluded from this offer. Expires 12/31/95.	**$25 off any Purchase of $300 or more** Some items may be excluded from this offer. Expires 12/31/95.
10% off One Purchase (Ready-made, non-sale items only) Some items may be excluded from this offer. Expires 12/31/95.	**Free membership in the Suit Club and complimentary necktie with the purchase of a suit.** Some items may be excluded from this offer. Expires 12/31/95.
$5 off a New Game, or One Free Game Rental Some items may be excluded from this offer. Expires 12/31/95.	**$10 off Hunter Fans; $15 off Casablanca Fans; Or $25 off Emerson Fans** (one item per coupon) Some items may be excluded from this offer. Expires 12/31/95.
10% off One Purchase of non-sale merchandise Some items may be excluded from this offer. Expires 12/31/95.	**10% off One Purchase** Some items may be excluded from this offer. Expires 12/31/95.

Shopping Secrets of Southern California	Shopping Secrets of Southern California
Graphaids	**Le Club Handbag Company**
Harpers	**Le Petit Jean**
Jackeez and Nicolz	**Lingerie for Less**
The Kitchen Warehouse	**The Liquidation Club**

10% off One Purchase

Some items may be excluded from this offer.
Expires 12/31/95.

20% off All Future Purchases

Some items may be excluded from this offer.
Expires 12/31/95.

10% off One Purchase
of non-sale merchandise

Some items may be excluded from this offer.
Expires 12/31/95.

5% off One Purchase of $50 or more

Some items may be excluded from this offer.
Expires 12/31/95.

10% off One Purchase

Some items may be excluded from this offer.
Expires 12/31/95.

$10 off a Purchase of $50 or more

Some items may be excluded from this offer.
Expires 12/31/95.

10% off One Purchase

Some items may be excluded from this offer.
Expires 12/31/95.

5% off One Purchase

Some items may be excluded from this offer.
Expires 12/31/95.

Shopping Secrets of Southern California	Shopping Secrets of Southern California
Luggage 4 Less	**National Fabrics and Foam**
Mark Friedman	**Old Tyme Ceiling Fan Co.**
Mom's the Word	**Panel It, The Kitchen Store**
Morrie's	**PCH Clothing Company**

$5 off one Purchase of $50 or More
(excluding remnants)

Some items may be excluded from this offer.
Expires 12/31/95.

10% off Any Ticketed Price

Some items may be excluded from this offer.
Expires 12/31/95.

$10 off Hunter Fans; $15 off Casablanca Fans; or $25 off Emerson Fans
(one item per coupon)

Some items may be excluded from this offer.
Expires 12/31/95.

Free Lamp with the purchase of a Living Room Set for $975 or more

Some items may be excluded from this offer.
Expires 12/31/95.

Free Delivery in Los Angeles

Some items may be excluded from this offer.
Expires 12/31/95.

10% off One Purchase

Some items may be excluded from this offer.
Expires 12/31/95.

$5 off One Purchase of $50 or More

Some items may be excluded from this offer.
Expires 12/31/95.

10% off One Purchase

Some items may be excluded from this offer.
Expires 12/31/95.

Shopping Secrets of Southern California	Shopping Secrets of Southern California
The Piano Outlet	**Rossi D'Italia Jewelry**
Shopping Secrets of Southern California	Shopping Secrets of Southern California
Pottery and Floral World	**Rubenfeld Kennedy Estate Jewelry**
Shopping Secrets of Southern California	Shopping Secrets of Southern California
Priscilla's Bridal	**Sacks SFO or Sacks SFO Kids**
Shopping Secrets of Southern California	Shopping Secrets of Southern California
Rapport International Home Furnishings	**Santa Barbara Ceramic Design Studio Outlets**

10% off One Purchase Some items may be excluded from this offer. Expires 12/31/95.	**Free Piano Lamp with Purchase of any new Piano** Some items may be excluded from this offer. Expires 12/31/95.
10% off One Purchase Some items may be excluded from this offer. Expires 12/31/95.	**10% off One Purchase** Some items may be excluded from this offer. Expires 12/31/95.
10% off One Purchase Mon.-Thurs. Some items may be excluded from this offer. Expires 12/31/95.	**Free Headpiece with purchase of a Bridal Gown** Some items may be excluded from this offer. Expires 12/31/95.
10% off One Purchase of Santa Barbara Ceramic Design StudiosCeramics Some items may be excluded from this offer. Expires 12/31/95.	**Free Gift with Purchase** Some items may be excluded from this offer. Expires 12/31/95.

Shopping Secrets of Southern California	Shopping Secrets of Southern California
Sara Designers Outlet	**Shopping Secrets of Southern California**
Sewing Machine Warehouse	**Sports Again**
Sid's Baby and Kids Furniture	**Steinberg's Discount Tack and Feed**
Sit 'n Sleep	**The Stork Shop**

Additional copies by mail only at $11.95 Send coupon to Box 24447 L. A., CA 90024-0447 Some items may be excluded from this offer. Expires 12/31/95.	**10% off One Outfit** Some items may be excluded from this offer. Expires 12/31/95.
10% off One Purchase Some items may be excluded from this offer. Expires 12/31/95.	**Buy a Sewing Machine and get the Extended Warranty for half price** Some items may be excluded from this offer. Expires 12/31/95.
10% off One Purchase of Dog Food (not on sale) Some items may be excluded from this offer. Expires 12/31/95.	**10% off a crib, stroller or car seat; or 15% off a 5 piece bedding set; or $30 off any bunk, twin or race car bed (sale items excluded)** Some items may be excluded from this offer. Expires 12/31/95.
$5 off a Purchase of $45 or more Some items may be excluded from this offer. Expires 12/31/95.	**Free local delivery, bed frame, mattress pad and pair of pillows, set-up and removal of old bed, with purchase of any Sealy, Serta or Simmons premium mattress set.** Some items may be excluded from this offer. Expires 12/31/95.

```
┌─────────────────────────┐  ┌─────────────────────────┐
│ Shopping Secrets of Southern California │  │ Shopping Secrets of Southern California │
│                         │  │                         │
│        Tool             │  │        The              │
│        Power            │  │      Typebox            │
│                         │  │                         │
│                         │  │                         │
│                         │  │                         │
└─────────────────────────┘  └─────────────────────────┘
```

Are you interested in receiving updates of this book?

Please take a minute to fill out the following. Use the back if you need more space. Thanks.

Name _____

Address _____

City, Zip _____

Are there any stores you think I should investigate (please include city)?

At which stores did you redeem coupons?

What features of the book did you find particularly useful?

As a service to readers of this book, additional copies are available to you at a discount. For additional copies send $11.95 per copy, plus the coupon in the coupon section, to the address below.

Shopping Secrets of Southern California
P. O. Box 24447, L.A., CA 90024-0447

10% off One Purchase
(Excluding Promotional Specials)

Some items may be excluded from this offer.
Expires 12/31/95.

$5 off a Purchase of $100 or more

Some items may be excluded from this offer.
Expires 12/31/95.